International Taxation Handbook

International Taxation Handbook

Policy, Practice, Standards, and
Regulation

Edited by

Colin Read
and
Greg N. Gregoriou

AMSTERDAM • BOSTON • HEIDELBERG • LONDON • NEW YORK • OXFORD
PARIS • SAN DIEGO • SAN FRANCISCO • SINGAPORE • SYDNEY • TOKYO
CIMA Publishing is an imprint of Elsevier

ELSEVIER

CIMA
PUBLISHING

HJ
2305
.I 58X
2007

CIMA Publishing is an imprint of Elsevier
Linacre House, Jordan Hill, Oxford OX2 8DP
30 Corporate Drive, Suite 400, Burlington, MA 01803, USA

First edition 2007

British Library Cataloguing in Publication Data
A catalogue record for this book is available from the British Library

Library of Congress Cataloguing in Publication Data
A catalogue record for this book is available from the Library of Congress

ISBN–13: 978-0-7506-8371-5
ISBN–10: 0-7506-8371-6

For information on all CIMA Publishing publications
visit our web site at http://books.elsevier.com

Typeset in 10/14 pts Melior by Charon Tec Ltd (A Macmillan Company), Chennai, India
www.charontec.com

Printed and bound in The Netherlands
07 08 09 10 11   10 9 8 7 6 5 4 3 2 1

Contents

Contents

Contents

About the editors

Colin Read is the Dean of the School of Business and Economics at SUNY College at Plattsburgh. He holds a Ph.D. from Queen's University in economics, a Juris Doctorate from the University of Connecticut, and a Master's of Taxation from the University of Tulsa. He has published numerous articles on economic theory, location theory, and the microeconomic underpinnings of information and taxation.

Greg N. Gregoriou is Associate Professor of Finance and coordinator of faculty research in the School of Business and Economics at the State University of New York, College at Plattsburgh. He obtained his Ph.D. (finance) from the University of Quebec at Montreal and is hedge fund editor for the peer-reviewed scientific journal *Derivatives Use, Trading and Regulation* published by Henry Stewart publications (UK), *Journal of Wealth Management* and the *Journal of Risk Management and Financial Institutions*. He has authored over 50 articles on hedge funds and managed futures in various US and UK peer-reviewed publications, including the *Journal of Portfolio Management, Journal of Derivatives Accounting, Journal of Futures Markets, European Journal of Operational Research, Annals of Operations Research, European Journal of Finance and Journal of Asset Management*. He has four books published by John Wiley. This is his fifth book with Elsevier.

About the contributors

Dr Paul U. Ali is an Associate Professor in the Faculty of Law, University of Melbourne and a Visiting Associate Professor in the Faculty of Law, National University of Singapore. Paul was previously a finance lawyer in Sydney. He has published several books and journal articles on finance and investment law, including, most recently, *Opportunities in Credit Derivatives and Synthetic Securitisation* (London, 2005), and articles in *Derivatives Use, Trading and Regulation*, *Journal of Alternative Investments*, *Journal of Banking Regulation* and *Journal of International Banking Law and Regulation*.

Markus Brem graduated from Munich University of Technology (Technische Universität München) and received his Ph.D. in agricultural economics at the Humboldt University of Berlin. In the period 2001–2003, he did research on hybrid governance, transfer pricing, and cross-border taxation at Kobe University and the Harvard Law School. He is now leading a research project titled 'Measuring Valuable Transactions in Global Companies', financed by the KPMG/University of Illinois Business Measurement Research Program. In 2005, he also held a Visiting Professor position at the Indian Institute of Management Ahmedabad, India. Professionally, he worked in the transfer pricing teams of KPMG, Voegele Partners, and NERA Economic Consulting. He is currently Executive Director and Partner of GlobalTransferPricing Business Solutions GmbH (www.Global TransferPricing.com), a specialized service firm in the field of transfer pricing analysis.

Alexandre B. Cunha is an Associate Professor at IBMEC Business School, Rio de Janeiro, Brazil. He has worked for the Brazilian Central Bank as a macroeconomics analyst and as an economist in the private sector. He holds a Ph.D. in Economics and an M.S. in Mathematics degrees from the University of Minnesota at Twin Cities. He has also received a B.A. in Economics from Rio de Janeiro State University and an M.A. in Economics from the Getulio Vargas Foundation, Rio de Janeiro, Brazil. His main research interests are monetary, fiscal, and exchange rate policies. Dr Cunha has been appointed a research fellow by the Brazilian Ministry of Science and Technology, and his research program has received several grants.

José Antônio de França is Professor of Universidade de Brasília, Master in Business Administration and is currently the Editor of *Revista Brasileira de Contabilidade* (*Brazilian Accounting Journal*, published by the Federal Accountancy Council) and is the chairman of the Brazilian Accounting Foundation.

Robert J. Franzese Jr is Associate Professor of Political Science at The University of Michigan, Ann Arbor. He earned Masters' degrees in Government (1992) and in Economics (1995) and a Ph.D. in Government (1996) from Harvard University. His publications include two books, *Macroeconomic Policies of Developed Democracies* (Cambridge, 2002) and *Institutional Conflicts and Complementarities: Monetary Policy and Wage Bargaining Institutions* (Kluwer, 2004), several articles in *American Journal of Political Science*, *Political Analysis*, *Annual Review of Political Science*, *European Union Politics*, *International Organization*, *Comparative Political Studies*, *Journal of Policy Analysis and Management*, *Empirica*, and *Political Science Quarterly*, plus chapters in eight edited volumes and three handbooks.

Carlo Garbarino is Professor of Taxation at Bocconi University, Milan, member of Istituto di Diritto Comparato and of the Steering Committee of the Ph.D. Program in International Economic Law of the same university. He holds a Ph.D. in Comparative and International Taxation, Master of Laws at the University of Michigan, is a Visiting Scholar at Yale University Law School, and a Visiting Professor at Université Sorbonne, Paris. He is also a member of the Faculty of Scuola Direzione Aziendale (SDA) – Bocconi and of the International Network for Tax Research – OECD, Paris. He is Coordinator of Comitato Tecnico Internazionale at Bocconi University, Editor of *EC Tax Review* and of *Diritto tributario internazionale*; Editor-in-Chief of *Fiscalitá Internazionale*; Director of the Series of volumes *Comparative and International Taxation*, Bocconi University Press – Egea, Milan; Editor of four volumes of *Aspetti fiscali delle operazioni internazionali*, 1995; *Convenzione Italia-USA contro le doppie imposizion. Commentario*, 2001; *Le Convenzioni dell'Italia in materia di imposte su reddito e patrimonio. Commentario*, 2002; *Aspetti internazionali della riforma fiscale*, Milan, 2004. He is author of *Manuale di tassazione internazionale*, Milan, 2005, and of three monographs (*La tassazione del reddito transnazionale*, Padova, 1990; *La tassazione delle operazioni sul capitale e sulle poste del patrimonio netto*, Milan, 1993, *Imposizione ed effettivitá*, Padova, 2003), as well as of about 60 publications on Italian, comparative, and international taxation.

Marcel Gérard is Professor of Economics and Taxation at FUCaM, the Catholic University of Mons. He also teaches at the Catholic University of Louvain,

Louvain-la-Neuve, and at the Ecole Supérieure des Sciences Fiscales in Brussels. A member of the CESifo and IDEP networks, and an expert to the OECD and EU Commission, he focuses his research activity on the taxation of company and savings, and more generally on the design of tax systems and public finance.

Jude C. Hays is Assistant Professor of Political Science at The University of Illinois, Urbana-Champaign. He earned Masters and Ph.D. degrees in Political Science at the University of Minnesota (2000), and has published several articles in *European Union Politics, International Organization, World Politics, International Studies Quarterly, Journal of Economic Behavior and Organization*, and others, chapters in two edited volumes and one handbook, plus a dissertation, *Globalization and the Crisis of Embedded Liberalism: The Role of Domestic Political Institutions*.

Jenny E. Ligthart is a Full Professor of Quantitative Economics at the Department of Economics of Tilburg University and the University of Groningen. In addition, she is the Director of the Netherlands Network of Economics (NAKE) – the Dutch national graduate school – and is a Senior Research Fellow at CentER and CESifo. Her research focuses on the macroeconomic repercussions of fiscal policy. Prior to joining Tilburg University, she worked for five years at the IMF's Fiscal Affairs Department in Washington, DC. She holds M.A. and Ph.D. degrees in Economics from the University of Amsterdam.

Alexsandro Broedel Lopes is Associate Professor of Accounting and Finance at the University of São Paulo, Brazil and Ph.D. student in Accounting and Finance (ABD) at the University of Manchester. He is a member of the Education Advisory Group of the International Accounting Standards Board (IASB), a Fellow of the Brazilian National Science Foundation (CNPQ), Research Director of Fucape, and Editor of the *Brazilian Business Review*. He is a former Doctoral Fellow at the London School of Economics and Research Assistant at the Financial Markets Group (2000/2001). He prepared the Education part of the ROSC project for the World Bank in Brazil. Alexsandro has a B.Sc. and a Doctoral degree in Accounting and Control from the University of São Paulo, and is interested in international capital market-based accounting research, business analysis and valuation, accounting for derivative financial instruments, and the link between accounting and corporate governance.

Robert W. McGee is a Professor at the Andreas School of Business, Barry University in Miami, Florida, USA. He has published more than 300 articles and more than 40 books in the areas of accounting, taxation, economics, law, and philosophy. His experience includes consulting with the governments of several former

Soviet, East European, and Latin American countries to reform their accounting and economic systems.

Irina Nasadyuk is a member of the Economics Faculty of the Department of International Economic Relations and Economic Theory at Odessa National University in Odessa, Ukraine. She has published several papers on tax evasion in transition economies. Irina is extensively involved in the Academic Fellowship Program of the Open Society Institute, facilitating the sustainability of reforms in higher education in Ukraine.

Gaëtan Nicodème is an economist at the European Commission's General Directorate for Economic and Financial Affairs, where he works on taxation and quality of public finance. He is also Assistant Professor at the Solvay Business School at the Free University of Brussels. His research focuses on corporate taxation, taxation of savings, and tax competition, with an emphasis on the European Union.

Jorge Katsumi Niyama is Professor and Coordinator of Master Program in Accounting at the Universidade de Brasilia. He received his Masters and Ph.D. degrees from the Universidade de São Paulo and a post-doctorate from the University of Otago, New Zealand. He is the author of *Contabilidade de Instituições Financeiras* (*Accounting for Financial Institutions*) and *Contabilidade Internacional* (*International Accounting*).

Paolo M. Panteghini was born in Brescia in 1965, and obtained a degree in Economics at the Università degli Studi di Brescia and a Ph.D. in Economics at the University of Pavia. He has done research at the University of Glasgow and the EPRU of Copenhagen. His main research interest is corporate taxation. He is also a Professor of Public Economics at the University of Brescia and a CESifo fellow.

Gwenaël Piaser has research interests essentially centering around microeconomic theory and applications. Professor Piaser obtained a Ph.D. in December 2001 from the University of Toulouse with a thesis mainly on public economics theory, shedding light on strategic interactions among individuals and governments in an environment where there is incomplete information. Professor Piaser has been a visiting researcher at CORE (Catholic University of Louvain) for three years and is a researcher at the University of Venice (Cá Foscari).

Fernando M.M. Ruiz is research assistant at the Catholic University of Mons, Academie Louvain, Belgium. He is a member of the IDEP, World Economic Survey Expert Group and Société Académique Vaudoise. His area of research is public economics, particularly tax competition and convergence in tax systems.

César Augusto Tibúrcio Silva is the Director of the School of Accountancy, Business, Economy and Information Science, and Professor of Management Accounting at the Universidade de Brasilia. He received his Doctorate from the Universidade de São Paulo, and is the author of *Contabilidade Básica* (*Basic Accounting*) and *Administração de Capital de Giro* (*Working Capital Management*).

Arilton Teixeira is a Director and an Associate Professor at the Capixaba Research Foundation (FUCAPE), Vitoria, Brazil. Dr Teixeira holds a Ph.D. in Economics from the University of Minnesota at Twin Cities. He has received an M.A. in Economics from the Catholic University, Rio de Janeiro, Brazil. His main research interests are growth and development economics and international trade. Dr Teixeira has been a visiting scholar at the research department of the Federal Reserve Bank of Minneapolis.

Thomas Tucha is a business economist with over six years of significant economic and corporate consulting expertise in the field of global transfer pricing. He has worked as a consultant with emphasis in the area of qualitative and quantitative transfer pricing analysis for several consulting companies, such as Voegele Partner GmbH, Frankfurt/Main, and NERA Economic Consulting GmbH, Munich. He was Assistant Professor in a joint research program between the University of Freiburg and KPMG, Frankfurt, on 'new approaches for margin analyses using econometric methodology'. As regards ongoing transfer pricing research, he is engaged in the research project 'Measuring Valuable Transactions in Global Companies', which is designed to generate advanced models of cross-border income allocation. Professionally, he focused on the development of models of quantitative valuation and was responsible for structuring strategic transfer pricing planning of MNE. In addition, he implemented such models into application software. His engagements frequently involved IT aspects and software implementation of transfer pricing models. Thomas Tucha's expertise spans a variety of analytical transfer pricing methods, including function and risk analysis, transfer pricing diagnostics and database-driven screening and margin analyses. Recently, he has specialized in the analysis of complex transfer pricing structures for international loss utilization projects and transfer pricing optimization systems on the basis of value chain analysis. He has been involved in the design and conceptualization of transfer pricing and expatriate documentation software systems, as well as in projects on cost allocation and global tax minimization analysis. His focus has been on the structuring and design of complex transfer pricing transactions and the implementation of strategic transfer pricing solutions.

He is a Partner at GlobalTransferPricing Business Solutions GmbH (www. GlobalTransferPricing.com).

Leonardo Vieira is an economist, senior adviser for Banco Central do Brasil (Central Bank of Brazil), and an expert in foreign transactions.

Gino Vita has worked for 24 years for the Canada Revenue Agency in various positions, including business file auditor, investigator for the investigation division, and national project coordinator. He has contributed to a number of international investigations and uncovered a number of tax-related schemes. Recently, Mr. Vita left the agency to take up the position of Senior Compliance Officer with the Financial Transaction and Report Analysis Centre of Canada (FINTRAC), Canada's Financial Intelligence Unit. Mr. Vita has a CMA designation as well as an executive MBA from the University of Quebec in Montreal and another from Paris-Dauphine in Paris, France.

Part 1

International Taxation
Theory

The Evolution of
International Taxation

Colin Read

Abstract
International taxation is becoming less and less about national sovereignty and increasingly about tax competition and the need for harmonization. While expanding spheres of economic influence meant that the first important steps of international taxation arose as the United States grappled with 50 semi-sovereign tax states and a growing influence around the world, many of our lessons now come from the experiences of the European Union countries. At the same time, the economics of international taxation theory increased in sophistication. The confluence of these influences could not come at a better time as emerging nations have the opportunity to, often for the first time, introduce new and integrated international taxation protocols. These countries can benefit from the collective insights before them, many of which are summarized in the articles assembled in this book.

1.1 Introduction

There was a time, before customs unions, free trade treaties, GATT, and other post-WW1 institutions, when international aspects of taxation were confined to tariffs and treaties. Innovations in transportation began to open up the trade in goods. Colonization and the heartland/hinterland political realities set up systems of trade in services. However, the resulting taxation implications of these innovations were often confined to excise taxes and customs duties or the domestic taxation of profits from these new multinational corporations. The spread of the Western economic model, 'innovations' in taxation avoidance, freer flows of capital resulting from balance of trade surpluses and the spread of capitalism all required innovations in the treatment of foreign profits, and, as such, the measurement of foreign costs and revenues. This is the traditional scope of international taxation. However, as firms become more clever in adjusting to new tax regimes, as broader customs unions (most notably the EU) give rise to more unified international taxation principles, and as a greater share of international trade becomes centered around the movement of services rather than goods, new international taxation principles soon arose. This is especially true as labor more easily commutes across borders, and as the definition of the value and location of a good or service changes with innovations such as the Internet and supply chain management. The articles in this book describe some of the innovations, in theory and practice, and their implications on tax policy in the developed and emerging nations.

In the first part of the book, we begin by describing the important implications of globalization on labor mobility, effective tax rates, and tax competition. In their quest to meld tax policy with economic growth, policymakers are now delving

5

into the academic literature on international taxation competitiveness to gain insights into optimal tax policy. The number of variables in play is forcing this increased sophistication. At one time, the policymaker could hold hostage their capital stock, exchange rate, and especially their labor force. Now, however, even the productivity of labor easily crosses borders in the Internet era of call-center outsourcing. The virtual worker can be located anywhere, which creates challenges for the taxation policymaker.

In the chapter entitled 'Summary, Description, and Extensions of the Capital Income Effective Tax Rate Literature', Professors Fernando M.M. Ruiz and Marcel Gérard assist us in the theoretical discussion of tax harmonization through their analysis of effective tax rates. They make a distinction important in international tax planning by differentiating between marginal and average tax rates in environments with technological progress, uncertainty, and competitive pressures. Their important conclusions regarding the endogeneity of effective tax rates on international variables is a point particularly relevant for international tax policymakers.

In a chapter entitled 'Empirical Models of International Capital-tax Competition', Professors Robert J. Franzese Jr and Jude C. Hays also model the inter-relationship between domestic and global politics and international tax competition. They create for us a foundation within which to evaluate international tax policy from a policy-maker's perspective. The goal of any tax policy should be the enhancement of the social welfare of the citizenry. Concepts of tax burden and efficiency must inevitably be used to validate the myriad tax regimes and their effects on international trade and capital movements. Nations are now coming to realize the strategic interdependence in their tax policymaking. This chapter makes a valuable contribution to that discussion. The authors point out some surprising implications about tax burdens that frustrate rather than further the goals of tax policymakers.

Professor Gwenaël Piaser continues this line of discussion in the chapter entitled 'Labor Mobility and Income Tax Competition'. The author also stresses the critical nature of our assumptions of mobility of capital, goods and services, and labor. This chapter streamlines the analysis by considering a two-country model that, while in the abstract, nonetheless nicely parallels the success of some countries, most notably Ireland, in increasing its mix of skilled workers and hence its tax revenue by decreasing its tax rate. This chapter also provides a nice theoretical foundation for some of the experiments currently being considered in the new Eastern European EU members.

We next follow up this theoretical discussion with a number of policy-oriented chapters devoted to optimal international tax policy in practice. The example of international tax policy innovation has often originated in the USA. However, the European Union now plays a leading role in tax harmonization. The European Union is a laboratory for the emerging insights into balancing international tax competition and cooperation. This second part of the book focuses on specific EU responses to international taxation within an environment of customs unions. Never before has there been such effective avenues for tax policy coordination. This is creating both an opportunity for the European Union to live up to its billing, and a laboratory for other countries to observe and emulate.

We begin by treating a challenge more prevalent as globalization becomes more significant – the need for securitization in global transactions. In 'Taxable Asset Sales in Securitization', Professor Paul Ali points out that various national policies on securitization more or less accomplish the various goals of corporations. These goals include raising of funds, improvement of their balance sheets, and better management of capital requirements. Professor Ali describes the method of securitization increasingly used to meet these requirements.

With the juxtaposition of greater global competition and greater cooperation within the EU, the tension between these two forces provide for an interesting study. As an example, Professors Markus Brem and Thomas Tucha make two important contributions to the book. These authors are concerned with the emergence of Advance Pricing Agreements (APAs) that allow reduced uncertainty in international tax planning. The innovations of APAs are a positive example of proactive policymaking designed to improve international commerce by improving the ability of a firm to tax plan. The authors point out that there are a variety of potential factors to be considered in international APAs, and discuss the importance of these factors on solutions chosen to meet idiosyncratic national needs.

The authors follow the discussion up with a discussion of the 'arm's length analysis' convention on transfer pricing, currently being considered by the Model Tax Convention group of the Organization for Economic Cooperation and Development (OECD). The authors describe a framework for the comparison of alternative APA and transfer pricing regimes, based on the notion of subtleties between risk insurable (or insured) and uncertainty as managed by related parties or entrepreneurs. In doing so, they authors help us better understand the best approaches to transfer pricing under the 'arm's length' methodology.

To close our discussion of innovations in international taxation, we include a chapter by Professor Gaëtan Nicodème entitled 'Corporate Tax Competition and Coordination in the European Union'. In that paper, Professor Nicodème adds to the transfer pricing mix the notion of thin capitalization, and presents some empirical results of his analysis of tax competition in the EU. The discussion includes particular responses by European Union countries to the tax competition and tax coordination dilemmas. This discussion rounds off the theoretical section of the book and acts as a springboard for the next part by discussing specific responses to the tax harmonization agenda through the institutions of International Financial Reporting Standards and the European Company Statute.

We then go on to outline various dimensions of corporate tax competition within the world's largest economic union. In 'Corporate Taxation in Europe: Competitive Pressure and Cooperative Targets', Professors Carlo Garbarino and Paolo M. Panteghini make the important observation that nations must balance both short-term and medium-term goals, as all the while they consider the effect of their policies on their economic union partners. They observe that the formation of a union both creates for more intimate competition while at the same time creating the opportunity for greater coordination. These strange bedfellows, when combined with policy learning and with competition from outside the union, create a dynamic policy mix. The authors use these insights to discuss the various ways the EU and the USA have embarked upon their international taxation policy reforms.

Professor Jenny Ligthart focuses on differential savings rates within the European Union in her paper entitled 'The Economics of Taxing Cross-border Savings Income: An Application to the EU Savings Tax'. She observes that innovations in international treaties and alliances are having the effect of reducing a country's tax policy potency. There has been a growing literature in the institutional arrangements of tax information sharing (see, for instance, the Gregoriou–Vita–Ali paper found elsewhere in this volume), there has been little work describing the economics of increased savings mobility. This chapter provides an excellent discussion of the political economy of global financial and taxation information sharing, a problem particularly vexing given the competing desire for domestic taxation autonomy.

In 'Tax Misery and Tax Happiness: A Comparative Study of Selected Asian Countries', Professor Robert W. McGee looks at public finance aspects of tax burdens within the Asian countries. The paper explores whether there has been a convergence of tax systems within these countries, and explores whether various tax policies are associated with greater social welfare.

Finally, we look at the broader global implications of increased capital and labor mobility. The countries outside the USA and the EU are in an interesting position. They have the opportunity to either reform or create their national taxation regimes based on the evolution of US and EU taxation principles. At the same time, however, they are able to create truly modern systems that respond to today's global marketplace. There is sometimes an advantage to the country that can adopt new practices without having to adapt their legacy practices.

We begin with an interesting paper that asks to what extent tax compliance is possible, from an ethical perspective. In 'The Ethics of Tax Evasion: Lessons for Transitional Economies', Irina Nasadyuk and Robert W. McGee place tax evasion into a historical perspective, and in doing so, draw forward three important insights – that tax evasion is viewed as ethical under certain circumstances, that the question of fairness is inextricably linked to this ethic, and that human rights abuses or corruption issues may indeed make for ethical tax evasion in the minds of the citizenry. This paper places tax compliance into a historical and philosophical perspective that appears quite obvious by the paper's conclusion.

In the second paper of this section on globalization, Professors Greg N. Gregoriou, Gino Vita, and Paul U. Ali discuss the dramatic rise of money laundering in their paper 'Money Laundering: Every Financial Transaction Leaves a Paper Trail'. They begin by defining money laundering, then describe its various degrees, and conclude with the economic costs associated with laundering on national economies and international commerce and taxation. They also discuss some efforts of countries to cooperate to reduce the incidence of money laundering.

We conclude with three responses from emerging nations. In 'Tax Effects in the Valuation of Multinational Corporations: The Brazilian Experience', Professors César Augusto Tibúrcio Silva, Jorge Katsumi Niyama, José Antônio de França, and Leonardo Vieira describe the experiences of Brazil on the valuation and taxation of multinational corporations. They point out that emerging nations must develop new institutions to deal with these new realities given rise by globalization. In their analysis, they focus on both the multinational corporation's experience and on the national experience.

We conclude this section and this book with a paper by Professors Alexandre B. Cunha, Alexsandro Broedel Lopes, and Arilton Teixeira, who collaborate to discuss the economics of reform in their chapter entitled 'The Economic Impacts of Trade Agreements and Tax Reforms in Brazil: Some Implications for Accounting Research'. The authors use a sophisticated general equilibrium model to describe the effects of tax reform in Brazil. By developing their general equilibrium model, the authors can better describe the welfare-enhancing effects of various types of internationalization, such as enhanced trade with Argentina or membership in the Free Trade Area of the Americas. They take note of the daunting task to include and reform emerging nations into a new taxation regime. They also leave us with the important message that emerging nations must improve accounting and taxation systems to enhance national well-being.

This combination of articles leaves the reader with one obvious conclusion. Never before has there been such a consciousness about the reality of tax competition and the need for tax harmonization. These lessons became acute as the European Union progressed toward greater harmonization. The lessons learned are in good time for emerging nations to learn from these hard-discovered experiences.

Summary, Description, and Extensions of the Capital Income Effective Tax Rate Literature

Fernando M.M. Ruiz and Marcel Gérard

Abstract

In this paper we summarize the capital income effective tax rate literature. An effective tax rate (ETR) can be defined as a measure intended to estimate the real tax burden on an economic activity. Departing from the cost of capital formulation, we describe the development of forward- and backward-looking marginal and average tax rates. We shed some light on the pros and cons of each approach, and we propose some simple extensions: a marginal effective tax with technological progress, an average effective tax with uncertainty and the entrance of rival firms, and an average effective tax rate on the cost of production.

2.1 Introduction

The main challenge for any empirical researcher studying taxation across countries is the selection of an appropriate measure for the tax. A priori, he could work with the statutory tax rates, but given the multiple provisions of the tax codes affecting the tax base, they do not represent a good approximation of the tax burden, resulting in a usual overestimation of the amount of the effective tax weight. In particular, in the case of income from capital, the taxable income differ from the true economic income on various respects. Among them, the most common are: the treatment of capital gains on realization rather than on an accrual basis generates a deferral which lowers the effective tax burden; the tax depreciation differs from the economic depreciation; imputed rental incomes are usually not taxed; etc.

To overcome that complexity and to obtain a summary measure that can be comparable and usable in an econometric analysis, economists have been working on the development of so-called effective tax rates for more than 20 years. Furthermore, those measures are important for the political debate in comparing the situation of local enterprises with respect to foreign competitors.

An effective tax rate (ETR) can be defined as a measure intended to estimate the real tax burden on an economic activity. Several estimates have been constructed in an attempt to find the 'true' effective tax rate. This chapter, as an extension of Gérard and Ruiz (2005), aims to summarize all different approaches estimating effective tax rates, and to shed some light on their pros and cons.

The different measures can be grouped in various forms, depending on what they assess or what kind of information they use. The answer to those questions gives, respectively, the classical separation between marginal ETR vs. average ETR and backward-looking ETR vs. forward-looking ETR. This classification can be sketched as in Figure 2.1, although some approaches might be included in more than one branch.[1]

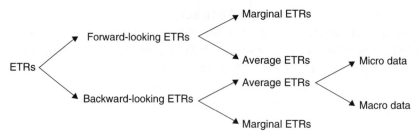

Figure 2.1   ETRs classification

2.2   Forward-looking ETRs

The forward-looking indicators intend to summarize the various provisions of the tax codes in a single measure, which assesses the real tax burden on a hypothetical project. Given the complexity of tax systems, a central question is whether we can obtain an accurate estimate. Before attempting an answer, let us show how they are constructed.

2.2.1   The cost of capital

The main concept surrounding the marginal ETR is a summary statistic, known as the 'cost of capital', which tries to capture all the features of the tax system. The cost of capital defines the rate of return that a firm must earn on an investment project before taxes just to break even.

Following Auerbach (1983) and Alworth (1988), we present an expression for the cost of capital from the neoclassical Jorgenson (1963) model. Though the cost of capital can be derived from a discrete time model, we will use the more common continuous time formulation. Let us assume a firm producing output using a single capital input ($F(K)$ and $F' > 0, F'' < 0$). The capital goods decay exponentially at a constant rate δ. Thus, the capital stock at time t is:

$$K_t = \int_{-\infty}^{t} e^{-\delta(t-s)} I_s \, ds, \tag{2.1}$$

where I_s is investment at date $s \leq t$. By differentiation of the above equation with respect to t, we obtain the net investment transition equation:

$$\dot{K}_t = I_t - \delta K_t. \tag{2.2}$$

The firm's optimization problem consists of choosing the investment plan at each time that maximizes the wealth of its owners. However, since the determination of an optimal investment path is contingent upon the determination of an optimal capital path, a more useful expression is obtained by determining the optimal size of the latter. Concisely, without personal taxes, owners' wealth is maximized with respect to K_t:

$$W = \int_0^\infty e^{-\rho t}(b_t F(K_t) - \tau Y - q_t I_t)\,dt \quad s.t.(2.2), \tag{2.3}$$

where ρ is the financial cost or the firm's discount rate, which will be clarified below. Additionally, b_t is the price of output, q_t the price of capital goods, τ the statutory tax rate ($0 \leqslant \tau \leqslant 1$) and Y is taxable income.

Taxable income is defined as output less depreciation allowances, immediate expensing or free depreciation and tax credits permitted by the tax authorities (A_l). Therefore,

$$Y = b_t F(K_t) - A_l q_t I_t. \tag{2.4}$$

Substituting the above equation in the firm's optimization problem (2.3) and denoting $A = \tau A_l$, the Euler condition, which must hold at the optimum yields:

$$C_t \equiv F'(K_t) = \frac{q_t}{b_t}\left(\delta + \rho - \frac{\dot{q}}{q_t}\right)\frac{1-A}{1-\tau}.$$

The term C_t is the cost of capital, expressing the shadow price of capital at time t. Hence, the firm will carry investment until the rate of return of the marginal investment is equal to the cost of the investment (the right-hand side of the equation). If inflation is neutral in the sense that $\dot{q}/q_t = \dot{b}/b_t = \pi$ and $q_t = b_t = 1$, the expression above reduces to:

$$C_t \equiv F'(K_t) = (\delta + \rho - \pi)\frac{1-A}{1-\tau}. \tag{2.5}$$

When the rate of allowances (A) or inflation (π) increases, the cost of capital declines. And when the depreciation rate (δ) or the discount rate (ρ) increases, the cost of capital follows the same direction. Additionally, an increase in the tax rate will raise the cost of capital, although it also raises A.

In the absence of taxes, equation (2.5) implicitly defines the demand for capital as a function of real interest rate ($K(r)$).[2] The firm will invest until the net return to one unit of capital equals the rate of return to savings:

$$F'(K_t) - \delta = r.$$

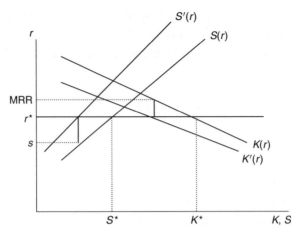

Figure 2.2   Capital demand and supply functions

Similarly, let us define capital supply as a function of real interest rate $(S(r))$,[3] and assume that the economy is small and open, implying that the real interest rate is determined internationally.

In Figure 2.2 we illustrate the situation of a capital importing country,[4] where domestic capital demand is K^*, funding given by residents is S^*, and the difference is supplied by foreigners.

If the return to capital is taxed, the real rate of return will differ from r^* and the capital demand curve will usually shift leftwards, reflecting the distortion in domestic investments. This tax distortion on the marginal investment can be observed by rearranging equation (2.5) to obtain:

$$F'(K_t) - \delta = r + \frac{(\tau - A)(\delta + r)}{(1 - \tau)},$$

where the second term measures the difference between the net return to capital and the real rate of return, indicating the extra earnings the company must achieve to pay the investor a return r. Nevertheless, this wedge is not necessarily positive, since a tax system may provide allowances and investment incentives causing a negative tax liability.

Like the capital demand, the capital supply curve will move left after the imposition of a personal tax on interest income, and savers will receive a post-tax real rate of return s. The presence of taxes imposes a wedge between the gross marginal rate of return (MRR) and the after-tax real rate of return, which could be disaggregated between the wedge generated by the corporate tax $(w_c = \text{MRR} - r^*)$ and the wedge generated by personal tax on savings $(w_p = r^* - s)$.

Sinn (1988) correctly points out that the distortion introduced by a tax on capital and savings does not have obvious implications for international capital movements. This is due to the fact that capital import is a rising function of taxes on domestic savings and a decreasing function of taxes on capital demand. Therefore, tax wedges should not be added together if we want to analyze the effect of taxes on international capital flows, although the variation in the demand for capital investment in the short run is probably more important than the variation in savings supply.

2.2.2 Marginal ETR

The main early study on marginal ETR (METR) levied on capital income is the work of King and Fullerton (1984), which is based on the papers of Jorgenson (1963), Hall and Jorgenson (1967), and King (1974), as a natural extension of the cost of capital approach. The study of King and Fullerton[5] is the first to compare METR for different countries (the USA, the UK, Sweden, and West Germany) following a uniform methodology.

The name marginal comes to indicate that the estimate measures the tax levied on a cash flow derived from a marginal increase of capital stock in a firm. In this way, the METR measures the actual incentives offered by the tax system for an additional investment. The central assumption is that the marginal benefit of the investment will equal the marginal cost, implying that the project does not generate rents over the interest rate.

The basic idea in King and Fullerton is founded on the wedge discussed in the previous section between the pre-tax real rate of return on a marginal investment (p) and the post-tax real rate of return to the saver who finances the investment (s). In summary, the METR is then the tax wedge expressed as a percentage of the pre-tax rate of return:[6]

$$\text{METR} = \frac{p - s}{p}. \tag{2.6}$$

As we mentioned before, the cost of capital measures the minimum rate of return the project must yield before taxes in order to provide the saver with the same net of tax return he or she would receive from lending at the market interest rate. In King and Fullerton, the pre-tax real rate of return is computed in a straightforward way. Abstracting from risk, wealth taxes on corporations, and tax treatment of inventories, one marginal euro of corporate investment in a real asset must yield a gross return equal to that in equation (2.5). Therefore, the pre-tax rate of return on the project is equal to the cost of capital less economic depreciation, $p = C - \delta$:

$$p = \frac{(1 - A)}{1 - \tau}(\rho + \delta - \pi) - \delta. \tag{2.7}$$

Considering now the post-tax real rate of return for the investor, this is equal to:

$$s = (1 - m)(r + \pi) - \pi - w_p, \tag{2.8}$$

where m is the marginal personal tax rate on interest income, r is the real rate of interest, π is the rate of inflation and w_p is the marginal personal tax rate on wealth.

The standard depreciation allowances, immediate expensing or free depreciation and tax credits (A), first stated in equation (2.4), can be expressed as:

$$A = f_1 A_d + f_2 \tau + f_3 g, \tag{2.9}$$

where f_1 is the proportion of the cost of an asset subject to the standard depreciation allowances (A_d), f_2 is the proportion of the cost qualifying for immediate expensing at corporate tax rate τ, and f_3 denotes the proportion qualifying for grants at the rate of grant g. The exact form of this expression depends on the provisions of the tax code. Considering only that the present value of standard allowances depends upon the pattern of tax depreciation, several formulas are allowed in the tax systems (declining balance, straight line, sum-of-the-years digits, etc.).[7] For instance, if depreciation is granted at a rate α on a declining balance basis on historical cost:

$$A_d = \int_0^\infty \tau a e^{-(a + \rho - \pi)t} \, dt = \frac{\tau a}{a + \rho - \pi}. \tag{2.10}$$

From expression (2.9) we can derive the following well-known proposition.

Proposition 1   In the absence of personal taxes and with equity finance, if the tax code allows for full immediate expensing of investment, the METR is equal to zero.

Proof   Under immediate expensing $A = \tau$, and replacing in equation (2.7), it follows immediately that METR $= 0$.

Finally, King and Fullerton link the firm's discount rate (ρ) with the market interest rate (i), depending upon the source of finance: Debt, new shares issues, and retained earnings. When choosing one of these sources, the firm will try to minimize its financial cost (see Alworth, 1988, Chapter 5).

If the project is financed by debt, the discount rate is net of tax interest rate, given that nominal interest income is taxed and nominal interest payments are tax deductible:

$$\rho = i(1 - \tau) \tag{2.11}$$

The discount rate for the other two sources of finance will depend on the personal tax system and the corporate tax system. King (1974) already defined the corporate tax system in terms of two variables, the corporate tax rate (τ – tax paid if no profits are distributed) and a variable θ, which measures the degree of discrimination between retentions and distributions. 'More formally, θ is defined as the opportunity cost of retained earnings in terms of net dividends foregone, that is the amount which shareholders could receive if one unit of retained earnings were distributed' (King, 1974, p. 23). Consequently, if one unit of dividend is distributed, θ goes to the shareholder and the remaining $1 - \theta$ goes in tax. In this way, the tax revenue on company profits is:

$$T = \tau Y + \frac{1 - \theta}{\theta} D,$$

where τ is the corporate tax, Y is the total taxable profit, $(1 - \theta)/\theta$ is the additional liability per unit of dividends received by the shareholder before personal tax and D is the gross dividend.

In the classical system of corporate tax,[8] $\theta = 1$ because no additional tax is collected or refunded. In an imputation system $\theta > 1$ because a tax credit is attached to dividends paid out. In the latter case, if we call n the rate of imputation, the total tax liability is $T = \tau Y - nD$ and $\theta = 1/(1 - n)$.

When the firm finances the investment with new equity, the investor requires a rate of return $i(1 - m)$ (the opportunity cost rate of return). If the project yields a return ρ, the net of tax dividend is equal to $(1 - m)\theta\rho$. Equating the latter with the opportunity cost, the firm's discount rate is:

$$\rho = \frac{i}{\theta}. \tag{2.12}$$

When the firm uses its retained earnings, the investor would require a yield $\rho(1 - z) = i(1 - m)$, where z is the effective personal tax rate on accrued capital gains, and the discount rate is given by:

$$\rho = i\left(\frac{1 - m}{1 - z}\right). \tag{2.13}$$

19

It follows from equations (2.7) and (2.8), and (2.11), (2.12) or (2.13), that in the absence of taxes, $p = s = r$.

The general formulas for the different sources of finance are not free of criticism. Scott (1987) reformulates the expression for debt and equity finance considering that the company wishes to maximize the present value of all net payments made to its shareholders and, therefore, they receive the same net of tax rate of return independently of the way they finance the firm. In the case of debt finance, he attacks the flaw that the firm's discount rate is independent of the shareholders. For equity finance, the expressions of King and Fullerton seem to ignore real returns in new shares and the problem of realization on accrued capital taxes.

King and Fullerton consider a domestic investment financed by domestic saving. However, the methodology can be extended to the complex taxation of international investments and multinational companies, as was done by Alworth (1988), OECD (1991), Gérard (1993), Devereux and Griffith (1998), and Devereux (2003), including in this framework the different methods of double taxation relief,[9] withholding taxes, transfer prices, etc.

Overall, a forward-looking METR constitutes a useful tool to simulate how changes in specific tax provisions affect the effective tax rates and to observe estimates isolated from other economic factors. However, the METRs that we obtain with this approach are not valid for all the investment projects of the economy, neither for an industry as a whole nor for changes in the sources of finance over time. It depends on the type of asset and industry composition of the investment, the way the project is financed, and the saver who provides the funds. To obtain a summary measure for the whole country, it is necessary to generate a weighted average of all possible combinations, having as weight a variable such as the proportion of capital stock for each particular choice. An alternative approach is to average the parameters before the effective tax is computed, as in Boadway et al. (1984) or McKenzie et al. (1997), who consider an average over sources of finance.

2.2.3 A simple extension to the marginal effective tax

A point completely ignored so far in the determination of the marginal effective tax is the static nature of the production function. In other words, we have neglected the existence and variation of technological progress that can have an important influence on the incentives to invest in a particular location and on the construction of an effective tax series comparable across countries.

For the sake of concreteness, let us assume that the technological progress is purely capital augmenting, i.e. $F(G_t K)$, where G represents the state of the art.

Defining the efficiency capital $k = G_t K$, we take this as the relevant input variable. The transition equation for this new state variable can be found from equation (2.2):[10]

$$\dot{k} = i - k(\delta - g),\qquad(2.14)$$

where g is the rate of technological growth.

Replacing the new production function in equations (2.3) and (2.4), and maximizing subject to (2.14), we obtain the Euler condition:

$$C_t \equiv F'(k_t) = (\delta + \rho - \pi - g)\frac{1 - A}{1 - \tau},$$

where, as expected, the rate of technological growth reduces the cost of capital.

This new variable is a country specific as much as inflation or the tax codes. Ignoring it can lead to some misleading interpretations of a capital income tax. For instance, two or more countries with equal inflation, tax rates, and tax base can be considered to have the same METRs in the traditional analysis. Nevertheless, if one of the countries is subject to a rapid technology change, it is normal, in some way, to put aside the statutory tax rate and to really consider a smaller effective tax.

Devereux et al. (2002) have constructed METR series for a number of countries. Following the analysis above, we can question the comparability across countries and through time of those values. From Figure 2.3 we can ask whether the high METRs at the beginning of the 1980s for Greece and Portugal have any meaning given

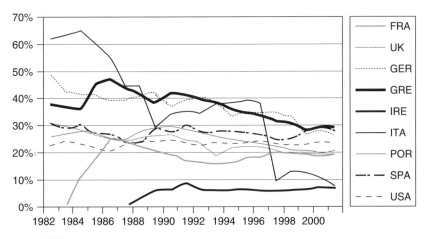

Figure 2.3   METRs

that they joined the EU in 1981 and 1986 respectively. Therefore a higher rate of technological growth is expected for them at that time than for the rest of the countries.

The backward-looking ETRs, presented below, are usually accused of containing too much fluctuation produced by the business cycle and the general economic conditions, which affect the profits of the firm. Along the same lines, we can argue that the forward-looking ETRs have too little fluctuation when ignoring technology change. While some economic parameters can be supposed to remain stable over time and across countries, the rate of technological growth is certainly not one of them.

On the other hand, the proposed approach has a clear limit in requiring a value for the variable g, although particular values for each industry might be constructed.

2.2.4   Average ETR

In the average ETR (AETR) popularized by Devereux and Griffith (1998), the firm has an investment project generating economic rents (i.e. the firm earns more than the capital costs). Here, instead of choosing the optimal size of capital stock, the firm faces mutually exclusive choices, such as setting a plant in one country or another, selecting the firm's technology, choosing the product type or quality, etc. Therefore, a firm would select project A over project B if the net present value of A were higher than that of B ($NPV_A > NPV_B$). Heavily drawing from Sørensen (2004), and keeping abstracting from debt finance, let us examine the similarities and differences between the marginal and average tax.

The AETR can be interpreted as influencing the investment location decision and the METR as determining the optimal level of investment conditional on one of the projects already chosen. In this way, now the tax will drive a wedge between the net present value before tax (NPV^*) and the net present value after tax (NPV):

$$NPV^* - NPVT = NPV,$$

where NPVT is the net present value of taxes. Rearranging terms we can express the AETR as the proportion of the value of the project paid in tax:

$$AETR = 1 - \frac{NPV}{NPV^*} = \frac{NPVT}{NPV^*}.$$

The NPVT is equal to the present value of tax paid less allowances:

$$NPVT = \int_0^\infty \tau(p + \delta)e^{-(\rho + \delta - \pi)t}\,dt - A = \frac{\tau(p + \delta)}{\rho + \delta - \pi} - A$$

and

$$\text{NPV}^* = \int_0^\infty p e^{-(\rho+\delta-\pi)t}\,dt = \frac{p}{\rho+\delta-\pi}$$

It follows that:

$$\text{AETR} = \frac{(\tau - A)(\rho + \delta - \pi) + \tau(p - \rho + \pi)}{p}. \tag{2.15}$$

As pointed out by Devereux (1998) and Sørensen (2004), this measure has some interesting properties, which are also valid, with minor changes, for the effective tax given in section 2.4.

Proposition 2 In the absence of personal taxes, when taxable income is smaller (larger) than true economic income, the AETR and the METR are smaller (larger) than the statutory tax rate, and when taxable income is equal to true economic income, the AETR is equal to the METR and to the statutory tax rate.

Proof For AETR or METR $< \tau$ we need that $A(\delta + r)/\delta > \tau$. From equation (2.4) we know that taxable income is smaller than economic income when depreciation allowances are higher than economic depreciation ($a > \delta$). Using equation (2.10) and replacing above, we have $(\delta + r)/\delta > (a + r)/a$ or $\delta < a$.
    The second part follows immediately from equation (2.10), making $a = \delta$ and replacing in equations (2.7) and (2.15).

Proposition 3 The AETR for a marginal investment is equal to the METR in the absence of personal taxes.

Proof For a marginal investment the economic rent is equal to zero. Hence, the net of tax value must equal the initial investment minus the net present value of economic depreciations:

$$\text{NPV}^* - \text{NPVT} = 1 - \int_0^\infty \delta e^{-(\rho+\delta-\pi)t}\,dt$$

$$\Rightarrow \tilde{p} = \frac{(1 - A)(\rho + \delta - \pi)}{(1 - \tau)} - \delta, \tag{2.16}$$

which is equal to the pre-tax rate of return, equation (2.5). Replacing equation (2.16) in (2.15) and setting $\tilde{p} = p$, we obtain:

$$\text{AETR} = \frac{(\tau - A)(r + \delta)}{(1 - \tau)\tilde{p}} = \text{METR}.$$

Proposition 4   In the absence of personal taxes, the AETR approaches the statutory tax rate for high rates of return.

Proof   As $p \to \infty$, it follows immediately from equation (2.15) that AETR $\to \tau$.

The last two propositions reflect the lower and upper bounds for the AETR. They can be summarized observing that the AETR can be written as a weighted average of the METR and the statutory rate. Using equations (2.16) and (2.17), we can write the AETR as:

$$\text{AETR} = \left(\frac{\tilde{p}}{p}\right)\text{METR} + \left(1 - \frac{\tilde{p}}{p}\right)\tau, \tag{2.17}$$

where for the marginal investment $\tilde{p} = p$ and AETR $=$ METR, and for high rates of return $(p \to \infty)$, AETR $= \tau$.

Proposition 5   In the absence of personal taxes, the AETR increases with profitability if and only if the statutory tax rate is higher than the METR.

Proof   It follows from differentiating equation (2.17) with respect to p.

Proposition 6   Under full immediate expensing the AETR approaches the statutory tax rate for high rates of return, in the absence of personal taxes.

Proof   It follows from Propositions 1 and 4.

The method of Devereux and Griffith is not the only one to calculate an ex-ante AETR. The Centre for European Economic Research and the University of Mannheim have developed the so-called European Tax Analyzer, which allows for the inclusion of more complex and realistic conditions. They have constructed a model-firm approach based on an industry-specific mix of assets and liabilities, including a large number of accounting items. Although the model derives the pre-tax and post-tax values of the firm in a more sophisticated way, making assumptions about the activities of the firm during a 10-year period, the notion of the AETR remains the same (see Jacobs and Spengel, 1999).

2.2.5   An extension to the EATR with uncertainty and the entrance of rival firms

Despite its great simplicity, the ex-ante AETR neglects the fact that the pre-tax rate of return on the project (p) is uncertain and subject to decline due to the appearance of future competitors attracted by extraordinary rents in the industry. Let us consider that assumption, and to model the pre-tax rate of return as a geometric Brownian motion with drift:

$$dp = -\alpha p\, dt + \sigma p\, dz \tag{2.18}$$

where dz is the increment of a Wiener process, $\alpha < 1$ is the drift parameter, and σ the variance parameter. Given that the project is expected to generate economic rents in the beginning, new similar projects will come and reduce the economic rent, a fact that is modeled with a negative trend.

As an example of a geometric Brownian motion with negative drift, we present in Figure 2.4 a sample path of equation (2.18) with a drift rate of 5% per year and a standard deviation of 25% per year. The graphic is built with monthly time intervals.

Now the expected NPV of the project is (see Dixit and Pindyck, 1994):

$$E[NPV^*] = E\left[\int_0^\infty p_t e^{-(\rho+\delta-\pi)t}\, dt\right] = \frac{p_0}{\rho + \delta - \pi + \alpha}$$

and the expected NPVT:

$$E[NPVT] = E\left[\int_0^\infty \tau(p_t + \delta)e^{-(\rho+\delta-\pi)t}\, dt - A\right] = \frac{\tau\delta}{\rho + \delta - \pi} - A + \frac{\pi p_0}{\rho + \delta - \pi + \alpha}.$$

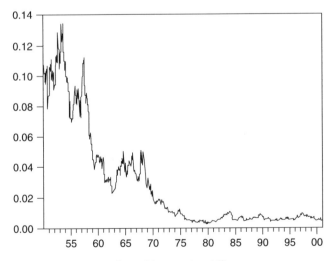

Figure 2.4   Geometric Brownian motion with negative drift

Therefore, the expected AETR is now:

$$E[\text{AETR}] = \frac{(\tau - A)(\rho + \delta - \pi) + \tau(p - \rho + \pi)}{p_0} + \frac{\delta\tau - A(\rho + \delta - \pi)}{p_0(\rho + \delta - \pi)}\alpha.$$

The parameter α reflects the expected rate of decline in the economic rent of the project. Whether the expected average tax is higher or smaller than expression (2.15) depends on country or industry specific values. Nevertheless, we can state the following proposition.

Proposition 7   In the absence of personal taxes, when taxable income is smaller (larger) than true economic income, the $E[\text{AETR}]$ is smaller (larger) than the AETR, and when taxable income is equal to true economic income, the $E[\text{AETR}]$ is equal to the AETR, to the METR, and to the statutory tax rate.

Proof   For $E[\text{AETR}] < \text{AETR}$, we need that $\delta\tau < A(r + \delta)$ and the proof follows as in Proposition 2.

As we can see in Figure 2.4, we are assuming a continuous decline in the rate of return to zero. Nonetheless, this fall in returns has a natural floor imposed by the rational expectation of the entrant firm as to the pre-tax rate of return for the marginal investment ($\tilde{p}$ in equation (2.16)). This lowest value will function as a reflecting barrier, because once it is touched the entry of competitive firms will stop. The expected NPV in this case will be:

$$E[\text{NPV}] = \frac{p_0}{\rho + \delta - \pi + \alpha} + Cp_0^{-\gamma}, \tag{2.19}$$

where $-\gamma < 0$ is the negative root of the fundamental quadratic $r + \delta + \alpha\xi - \sigma^2\xi$ $(\xi - 1)/2 = \phi(\xi)$. The first term in equation (2.19) is the expected NPV when returns continue towards zero and the second term is the increase in value because new entries will stop before zero. Using the Smooth Pasting Condition (for a discussion of the calculation of expected present values, see Dixit, 1993), we can calculate the value of the constant C:

$$F'(\tilde{p}) = 0$$

$$-\gamma C\tilde{p}^{-\gamma-1} + \frac{1}{\rho + \delta - \pi + \alpha} = 0$$

$$C = \frac{\tilde{p}^{1+\gamma}}{\gamma}\frac{1}{\rho + \delta - \pi + \alpha} > 0.$$

We can see that the second term in equation (2.19) is positive, showing that the floor increases the present value of returns by cutting off the downside potential. Then:

$$E[\text{NPV}] = \frac{p_0}{\rho + \delta - \pi + \alpha} + \frac{\tilde{p}^{1+\gamma}}{\gamma}\frac{p_0^{-\gamma}}{\rho + \delta - \pi + \alpha}.$$

For the marginal investment, the return must just cover its cost, implying that $\alpha = 0$ and $p_0 = \tilde{p}$. It follows that:

$$E[\text{NPV}] = \frac{1+\gamma}{\gamma}\frac{\tilde{p}}{\rho + \delta - \pi},$$

where the expected NPV is higher than the normal NPV because the presence of risk increases the cost of the irreversible investment. To be profitable, the investment must pay, in this case, the cost of capital incremented by the risk of the environment. In Pindyck (1991), this overcharge is associated with the value of an investment option. Delaying the investment is costly because it retards the realization of profits, but it is beneficial since it allows the company to watch the evolution of returns in the industry. Observe that the standard deviation of the returns affects the negative roots of the fundamental quadratic. Differentiating totally expression $\phi(\xi)$,

$$\frac{\partial \phi}{\partial \xi}\frac{\partial \xi}{\partial \sigma} + \frac{\partial \phi}{\partial \sigma} = 0$$

and evaluating it at $-\gamma$, $\partial\phi/\partial\xi > 0$, $\partial\phi/\partial\sigma > 0$, and therefore $\partial\xi/\partial\sigma < 0$ as σ increases, γ decreases and $(1+\gamma)/\gamma$ increases. The greater the amount of uncertainty over future values of p, the larger the excess return the firm will demand before it is willing to make the irreversible investment. Note also that when $\sigma \to 0$, $(1+\gamma)/\gamma \to 1$ and $E[\text{NPV}] \to \text{NPV}$, and all other results will tend towards the deterministic case presented earlier. Defining $(1+\gamma)/\gamma = \Gamma$, the expected METR is now:

$$E[\text{METR}] = \frac{\Gamma\tilde{p} - r}{\Gamma\tilde{p}},$$

which is higher than the METR and increases with the level of risk. The intuition behind this is that when the uncertainty on the return of the investment goes up, the value of the waiting option also increases because it is likely that returns will be smaller in the future, and the firm will only invest in a more profitable expected project. If a competitive firm enters when the returns are normal ($\tilde{p}$), it would just break even at the instant when entry takes place, and it would obtain lower returns thereafter. The entrance at that point cannot be justified and the entry threshold must exceed $\tilde{p}$ to compensate periods of supernormal returns and periods of subnormal returns. The level $\Gamma \tilde{p}$ will ensure a normal return on average.[11]

The advantages of the formula above are the facility of computation, given that they require only one additional variable, the variance of the returns (which can be considered as a join variance of prices, demand, and costs), and the readiness of calculation due to the possibility of using existing series. On the other hand, McKenzie (1994) has also developed an expression for an METR under risk and irreversibility of investments. Nevertheless, his derivation is more demanding in information because it ideally needs data on the demand and price of capital variances (although he uses an index of total unsystematic risk). Other kinds of risks, such as market risk, can be added to the cost of capital, equation (2.7), determining a risk premium as the covariance between the industry and market returns as a whole. Devereux (2003) follows that approach and derives an expression for the expected pre-tax rate of return.

2.3   Backward-looking ETRs

Backward-looking effective taxes use data from tax paid on income generated by previous investments, and hence they are not necessarily linked to future tax payments on new investments.

2.3.1   Average ETR

This methodology employs data on capital income tax paid (T) divided by a measure of the pre-tax income from capital. This ratio can be interpreted as an AETR. Moreover, Sørensen (2004) has shown that, under some assumptions, this tax is equal to the forward-looking AETR.

We define the pre-tax total income from capital as $p_t K_t$, where p_t is the average pre-tax rate of return and K_t is capital stock. The backward-looking AETR can be summarized as:

$$\text{AETR}^{\text{B}} = \frac{T_t}{p_t K_t}. \tag{2.20}$$

The total tax paid is equal to taxable income, given in equation (2.4), multiplied by the statutory tax rate. Under constant return to scale (using equation (2.7)), we can write:

$$T_t = \tau_t (p_t + \delta) K_t - AI_t. \tag{2.21}$$

Assuming that the economy has followed a 'golden rule' path where capital stock has grown at a constant rate equal to the real interest rate, so that $rK_t = I_t - \delta K_t$, we can substitute this expression in equation (2.21) to obtain:

$$T_t = ((\tau - A)(r + \delta) + \tau(p - r))K_t. \tag{2.22}$$

Finally, replacing this in equation (2.20), we find the relation between the backward-looking and forward-looking rates:

$$\text{AETR}^B = \frac{(\tau - A)(r + \delta) + \tau(p - r)}{p} = \text{AETR}^F.$$

It is important to highlight that this equation holds while the tax rules have remained constant over time ($a_t = a_{t-1} = \ldots$) and the economy has followed a 'golden rule' path. It is straightforward to show that, under constant return to scale, this is also equal to the METR if $p = \tilde{p}$. Notwithstanding, when capital stock grows at a constant rate equal to the real interest rate considering technological growth,[12] $\text{AETR}^B < \text{AETR}^F$ given that the rate of return remains constant and the amount of allowances increases ex-post, while ex-ante we need to consider a higher net present value of taxes because of the lower discount rate.

2.3.1.1 Micro data

In the backward AETR framework one can distinguish two approaches depending on the source of data used for the tax paid and the pre-tax income from capital. One approach uses micro or accounting firm-specific data and the other approach macro or aggregated economic data.

Generating an effective tax from micro data consists of taking the tax liabilities and profits from the financial statements of companies. The advantages of this method are that it can show the actual tax burden borne by companies and it can estimate an effective ex-post tax rate for different economic sectors and company sizes. Nevertheless, it has the shortcomings of being influenced by economic fluctuations and sectoral shocks, and it does not allow us to isolate features of tax systems. Additionally, the taxation of shareholders is completely omitted and the tax liability may contain tax payments or foreign source income from other locations where the company operates, producing a mismatch between numerator and denominator.

A number of studies have worked with micro AETR. Among them are Feldstein and Summers (1979), Feldstein et al. (1983), and Grubert and Mutti (2000). In the EU we can mention the recent studies of Buijink et al. (2000) and Nicodème (2001).

2.3.1.2 Macro data

The macro approach employs aggregate macroeconomic data of tax revenue and national accounts to compute the effective tax. The first of these methods is the use of corporate tax revenue expressed as percentage of GDP. Among the studies that utilize this method are Slemrod (2004) and Quinn (1997), or articles such as *The Economist* (2004). In spite of its simplicity and the availability of information to generate time series, this method is not really effective as regards corporate tax, given that by definition the GDP is the sum of all factor incomes. Mendoza et al. (1994) proposed the use of the corporate tax revenue plus an estimation of the capital income tax on individuals as a measure of the effective capital tax paid over the total operating surplus of the economy as a measure of the tax base. The main problem of this method is the assumption that households pay the same effective tax rates on capital and labor incomes, when in reality countries apply different statutory tax rates to income from different sources (see Haan and Volkerink, 2000). Martinez-Mongay (2000) adapted the method to use data available at the European Commission and the OECD, but he still considers that household income pays the same average tax rate regardless of the source of such income, whether labor or capital. Carey and Tchilinguirian (2000) observed that and other problems, such as the assumption that all self-employed income is assigned to capital and the lack of harmonization among the national accounts of the countries. They refined the estimates of Mendoza et al., obtaining a somewhat higher effective tax rate on capital, although in general, this change in level does not affect the evolution of the series over time or the cross-country comparison. Another work that applies an equivalent methodology is *Structures of the Taxation Systems in the European Union* (European Commission, 2003).

Overall, the main advantage of these methods is the facility of computation and the data availability. They also take into account implicitly all the elements of taxation. On the other hand, the measure of the effective tax is affected by business cycles, producing high variability in the estimates, having as a direct consequence the difficulty of linking the effective tax to changes in tax policies. Nevertheless, Mendoza et al. argued that this problem is attenuated by the fact that tax revenues and tax bases tend to move together, although this observation does not account for the possibility of carrying forward and carrying back losses, which causes a desynchronization with the cycle.

2.3.2 Marginal ETR

Recently, Gordon et al. (2003) proposed a marginal effective tax rate which may be estimated with ex-post data on tax revenue and income. Their idea is that there is a difference between the actual revenue raised under the current tax system and an estimated revenue, which would be collected under a hypothetical cash flow tax[13] (the so-called R-base tax, where R stands for real) that excludes financial income and replaces depreciation allowances by expensing for new investment. Given that a cash flow tax imposes a zero tax on the marginal investment (due to the absence of distinction between items of current expenditure and capital), the tax of Gordon et al. (2003) can be written as:

$$\text{METR}^{\text{B}} = \frac{(T - E)/K}{(T - E)/K + r(1 - \tau)},\tag{2.23}$$

where E is the tax that would be collected under a cash flow tax, and the other variables are as defined previously.

Sørensen showed that this backward-looking METR is equal to the forward-looking METR under the assumptions used in deriving equation (2.22). From that expression we know that, under full expensing:

$$E = \tau(p - r)K.$$

Therefore, the numerator of equation (2.23) is:

$$\frac{T - E}{K} = (\tau - A)(r + \delta).$$

Additionally, we can write equation (2.16) as:

$$\tilde{p} - r = \frac{(\tau - A)(r + \delta)}{1 - \tau}$$

and by substitution into equation (23), it follows that:

$$\text{METR}^{\text{B}} = \frac{(\tau - A)(r + \delta)}{(1 - \tau)\tilde{p}} = \frac{\tilde{p} - r}{\tilde{p}} = \text{METR}^{\text{F}}.$$

2.4 The cost of production approach

2.4.1 Marginal ETRC

An extension to the cost of capital discussed above is the cost of production introduced by McKenzie et al. (1997). They argue that other noncapital taxes also affect production and location decisions. Their model introduces (as in Jorgenson, 1963) a second production factor (labor) in computing the tax wedge between the marginal cost of production with and without taxes. Including a second input enables one to consider the substitution between them. Hence, the firm's maximization problem is now:

$$\max_{q,L,I} \int_0^\infty e^{-\rho t}[b_t F(K,L) - \tau Y - \varpi L(1 + \tau_L) - q_t I_t]dt \quad s.t.(2) \text{ and } F = F(K,L),$$

where labor price is assumed to be fixed and therefore taxes are fully borne by the firm. If payroll taxes (τ_L) are deducted from the corporate income tax, we have that taxable income is equal to:

$$Y = b_t F(K,L) - A_t q_t I_t - w(1 + \tau_L)L.$$

Solving first the firm's present value cost minimization problem for a constant level of output:

$$\min_{L,I} \int_0^\infty e^{-\rho t}(\varpi L(1 + \tau_L)(1 - \tau) + (1 - A)q_t I)dt.$$

We define the current-value Hamiltonian as:

$$H = wL(1 + \tau_L)(1 - \tau) + (1 - A)q_t I - \lambda(I - \delta K) - \nu(F(K,L) - F).$$

The FOCs are:

$$w(1 + \tau_L)(1 - \tau) - \nu F_L = 0$$

$$(1 - A)q_t - \lambda = 0$$

$$\dot{\lambda} - \rho\lambda = \lambda\delta - \nu F_K.$$

In the steady state we have:

$$\frac{F_k}{F_L} = \frac{q_t(1 - A)(\rho + \delta)}{w(1 + \tau_L)(1 - \tau)},$$

and using equation (2.5), we find that the usual marginal rate of technical substitution equals the ratio of input costs:

$$\frac{F_K}{F_L} = \frac{(p + \delta)}{w(1 + \tau_L)}.$$

This condition, jointly with the production function, gives the conditional factor demand functions for $L(F, \varphi)$ and $K(F, \varphi)$, where φ is a vector of prices, and the instantaneous cost function net of depreciations is:

$$\hat{C}(F, \varphi) = w(1 + \tau_L) L(F, \varphi) + pK(F, \varphi).$$

Thus, the firm's present value maximization problem becomes:

$$\max_q \int_0^\infty e^{-\rho t}(b_t F(K, L) - \hat{C}(F, \varphi))dt,$$

where the first-order condition is simply:

$$b_t = \hat{C}'_F(F, \varphi) \equiv MC(F, \varphi).$$

McKenzie et al. define the marginal effective tax rate on the cost of production (METRC) as the wedge between the gross of tax marginal cost and the net of tax marginal cost, $MC(F, \varphi) - MC(F, \varphi^0)$,[14] divided by the net of tax marginal cost. To keep symmetry with the previous analysis, let us express the tax as a percentage of the gross of tax marginal cost. Under a Cobb–Douglas constant return-to-scale production function, this is equal to the difference between geometric weighted averages of input costs over gross of tax average costs:

$$METRC = \frac{[w(1 + \tau_L)]^c p^d - w^c r^d}{[w(1 + \tau_L)]^c p^d}, \tag{2.24}$$

where c and d are the shares of labor and capital respectively. The similarity between expressions (2.24) with expression (2.6) is obvious under the assumption of no personal taxes.

Considering a Leontief production function,[15] where inputs are used in a fixed proportion:

$$METRC = \frac{[w(1 + \tau_L)] + p - w - r}{[w(1 + \tau_L)] + p} \tag{2.25}$$

Here the effective tax is simply the arithmetic weighted average of the marginal effective tax rates on the inputs, which is higher than the geometric weighted average, reflecting the impossibility for the firm to change.

In order to estimate the METRC it is necessary first to calculate the pre-tax rate of return on the various inputs.

This latter case is equivalent to the marginal tax developed by Gérard et al. (1997),[16] who consider labor incremented by a marginal investment, implying that input factors are used in a particular proportion. A similar formula was also used by Daly and Jung (1987).

2.4.2 Average ETRC

As a natural extension to the model, following the same reasoning as in Gérard (1993) and Devereux and Griffith (1998), we propose an average effective tax rate on the cost of production (AETRC), where factors receive a return other than their marginal product.

Ex-ante, a firm has a production project with a net present value before taxes:

$$\text{NPV}^* = \int_0^\infty (p + w')e^{-(\rho+\delta-\pi)t}\,dt = \frac{p + w'}{\rho + \delta - \pi},$$

where w' is the gross of tax return to labor (i.e. $w' = w(1 + \tau_L)$). Similarly as in section 2.2.4, the net present value of taxes is:

$$\text{NPVT} = \int_0^\infty \tau(p + \delta)e^{-(\rho+\delta-\pi)t}\,dt - A + \int_0^\infty \tau_L w e^{-(\rho+\delta-\pi)t}\,dt$$

$$1 = \frac{\tau(p + \delta)}{\rho + \delta - \pi} - A + \frac{\tau_L w}{\rho + \delta - \pi}.$$

Defining the average effective tax rate as the ratio of the two former expressions, we obtain:

$$\text{AETRC} = \frac{(\tau - A)(\rho + \delta - \pi) + \tau(p - \rho + \pi) + \tau_L w}{p + w'}.$$

We can show that if a marginal product requires a fixed proportion of capital and labor the AETRC is equal to the METRC. Given that for a marginal product we need it to pay the cost of capital plus the incremental labor costs per euro of capital:

$$\text{NPV}^* - \text{NPVT} = 1 - \int_0^\infty \delta e^{-(\rho+\delta-\pi)t}\,dt + \int_0^\infty w e^{-(\rho+\delta-\pi)t}\,dt.$$

From there we obtain expression (2.16), which is the pre-tax rate of return used in equation (2.25).

Similar propositions as before may be derived knowing that the AETRC can be rewritten as:[17]

$$\text{AETRC} = \left(\frac{\tilde{p} + w'}{p + w'}\right)\text{METRC} + \left(1 - \frac{\tilde{p} + w'}{p + w'}\right)\tau,$$

which shows that for very profitable projects the average tax tends to τ. The intuition when is that labor price remains fixed, payroll taxes and allowances become irrelevant for the determination of tax liability.

The general characteristic of the backward-looking AETRs is that they consider different kinds of taxes from various sources. In other words, they tend to aggregate taxes on different inputs, such as corporate income taxes, property taxes on real estate, payroll taxes, etc. That somewhat arbitrary classification and sharing leads us to include part of other inputs' income. For example, Mendoza et al. (1994) consider in the numerator taxes on income, profits and capital gains of corporations, taxes on immovable property, taxes on financial and capital transactions, and, indirectly, taxes on income of individuals. If the diverse inputs can be expressed in a one-to-one relationship, the ex-post tax will reduce to the AETRC. Therefore, it is more precise to consider the backward-looking AETRs as an approximation to the AETRC rather than to the AETR.

2.5   Conclusion: Advantages and disadvantages of using various ETRs

The forward-looking approach of King and Fullerton and Devereux and Griffith can add a number of endless complications as long as careful effort is made to incorporate all provisions of the tax codes and all ways that firms and individuals can respond to them. In this chapter, we have presented and developed some of those extensions and we have given the reference of many others. On the other hand, the backward-looking measures may take all complications implicitly into account, since they work with ex-post collected revenue data. Nevertheless, the real decisions whether to invest or not may be dominated by the current and expected tax rules. This suggests that a forward-looking indicator is the appropriate measure to assess incentives to invest. At this stage one is confronted with reality, which gives us the choice between working an incomplete, always perfectible forward-looking measure, and a sometimes misleading and biased backward-looking effective tax rate. The decision is not easy and the trade-off between completeness and bias is not clear. Both approaches can be justified or dismissed on different grounds. Therefore, we can state that none of the estimates can claim to be accurate. They can only indicate general trends. The final choice of the variable will depend on the particular phenomenon the researcher wants to study, although in the observation of general trends none of the methods should be disregarded.

The selection of a marginal vs. an average tax may have a more clear-cut outcome. Devereux and Griffith conceive the average tax as influencing mutually exclusive investment decisions and leave the place of determining the optimal level of investment for the marginal tax. Furthermore, the properties of these taxes permit the construction of different models, such as that of Devereux et al. (2002). However, in a competitive market, economic rents are not expected to last and marginal or average taxes could be used interchangeably.

Acknowledgments

Fernando Ruiz is indebted to IAP 5/26 for financial support.

Notes

1. Some authors call the forward-looking tax the effective tax and the backward-looking tax the implicit tax.
2. For the moment we abstract from the form the investment is financed, and we assume that the firm's discount rate is equal to the nominal interest rate ($\rho = i = r + \pi$).
3. This function will take a particular form in expression (2.8).
4. Similar conclusions follow for a capital exporting country.
5. The book is usually referred to by the name of the editors (King and Fullerton), although it was written by a larger team of economists.
6. Another measure presented in King and Fullerton is the tax wedge expressed as a percentage of the return to the saver.
7. Some of these formulas are in Hall and Jorgenson (1967).
8. See Appendix A for a discussion of different forms of corporate tax system. Lindhe (2002) analyzes how the various systems affect the cost of capital.
9. Tax relief methods intend to avoid the double imposition derived from taxing the same object in different jurisdictions. The main systems are presented in Appendix B.
10. The derivation of equation (2.14) is as follows. Taking equation (2.2) and multiplying by G we have $GK' = Gl - \delta k$. We can express K' as:

$$\dot{K} = \frac{d}{dt}\left(\frac{k}{G}\right) = \frac{G\frac{dk}{dt} - k\frac{dG}{dt}}{G^2}$$

$$= \frac{1}{G}\dot{k} - \frac{k}{G}g,$$

making

$$g = \frac{\frac{dG}{dt}}{G}.$$

Replacing the above, we obtain expression (2.14).

11. Note that the firm will invest when:

$$\frac{1+\gamma}{\gamma}\,\tilde{p} > \bar{p}.$$

In the absence of taxes and economic depreciations, we can write $\tilde{p} = r$ and the fundamental quadratic $\phi(\xi)$ satisfied by $-\gamma$ as:

$$\tilde{p} - (\tilde{p} + \alpha - \bar{p})\gamma - \frac{1}{2}\sigma^2\gamma(1+\gamma) = 0,$$

where after some rearranging we have:

$$\frac{1+\gamma}{\gamma}\,\tilde{p} = \bar{p} + \frac{1}{2}\sigma^2\gamma\,(1+\gamma),$$

which states that when returns are uncertain, the return must exceed the cost of capital (this result is equivalent to the one developed by Dixit and Pindyck, 1994, p. 145).

12. The 'real' interest rate in the case of technological growth is $r - g$, resulting in:

$$\text{AETR}^\text{B} = \frac{(\tau - A)(r + \delta) + \tau(p - r)}{p},$$

while

$$\text{AETR}^\text{F} = \frac{(\tau - A)(r + \delta - g) + \tau(p - r + g)}{p}.$$

13. A cash-flow tax estimates the tax burden on a cash-in/cash-out basis. If a company buys a machine using equity in year 0 for \$10 and it generates a cash inflow of \$15 in year 1, the taxable income would be \$−10 in year 0 and \$15 in year 1. This is equivalent to full immediate expensing. In other words, a cash flow tax is $\text{CFT} = \tau(F(K) - I)$, which, under similar assumptions as equation (2.22), simplifies to $\text{CFT} = \tau(p - r)K$, equal to E.

14. ϕ^0 is the vector of user prices for inputs that existed prior to the imposition of taxes, i.e. w and qr.

15. The general form for the effective tax in a CES production function is:

$$\text{METRC} = \frac{\left[[w(1+\tau_L)]^{-\rho\varepsilon}c^\varepsilon + p^{-\rho\varepsilon}d^\varepsilon\right]^{\frac{-1}{\rho\varepsilon}} - \left[w^{-\rho\varepsilon}c^\varepsilon + r^{-\rho\varepsilon}d^\varepsilon\right]^{\frac{-1}{\rho\varepsilon}}}{\left[[w(1+\tau_L)]^{-\rho\varepsilon}c^\varepsilon + p^{-\rho\varepsilon}d^\varepsilon\right]^{\frac{-1}{\rho\varepsilon}}},$$

where $\varepsilon = 1/(1 - \rho)$ is the elasticity of substitution.

16. Without personal taxes expression (2.27) in Gérard *et al.* (1997) reduces to $p'^* = p + w(1 + \tau_L)$.

17. Or more generally for the case of n inputs:

$$\text{AETRC} = \left(\frac{\bar{p} + \sum_{i=1}^{n} w'_j}{p + \sum_{i=1}^{n} w'_j}\right)\text{METRC} + \left(1 - \frac{\bar{p} + \sum_{i=1}^{n} w'_j}{p + \sum_{i=1}^{n} w'_j}\right)\tau,$$

where $w'_i = w_i/w_i(1 + t_j)$.

References

Alworth, J. (1988). *The Finance, Investment and Taxation Decisions of Multinationals*. Basil Blackwell.

Auerbach, A. (1983). Taxation, Corporate Financial Policy and the Cost of Capital. *Journal of Economic Literature*, 21(3):905–940.

Boadway, R., Bruce, N., and Mintz, J. (1984). Taxation, Inflation and the Effective Marginal Tax Rate on Capital in Canada. *Canadian Journal of Economics*, 17(1):62–79.

Buijink, W., Janssen, B., and Schols Y. (2000). Evidence of the Effect of Domicile on Corporate Average Effective Tax Rates in the European Union. MARC Working Paper 3/2000-11.

Carey, D. and Tchilinguirian, H. (2000). *Average Effective Tax Rates on Capital, Labour and Consumption*. OECD.

Daly, M. and Jung, J. (1987). The Taxation of Corporate Investment Income in Canada: An Analysis of Marginal Effective Tax Rates. *Canadian Journal of Economics*, 20(3):555–587.

Devereux, M. (2003). Measuring Taxes on Income from Capital. Working Paper 03/04 – IFS.

Devereux, M. and Griffith, R. (1998). The Taxation of Discrete Investment Choices. Working Paper 98/16 IFS.

Devereux, M., Lockwood, B., and Redoano, M. (2002). Do Countries Compete over Corporate Tax Rates? Discussion Paper 3400 – CEPR.

Dixit, A. (1993). *The Art of Smooth Pasting, Fundamentals of Pure and Applied Economics*, 55. Harwood Academic Publishers.

Dixit, A. and Pindyck, R. (1994). *Investment Under Uncertainty*. Princeton University Press.

The Economist (2004). A Taxing Battle, 29 January.

European Commission (2003). *Structures of the Taxation Systems in the European Union*. Technical Report.

Feldstein, M. and Summers, L. (1979). Inflation, Tax Rules and the Long Term Rate of Interest. *National Tax Journal*, 32:445–470.

Feldstein, M.S., Dicks-Mireaux, L., and Poterba, J. (1983). The Effective Tax Rate and the Pretax Rate of Return. *Journal of Public Economics*, 21(2):129–158.

Gérard, M. (1993). In: *Cost of Capital, Investment Location and Marginal Effective Tax Rate: Methodology and Application. Empirical Approaches to Fiscal Policy Modelling* (Heimler, A. and Meulders, D., eds). Chapman & Hall.

Gérard, M. and Ruiz, F. (2005). Marginal, Average and Related Effective Tax Rate Concepts. In *Taxation, Economic Policy and the Economy* (Kanniainen, V. and Kari, S., eds), pp. 17–39. University of Tampere, Finland.

Gérard, M., Beauchot, L., Jamaels, S., and Valenduc, C. (1997). *MESC (Marginal Effective Statutory Charge), An Extension of King–Fullerton Methodology*. II, No. 353. Universität Konstanz.

Gordon, R., Kalambokidis, L., and Slemrod, J. (2003). A New Summary Measure of the Effective Tax Rate on Investment. NBER Working Paper 9535.

Grubert, H. and Mutti, J. (2000). Do Taxes Influence Where US Corporations Invest? *National Tax Journal*, 53:825–840.

Haan, J. and Volkerink, B. (2000). Effective Tax Rates in Macroeconomics: A Note. Mimeograph.

Hall, R. and Jorgenson, D. (1967). Tax Policy and Investment Behavior. *American Economic Review*, 57(3):391–414.

Jacobs, O. and Spengel, C. (1999). *The Effective Average Tax Burden in the European Union and the USA*. ZEW.

Jorgenson, D. (1963). Capital Theory and Investment Behavior. *American Economic Review*, 53(2):247–259.

King, M. (1974). Taxation and the Cost of Capital. *Review of Economic Studies*, 41(1):21–35.

King, M. and Fullerton, D. (1984). *The Taxation of Income from Capital: A Comparative Study of the US, UK, Sweden and West Germany*. Chicago University Press.

Lindhe, T. (2002). Methods of Mitigating Double Taxation. Mimeograph.

Martinez-Mongay, C. (2000). ECFIN's Effective Tax Rates. Properties and Comparisons with other Tax Indicators. ECFIN/593/00.

McKenzie, K. (1994). The Implications of Risk and Irreversibility for the Measurement of Marginal Effective Tax Rates on Capital. *Canadian Journal of Economics*, 27(3):604–619.

McKenzie, K., Mintz, J., and Scharf, K. (1997). Measuring Effective Tax Rates in the Presence of Multiple Inputs: A Production Based Approach. *International Tax and Public Finance*, 4(3): 337–359.

Mendoza, E., Razin, A., and Tesar, L. (1994). Effective Tax Rates in Macroeconomics Cross-country Estimates of Tax Rates on Factor Incomes and Consumption. *Journal of Monetary Economics*, 34(3):297–323.

Nicodème, G. (2001). Computing Effective Corporate Tax Rates: Comparisons and Results. ECFIN E2/358/01.

OECD (1991). *Taxing Profits in a Global Economy: Domestic and International Issues*.

Pindyck, R. (1991). Irreversibility, Uncertainty, and Investment. *Journal of Economic Literature*, 29(3):1110–1148.

Quinn, D. (1997). The Correlates of Change in International Financial Regulation. *American Political Science Review*, 91(3):531–551.

Scott, M. (1987). A Note on King and Fullerton's Formulae to Estimate the Taxation of Income from Capital. *Journal of Public Economics*, 34(2):253–264.

Sinn, H. (1988). The 1986 Tax Reform and the World Capital Market. *European Economic Review*, 32(2–3):325–333.

Slemrod, J. (2004). Are Corporate Tax Rates, or Countries, Converging? *Journal of Public Economics*, 88(6):1169–1186.

Sørensen, P. (2004). *Measuring the Tax Burden on Capital and Labor*. CESifo Seminar Series.

Appendix A

There are several types of corporate tax system. The most important are:

- *Classical or separate entity system.* Under this system, the company and the shareholder are considered as two separate legal entities, each having to calculate its tax liability in an independent way. For example, if a company has a taxable income of 100 euros and the corporate rate in the country is 35%, the after-tax income is 65 euros. If all this income is distributed to a shareholder, the 65 euros will be taxed at the shareholder tax rate. Therefore, the total tax liability on company income before tax is $T = \tau Y$.

- *Full integration system.* In contrast with the previous system, full integration refers to the case where net income of the company (distributed or not) is included in the assessable income of the shareholders, implying that eventually no tax is paid at the company level.

- *Dividend exemption system.* As in the latter case, the corporate tax is integrated. But rather than integrating taxes at the shareholder level, dividends paid to shareholders are exempted from tax at the personal level.

- *Dividend deduction system.* Between the full integration and the dividend exemption systems, we have systems that attempt to reduce the tax rate on dividends. Under the dividend deduction system the company is considered as a taxpayer, but it is allowed to deduct $x\%$ of gross dividends distributed from the company's taxable income. Shareholders pay ordinary taxes on the dividends they receive.

- *Split-rate or two-rate system.* This is another method to reduce the tax rate on dividends by applying a lower rate on distributed profits than on undistributed profits.

- *Dividend imputation system.* The basic idea is that companies are taxed in their own right, and when they distribute income via dividends, a fraction of the tax paid by the company is imputed on the tax liability of the shareholder. In other words the tax liability for a shareholder is the difference between his personal income tax on dividends received and the credit based on the rate of imputation.

Appendix B

To avoid taxation of the same income in two different jurisdictions, the countries have adopted different methods of double taxation relief:

- *Exemption system.* Under this system, the income of the affiliate is taxed in one state and exempted in the other. Generally, the exemption system tends to assure the capital import neutrality, i.e. multinational companies of one country will bear an effective tax burden in foreign markets equal to multinational companies of other countries.

- *Credit system.* Taxes paid in the host country are used as a credit against the tax liability in the home country. If the company is consolidated in its worldwide income and receives full credit against tax liabilities for all taxes paid abroad, the regime tends to ensure the capital export neutrality. This means that the tax system will provide no incentives to invest at home rather than abroad, since the investors will face the same effective tax burden.

- *Deduction system*. Taxes paid in one state are allowable as deduction in determining the tax base in the second state.

Empirical Models of International Capital-tax Competition

Robert J. Franzese Jr and Jude C. Hays

Abstract

Many academic and casual observers contend that the dramatic post-1970s rise in international capital mobility and the steadily upward postwar trend in trade integration, by sharpening capital's threat against domestic governments to flee 'excessive and inefficient' taxation, has forced and will continue to force welfare/tax-state retrenchment and tax-burden shifts away from more mobile capital (especially financial capital) and toward less mobile labor (especially manual labor). Several important recent studies of the comparative and international political economy of policy change over this period challenge such claims, whereas others find more support. We offer a brief review and comparison of these arguments, emphasizing that all imply a strategic interdependence in fiscal policymaking that, in turn, implies a spatial interdependence in tax-policy data, which these previous studies tended to ignore. We then briefly summarize our own preliminary explorations of alternative strategies for estimating empirical models of such interdependent processes and, finally, we explore the empirical record regarding globalization and tax competition, applying the spatial-lag model in a reanalysis of the capital-tax regressions in Hays (2003).

3.1   Introduction

This paper studies globalization, i.e. international economic integration, and capital taxation, emphasizing the implied strategic dependence in fiscal policymaking and the resultant spatial interdependence of fiscal-policy data. Many academic and casual observers argue that the dramatic post-1972 rise in global capital mobility and the steady postwar rise in trade integration sharpen capital's threat against domestic governments to flee 'excessive and inefficient' taxation and public policies. This, the standard view holds, has forced and will continue to force welfare- and tax-state retrenchment and tax-burden shifts from more mobile capital (especially financial) toward less mobile labor (especially skilled manual).

Several important studies of the comparative and international political economy of tax and welfare policies over this era have recently challenged such claims on at least four distinct bases. Garrett (1998) argued that certain combinations of left government with social-welfare, active-labor-market, coordinated-bargaining, and related policies can be as or more efficient than neoliberal state-minimalism and conservative government and, therefore, that capital will not flee such efficient combinations. Boix (1998) argued that public (human and physical) capital-investment strategies comprise an alternative to neoliberal minimalism that is sufficiently efficient economically to retain and possibly attract capital and politically effective enough to maintain left electoral competitiveness. Hall and Soskice (2001) argued that complex national networks of political–economic institutions confer *comparative* advantages in differing productive activities, which, as Mosher and Franzese (2002) elaborated, implies that, *if international tax competition remains sufficiently muted*, capital mobility and trade integration would spur institutional and policy specialization, which, in this context, means cross-national welfare/tax-state variation rather than convergence or global retrenchment. Swank (2002) argued that the institutional structure of the polity and of the welfare/tax system itself shape domestic policy responses to capital (and trade) integration. We review such arguments and offer a preliminary evaluation, specifying empirical models that, unlike these and other previous efforts, embody the spatial relationships central to such diffusion processes.

Two recent studies (Hays, 2003; Basinger and Hallerberg, 2004), however, do recognize the strategic interdependence implicit in tax-competition arguments and incorporate the implied spatial interdependence into their empirical analyses.[1] As we show elsewhere (Franzese and Hays, 2004, 2006) and will summarize later, though, least-squares estimation of such spatial empirical models (S-OLS) suffers important statistical flaws that, in particular, jeopardize any conclusions drawn from hypothesis tests related to the crucial parameter, the coefficient on the 'spatial lag', which gauges the strength of interdependence. We reanalyze Hays's (2003) model by an alternative estimation strategy, spatial two-stage-least-squares instrumental variables (S-2SLS-IV) that, in our previous Monte Carlo experiments, produced unbiased hypothesis tests.

3.2 Globalization, tax competition, and convergence

In theory, strong inter-jurisdictional competition undermines the tax-policy autonomy of individual tax authorities, inducing tax rates to converge, especially those levied upon more mobile assets. Such inter-jurisdiction competition intensifies as capital becomes more liquid and more mobile across borders. Indeed, many scholars of domestic and international fiscal competition (e.g. Zodrow and Mieszkowski, 1986; Wilson, 1986, 1999; Wildasin, 1989; Oates, 2001) expect such intense inter-jurisdiction competition to engender a virtually unmitigated race to some (*ill-defined*: see below) bottom. As a central exemplar, most scholarly and casual observers see the striking post-1970s rise in international capital mobility and steady postwar increase in trade integration as forcing welfare- and tax-state retrenchment and a shift in tax-burden incidence from relatively mobile (e.g. capital, especially financial capital) toward more immobile (e.g. labor, especially less-flexibly-specialized types).[2] Growing capital-market integration and asset mobility across jurisdictions enhances such pressures, the argument holds, by sharpening capital's threat against domestic governments to flee 'excessive and inefficient' welfare and tax systems.

Several notable recent studies of the comparative and international political economy of policy change over this period challenge these claims. First, empirically, some contest whether *globalization* in general and capital mobility in particular have actually significantly constrained public policies broadly and capital-tax policy specifically. Hines (1999), after reviewing the empirical economics literature, concluded that national tax systems affect the investment location decisions of multinational corporations and firms do seize opportunities to avoid taxes. Rodrik (1997), Dehejia and Genschel (1999), Genschel (2001), and others argued that this has increasingly constrained governments' policy-latitude in recent years. Quinn (1997), Swank (1998, 2002), Swank and Steinmo (2002), Garrett and Mitchell (2001), and others, however, did not find these trends to have constrained governments' tax policies much or at all. The theoretical explanation for the latter kinds of results, occasionally implicit, seems that other cross-national differences also importantly affect investment-location decisions, affording governments some room to maneuver. Hines (1999, p. 308), for example, found commercial, regulatory, and other policies, and labor-market institutions, intermediate-supply availability, and final-market proximity, among other factors, to be key in corporate investment-location decisions. Moreover, other factors than capital mobility affect governments' tax policies. For example, Swank (2002, see pp. 252–256 in particular) argued that corporate and capital tax rates depend on funding requirements of programmatic outlays, macroeconomic factors like inflation and economic growth, and partisan politics. Controlling for such factors, he found little relationship between taxation and capital mobility.

On closer inspection, these recent challenges to simplistic *globalization-induces-welfare/tax-state-retrenchment* views have at least four distinct bases. Garrett (1998) argued that certain combinations of left government and social-welfare, active-labor-market, and related policies with coordinated bargaining can be as or more efficient than neoliberal state-minimalism and conservative government. Therefore, he argues, capital will not flee such efficient combinations. Boix (1998) argued that public human- and physical-capital investment strategies comprise an alternative to neoliberal minimalism that is sufficiently efficient economically to retain, and perhaps attract, capital, and politically effective enough to maintain left electoral competitiveness. Hall et al. (2001) argued that complex national networks of political–economic institutions confer *comparative* advantages in differing productive activities, which, as Mosher and Franzese (2002) elaborated, implies capital mobility and trade integration could (*if international tax competition remains sufficiently muted*: see below) spur institutional and policy specialization, which would imply persistent welfare/tax-system variation or even divergence rather than convergence or global retrenchment. These three views fundamentally question whether international economic integration actually creates economic pressures to retreat from welfare/tax-state commitments (or at least whether all aspects of globalization do so, so strongly: see below).

Swank's (2002) argument that the institutional structures of the polity and of the welfare system itself shape the domestic policy response to integration represents a fourth basis for challenge. His view does not fundamentally challenge claims of the exclusively superior macroeconomic efficiency of neoliberal minimalism but, rather, stresses the primacy of domestic political conditions – the policymaking access, cohesion and organization, and relative power of contending pro- and anti-welfare/tax interests – in determining the direction and magnitude of welfare/tax-policy reactions to economic integration. Specifically, he argued and found that inclusive electoral institutions, social-corporatist interest representation and policy-making, centralized political authority, and universal welfare systems relatively favor the political access and potency of pro-welfare/public-policy interests and bolster supportive social norms in the domestic political struggle over the policy response to integration. The opposite conditions favor anti-tax/welfare interests and norms in this struggle. Capital mobility and globalization therefore induce increased welfare/tax-state largesse in previously generous states and retrenchment in tight ones – i.e. divergence rather than convergence. Swank's approach is, thus, the most directly and thoroughly political of these critiques. It is also perhaps the most thoroughly explored empirically, offering comparative-historical statistical and qualitative analyses of six alternative versions of the *globalization-induces-retrenchment* thesis: A simple version (a regression including one of five capital-openness measures), and five others he terms the *run-to-the-bottom* (capital openness times lagged welfare-policy), *convergence* (capital openness times the gap from own to cross-country mean welfare-policy), *nonlinear* (capital openness and its square), *trade-and-capital-openness* (their product), *capital-openness-times-fiscal-stress* (deficits times capital openness), and *capital-flight* (net foreign direct investment) versions. He found little support for any globalization-induces-retrenchment argument and, indeed, some indications that capital mobility tends on average to enhance welfare effort (perhaps supporting those stressing its effect in increasing popular demand for social insurance against global risks).[3]

Basinger and Hallerberg (2004), in a sense, take the implied next step of Swank's central point. Swank stressed the domestic political and political–economic institutions and structures of interest that shape governments' policy responses to economic integration. It then follows, however, as Basinger and Hallerberg (2004, p. 261) summarize, '[if] countries with higher political costs are less likely themselves to enact reforms, [then this] also reduces competing countries' incentives to reform regardless of their own political costs'. That is, the magnitude of the tax-competition pressures that economic integration places upon one government's fiscal policies depend upon the policy choices of its competitors, which is precisely the strategic interdependence that we emphasize here as well.

Such critiques underscore that the *bottom* toward which globalization and capital mobility may push tax-competing states may not be that of neoliberal minimalism. Insofar as alternative economic advantages allow some states to retain higher tax rates, or insofar as restraining political conditions prevent some from reaching neoliberal minimum, the competitive pressures on all states diminish, more so, of course, the more economically integrated and important are those states whose domestic political–economic conditions allow such maneuvering room or raise such constraints. Furthermore, if, as Mosher and Franzese (2002) suggest, national economic-policy differences contribute to *comparative* advantages – which, if they do, they do regardless of their *absolute* efficiency – then both trade and global *fixed-capital* integration would actually enhance economic pressures toward specialization, i.e. divergence and not convergence. From this view, international *liquid-capital* mobility alone, through the tax competition it engenders, produces whatever 'races' may occur. In this case, interestingly, such competitive races would occur regardless and independent of the efficiency of the tax systems in question or of the public policies they support. Furthermore, as both Hays (2003) and Basinger and Hallerberg (2004) stressed, the race need not be to the *bottom*; Rather, the competitiveness and the destination of the race depend on the constellation of domestic political–economic conditions present in, and the economic integration of, the international system. Conversely, as Mosher and Franzese (2002) emphasized, zero offers no inherent *bottom* to such tax-cut races as may occur. In the competition for liquid portfolio capital specifically, governments would always have incentives to cut taxes further, perhaps deep into subsidy; Only their abilities to tax other less liquid and/or mobile assets and to borrow limit (in an internationally interdependent manner, as just noted) those races.

Thus, international tax-competition arguments, in any of their conventional forms and throughout each of these critiques, imply cross-national (i.e. spatial) interdependence in the rates of capital taxation. Whatever pressures upon domestic policymaking may derive from rising (liquid-portfolio) capital mobility, their nature and magnitude will depend on the constellation of tax (and broader economic) systems with which the domestic economy competes.

3.3 A stylized theoretical model of capital-tax competition

We leverage Persson and Tabellini's (2000, Chapter 12) formal–theoretical model to demonstrate further that tax competition implies spatial interdependence. The model's essential elements are as follows. In two jurisdictions (i.e. countries), denote the domestic and foreign capital-tax rates as τ_k and τ_k^*. Individuals can invest in either country, but foreign investment incurs *mobility costs*. Taxation follows the source (not the residence) principle. Governments use revenues from taxes levied on capital and labor to fund a fixed amount of spending.[4] Individuals differ in their relative labor-to-capital endowment, denoted e^i, and make labor-leisure, l and x, and savings-investment, $s = k + f$ (k = domestic; f = foreign), decisions to maximize quasi-linear utility, $\omega = U(c_1) + c_2 + V(x)$, over leisure and consumption and in the model's two periods, c_1 and c_2, subject to a time constraint, $1 + e^i = l + x$, and budget constraints in each period, $1 - e^i = c_1 + k + f + \equiv c_1 + s$ and $c_2 = (1 - \tau_k)k + (1 - \tau_k^*)f - M(f) + (1 - \tau_l)l$.

The equilibrium economic choices of citizens i in this model are as follows:

$$s = S(\tau_k) = 1 - U_c^{-1}(1 - \tau_k) \tag{3.1}$$

$$f = F(\tau_k, \tau_k^*) = M_f^{-1}(\tau_k - \tau_k^*) \tag{3.2}$$

$$k = K(\tau_k, \tau_k^*) = S(\tau_k) - F(\tau_k, \tau_k^*). \tag{3.3}$$

With labor, $L(\tau_l)$, leisure, x, and consumption, c_1, c_2, implicitly given by these conditions, this leaves individuals with indirect utility, W, defined over the policy variables, tax rates, of:

$$W(\tau_l, \tau_k) = U\{1 - S(\tau_k)\} + (1 - \tau_k)S(\tau_k) + (\tau_k - \tau_k^*)F(\tau_k, \tau_k^*) - M\{F(\tau_k, \tau_k^*)\}$$
$$+ (1 - \tau_l)L(\tau_l) + V\{1 - L(\tau_l)\}. \tag{3.4}$$

Facing an electorate with these preferences over taxes, using a Besley–Coate (1997) citizen-candidate model wherein running for office is costly and citizens choose whether to enter the race by an expected-utility calculation, some citizen candidate will win and set tax rates to maximize his or her own welfare. The model's stages are: (1) Elections occur in both countries; (2) Elected citizen-candidates set their respective countries' tax rates; (3) All private economic decisions are made. In this case, the candidate who enters and wins will be the one with endowment e^p such that s/he desires to implement the following *Modified Ramsey Rule*:

$$\frac{S(\tau_k^P) - e^P}{S(\tau_k^P)}[1 + \varepsilon_l(\tau_k^P)] = \frac{L(\tau_l^P) + e^P}{L(\tau_l^P)}\left[1 + \frac{S_\tau(\tau_k^P) + 2F_\tau^*(\tau_k^{P^*}, \tau_k^P)\tau_k}{S_\tau(\tau_k^P)}\right]. \quad (3.5)$$

Equation (3.5) gives the optimal capital-tax-rate policy for the domestic policy-maker to choose, which, as one can see, is a function of the capital tax-rate chosen abroad. The game is symmetric, so the optimal capital tax-rate for the foreign policymaker to choose looks identical from his or her point of view and, importantly, depends on the capital tax-rate chosen domestically. That is, equation (3.5) gives best-response functions $\tau_k = T(e^P, \tau_k^*)$ and $\tau_k^* = T^*(e^P, \tau_k)$ for the foreign and domestic policymaker respectively. In words, the domestic (foreign) capital-tax rate depends on the domestic (foreign) policymaker's labor-capital endowment and the foreign (domestic) capital tax rate – i.e. capital taxes are strategically interdependent. The slope of these functions, $\partial T/\partial \tau_k^*$ and $\partial T^*/\partial \tau_k$, can be either positive or negative. An increase in foreign tax rates induces capital flow into the domestic economy, but the domestic policymaker may use the increased tax base to lower tax rates or to raise them (the latter to seize the greater revenue opportunities created by the decreased elasticity of this base). Figure 3.1 plots these reaction functions assuming that both slope positively. The illustrated comparative static shows an increase in the domestic policymaker's labor-capital endowment. This change shifts the function T outward, raising the equilibrium capital-tax rate in both countries.

Although formal tax-competition models, like Persson and Tabellini's (or Hays' or Basinger and Hallerberg's), clearly demonstrate the strategic ('spatial'[5]) interdependence of capital taxes, as any of the alternative arguments reviewed above would also imply, very few scholars have empirically modeled that interdependence directly. Not all tax/welfare-state retrenchment arguments, however, necessarily involve tax competition. Iversen and Cusack (2000), for example, argue that structural change in the labor force, specifically deindustrialization, is the primary force pushing welfare/tax-state retrenchment. Pierson (2001) concurs in part, but also emphasizes *path dependence* (technically, state dependence), namely the accumulation and entrenchment of interests (or their absence) behind

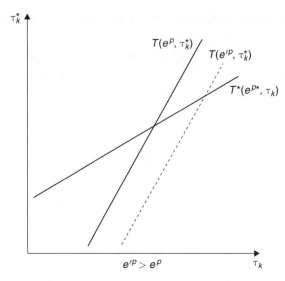

$e'^p > e^p$

Figure 3.1 Best response functions. Reprinted from Persson, T. and Tabellini, G. (2000). *Political Economics: Explaining Economic Policy*, p. 334, by permission of The MIT Press, Cambridge, MA. © 2000 Massachusetts Institute of Technology)

welfare/tax-state policies and institutions. Rodrik (1998), and Cameron (1978) before him, stressed instead the added demand from some domestic interests for certain social policies that increased economic exposure would engender. Such forces – labor-force structural change, domestic-interest entrenchment and/or change – may be related to, or even partly caused by, aspects of globalization, but ultimately these are domestic arguments, or arguments about domestic factors that modify responses to *exogenous* external trends, and therefore do not by themselves imply a strategic interdependence among policy choices, as do the tax-competition arguments reviewed above.

We term the former sorts of 'domestic factors' or 'exogenous external' or 'domestic factors–conditional responses to exogenous external' approaches *Open Economy–Comparative Political Economy* (OE-CPE), and the latter, pure tax-competition arguments exemplify the (internationally) strategic-interdependence approaches we term *International Interdependence–Political Economy* (II-PE). Of course, the two are easily combined in *(Open-Economy) Comparative and International Political Economy* (C&IPE) models that reflect both domestic factors and/or domestically modified responses to exogenous-external conditions on the one hand and international interdependence on the other. We (re-)analyze one such C&IPE empirical model of globalization and capital-tax competition (Hays, 2003) in the section after next, but first we explain the serious econometric challenges to estimating and, a fortiori, distinguishing these alternatives and some (partially successful) approaches to surmounting these challenges.

3.4 Econometric issues in estimating C&IPE empirical models from spatially interdependent data

Open-economy CPE explicitly recognizes the potentially large effects of external conditions on domestic political and economic outcomes, often emphasizing how domestic institutions, structure, and contexts shape the degree and nature of domestic exposure to such external (i.e. foreign or international) conditions and/or moderate the domestic policy and outcome responses thereto. This produces characteristic theoretical and empirical models of the following sort:

$$\mathbf{y}_{it} = \xi_{it}\beta_0 + \eta_t\beta_1 + (\xi_{it} \cdot \eta_t)\,\beta_3 + \varepsilon_{it}. \tag{3.6}$$

In equation (3.6), the incidence, impact, and/or effects of global conditions, η_t, on domestic policies/outcomes, $\mathbf{y}_{it}$, are conditioned by domestic institutional–structural–contextual factors, ξ_{it}, and so differ across spatial units (countries). Welfare/tax-state retrenchment examples of such an approach include the aforementioned Iversen–Cusack or Cameron–Rodrik arguments. The exogenous-external conditions, η_t, in those cases might reflect technological or other progress in production, shipping, or financial processes.[6] The domestic institutional, structural, or contextual conditions, ξ_{it}, in these examples that affect policies/outcomes and/or moderate domestic policy/outcome responses to these exogenous-external trends might include union density, existing industrial structure, and partisan electoral competitiveness. In empirical specifications of such OE-CPE models, researchers would typically leave to FGLS or PCSE 'corrections' any spatial correlation distinct from that induced by the common or correlated responses to the *exogenous*-external conditions.

II-PE approaches and models, contrarily, explicitly incorporate the interdependence of domestic and foreign policies/outcomes, as implied, for example, by tax competition. C&IPE combines the two to produce characteristic theoretical and empirical models of the following sort:

$$\mathbf{y}_{it} = \rho\sum_{j\neq i} w_{ij}\mathbf{y}_{j,t} + \xi_{it}\beta_0 + \eta_t\beta_1 + (\xi_{it} \cdot \eta_t)\,\beta_3 + \varepsilon_{it}, \tag{3.7}$$

where $y_{j,t}$, the outcomes in the other $(j \neq i)$ units in some manner (given by ρw_{ij}) directly affect the outcome in unit i. Note that w_{ij} reflects the degree of connection from j to i, and ρ reflects the impact of the outcomes in the other $(j \neq i)$ units, as weighted by w_{ij}, on the outcome in i. In the substantive venue of tax competition, for example, the w_{ij} could gauge the similarity or complementarity i's and j's economies or of their (capital or goods-and-services) trade bundles. The rest of the right-hand-side model reflects the domestic political economy, including the domestic-context-conditional effects of exogenous external conditions as described in the OE-CPE model (3.6).

Econometrically, as we summarize below (working from Franzese and Hays, 2004, 2006), obtaining 'good' (unbiased, consistent, efficient) estimates of coefficients and standard errors in such C&IPE models and distinguishing OE-CPE processes from II-PE processes are *not* straightforward. The first and foremost considerations are the relative and absolute theoretical and empirical precisions of the alternative OE-CPE and II-PE parts of the model, i.e. the *interdependence* parts and the *common, correlated, or domestic-context-conditional responses to common, correlated, or domestic-context-conditioned exogenous-external factors* (henceforth *common-conditions*) parts. To elaborate: The relative and absolute accuracy and power with which the spatial-lag weights, w_{ij}, reflect and can gain leverage upon the actual *interdependence* mechanisms operating and with which the domestic and exogenous-external parts of the model can reflect and gain leverage upon the *common-conditions* alternatives critically affect the empirical attempt to distinguish and evaluate their relative strength because the two mechanisms produce similar effects so that inadequacies or omissions in the specification of the one tend, quite intuitively, to induce overestimation of the importance of the other. However, secondarily, even if the *common-conditions* and *interdependence* mechanisms are modeled perfectly, the spatial-lag regressor(s) in this model will be endogenous (i.e. they will covary with the residuals), so estimates of ρ will suffer simultaneity biases. Moreover, as with the primary (relative) omitted-variable or misspecification biases mentioned first, these simultaneity biases in estimating the strength of *interdependence* induce biases in the opposite direction in estimating OE-CPE mechanism strength.

Equation (3.7) can be rewritten in matrix notation thus:

$$\mathbf{y} = \rho \mathbf{W} \mathbf{y} + \mathbf{X} \boldsymbol{\beta} + \varepsilon, \tag{3.8}$$

where $\mathbf{y}$ is an $NT \times 1$ vector of observations on the dependent variable stacked by unit (i.e. unit 1, time 1 to T, then unit 2, time 1 to T, etc. through unit N), and

W is an $NT \times NT$ block-diagonal spatial-weighting matrix (with elements w_{ij}). Thus, **Wy** is the spatial lag, given in scalar notation as the first term on the right-hand side of equation (3.2). The diagonal elements of the off-diagonal $T \times T$ blocks in **W**, which reflect the contemporaneous effect of the column unit on the row unit, are the w_{ij} that reflect the degree of connection from unit j to i – so, unlike a variance–covariance matrix, **W** need not be symmetric. ρ, the spatial autoregressive coefficient, reflects the impact of the outcomes in the other ($j \neq i$) spatial units, as weighted by w_{ij}, on the outcome in i. Thus, ρ gauges the overall strength of diffusion, whereas the w_{ij} describe the relative magnitudes of the diffusion paths between the sample units.

Generally, the set of w_{ij} is determined by theoretical and substantive argumentation as to which units will have greatest affect on outcomes in other units; ρ values are the coefficients to be estimated on these spatial lags. For example, operationalization of the tax-competition argument would be weights, w_{ij}, based on the trade or capital-flow shares of countries j in country i's total. The inner product of that vector of weights with the stacked dependent variable **y** then gives the weighted sum (or average) of **y** in the other countries j in that time-period as a right-hand-side variable in the regression. The matrix **Wy** just gives the entire set of these vector inner products – in this case, the trade- or capital-flow-weighted averages – for all countries i.[7] **X** is a matrix of NT observations on K exogenous regressors – in our case, η, ξ, and $\eta \cdot \xi - \beta$ is a $K \times 1$ vector of coefficients thereupon, and ε is an $NT \times 1$ vector of residuals, with the usual properties assumed.

In Franzese and Hays (2004, 2006), we demonstrate analytically, in the simplest possible case (one domestic factor, X, two countries, 1 and 2, and conditionally $i.i.d.$ errors, ε) that OLS estimates of equation (3.7) (or the identical (3.8)) will suffer simultaneity bias and, obviously, that OLS estimates of equation (3.7) omitting the spatial lag will suffer omitted-variable bias, and we specify those biases insofar as possible.

This simple case highlights that OLS estimates of equation (3.7) will suffer simultaneity (endogeneity) bias:

$$Y_1 = \beta_1 X_1 + \rho_{12} Y_2 + \varepsilon_1 \tag{3.9}$$

$$Y_2 = \beta_2 X_2 + \rho_{21} Y_1 + \varepsilon_2. \tag{3.10}$$

The left-hand side of equation (3.9) is on the right-hand side of equation (3.10) and vice versa: Textbook endogeneity. In words: Country 2 affects country 1, but country 1 also affects country 2. The resultant bias in OLS estimates of ρ can be shown (with a little further simplification) to equal:

$$\hat{\rho}_{12} = \rho_{12} + \frac{\rho_{21}\text{Var}(\varepsilon_1)(1 - \rho_{21}\rho_{12})}{\beta_2^2 + \rho_{21}^2\text{Var}(\varepsilon_1) + \text{Var}(\varepsilon_2)}. \tag{3.11}$$

which, assuming $\rho_{12}\rho_{21} < 1$, implies that OLS estimates of diffusion from country j to i will have bias of the same sign as the diffusion from i to j (N.B. all terms except ρ_{21} in equation (3.11) are necessarily positive). This means that, if 'feedback' from j to i and i to j reinforce (both positive as in Figure 3.1, or both negative), then OLS estimates of interdependence will be inflated. If feedback is dampening (e.g. opposite slopes in Figure 3.1), which is probably less likely in most substantive contexts (but possible in Persson and Tabellini's model, as noted), OLS estimates will be attenuated. We can also show, moreover, that this bias in the estimated strength of interdependence, ρ, induces an attenuation bias in the estimate of β, the effect of X (i.e. domestic and/or exogenous-external factors):

$$\hat{\beta}_1 = \beta_1 - \frac{\beta_1\text{Var}(\varepsilon_1)\,\rho_{21}^2}{\beta_2^2 + \rho_{21}^2\text{Var}(\varepsilon_1) + \text{Var}(\varepsilon_2)}. \tag{3.12}$$

Thus, typically, OLS estimates of C&IPE models will tend to overestimate the importance of interdependence – e.g. tax competition – and underestimate that of domestic, exogenous-external, and/or domestic-context-conditional exogenous-external mechanisms (i.e. OE-CPE arguments).

On the other hand, OLS estimates of OE-CPE models that ignore interdependence, i.e. that omit spatial lags, will suffer the converse omitted-variable biases, which we have (more easily, using the usual omitted-variable-bias formula) shown in the simplest case to equal:

$$\hat{\beta}_1 = \beta_1 + \frac{\rho_{12}\rho_{21}\beta_1}{1 - \rho_{12}\rho_{21}} \tag{3.13}$$

$$\hat{\beta}_2 = \beta_2 + \frac{\rho_{12}\rho_{21}\beta_2}{1 - \rho_{12}\rho_{21}}. \tag{3.14}$$

Again, if feedback is reinforcing (same-signed ρ_{12}, ρ_{21}) these are inflation biases and if feedback is dampening these are attenuation biases. Thus, in the positive-feedback case that we suspect is more common, OLS estimates of OE-CPE models that ignore *interdependence* will tend to overestimate the power of domestic, exogenous-external, and/or domestic-context-conditional exogenous-external explanations. Finally, this conclusion holds as a matter of degree also: Insofar as *interdependence* is inadequately specified, absolutely and relatively to the alternative OE-CPE argument specification, the latter will tend to be overestimated and the former underestimated, and vice versa.

Our simulations suggested that these omitted-variable biases of excluding *interdependence* are of greater concern than the simultaneity biases of including them in OLS regressions, under a fairly wide range of plausible substantive conditions. Therefore, regarding the substantive application at hand here, researchers unambiguously do better to include the spatial lags needed to specify correctly the strategic interdependence implied by tax-competition arguments than to ignore/omit that implication. However, we also showed that simultaneity biases from including spatial lags in OLS regressions to reflect interdependence can be appreciable, that they tend toward overestimating the central quantity of interest here (ρ), and, worse still, that underestimation of the variance–covariance of its estimate (i.e. its standard error) also prevails.[8] Thus, on the one hand, hypothesis tests that fail to model the interdependence mechanism at all, i.e. OE-CPE models, will obviously fail to find such interdependence (e.g. tax competition) and, somewhat less obviously, tend to overestimate the importance of domestic and exogenous-external conditions; On the other hand, however, hypothesis tests based on OLS estimations of *correctly specified* models like equation (3.7) would be biased in favor of finding strong tax-competition effects, perhaps greatly so because the relevant *t*-statistics have inflated numerators and deflated denominators, and would tend to understate the importance of domestic and exogenous-external effects.

Fortunately, one can estimate models like equations (3.7) or (3.8) of interdependent processes, such as tax competition, by two-stage-least-squares instrumental variables (2SLS-IV) or by maximum likelihood (ML), to obtain consistent estimates of ρ and of β. In fact, the former is not difficult to implement[9] because the spatial structure of the data itself suggests potential instruments. Valid instruments must satisfy that their (asymptotic) covariance with the endogenous regressor – here, the spatially lagged outcomes in the other countries – is nonzero, and preferably large, whereas their (asymptotic) covariance with the residual in that equation is zero. Stated more intuitively: Valid instruments must affect the variable for which they instrument, preferably greatly, but must *not* affect the dependent variable except insofar as they affect the variable being instrumented. In the tax-competition context, this means that valid instruments must predict the tax policies of competitor countries but not affect the tax policies of the domestic country except insofar as they affect those foreign countries' tax policies. Thus, all of the **X** variables in equation (3.8), i.e. the foreign countries' own domestic, exogenous-external, and domestic-context-conditional-external factors,[10] are candidate instruments! One simply uses the spatial lags of $\mathbf{X}$, $\mathbf{WX}$ (i.e. the same $\mathbf{W}$ already used to generate the spatial lag itself, $\mathbf{Wy}$), as instruments for the spatial lag in the first stage of the 2SLS-IV estimation. Fortunately, too, our Monte Carlo experiments show that such 2SLS-IV estimates not only produce consistent estimates, but also essentially unbiased ones, even at relatively small sample sizes. Moreover, the accompanying 2SLS-IV standard-error estimates accurately reflected the true sampling variability of the 2SLS-IV coefficient estimates across all sample sizes and parameter conditions explored. This suggests spatial 2SLS-IV, unlike spatial OLS, will produce unbiased hypothesis tests.

Unfortunately, 2SLS-IV estimates are not typically very efficient and, indeed, are routinely outperformed in mean-squared-error terms by simple OLS estimates (and usually by the ML estimates also). That is, spatial 2SLS-IV suffers the typical IV problem of weak instruments. In other words, spatial 2SLS-IV estimates have larger standard errors than alternative estimators, often large enough to more than offset their unbiasedness, but, in their defense, as noted above, at least they honestly report these larger standard errors. Furthermore, as is virtually always true, perfectly exogenous instruments cannot be guaranteed. In the spatial 2SLS-IV context, the problem of *quasi-instruments* (Bartels, 1991) will arise in the presence of what we call *cross-spatial endogeneity*. That is, foreign countries' domestic and exogenous-external explanators will not be valid instruments for foreign countries' outcomes if the outcome in the domestic country correlates for some reason with the explanators in the foreign country. In our context, this would mean if tax policies in one country somehow affected other countries' domestic conditions. Canadian taxes affecting German election outcomes, for example, might seem implausible so, on this basis, the proposed spatial instruments may have a strong claim to exogeneity.[11] However, cross-spatial endogeneity can also arise without such direct 'diagonal causal arrows' from one country's outcomes to others' explanatory (domestic) factors because, intuitively, combinations of 'horizontal' and 'vertical' arrows can make 'diagonal' ones. That is, if the more usual sort of endogeneity problems exist, wherein $\mathbf{y}$ (tax policies) causes $\mathbf{X}$ (e.g. domestic industrial structure), and spatial correlation among the $\mathbf{X}$ variables exists also (e.g. industrial structure correlates across countries), then the 'diagonal' that violates spatial-instrument validity, covariance of $\mathbf{WX}_j$ with $\mathbf{y}_i$, emerges. In sum, therefore, we can believe the instrumentation assumptions necessary for consistency (and asymptotic efficiency[12]) of spatial 2SLS-IV estimates of the strength of interdependence if we believe (a) direct effects from $\mathbf{y}_i$ to $\mathbf{X}_j$ do not exist and (b) the $\mathbf{X}$ variables are either spatially uncorrelated or exogenous to $\mathbf{y}$.[13]

Researchers interested in spatial interdependence, which necessarily includes those interested in tax competition, therefore face a troubling dilemma. They obviously must specify empirical models that reflect the dependence of one country's policies on those of their competitors; Interdependence, after all, is the core of their argument, and the testing for and gauging of it the core of their empirical estimations. In fact, though, even researchers uninterested in interdependence per se, and interested only in comparative- or open-economy-comparative-political-economy questions, must specify empirical models that reflect spatial interdependence (if it exists) to avoid potentially severe omitted-variable biases in their quantities of interest. Indeed, one way to phrase our primary conclusion from these econometric explorations would be to emphasize that accurate and powerful specification of the alternative is as critical to scholars solely interested in C&IPE from either the CPE or IPE angle as it is to those interested in C&IPE jointly. Any insufficiency in the specification of the one side will tend to bias our conclusions toward the other. Beyond this, however, i.e. even after we are fully satisfied (or as satisfied as we can be) with the domestic, exogenous-external, and interdependent aspects of our model specification, the researcher into substantive contexts like tax competition still faces a dilemma in choosing estimators. Spatial 2SLS-IV estimates seem to perform well in terms of coefficient unbiasedness and accuracy of reported standard errors and so should tend to produce unbiased hypothesis tests. However, these tests may be relatively weak (lack power) given that the estimators are inefficient; Moreover, the spatial 2SLS-IV estimates are sufficiently inefficient that one would prefer the simpler spatial OLS point estimates on mean-squared error grounds.

One reasonable approach to this dilemma would be to report point estimates of the strength of diffusion, ρ, and other model coefficients, β, from the smaller mean-squared-error S-OLS or S-ML procedure, but to report the hypothesis tests with better unbiasedness properties from the 2SLS-IV procedure, being sure to acknowledge the latter's lack of power, which means to avoid drawing conclusions from failures to reject even more so than one always should, even with more powerful tests. However, this approach leaves ambiguous which standard errors to report. Standard errors from S-OLS tend to be 'inaccurately too small' and, as we also showed in Franzese and Hays (2004, 2006), PCSEs will not necessarily help with this particular problem. Standard errors from spatial 2SLS-IV, conversely, tend to be 'accurately too large' and refer to different point estimates besides. (S-ML standard errors have proven reasonably accurate under many conditions, but unfortunately somewhat erratic in others, which is why we eschew them here.) At this point, the best we can offer is the advice to show readers both and refer them to our Monte Carlo experiments to decide for themselves which or which combination of estimates they prefer, as none statistically dominates.

3.5 Spatial-lag empirical models of capital-tax competition

Although all theoretical models of and arguments regarding tax competition clearly, indeed inherently, imply the spatial interdependence of capital taxes, few scholars have empirically modeled such interdependence directly. Two recent exceptions (Hays, 2003; Basinger and Hallerberg, 2004), however, do estimate spatial-lag models of international capital-tax competition, using S-OLS. In the next section, we discuss the empirical work in these two papers and then conduct a reanalysis of the regression models in Hays (2003). Our empirical results support the conclusion of strong international interdependence in capital-tax policy.

Hays (2003) argued that the effect of globalization – specifically, increased international capital mobility – on a country's capital tax rate depends on its capital endowment and political institutions. Thus, his theoretical argument is of the OE-CPE variety. An exogenous increase in international capital mobility affects the capital tax rate in two ways. First, it shifts the revenue-maximizing tax rate downward. Second, by making the supply of capital more elastic, it increases the marginal gain from increasing (decreasing) the capital tax rate when it is below (above) the revenue-maximizing level. How much globalization reduces the revenue-maximizing tax rate depends on a country's capital endowment: The drop is large for capital-rich countries and relatively small for capital-poor ones. The impact of increasing the elasticity of the supply of capital on tax rates, conversely, is a function of a country's political institutions. In brief, the capital-supply elasticity determines the marginal revenue gain from changing tax rates while political institutions determine the marginal cost of changing tax rates. Hays's theoretical argument explains why increased international capital mobility will have the greatest negative impact on capital-tax rates in relatively closed and capital-rich countries with majoritarian political institutions (e.g. the UK).

To test this hypothesis, Hays estimated a spatial-lag model with a temporal lag and country-fixed effects. The Mendoza et al. (1997) capital-tax rates are the dependent variable; The key independent variables are the degree of capital mobility – measured by Quinn's (1997) indices of capital and financial openness – and capital mobility interacted with a measure of each country's capital endowment and its consensus-democracy score (Lijphart, 1999).[14] For each country, Hays (2003) used the average tax rate, i.e. the average of the dependent variable, $\mathbf{y}$, in the $N-1$ other countries as the spatial lag. In other words, all the off-diagonal elements of the spatial weighting matrix from equation (3.8) are set to $1/(N-1)$. For Hays's original purposes, this spatial lag controls for the possibility that the observed changes in capital taxation are being driven by tax competition between countries.[15] Hays estimated the model using OLS and reported panel-corrected standard errors (PCSEs).

For their part, Basinger and Hallerberg (2004) estimated spatial-lag models to test the following hypotheses derived from their theoretical model of tax competition: (1) Countries will undergo tax reform more frequently if the political costs of such reforms are low and/or the decisiveness of reforms in determining the patterns of investment flows is high; (2) Countries will engage in tax reform when the political costs of reform in competitor countries is low; (3) The domestic political costs of reform and the decisiveness of reform will determine the sensitivity of countries' tax policies to tax changes in their competitors. Basinger and Hallerberg (2004) included both spatially weighted $\mathbf{X}$ variables and spatially weighted $\mathbf{Y}$ variables (i.e. spatial lags) on the right-hand side of their regression models. Hypothesis 1 is operationalized with a set of domestic $\mathbf{X}$ variables; They tested Hypothesis 2 using a set of spatially weighted $\mathbf{X}$ variables and Hypothesis 3 with the spatial lags interacted with domestic $\mathbf{X}$ variables.

The dependent variable in their empirical analysis is the change in the capital-tax rate. In addition to the Mendoza et al. (1997) capital-tax rates, the same variable Hays (2003) used, Basinger and Hallerberg (2004) considered also the top marginal capital-tax rates (of both central government and overall). They identified two kinds of domestic political costs as independent variables: Transaction and constituency costs. *Ideological distances* between veto players were used to measure transaction costs. The greater the ideological distance between political actors that can block policy change, the harder is altering the status quo (in this case, adopting capital-tax reform). *Partisanship* was used to measure constituency costs; The constituency costs associated with capital-tax reform will be higher when left governments are in power. A third independent variable of interest, the degree of capital mobility, was measured using capital controls on outflows (based on Quinn's data). The degree of capital mobility determines the decisiveness of capital taxes in determining the location of international investments.

Basinger and Hallerberg (2004) used four different spatial-weighting matrices: A symmetric $1/(N-1)$ weighting matrix, which makes the spatial lag for each unit equal to the simple average of the $\mathbf{Y}$ values in the other units (as in Hays), and three weighted averages using, respectively, GDP, FDI, and Fixed Capital Formation (FCF) as weights. The last three spatial-weighting matrices have cell entries that differ across columns, but the rows are identical. For example, for every country (row) in the sample, the USA (column) – because of its large GDP, capital stock, and flows of FDI – is weighted more heavily than Finland (another column), but the effect of American tax rates on other tax rates is the same for all countries (in every row). American tax rates (column) have the same effect on Canada (row) as they do on Austria (another row), for example. These spatial weights are time varying (because the GDP, FDI, and FCF of each country changes over time). Like Hays, Basinger and Hallerberg (2004) included country-fixed effects in their models, but, unlike Hays, they did not lag the dependent variable directly. They did include the lagged level of the tax rate, though, which makes their model with changes as the dependent variable essentially the same as a partial-adjustment (lagged-dependent-variable) model in levels like the one Hays estimates. Finally, Basinger and Hallerberg (2004) also estimated their models by OLS with panel-corrected standard errors.

Both Hays (2003) and Basinger and Hallerberg (2004) found the coefficient on the spatial lag to be positive and statistically significant – i.e. both found strong evidence of tax competition. The problem with both analyses, however, is that neither accounts for the endogeneity of the spatial lag, which renders biased and inconsistent the S-OLS estimator used. As we showed in Franzese and Hays (2004, 2006), the simultaneity bias in these circumstances would be toward exaggeration of the strength of interdependence and would also entail an induced downward bias in the estimated effects of *common conditions*. Furthermore, both may have underspecified the *common-conditions* sorts of arguments they include as well, which, again as we showed in Franzese and Hays (2004, 2006), would tend further to depress those estimated effects and inflate the estimated strength of interdependence. We therefore conduct now a reanalysis of Hays's (2003, p. 99)[16] regressions using a new spatial-weight matrix and two consistent estimators – spatial two-stage least squares and spatial maximum likelihood (Tables 3.1 and 3.2). We also re-estimate the regressions, including a set of period dummies to control better for common shocks (Table 3.3).[17] The results show that Hays may have overestimated the coefficient on the spatial lag with consequences for some of the other estimates. In particular, the original results for the mediating effect of the capital endowment on capital-account openness are not very robust across alternative estimators. However, the consensus democracy results are robust and tend to be even stronger (i.e. larger coefficients and higher levels of statistical significance) when the consistent estimators are used.

Table 3.1 Capital tax rates and international capital mobility (capital-account openness)

Independent variables	Capital-account openness	Capital-account openness	Capital-account openness	Capital-account openness	Capital-account openness	Capital-account openness
Capital mobility	1.918**	2.223**	2.159**	1.620*	1.695*	1.729*
	(0.919)	(0.930)	(1.045)	(0.859)	(0.996)	(1.013)
Capital mobility interacted with:						
Capital endowment	−0.070*	−0.069*	−0.069**	−0.033	−0.0425	−0.048
	(0.040)	(0.040)	(0.033)	(0.039)	(0.030)	(0.040)
Consensus democracy	0.484	0.746*	0.691	1.245***	1.053**	1.121**
	(0.431)	(0.434)	(0.472)	(0.428)	(0.485)	(0.534)
Corporatism	−1.186	−2.229	−2.008	−3.047**	−2.578*	−2.453
	(1.339)	(1.359)	(1.399)	(1.318)	(1.357)	(1.641)
Left government	0.370*	0.286	0.304	0.304	0.321	0.331
	(0.196)	(0.195)	(0.209)	(0.186)	(0.196)	(0.215)
Population	−1.7ge-07	−9.77e-06**	−7.74e-06*	5.79e-07	3.88e-07	0.001
	(3.49e-06)	(3.98e-06)	(4.03e-06)	(3.30e-06)	(3.60e-06)	(0.004)
European Union	−0.204	−0.465***	−0.410**	−0.520***	−0.440**	−0.442***
	(0.161)	(0.170)	(0.185)	(0.161)	(0.176)	(0.168)
Temporal lag	0.834***	0.754***	0.771***	0.686***	0.723***	0.706***
	(0.034)	(0.039)	(0.028)	(0.043)	(0.031)	(0.038)
Spatial lag		0.280***	0.221***	0.0316***	0.237***	0.267***
		(0.066)	(0.048)	(0.049)	(0.035)	(0.044)
Obs.	465	465	465	465	465	465
Estimation	Nonspatial OLS	Spatial OLS	Spatial 2SLS	Spatial OLS	Spatial 2SLS	Spatial ML
Diffusion		Uniform	Uniform	Nonuniform	Nonuniform	Nonuniform

Notes: The regressions were estimated with fixed country effects (coefficients for country dummies not shown).
For the OLS estimates, panel-corrected standard errors are given in parentheses.
For the 2SLS estimates, robust standard errors clustered by year are given in parentheses.
For the ML estimates, robust standard errors are given in parentheses.
*** Significant at 1%; ** Significant at 5%; * Significant at 10%.

Table 3.2   Capital tax rates and international capital mobility (financial openness)

Independent variables	Financial openness	Financial openness	Financial openness	Financial openness	Financial openness	Financial openness
Capital mobility	0.858***	0.988***	0.958**	0.725**	0.758**	0.741**
	(0.338)	(0.342)	(0.359)	(0.313)	(0.345)	(0.322)
Capital mobility interacted with:						
Capital endowment	−0.029*	−0.034**	−0.033**	−0.024*	−0.025**	−0.028*
	(0.015)	(0.016)	(0.013)	(0.014)	(0.011)	(0.014)
Consensus democracy	0.209	0.306*	0.283*	0.422***	0.369**	0.369**
	(0.154)	(0.157)	(0.165)	(0.151)	(0.161)	(0.168)
Corporatism	−0.534	−0.817*	−0.751	−0.888**	−0.799	−0.656
	(0.471)	(0.490)	(0.603)	(0.451)	(0.567)	(0.612)
Left government	0.099*	0.085	0.088	0.089*	0.0916	0.095
	(0.054)	(0.054)	(0.057)	(0.051)	(0.055)	(0.059)
Population	2.45e-07	−2.10e-06*	−1.55e-06	2.13e-07	2.21e-07	0.000
	(1.04e-06)	(1.23e-06)	(1.11e-06)	(9.83e-07)	(9.79e-07)	(0.001)
European Union	−0.075*	−0.148***	−0.131**	−0.156***	−0.136***	−0.131***
	(0.046)	(0.050)	(0.050)	(0.045)	(0.045)	(0.044)
Temporal lag	0.825***	0.751***	0.768***	0.682***	0.718***	0.702***
	(0.036)	(0.040)	(0.030)	(0.044)	(0.031)	(0.038)
Spatial lag		0.261***	0.200***	0.309***	0.231***	0.261***
		(0.066)	(0.053)	(0.047)	(0.036)	(0.043)
Obs.	465	465	465	465	465	465
Estimation	Nonspatial OLS	Spatial OLS	Spatial 2SLS	Spatial OLS	Spatial 2SLS	Spatial ML
Diffusion		Uniform	Uniform	Nonuniform	Nonuniform	Nonuniform

Notes: The regressions were estimated with fixed country effects (coefficients for country dummies not shown).
For the OLS estimates, panel-corrected standard errors are given in parentheses.
For the 2SLS estimates, robust standard errors clustered by year are given in parentheses.
For the ML estimates, robust standard errors are given in parentheses.
*** Significant at 1%. ** Significant at 5%. * Significant at 10%.

Table 3.3 Capital tax rates and international capital mobility (fixed period effects)

Independent variables	Capital-account openness	Capital-account openness	Capital-account openness	Financial openness	Financial openness	Financial openness
Capital mobility	2.162**	1.993*	2.397**	0.918***	0.843**	0.974***
	(0.909)	(1.0115)	(0.941)	(0.327)	(0.345)	(0.309)
Capital mobility interacted with:						
Capital endowment	−0.048	−0.039	−0.067*	−0.028	−0.024*	−0.035**
	(0.045)	(0.032)	(0.038)	(0.017)	(0.012)	(0.015)
Consensus democracy	1.156**	1.287**	1.096**	0.417**	0.447***	0.380**
	(0.506)	(0.507)	(0.514)	(0.168)	(0.159)	(0.161)
Corporatism	−3.373**	−3.464**	−2.935*	−1.070**	−1.061*	−0.853
	(1.487)	(1.318)	(1.548)	(0.515)	(0.545)	(0.585)
Left government	0.186	0.203	0.199	0.059	0.06171	0.063
	(0.188)	(0.203)	(0.203)	(0.051)	(0.056)	(0.055)
Population	−6.03e-06	−2.40e-06	−0.008*	−1.04e-06	−2.37e-07	−0.002
	(4.25e-06)	(5.67e-06)	(0.004)	(1.18e-06)	(1.58e-06)	(0.001)
European Union	−0.649***	−0.627***	−0.654***	−0.193***	−0.186***	−0.191***
	(0.192)	(0.195)	(0.187)	(0.058)	(0.056)	(0.053)
Temporal lag	0.723***	0.713***	0.724***	0.719***	0.708***	0.720***
	(0.044)	(0.033)	(0.038)	(0.045)	(0.033)	(0.038)
Spatial lag	0.157**	0.243***	0.118**	0.166***	0.247***	0.128**
	(0.068)	(0.076)	(0.059)	(0.060)	(0.070)	(0.057)
Obs.	465	465	465	465	465	465
Estimation	Spatial OLS	Spatial 2SLS	Spatial ML	Spatial OLS	Spatial 2SLS	Spatial ML
Diffusion	Nonuniform	Nonuniform	Nonuniform	Nonuniform	Nonuniform	Nonuniform

Notes: The regressions were estimated with fixed country and period effects (coefficients for country and period dummies not shown).
For the OLS estimates, panel-corrected standard errors are given in parentheses.
For the 2SLS estimates, robust standard errors clustered by year are given in parentheses.
For the ML estimates, robust standard errors are given in parentheses.
*** Significant at 1%; ** Significant at 5%; * Significant at 10%.

Hays (2003) used two policy measures of international capital mobility from Quinn: Capital-account openness and financial openness. The first variable is specific to restrictions on capital-account transactions. The second, a broad measure of financial openness, reflects restrictions on either capital- or current-account transactions. Both of these measures vary across countries but have a common time-trend towards liberalization. Therefore, thinking of capital mobility as representing a common external variable makes sense. Table 3.1 presents the results of our reanalysis for the capital-account openness models. The original estimates are reported in the second column, labeled 'Spatial OLS' and 'Uniform diffusion'. By uniform diffusion we mean that Hays used a spatial-weighting matrix with off-diagonal elements that all take a value of $1/(N-1)$. In our reanalysis, we also include a nonuniform weighting matrix based on observed cross-national correlations in capital-tax rates. For each country's row in the spatial-weighting matrix we enter ones for the countries with which its capital-tax rates have a statistically significant positive correlation. We then row-standardize the resulting spatial-weighting matrix.[18] The weighting matrix is nonuniform in the sense that, unlike in the uniform case, Country A's importance in determining Country B's capital-tax rate may not be the same as Country B's importance in determining Country A's tax rate.[19]

We report nonspatial OLS estimates in the first column of Table 3.1 to demonstrate the sizable omitted-variable bias (seen relative to the other columns) when the spatial lag is omitted. Notably, the nonspatial OLS estimate for the consensus-democracy interaction term is about 35% smaller than the original S-OLS estimate and statistically insignificant. Then, two things worry us about Hays's original estimates in the second column. First, he uses S-OLS, which is likely to inflate the estimate of the crucial ρ coefficient because the spatial lag is endogenous. This simultaneity bias induces bias in the other coefficient estimates as well (Franzese and Hays, 2004, 2006). Second, Hays used a uniform spatial-weighting matrix. Each country's capital-tax rate in the sample is assumed equally important in determining every other country's tax rate. This convenience assumption gives a simple unweighted average of the capital-tax rates in the other countries as the spatial lag. If this assumption is wrong, which it almost certainly is in this case, the spatial lag contains measurement error, which may cause attenuation bias in the spatial-lag coefficient estimate (and induced biases in the other coefficient estimates).[20] Note that the feared simultaneity and measurement-error biases work in opposite directions here.

The estimates in the third and fourth columns are consistent with our expectations. First, when we estimate by S-2SLS, the estimated coefficient on the spatial lag drops from 0.280 to 0.221 (a 21% reduction) and, when we use the non-uniform spatial-weighting matrix, the estimate increases to 0.316 (+13%). Columns 5 (S-2SLS) and 6 (S-ML) make both 'corrections': One of the two consistent estimators and the nonuniform spatial-weighting matrix. The results, which are very similar across the two estimators, suggest that, on balance, Hays overestimated the coefficient on the spatial lag (i.e. the simultaneity bias seemed to have dominated) and so underestimated the coefficients on the capital-mobility variable and the capital-mobility-times-consensus-democracy interaction variable (induced biases). In more general terms, due to the endogeneity of the spatial lag, Hays (2003) seems to have overestimated the importance of international factors (tax competition) at the expense of domestic (consensus democracy) and common external factors (capital mobility), which is just what our simulations (Franzese and Hays, 2004, 2006) would lead us to expect. Our reanalysis of Hays's financial-openness model in Table 3.2 tells a similar story.

First, nonspatial OLS produces serious omitted variable bias (column 1, Table 3.2). Second, Hays (2003) probably overestimated the coefficient on the spatial lag and underestimated the coefficients on the capital-mobility and consensus-democracy interaction variables (columns 5 and 6 vs. column 2). In Table 3.3, finally, we include period dummies in the models to control more thoroughly for common shocks. Again, we expect this will cause S-OLS to underestimate the coefficient on the spatial lag for the same reason adding unit dummies causes OLS to underestimate the coefficient on temporal lags: Hurwicz or Nickell bias.[21] We expect to find an analogous spatial-Hurwicz bias in the spatial-lag estimates here (Hurwicz, 1950). Again, the results from our reanalysis are largely consistent with this expectation. The estimated coefficient on the spatial lag in the capital-account-openness model drops by 50% from 0.316 to 0.157 (column 4, Table 3.1 vs. column 1, Table 3.3) with the addition of the period dummies. In the financial-openness model, the ρ estimate is 46% smaller with period dummies (column 4, Table 3.2 vs. column 4, Table 3.3).[22]

3.6 Conclusion

Theoretically and substantively, we expect international interdependence in capital-tax policy. Empirically, Hays (2003) and Basinger and Hallerberg (2004) demonstrated such interdependence using spatial-lag models that specify one country's capital tax rate to depend on the capital tax rates in other countries. However, estimating spatial-lag models is, to be brief, a tricky business. In this paper, we highlighted two problems caused by the endogeneity of the spatial lag and measurement error. Our reanalysis of Hays's (2003) regressions suggests that both these problems are present, although his key substantive conclusions remain qualitatively unchanged. International capital-tax competition is very real and rather stiff in general, but it does not imply some unmitigated *race to the bottom*. The stiffness of the competition depends on what competitors are doing and that depends on the competitors' domestic political–economic and exogenous global contexts. The response to the competition that does emerge depends on the home countries' domestic political–economic contexts and exogenous global contexts.

Acknowledgments

This research was supported in part by NSF grant no. 0318045. We thank Chris Achen, James Alt, Kenichi Ariga, Neal Beck, Jake Bowers, Kerwin Charles, Jakob de Haan, John Dinardo, John Freeman, Mark Hallerberg, Mark Kayser, Achim Kemmerling, Hasan Kirmanoglu, Xiaobo Lu, Thomas Pluemper, Dennis Quinn, Megan Reif, Frances Rosenbluth, Ken Scheve, Phil Schrodt, Wendy Tam-Cho, and Gregory J. Wawro for useful comments on this and/or previous and/or subsequent work in our broader methodological project on spatial-econometric models for political science. We are grateful to Mark Hallerberg and Duane Swank for providing their data to us. Xiaobo Lu also provided excellent research assistance. We alone are responsible for any errors.

Notes

1. Hays (2003), however, makes a small-country assumption in his theoretical model to simplify the formal model by eliminating the role of strategic interdependence.
2. Unskilled labor is usually relatively mobile within (national) jurisdictions but highly immobile across jurisdictions, especially those borders delineating strongly differentiated ethnic, linguistic, religious, and cultural societies. Some types of skilled labor are highly specialized into specific productive activities, which may limit intra- and inter-jurisdictional mobility; Other types, some *human capitalists* for example, may be relatively mobile across jurisdictions.
3. Franzese (2003) offers a more complete review of Swank (2002).
4. Government consumption is not only fixed but also entirely wasted, i.e. it enters no one's utility function.
5. The issues grouped in the econometric literature under the heading *spatial* interdependence need not actually have geometric or geographic *space* as the metric of dependence, as the tax-competition venue illustrates nicely. Competitors or closer competitors for capital need not

share borders or be geographically closer but, rather, are closer by some economic considerations (which may include geographic proximity, certainly).

6. Equation (3.6) models these exogenous-external conditions as common to all units (N.B. no subscript i) but, generally, they will at least correlate across units.

7. Another common spatial-lag specification, frequently used to specify contiguity, leader-emulation, or cultural-connection mechanisms of interdependence, for example, is to consider outcomes from unit or set of units j, but not the outcomes from other units, to diffuse to the outcome in i. For example, only outcomes from countries with similar religious or political heritage diffuse. This implies the weights are 1 (for sums; $1/(N-1)$ for averages) or 0, so diffusion either occurs from some j to some i or it does not, but otherwise the math is the same.

8. Furthermore, PCSEs did not seem to help much in this last regard.

9. The latter is not so much difficult as computationally intensive. These two methods are the ones we explored and most commonly discussed, but are not exhaustive of those potentially capable of returning 'good' estimates of β and ρ.

10. The exogenous-external factors may seem not to satisfy the intuitive statement of valid instruments because they enter both domestic- and foreign-country tax policies. However, they enter both exogenously so, although they do not provide much leverage or power to the instrumentation – they do so only insofar as they are domestic-context conditioned and this context conditioning correlates (exogenously) across countries – they are nonetheless valid.

11. On the other hand, Persson and Tabellini (2000) discussed just such 'strategic delegation' as one implication of their model. Voters in one country have incentives to support a citizen-candidate of greater or lesser capital-labor endowment than themselves precisely because they internalize the effect on their own capital-tax rates of foreign elections.

12. *Asymptotic efficiency* should not at all be confused with *efficiency*. The former is an extremely weak property, stating only that as sample sizes *approach infinity* estimates *become* the most efficient ones and nothing at all necessarily about the relative or absolute efficiency of the estimates along the path they follow as sample sizes approach infinity. Furthermore, if one had infinite samples, efficiency would be virtually irrelevant.

13. The latter of the two parts of (b) is of course the usual regressor-exogeneity assumption necessary to the unbiasedness and consistency of all LS estimators. However, violation of it alone produces biased and inconsistent estimates of β, not of ρ (except insofar as bias in the former induces bias in the latter, which, by usual induced-bias intuition, only occurs in some dampened proportion to the degree to which a typical single country's domestic $\mathbf{X}$ correlates with the foreign $\mathbf{y}$ in its spatial lag, which is not usually very much).

14. The capital-endowment data are from the Penn World Tables. Hays used the capital stock per worker in 1965 as a measure of each country's initial capital endowment.

15. While Hays's regression models allowed for tax competition, his theoretical model made a small-country assumption and so did not, because the global after-tax return to capital is exogenous to small countries. Tax competition is not inconsistent with his theory, but Hays's original focus is on strategic interaction (among producer groups) within countries rather than on tax competition between countries.

16. Table 3.2 reports the original estimates as well.

17. Neither Hays nor Basinger and Hallerberg reported results that included period dummies. (Period dummies are a simple method to control for common shocks.) This is problematic in

that if common shock variables are underspecified, estimated coefficients on spatially weighted variables are likely to be inflated (Franzese and Hays, 2004, 2006). However, Basinger and Hallerberg argued that period dummies create a multicolinearity problem for their models. Distinguishing common shocks from uniform, $1/(N-1)$, diffusion is especially difficult, and Franzese and Hays (2003) argued that such period dummies may also create a spatial-Hurwicz/Nickell bias in the estimates for spatial-lag coefficients. Whether the benefits of period dummies outweigh the costs is ambiguous and probably should be assessed on a case-by-case basis.

18. Row standardization replaces the ones in each country's row in the weighting matrix with $1/N$, where N is the number of countries with which its tax rate is correlated. In other words, if a country's capital tax rate is positively correlated with five other countries, the appropriate cells in the weighting matrix take a value of 0.2. This procedure normalizes the sums across rows of cell entries to one in each row.

19. For example, if Country A's tax rate is correlated with five other countries and Country B's tax rate is only correlated with Country A, the importance of Country A's tax rate (i.e. its weight in the spatial-weighting matrix) in determining Country B's tax rate will be greater than the reverse.

20. We see no strong reason to think this measurement error would be systematic.

21. For a discussion of this bias, see Beck and Katz (2004) on estimating dynamic models with TSCS data.

22. Interestingly, when period dummies are included in the models, the two consistent estimators (S-2SLS and S-ML) give very different estimates, particularly of the spatial-lag coefficient. In both the capital-account and financial-openness models, the S-2SLS estimates are approximately two times larger than the S-ML estimates. We suspect this problem results from an eigenvalue-approximation simplification of the likelihood function employed in Stata's spatial-regression package, which approximation we suspect performs poorly in the presence of high colinearity between the spatial lag and the other regressors. The correlation between period dummies and a spatial lag reflecting a uniform interdependence process is high (and grows with N, the number of units, reaching perfect colinearity at $N = \infty$).

References

Bartels, L. (1991). Instrumental and 'Quasi-instrumental' Variables. *American Journal of Political Science*, 35(3):777–800.

Basinger, S. and Hallerberg, M. (2004). Remodeling the Competition for Capital: How Domestic Politics Erases the Race to the Bottom. *American Political Science Review*, 98(2):261–276.

Beck, N. and Katz, J. (2004). Time-series-cross-section Issues: Dynamics, 2004. Paper Presented at the 2004 Summer Meeting of the Society for Political Methodology, Palo Alto, CA.

Boix, C. (1998). *Political Parties, Growth and Equality*. Cambridge University Press, New York.

Cameron, D. (1978). The Expansion of the Public Sector: A Comparative Analysis. *American Political Science Review*, 72(4):1243–1261.

Dehejia, V. and Genschel, P. (1999). Tax Competition in the European Union. *Politics and Society*, 27(3):403–430.

Franzese, R. (2003). Multiple Hands on the Wheel: Empirically Modeling Partial Delegation and Shared Control of Monetary Policy in the Open and Institutionalized Economy. *Political Analysis*, 11(4):445–474.

Franzese, R. and Hays, J. (2003). Diagnosing, Modeling, Interpreting, and Leveraging Spatial Relationships in Time-series-cross-section Data. National Science Foundation Proposal.

Franzese, R. and Hays, J. (2004). Empirical Modeling Strategies for Spatial Interdependence. Paper Presented at the 2004 Summer Meeting of the Society for Political Methodology, Palo Alto, CA.

Franzese, R. and Hays, J. (2006). Spatial Econometric Models for the Analysis of TSCS Data in Political Science. Unpublished manuscript, previously presented at the 2005 meetings of the American Political Science Association.

Garrett, G. (1998). *Partisan Politics in the Global Economy*. Cambridge University Press, Cambridge.

Garrett, G. and Mitchell, D. (2001). Globalization, Government Spending and Taxation in the OECD. *European Journal of Political Research*, 39(2):145–177.

Genschel, P. (2001). Globalization, Tax Competition, and the Fiscal Viability of the Welfare State. MPIfG Working Paper, 01/1.

Hays, J. (2003). Globalization and Capital Taxation in Consensus and Majoritarian Democracies. *World Politics*, 56(1):79–114.

Hines, J. (1999). Lessons from Behavioral Responses to International Taxation. *National Tax Journal*, 52(2):305–322.

Hurwicz, L. (1950). Least Squares Bias in Time Series. In: *Statistical Inference in Dynamic Economic Models* (Koopmans, T.C., ed.), pp. 365–383. Wiley, New York.

Iversen, T. and Cusack, T. (2000). The Causes of Welfare State Expansion: Deindustrialization or Globalization? *World Politics*, 52(3):313–349.

Lijphart, A. (1999). *Patterns of Democracy: Government Forms and Performance in Thirty-six Countries*. Yale University Press, New Haven, CT.

Mendoza, E., Razin, A., and Tesar, L. (1997). On the Ineffectiveness of Tax Policy in Altering Long-run Growth: Harberger's Superneutrality Conjecture. *Journal of Public Economics*, 66(1):99–126.

Mosher, J. and Franzese, R. (2002). Comparative Institutional Advantage: The Scope for Divergence within European Economic Integration. *European Union Politics*, 3(2):177–204.

Oates, W. (2001). Fiscal Competition and European Union: Contrasting Perspectives. *Regional Science and Urban Economics*, 31(2–3):133–145.

Persson, T. and Tabellini, G. (2000). *Political Economics: Explaining Economic Policy*. MIT Press, Cambridge, MA.

Pierson, P. (ed.) (2001). *The New Politics of the Welfare State*. Oxford University Press, Oxford.

Quinn, D. (1997). The Correlates of Change in International Financial Regulation. *American Political Science Review*, 91(3):531–552.

Rodrik, D. (1997). *Has Globalization Gone Too Far?* Institute for International Economics, Washington, DC.

Rodrik, D. (1998). Why Do More Open Economies Have Bigger Governments? *Journal of Political Economy*, 106(5):997–1032.

Swank, D. (1998). Funding the Welfare State: Globalization and the Taxation of Business in Advanced Market Economies. *Political Studies*, 46(4):671–692.

Swank, D. (2002). *Global Capital, Political Institutions, and Policy Change in Developed Welfare States*. Cambridge University Press, New York.

Swank, D. and Steinmo, S. (2002). The New Political Economy of Taxation in Advanced Capitalist Democracies. *American Journal of Political Science*, 46(3):477–489.

Wildasin, D. (1989). Interjurisdictional Capital Mobility: Fiscal Externality and a Corrective Subsidy. *Journal of Urban Economics*, 25(2):193–212.

Wilson, J. (1986). A Theory of Interregional Tax Competition. *Journal of Urban Economics*, 19(3):296–315.

Wilson, J. (1999). Theories of Tax Competition. *National Tax Journal*, 52(2):269–304.

Zodrow, G. and Mieszkowski, P. (1986). The New View of the Property Tax: A Reformulation. *Regional Science and Urban Economics*, 16(3):309–327.

Labor Mobility and Income Tax Competition

Gwenaël Piaser

Abstract

This chapter provides a model of nonlinear income taxation in a context of international mobility. We consider two identical countries, in which each government chooses noncooperatively a redistributive taxation. If both governments are Rawlsian, the mobility of unskilled workers has no influence on the income tax equilibrium. The mobility of skilled workers reduces the redistribution of income: At optimum, by decreasing income tax, a government attracts skilled workers and thus increases its total tax revenue. If we consider more general welfare functions, the mobility of unskilled workers matters. Finally, if the costs to move are low, at equilibrium, labor supplies are not distorted.

4.1 Introduction

Conventional wisdom suggests that mobility across countries leads to a 'race to the bottom': Generous countries will see their low-skilled population increase and at the same time their more skilled workers emigrate to escape high tax rates. This will make redistribution and social programs more difficult as any economic integration would cause reductions in social programs, or less progressive tax schedules. In such a situation one would conclude that free migration constrains the shape of possible redistribution schemes for each government. This effect of international competition with a mobile factor has already been studied in the literature (for a more detailed survey, see Cremer et al., 1996; Wilson, 1999), especially for capital income taxation. The primary objective of the current chapter is to provide a model of income tax competition between two countries for the case of mobile workers. Since most papers on income tax competition focus on linear income taxes (e.g. Gordon, 1983; Wildasin, 1991, 1994), our work will consider nonlinear income taxes.

Optimal nonlinear taxation usually consists of transferring income from the rich to the poor. In this context, Bertrand competition between governments leads to an unsatisfactory equilibrium: Trying to attract skilled workers in order to increase tax revenue, each government has an incentive to reduce the tax rate on high wages. If there is no restriction on mobility, the *laissez-faire* is the only outcome of the competition game. Using Swiss data, Kirchgässner and Pommerehne (1996) showed that fiscal competition has an empirical impact. Their results strongly suggest that high income earners choose their place of residence depending on the amount of income tax they have to pay. But they have also shown that even if fiscal competition matters, there is no 'race to the bottom' – neighboring regions exhibit very different taxation policies. In the remainder of this chapter, we will consider different restrictions on mobility and their consequences on the equilibrium. Workers will have different costs to move, depending on their preferences.

The consequences of labor mobility on redistribution have already been studied in the literature. Hamilton et al. (2002) considered only a particular case: The governments are Rawlsian,[1] income taxes are linear, and the unskilled workers are perfectly mobile while the skilled workers are perfectly immobile. They showed that in that case international mobility does not affect redistribution: A Rawlsian government has no incentive to attract unskilled workers as long as it maximizes their per-person utility by transferring income to them. It has an incentive to attract skilled workers who pay taxes, but in their model these skilled workers are immobile. This chapter generalizes this result as we will consider nonlinear taxation and allow for any kind of mobility.

Hamilton and Pestieau (2001) have studied nonlinear income tax competition. They have considered both Rawlsian, despotic governments and majority voting outcomes under different assumptions on the mobility of workers. Their assumptions on mobility are quite restrictive: Workers are perfectly mobile or perfectly immobile and both kinds of workers cannot be mobile together. Moreover, they consider small, open economies: Each country does not anticipate any effect of its own redistribution scheme on international migration. In the following we consider the opposite assumption: Our governments are strategic players who anticipate that their taxes affect migration.[2]

Hindriks (1999) provided a model close to ours. The author discussed the level of redistribution when workers are imperfectly mobile, but he did not allow for imperfect information between government and workers. Moreover, labor supply was taken as exogenous. On the contrary, we will focus on imperfect information.

Finally, from a technical point of view, this chapter is close to Rochet and Stole (2002), which analyzed the competition between two principals in a duopoly framework with random participation. In our model the cost of mobility plays the same role as the random participation in limiting the effect of the Bertrand competition.

This chapter extends Hindriks's (1999) analysis to the asymmetric information case. To achieve this purpose, we will use some of the technical tools proposed by Rochet and Stole (2002). Equivalently, this chapter extends the results of Hamilton and Pestieau (2001) to the strategic case.

The chapter is organized as follows. Section 4.2 introduces the basic framework of the study. Then the basic properties of the optimal taxation are addressed in section 4.3. Sections 4.4 and 4.5 derive the properties of the competitive outcome under different assumptions on the welfare criterion. Finally, section 4.6 concludes.

4.2 Model

For tractability, the discrete-type setting of Stiglitz (1982) is adopted. Hence, we consider an economy with two kinds of agents: The workers (who are also tax-payers) and two governments.

4.2.1 Workers

The workers are characterized by their identical preferences and different abilities. The preferences can be formalized by a quasi-linear utility function $U(.,.)$:

$$U(Z,L) = Z - v(L),$$

where $Z = I - T(I)$ is the after-tax income, with I being the before-tax income, L is the labor supply, and $T(.)$ is the tax schedule set by the government. The function $v(.)$ is the disutility of labor, satisfying: $v(0) = 0$, $v' > 0$, $v'(0) = 0$, and $v'' > 0$. Ability is denoted by w, which is also the (constant) marginal productivity. We assume that there are two types of workers: Skilled workers who have a high productivity and unskilled workers who have a low marginal productivity. Formally: $w \in \{w_1, w_2\}$, with $w_1 < w_2$.

Since the labor market is competitive, wages are equal to the marginal productivities of workers, implying $I = w_k L$ (with $i = 1,2$). The utility can be written as a function of I:

$$U_k = I - T(I) - v\left(\frac{I}{w_k}\right).$$

We denote by p_1 the proportion of unskilled workers in a given region and p_2 the proportion of skilled workers in a given region. Therefore, $p_1 + p_2 = 1$.

There are two countries denoted by $i = A,B$. Workers can move (once) from their native country to the foreign country. For a worker of ability w_k, born in country A, the cost of changing country is $(1 - x)\sigma_k$, with x denoting a preference parameter depending upon the individual, $x \in [0,1]$, and σ_k a preference parameter depending upon the individual productivity. The variable x can be interpreted as a personal mobility parameter. Therefore, a worker with $x = 0$ is the least mobile, while a worker with $x = 1$ is the most mobile. The variable σ_k can also be interpreted as a mobility parameter. The higher is σ_k, the less mobile is a worker with ability w_k.

The variables (x, w) are private information: They are only known by the worker. We assume that x is uniformly distributed (for either skilled or unskilled workers) on the segment $[0,1]$. The whole population in each country is equal to 1.

4.2.2 Governments

The governments are both benevolent.[3] They have the same preferences over the utility space represented by the same welfare function $W(U_1, U_2)$. We will consider only two particular cases, the Rawlsian case:

$$W(U_1, U_2) = \min\{U_1, U_2\}$$

and the 'quasi-utilitarian' case:

$$W(U_1, U_2) = \alpha U_1 + U_2,$$

where α is an exogenous weight such that $\alpha > p_1/p_2$.

Therefore, we restrict our analysis to welfare functions which do not depend on the proportion p_2. The governments are only interested in gross inequalities between workers. Note that if we include p_2 in the welfare function some undesirable effects may result: Attracting skilled workers may increase the total welfare even if utilities remain the same.

The second welfare function is not exactly the utilitarian social welfare function, it will be used to test the robustness of the results obtained in the Rawlsian case. Introducing a real utilitarian welfare function would complicate the technical analysis of the model. Moreover, assuming that $\alpha > p_1/p_2$, governments have a clear behavior: Their preferences are biased towards the unskilled workers. Thus, without ambiguity, they want to redistribute wealth from skilled to unskilled workers.

The governments choose their income tax schedule noncooperatively under a budget constraint. The taxation has a unique purpose: Redistribution from the 'rich' to the 'poor'. The governments do not need to finance public goods.

Given the two income tax schedules, $T_A(.)$ and $T_B(.)$, a worker from country A chooses to move if and only if:

$$\max_I \left[I - T_A(I) - v\left(\frac{I}{\omega}\right) \right] \leq \max_I \left[I - T_B(I) - v\left(\frac{I}{\omega}\right) \right] - \left(x - \frac{1}{2} \right) \sigma_1.$$

We denote by $P_1[T_A(.), T_B(.)]$ the proportion of unskilled workers who choose to live in country B, given the two tax policies. In the same way, we denote by $P_2[T_A(.), T_B(.)]$ the proportion of skilled workers who choose to live in country B, given the two tax policies.

4.3 Autarky

The results presented in this section have been obtained by Stiglitz (1982). To characterize the optimal tax policy, we derive a 'revelation mechanism'. For our purpose, a mechanism consists of a set of specific after- and before-tax income. The government maximizes the welfare function with respect to (I_1, Z_1, I_2, Z_2) under the two incentive constraints and the budget constraint:

$$\max W\left[Z_1 - v\left(\frac{I_1}{w_1}\right), Z_2 - v\left(\frac{I_2}{w_2}\right)\right]$$

s.t.

$$Z_1 - v\left(\frac{I_1}{w_1}\right) \geq Z_2 - v\left(\frac{I_2}{w_1}\right),$$

$$Z_2 - v\left(\frac{I_2}{w_2}\right) \geq Z_1 - v\left(\frac{I_1}{w_2}\right),$$

$$p_1(I_1 - Z_1) + p_2(I_2 - Z_2) = 0.$$

This program can be written as:

$$\max W(U_1, U_2),$$

s.t.

$$U_1 + v\left(\frac{I_1}{w_1}\right) - v\left(\frac{I_1}{w_2}\right) - U_2 \leq 0, \tag{4.1}$$

$$U_2 + v\left(\frac{I_2}{w_2}\right) - v\left(\frac{I_2}{w_1}\right) - U_1 \leq 0, \tag{4.2}$$

$$p_1\left[I_1 - U_1 - v\left(\frac{I_1}{w_1}\right)\right] + p_2\left[I_2 - U_2 - v\left(\frac{I_2}{w_2}\right)\right] = 0. \tag{4.3}$$

The government maximizes with respect to (U_1, I_1, U_2, I_2). We denote by δ_1 the Lagrangian multiplier associated with constraint (4.1), by δ_2 the Lagrangian multiplier associated with constraint (4.2), and by λ the multiplier associated with the budget constraint (4.3).

79

To clarify and simplify the notation, we will adopt the following definitions. We define I_2^{fb} and I_1^{fb} as the two before-tax incomes that would be optimal without asymmetric information. Formally, they are defined by the following equations:

$$v'\left(\frac{I_2^{fb}}{\omega_2}\right) = \omega_2,$$

$$v'\left(\frac{I_1^{fb}}{\omega_1}\right) = \omega_1.$$

Proposition 1 (Mirrlees, 1971; Stiglitz, 1982). If we consider a pure Rawlsian government or a quasi-utilitarian government with $\alpha > p_1/p_2$ at the optimum, constraint (4.1) is binding, the labor supply (or the before-tax income) of the skilled workers is not distorted, $I_2 = I_2^{fb}$, and the labor supply of the unskilled individuals is distorted: $I_1 < I_1^{fb}$.

The assumption $\alpha > p_1/p_2$ guarantees that the government wants to redistribute wealth from skilled to unskilled workers. If we assume $\alpha = p_1/p_2$, then the *laissez-faire* is optimal and thus fiscal competition is not an issue. If $\alpha < p_1/p_2$, government's preferences are biased towards skilled workers and redistribution occurs from the 'poor' to the 'rich'. Since we want to model interactions between redistribution and tax competition, the former assumption seems to be the most appropriate.

It must also be noticed that the optimal taxation exhibits an important feature. The labor supply of the less skilled individuals is distorted in order to reduce the incentives for the skilled to misreport their type. It shapes the form of the tax function, which cannot be convex everywhere. International mobility affects this property when the moving cost is sufficiently low, as is shown in the following sections.

4.4 Rawlsian governments

First, we consider two Rawlsian governments. Moreover, each government chooses its tax function taking the tax function of the other country as given and anticipating correctly the migration induced by taxes. Equilibrium is a fixed point at which no worker wants to move and no government wants to change its redistribution policy (given the policy of the other country):

Definition 1. The tax policies of the two governments, $T_A(.)$ and $T_B(.)$, are a Nash equilibrium if and only if:

$$\forall_i, \forall_j \neq i, T_i(.) =$$

$$\text{argmax } W\left[U_1\left(I_{i1} - T_i(I_{i1}) - \nu\left(\frac{I_{i1}}{\omega_1}\right)\right), U_2\left(I_{i2} - T_i(I_{i2}) - \nu\left(\frac{I_{i2}}{\omega_2}\right)\right)\right]$$

under the budget constraint:

$$p_1 P_1\left[T_i(.), T_j(.)\right] T_i(I_{i1}) + p_2 P_2\left[T_i(.), T_j(.)\right] T_i(I_{i2}) = 0,$$

where for $k = 1,2$:

$$I_{ik} = \frac{\text{argmax}}{I}\left[I - T_i(I) - \nu\left(\frac{I}{\omega_k}\right)\right].$$

We adopt the Rothschild–Stiglitz–Nash concept of equilibrium. This could be controversial. Since budget constraint depends on the proportions of both kinds of workers, after migration from one country to the other due to a change in the fiscal policy of one country, the budget constraint is no longer balanced. We keep this concept of equilibrium for two main reasons. First, there is no consensus on an alternative definition of equilibrium. By choosing another concept of equilibrium, we allow the agents to have a behavior inconsistent with the usual assumption (agents are Nash players) made in the economic literature. Second, as our model is static, we cannot introduce explicitly public debt. Thus, to keep the model simple and consistent with previous models, we will make a sharp assumption. We will consider that if a government chooses a taxation policy that leads to a public deficit, given the policy chosen by the other government, its policy is enforced at the cost of an infinite welfare loss. Given this last assumption, payoffs are well defined, and one can apply the Nash concept of equilibrium.

We solve this game by using the 'revelation principle', i.e. we assume that there is no restriction to consider that both governments offer truthful mechanisms. In a more general setting, if competition between two principals is taken into account there is some loss of generality in restricting the analysis to this set of mechanisms. In our context, the agent cannot deal simultaneously with both principals. An agent works and pays taxes in country A or in country B. In this case, Martimort and Stole (2002) argued that the revelation principle applies as long as we consider only pure strategy equilibria.[4]

Moreover, we will only consider the first-order conditions and assume that they are sufficient to characterize the best strategies.

Government A chooses a taxation which can be summarized by the t-uple $(I_{A1}, U_{A1}, I_{A2}, U_{A2})$. A worker with preference x and ability ω_k from country B, moves if and only if:

$$U_{Ak} - (1-x)\sigma_k \geq U_{Bk},$$

i.e. if and only if:

$$x \geq 1 + \frac{(U_{Bk} - U_{Ak})}{\sigma_k}.$$

In the same way, a worker (x, ω_k) from country A, moves if and only if:

$$x \geq 1 + \frac{(U_{Ak} - U_{Bk})}{\sigma_k}.$$

Given the two taxations, the proportion of workers with ability ω_k who live in B is:

$$p_k P_k (U_{Ak}, U_{Bk}),$$

where:

$$
P_k(U_{Ak}, U_{Bk}) =
\begin{cases}
0 & \text{if } \dfrac{(U_{Bk} - U_{Ak})}{\sigma_k} < 0, \\
1 - \dfrac{(U_{Bk} - U_{Ak})}{\sigma_k} & \text{if } 0 \leq \dfrac{(U_{Bk} - U_{Ak})}{\sigma_k} \leq 1, \\
1 & \text{if } \dfrac{(U_{Bk} - U_{Ak})}{\sigma_k} > 1.
\end{cases}
$$

The governments do not observe the worker preference x. As long as they do not use random taxation, they cannot design mechanisms which reveal this information. This property is a consequence of the additive moving cost. We also assume that a government cannot discriminate between immigrants and native inhabitants. In this context, the optimal mechanism is still a set of specific after- and before-tax incomes.

First, we consider two Rawlsian governments. Since we can restrict our analysis to truthful mechanisms, we impose that workers reveal their type. This gives two incentive constraints similar to (4.1) and (4.2), and the budget constraint becomes:

$$p_1 P_1(U_{A1},U_{B1})\left[U_{B1} + v\left(\frac{I_{B1}}{w_1}\right) - I_{B1}\right] + p_2 P_2(U_{A2},U_{B2})\left[U_{B2} + v\left(\frac{I_{B2}}{w_2}\right) - I_{B2}\right] = 0.$$

(4.4)

The government still maximizes the social welfare function with respect to $(I_{B1},U_{B1},I_{B2},U_{B2})$. The program of the government B is similar to the autarky case, except that the number of skilled and unskilled workers in country B is now endogenous. In mathematical terms:

$$\max U_{B1},$$

s.t.

$$U_{B1} + v\left(\frac{I_{B1}}{w_1}\right) - v\left(\frac{I_{B1}}{w_2}\right) - U_{B2} \leq 0,$$

$$U_{B2} + v\left(\frac{I_{B2}}{w_2}\right) - v\left(\frac{I_{B2}}{w_1}\right) - U_{B1} \leq 0,$$

$$p_1 P_1(U_{A1},U_{B1})\left[U_{B1} + v\left(\frac{I_{B1}}{w_1}\right) - I_{B1}\right] + p_2 P_2(U_{A2},U_{B2})\left[U_{B2} + v\left(\frac{I_{B2}}{w_2}\right) - I_{B2}\right] = 0.$$

We assume that the best reply of government B is fully characterized by the first-order conditions of this program: This problem has an interior solution and the second-order conditions are always satisfied.

Given this, it is convenient to define a threshold value for σ_2:

$$\tilde{\sigma} = p_1\left[I_2^{\text{fb}} - v\left(\frac{I_2^{\text{fb}}}{w_2}\right)\right] = p_1\left[I_1^{\text{fb}} - v\left(\frac{I_1^{\text{fb}}}{w_2}\right)\right].$$

Given the properties of the function v, it is easy to see that $\tilde{\sigma} > 0$. One can interpret $\tilde{\sigma}$ as the maximum difference between the income tax paid by the skilled workers and the income tax paid by the unskilled, such that skilled workers have no incentive to misreport their type. The quasi-linearity of the utility function allows us to define easily such a value.[5]

As we consider similar countries, we restrict the analysis to symmetric equilibria in which there is no migration:

$$P_1(U_{A1},U_{B1}) = P_2(U_{A2},U_{B2}) = 1.$$

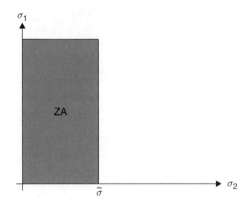

Figure 4.1   Rawlsian governments

Proposition 2.   At equilibrium, the optimal allocations have the following properties:

- If $\sigma_2 \in [\tilde{\sigma}, +\infty[$, the incentive constraint (4.2) is binding: The labor supply of the skilled worker is not distorted while the labor supply of the unskilled worker is distorted. Each skilled worker pays a total income tax smaller than σ_2.
- If $\sigma_2 \in [0, \tilde{\sigma}[$, none of the incentive constraints is binding, so labor supplies are not distorted. Each skilled worker pays a total income tax equal to σ_2.
- For any given σ_2, the tax policy does not depend on σ_1.

The proposition can be summarized by Figure 4.1.

There are two regimes of taxation, depending the value of σ_2. If σ_2 is small, tax policy does not involve any distortion (Area ZA in Figure 4.1). On the contrary, if σ_2 is large enough, the tax polices are less redistributive but qualitatively similar to the tax policy in autarky.

This result recalls that of Rochet and Stole (2002), but the framework and the intuition are quite different. A government has three relevant constraints here. First, it must respect a budget constraint. Second, the government has to leave enough rent to skilled workers in order to dissuade them from misreporting their type, which is formalized by the incentive constraint (4.2). But here the government also has to prevent migration of the skilled workers (which is new compared to the autarky case).

If σ_2 is small, moving from one country to the other is quite easy, then the third constraint prevails: In order to prevent migration, sufficient rent is given to skilled workers and they have no incentive to misreport their type. If σ_2 becomes higher, it is easier to prevent migration, therefore the government leaves less rent to the skilled workers, who may have an incentive to misreport their type.

By assuming extreme values for mobility, we can deduce from Proposition 2 two interesting corollaries. First, if skilled individual are immobile, i.e. if σ_2 goes to infinity, the budget constraint becomes:

$$p_1 P_1(U_{A1}, U_{B1}) \left[U_{B1} + v\left(\frac{I_{B1}}{\omega_1}\right) - I_{B1} \right] + p_2 \left[U_{B2} + v\left(\frac{I_{B2}}{\omega_2}\right) - I_{B2} \right] = 0. \quad (4.5)$$

The program of government B remains similar. It maximizes the utility of the less skilled workers:

$$\max U_{B1}.$$

Since we restrict our analysis to truthful mechanisms, we impose the two incentive constraints (4.1) and (4.2), and the budget constraint (4.5).

Corollary 1. If σ_2 goes to infinity then at equilibrium, the tax policy does not depend on σ_1 and does not differ from the autarky case.

This corollary is a straightforward generalization of Hamilton et al.'s (2002) main result and the intuition is the same. A Rawlsian government has no incentive to attract unskilled workers. On the contrary, a Rawlsian government has incentives to attract skilled workers who pay taxes, but here, skilled workers cannot move.

Second, if unskilled workers are immobile, i.e. if σ_1 goes to infinity, the budget constraint becomes:

$$p_1 \left[U_{B1} + v\left(\frac{I_{B1}}{\omega_1}\right) - I_{B1} \right] + p_2 P_2(U_{A2}, U_{B2}) \left[U_{B2} + v\left(\frac{I_{B2}}{\omega_2}\right) - I_{B2} \right] = 0. \quad (4.6)$$

The program of the government remains similar:

$$\max U_{B1}.$$

We impose the two incentive constraints (4.1) and (4.2), and the budget constraint (4.6).

Corollary 2. When σ_1 goes to infinity, the equilibrium is unchanged: σ_2 remains irrelevant.

4.5 Quasi-utilitarian criterion

Proposition 2 contrasts with the results obtained by Hindriks (1999). Opposite to our model, his optimal transfer policy depends on the variable σ_1. This important difference does not come from his assumption on information, but from the objective of the governments. Considering other welfare functions we get optimal tax policies which depend on σ_2 and σ_1. The following example shows this.

Let us consider the case where the government of country B maximizes the social welfare:

$$\max \alpha U_{B1} + U_{B2}$$

under the incentive constraints (4.1) and (4.2), and the budget constraint (4.4).

We keep the same concept of equilibrium, i.e. Nash equilibrium, the revelation principle still applies, and because countries are similar, we restrict attention to symmetric equilibria.

Proposition 3. If both governments have a quasi-utilitarian objective, then at equilibrium:

- If $\sigma_2 \notin \tilde{S}$ none of the incentive constraints is binding – labor supplies are not distorted. Each skilled worker pays a total income tax T_2.
- If $\sigma_2 \in \tilde{S}$ the incentive constraint (4.2) is binding – the labor supply of the skilled worker is not distorted, while the labor supply of the unskilled workers is distorted. Each skilled worker pays a total income tax smaller than T_2.

Where

$$\tilde{S} = \left\{ s > 0, \left[1 - \frac{p_1}{\alpha p_2} - \frac{\tilde{\sigma}}{\alpha \sigma_1} \right] s > \tilde{\sigma} \right\}$$

and

$$T_2 = - \frac{\left(1 - \alpha \dfrac{p_2}{p_1} \right) \sigma_1}{\dfrac{p_2}{p_1} + \alpha \dfrac{p_2}{p_1} \dfrac{\sigma_1}{\sigma_2}}.$$

The intuition behind this proposition can be explained using Figure 4.2, which represents the set $\tilde{S}$.

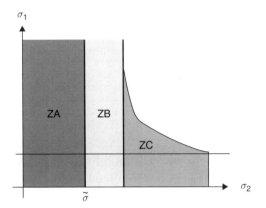

Figure 4.2   Quasi-utilitarian governments

The area in which labor supplies are not distorted can be divided into three subareas: ZA, ZB, and ZC.

First, the domain of values of σ_2 where labor supplies are not distorted is enlarged: The area ZB is added to ZA. If the welfare of skilled workers affects social welfare, then it is less costly for a government to reduce tax on skilled workers to attract them. The shape of the area ZB does not depend on σ_1, and if α goes to infinity the area ZB vanishes.

Second, now σ_1 matters. In the autarky case, a government would be better off with fewer unskilled workers in its country: Fewer unskilled workers means less taxes on skilled workers (or higher transfers to the less skilled workers for a Rawlsian government). Then, if σ_1 is small, a government has an incentive to reduce transfers to the unskilled workers (which reduce their welfare) to make them move. This effect is represented by the area ZC. Moreover, if σ_1 goes to infinity, the unskilled workers become immobile and the area ZC vanishes. If σ_1 goes to zero the mobility of the unskilled workers becomes a crucial variable and the tax paid by the skilled workers, T_2, also goes to zero.

Finally, this counter-intuitive behavior is emphasized by the specification of the welfare function. Since it does not depend on p_2, a government has the same utility, whatever the number of the 'poor' living in its country. As long as the government cares for the welfare skilled workers, as the number of unskilled workers increases, the social welfare decreases.

Proposition 3 is a generalization of Proposition 2. If $1/\alpha$ goes to 0, the conditions $\sigma_2 \in \tilde{S}$ and $\sigma_2 \in [0,\tilde{\sigma}[$ are equivalent and $T_2 = \sigma_2$.[6] From this we can conclude that if α is sufficiently high, the influence of σ_1 on the optimal tax policy is quite low.

The conclusions from Proposition 3 allow us to demonstrate two properties. First, the neutrality of σ_1 no longer holds if we consider more general welfare functions. Second, the role of welfare criterion, which can imply counter-intuitive and questionable behavior of governments.

4.6 Conclusion

In this chapter it has been shown how mobility affects the possibility of redistribution, and the shape of the taxation policy has been defined. In this analysis the key variable is the mobility of skilled workers, who are considered to be the 'victims' of redistribution. If they can move, they use the competition between the two governments to reduce their income tax rate. On the other hand, the ability to move of the unskilled workers does not affect the optimal tax policy of Rawlsian governments.[7] Moreover, if the cost to move for the skilled workers is small, the equilibrium of the game leads to first best allocations, i.e. efficient labor supplies. This does not mean that fiscal competition has no effect on the redistribution. On the contrary, redistribution is reduced by this competition. Finally, the role of the welfare function has been stressed using one particular example: If the government cares about the whole population, the tax system exhibits 'counter-intuitive behavior'. Despite being benevolent definition, the government induces the less rich part of the population to migrate to other countries.

From a technical point of view, even if we use a standard model, some assumptions are restrictive in different ways. The welfare function plays a central role in our model. As has been said, these results have been derived using two particular welfare functions. Introducing generalized welfare functions would give intuition on the robustness of the main conclusions of this chapter. Also, a tractable discrete-type model has been considered, but even in a more traditional setting discrete and continuous models are not strictly equivalent.

The existence of nonsymmetric equilibria remains an open question. As long as we consider symmetric countries, focusing on symmetric equilibria makes sense. But a clear possible extension would be to take asymmetric countries into account, and then we would have no reason to focus on these particular outcomes of the game. As capital taxation is an important question in economic literature, introducing a generalized production function including capital as production factor and capital taxation (as in Huber, 1999) would also probably give new results.

Finally, the importance of mobility costs of the skilled workers has been stressed. It would be interesting to try to get empirical estimations for these costs.

This could have interesting consequences for fiscal policy. For example, Kirchgässner and Pommerehne (1996) have suggested that fiscal competition has a significant effect in Switzerland. However, this competition could be less important in the European Union, because costs to move are higher.

Acknowledgments

I would like to thank Salvador Barrios, François Boldron, Eloisa Campioni, Vidar Christiansen, Clemens Fuest, Nicolas Gravel, Jean Hindriks, Sylvain Latil, Jean-Marie Lozachmeur, Maurice Marchand, Pierre Pestieau, and Eric Strobl for their remarks, their comments and their help. I want also to thank audiences in Lille, Montpellier, Munich, Stockholm, and Paris for their comments and suggestions. The usual caveats apply.

Notes

1. A Rawlsian government would the maximize the utility of the least advantaged resident.
2. Our model does not generalize that of Hamilton and Pestieau (2001). Both assumptions on strategic behavior of the government can be justified.
3. We take the separation between the two countries as given. Obviously, the merge of the two governments would be welfare improving. For a discussion on principals' separation, see Martimort (1999).
4. For a discussion on the revelation principle and exclusive dealing in a more general setting, see Page and Monteiro (2003).
5. I thank Nicolas Gravel, who made that point.
6. If $1/\alpha$ goes to 0, the conditions $\sigma_2 \notin \tilde{S}$ and $\sigma_2 \in [\tilde{\sigma}, +\infty[$ become equivalent as well.
7. The results would be exactly the contrary if we had considered 'despotic' governments, i.e. governments which maximize the utility of the richest workers.

References

Cremer, H., Fourgeaud, V., Leite-Monteiro, M., Marchand, M., and Pestieau, P. (1996). Mobility and Redistribution: A Survey. *Public Finance*, 51(3):325–352.

Gordon, R. (1983). An Optimal Taxation Approach to Fiscal Federalism. *Quarterly Journal of Economics*, 98(4):567–585.

Hamilton, J. and Pestieau, P. (2001). Optimal Income Taxation and the Ability to Distribution: Implication for Migration Equilibria. CORE Discussion Paper No. 2002-35.

Hamilton, J., Lozachmeur, J.-M. and Pestieau, P. (2002). Rawlsian Government and the Race to the Bottom. *Economics Bulletin*, 8(2):1–6.

Hindriks, J. (1999). The Consequences of Labour Mobility for Redistribution: Tax vs. Transfer Competition. *Journal of Public Economics*, 74(2):215–223.

Huber, B. (1999). Tax Competition and Tax Coordination in an Optimum Tax Model. *Journal of Public Economics*, 71(3):441–458.

Kirchgässner, G. and Pommerehne, W. (1996). Tax Harmonization and Tax Competition in the European Union: Lessons from Switzerland. *Journal of Public Economics*, 60(3):351–371.

Martimort, D. (1999). Renegotiation Design with Multiple Regulators. *Journal of Economic Theory*, 88(2):261–293.

Martimort, D. and Stole, L. (2002). The Revelation and Delegation Principles in Common Agency Games. *Econometrica*, 70(4):1659–1673.

Mirrlees, J. (1971). An Exploration in the Theory of Optimum Income Taxation. *Review of Economic Studies*, 38(2):175–208.

Page, F. and Monteiro, P. (2003). Three Principles of Competitive Nonlinear Pricing. *Journal of Mathematical Economics*, 39(1):63–109.

Rochet, J.-C. and Stole, L. (2002). Nonlinear Pricing with Random Participation. *Review of Economic Studies*, 69(1):277–311.

Stiglitz, J. (1982). Self-selection and Pareto Efficient Taxation. *Journal of Public Economics*, 17(2):213–240.

Wildasin, D. (1991). Income Redistribution in a Common Labor Market. *American Economic Review*, 81(4):757–773.

Wildasin, D. (1994). Income Redistribution and Migration. *Canadian Journal of Economics*, 27(3):637–656.

Wilson, J. D. (1999). Theories of Tax Competition. *National Tax Journal*, 52(2):269–304.

Appendix A: Proof of Proposition 1

See Stiglitz (1982).

Appendix B: Proof of Proposition 2

The program of government B:

$$\max U_{B1},$$

s.t.

$$U_{B1} + \nu\left(\frac{I_{B1}}{\omega_1}\right) - \nu\left(\frac{I_{B1}}{\omega_2}\right) - U_{B2} \leq 0,$$

$$U_{B2} + \nu\left(\frac{I_{B2}}{\omega_2}\right) - \nu\left(\frac{I_{B2}}{\omega_1}\right) - U_{B1} \leq 0,$$

$$p_1 P_1(U_{A1}, U_{B1})\left[U_{B1} + \nu\left(\frac{I_{B1}}{\omega_1}\right) - I_{B1}\right] + p_2 P_2(U_{A2}, U_{B2})\left[U_{B2} + \nu\left(\frac{I_{B2}}{\omega_2}\right) - I_{B2}\right] = 0.$$

The Lagrangian of the problem:

$$L = U_{B1} - \delta_2 \left[U_{B1} + v\left(\frac{I_{B1}}{w_1}\right) - v\left(\frac{I_{B1}}{w_2}\right) - U_{B2} \right]$$

$$- \delta_1 \left[U_{B2} + v\left(\frac{I_{B2}}{w_2}\right) - v\left(\frac{I_{B2}}{w_1}\right) - U_{B1} \right]$$

$$+ \lambda \left[p_1 P_1(U_{A1}, U_{B1}) \left[U_{B1} + v\left(\frac{I_{B1}}{w_1}\right) - I_{B1} \right] \right.$$

$$\left. + p_2 P_2(U_{A2}, U_{B2}) \left[U_{B2} + v\left(\frac{I_{B2}}{w_2}\right) - I_{B2} \right] \right],$$

where λ, δ_1, and δ_2 are the multipliers associated with the constraints. The general methodology is the following. The first-order conditions with respect to $(I_{B1}, U_{B1}, I_{B2}, U_{B2})$ characterize the best reply of government B to government A's policy. We set $U_{B1} = U_{A1}$ and $U_{B2} = U_{A2}$. The first-order conditions are then:

$$1 - \delta_2 + \delta_1 - \lambda p_1 + p_1 \frac{\lambda}{\sigma_1} \left[I_{B1} - v\left(\frac{I_{B1}}{w_1}\right) - U_{B1} \right] = 0,$$

$$-\delta_1 + \delta_2 - \lambda p_2 + p_2 \frac{\lambda}{\sigma_2} \left[I_{B2} - v\left(\frac{I_{B2}}{w_2}\right) - U_{B2} \right] = 0,$$

$$-\delta_1 \left[\frac{1}{w_2} v'\left(\frac{I_{B2}}{w_2}\right) - \frac{1}{w_1} v'\left(\frac{I_{B2}}{w_1}\right) \right] + \lambda p_2 \left[1 - \frac{1}{w_2} v'\left(\frac{I_{B2}}{w_2}\right) \right] = 0,$$

$$-\delta_2 \left[\frac{1}{w_1} v'\left(\frac{I_{B1}}{w_1}\right) - \frac{1}{w_2} v'\left(\frac{I_{B1}}{w_2}\right) \right] + \lambda p_1 \left[1 - \frac{1}{w_1} v'\left(\frac{I_{B1}}{w_1}\right) \right] = 0.$$

The budget constraint becomes:

$$p_1 \left[U_{B1} + v\left(\frac{I_{B1}}{w_1}\right) - I_{B1} \right] + p_2 \left[U_{B2} + v\left(\frac{I_{B2}}{w_2}\right) - I_{B2} \right] = 0.$$

The incentive constraints remain unchanged. We consider solutions to the latter conditions, such that $\delta_1 \geq 0$, $\delta_2 \geq 0$ and $\lambda \geq 0$. If we find a solution, by construction it will be a symmetric equilibrium of the game. As we consider symmetric equilibria, we use the following notation: $U_{A1} = U_{B1} = U_1$, $U_{A2} = U_{B2} = U_2$, and $I_{A1} = I_{B1} = I_1$, and $I_{A2} = I_{B2} = I_2$.

Tedious but straightforward computations show that:

- If $\sigma_2 < \sigma$, the countries adopt the following policy: $I_2 = I_2^{\text{fb}}$, $I_1 = I_1^{\text{fb}}$, $U_2 = I_2^{\text{fb}} - \sigma_2 - v\left(\frac{I_2^{\text{fb}}}{w_1}\right)$, and $U_1 = I_1^{\text{fb}} - \sigma_1 - v\left(\frac{I_1^{\text{fb}}}{w_1}\right)$. It implies that skilled workers pay an income tax $T_2 = \sigma_2$ and unskilled workers receive a transfer
$$T_1 = -\frac{p_2}{p_1}\sigma_2.$$

- If $\sigma_2 > \sigma$, the equilibrium policy implies that $T_2 < \sigma_2$.

Appendix C: Proof of Corollaries 1 and 2

Proofs of Corollaries 1 and 2 are similar to the proof of Proposition 2.

Appendix D: Proof of Proposition 3

The program of government B:
$$\max \alpha U_{B1} + U_{B2},$$

s.t.

$$U_{B1} + v\left(\frac{I_{B1}}{w_1}\right) - v\left(\frac{I_{B1}}{w_2}\right) - U_{B2} \le 0,$$

$$U_{B2} + v\left(\frac{I_{B2}}{w_2}\right) - v\left(\frac{I_{B2}}{w_1}\right) - U_{B1} \le 0,$$

$$p_1 P_1(U_{A1}, U_{B1})\left[U_{B1} + v\left(\frac{I_{B1}}{w_1}\right) - I_{B1}\right] + p_2 P_2(U_{A2}, U_{B2})\left[U_{B2} + v\left(\frac{I_{B2}}{w_2}\right) - I_{B2}\right] = 0.$$

The Lagrangian of the problem:

$$L = \alpha U_{B1} - U_{B2} - \delta_2\left[U_{B1} + v\left(\frac{I_{B1}}{w_1}\right) - v\left(\frac{I_{B1}}{w_2}\right) - U_{B2}\right]$$

$$- \delta_1\left[U_{B2} + v\left(\frac{I_{B2}}{w_2}\right) - v\left(\frac{I_{B2}}{w_1}\right) - U_{B1}\right]$$

$$+ \lambda\left(p_1 P_1(U_{A1}, U_{B1})\left[U_{B1} + v\left(\frac{I_{B1}}{w_1}\right) - I_{B1}\right]\right.$$

$$\left. + p_2 P_2(U_{A2}, U_{B2})\left[U_{B2} + v\left(\frac{I_{B2}}{w_2}\right) - I_{B2}\right]\right),$$

where λ, δ_1, and δ_2 are the multipliers associated with the constraints.

We keep the same methodology. The first-order conditions give the best reply of government B to the government A policy. We set $U_{B1} = U_{A1}$ and $U_{B2} = U_{A2}$, and we take arbitrary values for U_{B1} and U_{B2}. The first-order conditions become:

$$\alpha - \delta_2 + \delta_1 - \lambda p_1 + p_1 \frac{\lambda}{\sigma_1}\left[I_{B1} - v\left(\frac{I_{B1}}{w_1}\right) - U_{B1}\right] = 0,$$

$$1 - \delta_1 + \delta_2 - \lambda p_2 + p_2 \frac{\lambda}{\sigma_2}\left[I_{B2} - v\left(\frac{I_{B2}}{w_2}\right) - U_{B2}\right] = 0,$$

$$-\delta_1\left[\frac{1}{w_2}v'\left(\frac{I_{B2}}{w_2}\right) - \frac{1}{w_1}v'\left(\frac{I_{B2}}{w_1}\right)\right] + \lambda p_2\left[1 - \frac{1}{w_2}v'\left(\frac{I_{B2}}{w_2}\right)\right] = 0,$$

$$-\delta_2\left[\frac{1}{w_1}v'\left(\frac{I_{B1}}{w_1}\right) - \frac{1}{w_2}v'\left(\frac{I_{B1}}{w_2}\right)\right] + \lambda p_1\left[1 - \frac{1}{w_1}v'\left(\frac{I_{B1}}{w_1}\right)\right] = 0.$$

The budget constraint becomes:

$$p_1\left[U_{B1} + v\left(\frac{I_{B1}}{w_1}\right) - I_{B1}\right] + p_2\left[U_{B2} + v\left(\frac{I_{B2}}{w_2}\right) - I_{B2}\right] = 0.$$

The incentive constraints remain unchanged. We consider symmetric solutions to the latter conditions. We keep the same notation.

Again, tedious but straightforward computation shows that:

- If $\sigma_2 \notin \tilde{S}$, the equilibrium policy involves:

$$I_2 = I_2^{fb}, I_1 = I_1^{fb}, U_2 = I_2^{fb} + \frac{\left(1 - \alpha \frac{p_2}{p_1}\right)\sigma_1}{\frac{p_2}{p_1} + \alpha \frac{p_2}{p_1}\frac{\sigma_1}{\sigma_2}} - v\left(\frac{I_2^{fb}}{w_2}\right), \text{ and}$$

$$U_1 = I_1^{fb} + \frac{p_2}{p_1}\frac{\left(1 - \alpha \frac{p_2}{p_1}\right)\sigma_1}{\frac{p_2}{p_1} + \alpha \frac{p_2}{p_1}\frac{\sigma_1}{\sigma_2}} - v\left(\frac{I_1^{fb}}{w_1}\right).$$

It implies that skilled workers pay an income tax $T_2 = -\dfrac{\left(1-\alpha\frac{p_2}{p_1}\right)\sigma_1}{\frac{p_2}{p_1}+\alpha\frac{p_2}{p_1}\frac{\sigma_1}{\sigma_2}}$, and

unskilled workers receive a transfer $T_1 = \dfrac{p_2}{p_1}\dfrac{\left(1-\alpha\frac{p_2}{p_1}\right)\sigma_1}{\frac{p_2}{p_1}+\alpha\frac{p_2}{p_1}\frac{\sigma_1}{\sigma_2}}$. The assumption

$\alpha > p_1/p_2$ insures that T_2 is positive and T_1 is negative.

- If $\sigma_2 \in \tilde{S}$ and if country A adopts the policy described in the proof, the best response of country B is to adopt the same policy. We can deduce that the

  tax paid by the skilled workers is less than $T_2 = -\dfrac{\left(1-\alpha\frac{p_2}{p_1}\right)\sigma_1}{\frac{p_2}{p_1}+\alpha\frac{p_2}{p_1}\frac{\sigma_1}{\sigma_2}}$.

Part 2

Optimal International Taxation in Practice – Innovations and the EU

Taxable Asset Sales in
Securitization

Paul U. Ali

Abstract

Securitization is one of the most important ways in which banks and corporations raise funds (significant savings in fundraising can be achieved as the funds raised in a securitization are priced on the creditworthiness of the securitized assets, not the creditworthiness of the bank or corporation), enhance their balance sheets (by removing certain assets from their balance sheets and ensuring the funds raised on the security of those assets do not appear as liabilities on their balance sheets) and, in the case of banks, manage their regulatory capital requirements (the capital held against the securitized assets can be released and deployed more profitably by the bank). These objectives are achieved by isolating a nominated pool of assets in an orphan entity and having that entity issue debt securities which are serviced out of the cashflows generated by the assets, in a form of securitization known as cash or true sale securitization.

5.1   Introduction

Securitization is one of the most important ways in which banks and corporations raise funds. Significant savings in fundraising can be achieved as the funds raised in a securitization are priced on the creditworthiness of the securitized assets (not the creditworthiness of the bank or corporation), enhance their balance sheets (by removing certain assets from their balance sheets and ensuring the funds raised on the security of those assets do not appear as liabilities on their balance sheets) and, in the case of banks, manage their regulatory capital requirements (the capital held against the securitized assets can be released and deployed more profitably by the bank). These objectives are achieved by isolating a nominated pool of assets in an orphan entity and having that entity issue debt securities which are serviced out of the cashflows generated by the assets, in a form of securitization known as cash or true sale securitization. However, careful structuring of these transactions is necessary to avoid negative international tax consequences.

The efficacy of securitization transactions, which depends, in turn, upon the efficacy of the individual components of the transaction, is now necessarily a matter that runs across borders (Schwarcz, 1998). This is due to three factors. First, many securitizations involve the issue of debt securities into foreign markets due, for example, to local demand for such securities having been satiated, with the issuer being forced to look to foreign markets to sell the securities. This is also necessary where the issuer is located in an offshore jurisdiction while the likely investors are located in onshore jurisdictions. That leads to the second factor. Many of the issuers in securitization transactions are located in offshore jurisdictions, such as the Cayman Islands, Channel Islands, or the British Virgin Islands, for corporate,

99

regulatory, or taxation reasons. The third factor relates to the assets being securitized themselves. Those assets may be diversified by geographic region.

A critical element in the economic viability of cash securitizations is ensuring neutrality for any taxation imposts on the transfer of assets from the bank or corporation to the orphan entity. In many active securitization markets, imposts in the form of stamp duty are levied by the revenue authorities on sales of assets (including receivables and real property mortgages). Moreover, failure to pay the requisite taxation impost may lead to the invalidation of the asset sale. This arises both in the case of purely domestic securitizations (where the securitized assets, the orphan entity, and the investors are situated in the same taxation jurisdiction) and international or cross-border securitizations (where some or all of the securitized assets are situated in a different taxation jurisdiction to that of the orphan entity). The latter is a common feature of many bank securitizations where a multi-jurisdiction loan portfolio is being securitized (that is, the borrowers are spread across multiple jurisdictions) and of offshore securitizations where the orphan entity is incorporated in an offshore jurisdiction.

This chapter outlines the structure of cash securitizations and also discusses the way in which asset transfers are structured to avoid the imposition of stamp duty and similar taxation imposts.

5.2 Cash securitizations

Cash securitizations, which are the more common of the two main forms of both domestic and international securitizations (the other being synthetic securitizations), involve the combination of two well-known concepts: The transfer of assets from the originator of the assets (or a warehouse facility provider) to a securitization vehicle, and the issue of securities to investors in the capital markets by the securitization vehicle (Ali and de Vries Robbe, 2003). The proceeds obtained from the issue of securities are employed by the securitization vehicle to finance the acquisition of the assets from the originator or warehouse facility provider, while the cashflows generated by those assets are used to meet the securitization vehicle's obligations to pay principal and interest on the securities (Ali and de Vries Robbe, 2003).

The efficacy of any cash securitization depends upon two key factors. First, the securitization vehicle must be structured in a manner so that it is bankruptcy remote from the originator and, second, the transfer of the securitized assets must constitute a true sale to the securitization vehicle. It is also essential, when structuring a true sale of assets, to ensure that the true sale does not attract stamp duty or a similar taxation impost.

5.3   Bankruptcy remoteness of the securitization vehicle

Bankruptcy remoteness means, in essence, that the solvency of the securitization vehicle and its ability to meet its obligations in respect of the securities issued by it will not be impaired by the insolvency of the originator. This can ordinarily be achieved by ensuring that the securitization vehicle is independent of the originator, thus insulating the former against the risk that persons with claims against the latter will be able to pierce the corporate veil between the two entities, leading to the pooling of the entities' assets. This requires an assessment of the law of jurisdictions in which the originator and securitization vehicle are located. In international securitizations, the jurisdictions may be identical (with only the securitized assets being located in a different jurisdiction) or different (particularly where the securitization vehicle is located in an offshore jurisdiction). In common-law jurisdictions such as Australia, this entails taking the following steps (Kravitt, 1996; Ali and de Vries Robbe, 2003):

1.   The originator does not own the securitization vehicle (often the entire share capital of the securitization vehicle is placed in a charitable or non-charitable purpose trust and the trustee of the trust is independent of the originator).
2.   The directors (and any other officers) of the securitization vehicle are independent of the originator (at the very least, they must not be employees of the originator).
3.   The securitization vehicle reports its assets and liabilities separately from the originator and files separate tax returns.
4.   The securitization vehicle's assets are not commingled with the originator's assets.
5.   Dealings (including the transfer of the assets to be securitized) between the originator and the securitization vehicle are undertaken on commercially defensible terms.

5.4   True sale of the securitized assets

If the dealings between the originator and the securitization vehicle are not undertaken on commercially defensible grounds, they may be taken by a court to be evidence of the influence wielded by the originator, leading to the erosion of the corporate veil between the two entities and thus undermining bankruptcy remoteness. In addition, dealings which are not on commercially defensible terms are at risk of being characterized by a court as fraudulent conveyances or voidable preferences and therefore the subject matter of those dealings can be appropriated by the originator's creditors on its insolvency. To avoid either of these findings, the transfer of assets from the originator to the securitization vehicle must be priced fairly. The pricing of the assets may also have taxation consequences, particularly as regards over-collateralization, where the assets are effectively being transferred for less than their aggregate face value.

Furthermore, to also ensure bankruptcy remoteness and to avoid the pooling of assets between the two entities, the transfer of assets from the originator to the securitization vehicle must constitute an absolute assignment or true sale of those assets. This means, as a matter of law, the originator must divest itself of all of the risks and the entire benefit of the assets to be securitized. This requires an assessment of the law not only of the jurisdictions in which the originator and securitization vehicle are located, but also of the law of the jurisdiction in which the assets are located. In a purely domestic securitization, these jurisdictions will be identical, but an international securitization may involve, as a minimum, an examination of two (for example, where the securitization vehicle is located in an offshore jurisdiction) or three jurisdictions (for example, where the securitization vehicle and the assets are located in different jurisdictions to that of the originator). In practice, the number of jurisdictions to be examined will often be considerably higher in the case of securitized assets that have been diversified by geographic region (for example, where a bank is securitizing a multi-jurisdiction loan portfolio). While the law of the jurisdiction in which the assets are located will, as a general rule, determine the efficacy of the sale itself (that is, whether the assets can be sold), an examination of the law of the jurisdictions of the originator and issuer is also necessary to determine whether those parties have the necessary legal capacity to consummate any such sale and whether such a sale is at risk of invalidation by the insolvency laws of those jurisdictions.

In determining whether there has been a true sale of the assets under the law of jurisdiction in which the assets are located, two factors are decisive (Schwarcz, 1993):

1. Can the securitization vehicle recover any fall in value of the securitized assets from the originator?
2. Has the originator retained any rights to the benefit of any increase in value of the securitized assets?

Both of the questions posed above must be answered in the negative if the transfer of the assets is to be accorded the status of a true sale. In contrast, answering either or both of the above questions in the positive will lead to recharacterization of the transfer by a court as a conditional assignment or an assignment by way of security. The originator will, in the latter situation, be taken not to have relinquished the entire benefit of, and the risks associated with, the assets, and the relationship between the two entities will not be one of seller and buyer (as in the case of an absolute assignment or true sale) but of mortgagor and mortgagee (as in the case of an assignment by way of security or mortgage).

A true sale, in common-law jurisdictions such as Australia, requires, as a minimum, a divestiture in favor of the securitization vehicle of the originator's entire beneficial interest in or equitable title to the securitization vehicle. This can be effected as an absolute assignment either at law (where legal title to the assets is passed to the securitization vehicle and the entire equitable title to the assets which has not been severed from the legal title passes also with the legal title) or in equity (where the entire equitable title is severed from the legal title and passed on to the securitization vehicle with legal title being retained by the originator) (Worthington, 1996; Ali, 2002). The transfer in its entirety of the equitable title to the assets, whether as part of the legal title to the assets or following its severance from the legal title, is sufficient to effect a transfer of the entire benefit and risks of the securitized assets from the originator to the securitization vehicle.

However, should the originator retain a right to share in the profits of the securitized assets or remain liable to make good, either in whole or in part, any losses incurred by the securitization vehicle on the assets, the originator will be viewed by a court as not having passed the entirety of its beneficial interest in the securitized assets on to the securitization vehicle (Ali and de Vries Robbe, 2003). This retention of a beneficial interest in the securitized receivables means that the transfer does not have the character of an absolute assignment but will rather be characterized as an assignment by way of security (Ali, 2002). The use of the proceeds from the issue of the securities by the securitization vehicle to acquire the securitized assets will be seen not as the payment of the purchase price for the sale of the assets, but, instead, as the extension of a loan by the securitization vehicle to the originator secured over the securitized assets.

The dealing between the two entities is thus in the nature of a mortgage. The securitization vehicle can be treated as having a fixed claim against the originator for the payment of an amount equivalent to the quantum of the proceeds exchanged by it for its interest in the securitized assets and, like any other mortgagee, can, should there be a shortfall between the value of the assets and the amount advanced by it to the originator, claim that shortfall from the originator. In addition, the originator (like any other mortgagor), not the securitization vehicle, will take the benefit of any increase in value of the securitized assets above the amount advanced to the originator.

Moreover, the originator's retention of a beneficial interest in the securitized assets means that those assets, even though the majority of the beneficial interest has passed to the securitization vehicle, can still be attached by the originator's creditors, in the event of the originator's insolvency. That beneficial interest, since it constitutes property, will continue to form part of the pool of assets available for distribution, on insolvency, to the originator's creditors. Accordingly, the failure of the transfer of assets to satisfy the requirements for a true sale means that, regardless of the fact that the originator does not own or control the securitization vehicle, the securitization vehicle will not be bankruptcy remote from the originator and the securitized assets will be pooled with the originator's assets.

The absence of a true sale will also abrogate the very rationale for the securitization. The investors in the securities issued by the securitization vehicle will remain exposed to the credit risk of the originator and, accordingly, will be in no different a position to creditors that have advanced funds directly to the originator. The funds raised by the securitization vehicle (and which are to be passed on to the originator in the form of the purchase price for the securitized assets) will not be priced on a basis that reflects only the creditworthiness of the securitized assets, but will also take into account the originator's creditworthiness. In addition, without a true sale, the originator will not be able to remove the securitized assets from its balance sheet (and the funds received from the securitization vehicle will need to be accounted for as a liability rather than an asset on the originator's balance sheet). Nor, if the originator is a bank, will it be able to release the regulatory capital held by it against the assets being securitized.

The true sale of the securitized assets is thus an integral component of all cash securitizations. Care, however, must be taken when structuring the sale to ensure that not only is the risk of recharacterization avoided or minimized, but also that the sale is neutral as regards stamp duty and similar taxation imposts. This is a particularly onerous matter as regards international securitizations, where the questions as to the efficacy of the sale and its neutrality must be examined in all jurisdictions in which the securitized assets are located.

5.5   True sales and legal assignments

Stamp duty is a document-based impost. Accordingly, while a sale of assets (such as the assets the subject of a securitization) may constitute a sale of dutiable assets, it is the writing that evidences the sale, rather than the sale itself, that attracts stamp duty.

The assets that are the subject of a securitization are ordinarily debts or other intangibles (or choses in action). For instance, RMBS (Residential Mortgage-Backed Securities) and CMBS (Commercial Mortgage-Backed Securities) securitizations both involve the securitization of loans secured over real property, while CDOs (Collateralized Debt Obligations) typically involve the securitization of corporate loans (and, less commonly, corporate bonds, the debt securities issued in other securitizations, project finance transactions and other structured finance transactions, sovereign debt, and municipal debt). Other important classes of assets that have been securitized include auto loans, credit card debts, and student loans.

In common-law jurisdictions such as Australia, an absolute assignment of debts or other intangibles can, as noted above, be effected at law or in equity. As regards the first method, a debt can only be assigned at law if the assignment complies with the statutory framework specifically established for legal assignments of intangibles (Ali, 2002). A key requirement is that the assignment of the debt must be evidenced in writing. Accordingly, while a legal assignment will effect a transfer to the securitization vehicle of legal title to the debt being securitized and perfect the rights of the securitization vehicle in the debt at law, any such writing will attract the application of stamp duty (unless the assignment has the benefit of a statutory exemption). In addition, the legal assignment of the intangibles comprising the mortgages or other security interests that support the repayment of the securitized debts (as in the case of RMBS, CMBS, and auto loan securitizations) may also constitute a dutiable transfer, as well as having to be registered (and thus attracting a separate registration fee for each individual mortgage or security interest in the pool of securitized assets). This is relevant not only to purely domestic securitizations, involving, for example, Australian assets and an Australian securitization vehicle, but also to international securitizations where some or all of the securitized assets are situated in a different jurisdiction to the securitization vehicle. The securitized assets, as debts, will be taken to be situated in the jurisdiction in which legal action can be taken to enforce the debt – that is, the jurisdiction where the debtor is incorporated, has its principal place of business, or is otherwise taken to be located.

These shortcomings with legal assignments, when coupled with the requirement that notice of the assignment, for that assignment to be effective at law, must be given to the underlying debtor (thus potentially disrupting the relationship between the originator and the debtor) and the inability to assign future debts at law (meaning that a fresh assignment must be effected in respect of each future addition to the securitized pool of assets) has meant that legal assignments are rarely employed in cash securitizations (Ali and de Vries Robbe, 2003).

5.6   True sales and equitable assignments

An equitable assignment of a debt, in contrast, suffers none of the shortcomings identified above with legal assignments. The efficacy of an equitable assignment is not dependent upon notice of the assignment being given to the underlying debtor (thus leaving the relationship between the originator and the debtor intact), unless the debt is subject to an anti-assignment clause under which the prior consent of the debtor must be sought (McCormack, 1999). Both present and future debts can be subject of an equitable assignment (so that a generic class of debts can be assigned). Furthermore, equitable assignments can be readily structured to avoid the imposition of stamp duty and similar taxation imposts. There is, however, a major drawback with equitable assignments. The originator retains legal title to the assigned debt and, unless the securitization vehicle elects to give notice of the assignment to the underlying debtor, that debtor will continue to make payments on the debt to the originator and remain free to reduce its liability on the debt to the originator by exercising rights of set-off against the originator.

Avoiding the imposition of stamp duty and similar taxation imposts is accomplished by ensuring that the assignment of the debts being securitized is not reduced to writing. The method commonly selected is one which combines a written offer with acceptance by conduct. The originator offers to assign certain designated debts (or an entire generic class of debts) to the securitization vehicle and the latter accepts that offer simply by remitting a portion of the proceeds from the issuance of the securities equivalent to the purchase price nominated in the offer to the originator. The written offer is not evidence of the assignment as, on its own, it does not constitute a binding contract between the originator and the securitization vehicle to assign the designated debts (that contract only comes into existence on the securitization vehicle's payment of the purchase price).

Nor does this method of assignment run foul of the requirement in the property-law statutes of many common-law jurisdictions (including Australia) that assignments of equitable interests, whether of real or personal property, must be made in writing in order to be valid. Having to comply with this requirement would render the assignment subject to stamp duty (in the absence of an express statutory exemption). It is, however, possible to interpret this requirement as applying only to equitable interests in existence at the time of assignment. Where debts are being securitized and the originator holds legal title to the debts, the assignment in equity of those debts to the securitization vehicle does not need to be made in writing, as at the time of the assignment there are no existing equitable interests in the debts separate from the legal title to those debts (Ali, 2002). It is, in fact, the assignment itself that effects a severance of the equitable title to the debts from the legal title held by the originator and brings into being a separate equitable interest in the debts (Ali, 2002).

5.7   Replenishment

Many securitization structures, particularly CDOs, incorporate lightly dynamic features enabling the manager of the transaction to replenish and substitute securitized assets (de Vries Robbe and Ali, 2005).

Replenishment refers to the situation where the manager tops up the securitized assets by purchasing new assets as existing assets in the securitized pool amortize or are prepaid or repaid (de Vries Robbe and Ali, 2005). Again, the introduction of the new assets into the pool can be effected via the method of equitable assignment described above to ensure that the replenishment of the securitized pool does not result in dutiable transfers of assets.

5.8   Substitution

The substitution of assets, in contrast to replenishment, raises more complex issues, both in relation to the taxation status of the relevant transfer and as regards the validity of that transfer. While replenishment involves the purchase by the securitization vehicle of new assets, substitution refers to the situation where existing assets in the securitized pool are exchanged for new assets because the former no longer qualify for inclusion in that pool (de Vries Robbe and Ali, 2005).

Substitution is primarily used to preserve the credit quality of the securitized pool. For this reason, it is vitally important to ensure that the ability of the manager to call for an exchange of assets from the originator does not translate into a blanket obligation on the part of the originator to make good any deterioration in the credit quality of the securitized assets by taking back the credit-impaired assets and replacing them with unimpaired new assets. Such an obligation could well be viewed by a court as the conferral of a right, common to the holder of a mortgage or other security interest (but alien to that of a buyer), upon the securitization vehicle to recover any fall in value of the securitized assets from the originator.

The other key concern with the substitution of assets relates to stamp duty. A substitution of assets involves two assignments of assets: An assignment of new assets from the originator to the securitization vehicle and a reassignment of existing assets from the securitization vehicle to the originator. The first assignment can simply be effected in the same way as the original assignment of the existing assets.

The second assignment can, however, be problematic from a stamp duty perspective. This assignment will necessarily involve an assignment of existing equitable interests (being the securitization vehicle's equitable title to the assets being replaced), and as such must be reduced to writing and will attract the application of stamp duty or similar taxation impost (unless the assignment has the benefit of a statutory exemption).

One intriguing method of dealing with this issue has been advanced but, unfortunately, in the absence of a statutory exemption from stamp duty, it can be dismissed as of little legal merit. Some market participants have advocated characterizing the reassignment of the assets being replaced not as an assignment (which would attract the consequences outlined above), but as a disclaimer of the equitable interest in those assets in favor of the originator. There are two problems with this suggestion. First, a disclaimer that takes effect as a directed vesting of assets in a specific person (since the clear intention here is that it is the originator and not any other person who should obtain the equitable interest in question) will almost certainly be treated as an assignment by a court since, as a matter of law, one cannot disclaim or abandon property in favor of a specific person. Second, if, on the other hand, the disclaimer is to be interpreted according to its terms and that the assets in question are seen as having being abandoned by the securitization vehicle (with the effect that the originator is in an analogous position to a person who acquires title by finding such assets), the likely result is that there will be no equitable interests to be found by the originator – the abandonment of debts is very likely to be treated by a court as a release of the debts, with their resulting extinguishment.

Perhaps a more effective means of dealing with the reassignment issue is to look more closely at the original assignment of assets. The original assignment, as noted above, effects a severance of the equitable title to the assets being securitized from the legal title to those assets. This has the effect of constituting the originator the trustee of the securitized assets for the benefit of the securitization vehicle. In analogous fashion, the reassignment of the assets could be effected via a sub-trust. This would effect a second severance of the equitable title and constitute the securitization vehicle the trustee of the reassigned assets for the benefit of the originator. Importantly, the conferral of the benefit of those assets on the originator involves the assignment of a severed equitable interest in the assets, not the existing interest held by the securitization vehicle and, consequently, it is arguable that there is no assignment of an existing equitable interest that must be reduced to writing. The above characterization is, however, not without risk. One needs to inquire how a court might view a situation where the sole beneficiary of a trust elects to create a sub-trust subsequently over part of the trust estate solely in favor of the trustee! (The use of a trust analogous to the proceeds trust found in retention of title clauses is unlikely to be of assistance: The creation of a single trust with the originator as the trustee would still involve the assignment of an existing equitable interest back to the originator, where assets that were originally held for the benefit of the securitization vehicle are nominated as now being held for the trustee's benefit, and making the securitization vehicle the trustee would, again, involve a sub-trust.)

5.9   Conclusion

Banks and corporations routinely use securitization to raise funds and improve their balance sheets and, in the case of banks, manage their regulatory capital requirements. The most common form of securitization involves the sale of assets to a securitization vehicle with the acquisition financed via the issue of securities. A key factor in the economic viability of these cash securitizations is achieving neutrality for the sale of assets as regards stamp duty or similar taxation imposts on transfers of assets. It is possible to achieve that objective by structuring the sale of assets as an absolute assignment in equity.

This is a vital aspect of both domestic and international securitizations. In many cases, the assets being securitized will comprise the multi-jurisdictional loan portfolios of international commercial banks. In other instances, the securitization vehicle may be established in a jurisdiction, such as an offshore jurisdiction, different to the jurisdictions in which the originator and the securitized assets are located. The issue that arises is thus not merely the efficacy and neutrality of the true sale under the law of a single jurisdiction, but the efficacy and neutrality of the true sale under the laws of the various jurisdictions in which the securitized assets are located, as well as the capacity of the originator and securitization vehicle to execute the sale free from the risk of a claw-back on insolvency, under their own laws.

Cash securitizations now often include replenishment and substitution features. As with the original sale of assets to the securitization vehicle, the replenishment of assets can be achieved in a manner that is stamp duty neutral. That may not, however, be the case with the substitution of assets (where assets held by the securitization vehicle of diminished credit quality are exchanged for fresh assets with the originator). The reassignment of assets to the originator potentially constitutes a dutiable transfer. Nonetheless, it may be possible through the use of careful structuring to avoid such a result.

References

Ali, P.U. (2002). *The Law of Secured Finance*. Oxford University Press, Oxford.

Ali, P.U. and de Vries Robbe, J.J. (2003). *Synthetic, Insurance and Hedge Fund Securitisations*. Thomson, Sydney.

de Vries Robbe, J.J. and Ali, P.U. (2005). *Opportunities in Credit Derivatives and Synthetic Securitisation*. Thomson Financial, London.

Kravitt, J.H.P. (1996). *Securitization of Financial Assets*, 2nd edn. Aspen Law & Business, New York.

McCormack, G. (1999). Debts and Non-assignment Clauses. *Journal of Business Law*, 422–445.

Schwarcz, S.L. (1993). The Parts are Greater than the Whole: How Securitization of Divisible Interests can Revolutionize Structured Finance and Open the Capital Markets to Middle-market Companies. *Columbia Business Law Review*, 139–167.

Schwarcz, S.L. (1998). The Universal Language of Cross-border Finance. *Duke Journal of Comparative and International Law*, 8:235–254.

Worthington, S. (1996). *Proprietary Interests in Commercial Transactions*. Clarendon Press, Oxford.

Globalization, Multinationals, and Tax Base Allocation: Advance Pricing Agreements as Shifts in International Taxation?

Markus Brem and Thomas Tucha

Abstract

This chapter elaborates on the emergence of so-called Advance Pricing Agreements (APA) in international taxation and corresponding APA programs in individual countries. It refers to how globalizing business processes trigger governance change at the nation state level regarding the identification and allocation of the tax base of multinational companies. The introduction of APA programs and the generation of APAs are considered to be an example of such governance change. On the basis of a governance choice model, the chapter seeks to identify factors which might explain variation in the evolution of national APA programs and the implementation of individual APAs between the multinational corporate taxpayer and the national tax authorities. Differences in institutions, economic conditions, and the actors involved appear to be factors explaining variation across countries.

6.1 Introduction

Taxing multinational companies has become a fuzzy enterprise for both the taxpayer and the tax collector. While the globalization of international business structures has developed at an impressive speed and scope, the international institutions, regimes, and organizations regulating such cross-border businesses still seem to be in their infancy. International taxation appears to lack governance structures which correspond to expanding global business activities, especially with respect to transfer pricing and cross-border income allocation of multinational group companies.

Although the OECD tries to play the role of a standard setter by developing a certain degree of international standards and regimes (OECD, 1995a, b), international taxation governance still appears to be in need of an administrative shift from domestic to global governance in terms of regulation and procedure. However, nowadays it seems obvious that globalization lacks global institutions and coordination (Garcia, 2005, p. 12; Cf. also Tanzi and Zee, 2000; Roin, 2002), including enforceable governance for both the taxpayer and the tax authority. A large volume of pending litigations on international tax issues demonstrates this lack of global institutions.[1]

A recent development for avoiding disputes ex-ante in many industrialized countries and individual Advance Pricing Agreements (APAs) between multinational corporate taxpayers and tax authorities are the advance ruling systems and so-called APA programs. APAs are mostly used in the field of transfer pricing to resolve international tax controversies.[2] They can be labeled as a sort of negotiation mechanism between sovereign states and between the multinational taxpayer with taxing state(s) to resolve tax transfer pricing disputes (Waegenaere et al., 2005).

This chapter examines factors which may explain differences between countries in terms of the existence of APA programs and the use of individual APAs. It proposes a mechanism to explain the existence of APAs and – as we hypothesize – its temporary deployment in international taxation. It also reveals possible reasons as to why certain countries have introduced APA programs and what relevance APAs may play in international taxation in the future. To provide for the contextual nature of APAs, some key features of transfer pricing are presented first.

6.2   Transfer pricing and APAs

Cross-border business between foreign affiliated parties of multinational corporate company groups is of increasing importance in today's business world. Depending upon the countries involved, a large share of the total cross-border exchange of business transactions is coordinated within the boundaries of multinational companies (MNCs) at the turn of the 21st century (Feldstein et al., 1995; Owens, 1998; *The Economist*, 2001; European Commission, 2001; OECD, 2001a; Whalley, 2001; Neighbour, 2002 (reporting a share of up to 60%)). With the continuing globalization process in the modern business world, we can expect this proportion to increase significantly for many countries in the near future. Alongside this development, several multinational groups have been changing their organizational and business structures. For example, many MNCs are organized along business lines irrespective of legal entity structures (Buckley and Casson, 2000; Wilkinson and Young, 2002; Lengsfeld, 2005; Brem and Tucha, 2006).

6.2.1   Transfer pricing and MNCs

While new business structures seem to ignore national borders, taxing income generated through such business is still governed on a national basis through country-specific accounting and taxation principles and provisions allocating the jurisdiction's tax base. The rules vary significantly across different countries and even between countries within comparatively harmonized economic regions (European Commission, 2001), which are subject to domestic legal and administrative traditions. This variation in tax rules across national tax jurisdictions (countries) causes different degrees of complexity and uncertainty for both the tax authority and the taxpayer regarding tax base allocation (cf. Messere, 1993; OECD, 2003). Transfer pricing is a prominent example of such complexity and controversy.

Transfer pricing refers to the pricing of goods, services, capital and technology inputs, managerial skills, financial services, shared/support services, etc. if they are transferred between affiliates of MNCs. With respect to today's global business structures, intra-group transfers of technology, management services, and financial loans move around within the MNC family. Intermediate goods such as parts, components, and sub-assemblies flow downstream for further processing within the boundaries of the MNC (or coordinated by it) before a final sale to third parties generates revenue at the outbound side of the multinational organization (B-to-C or B-to-B). At the same time, some affiliates may provide shared services to group business services (legal, accounting, advertising, IT, etc.) on behalf of the group, or its headquarters (Eden, 1998; Eden and Kurdle, 2005; Brem and Tucha, 2006).

In tax terminology, the pricing of intra-group transactions is normally assessed by means of so-called transfer pricing methods (TPMs), of which at least six categories are internationally recognized for tax purposes.[3] The basic framework for applying TPMs is provided by the internationally accepted 'arm's length principle' (ALP) (OECD, 1995a, Article 9(1)), which provides that a transfer price shall be in accordance with a price the two parties would have agreed on as third parties in a comparable market transaction. With respect to the comparability of related-party transactions and market transactions, and given the limitations in comparable data availability, the combination of ALP and TPMs provides much room for interpretation, discretionary power, design options, and transfer price manipulation, affecting the tax base allocation.

With the emergence of national documentation requirements implemented by an increasing number of national tax authorities to enforce ALP (OECD, 1995a), MNCs are now becoming increasingly aware of the need to set appropriate ('nonmanipulated') transfer prices for delivering goods and services within an MNC. However, intra-group transactions are regularly associated with intra-group intangible trade, such as patents, trademarks, financial services, etc. This often leaves both the taxpayer and the tax authorities puzzled on pricing individual related-party transactions and/or offsetting with other related-party transactions. Also, various facets of tangible related-party transactions (e.g. goods, services) open a wide range of possible interpretations as to what is the appropriate arm's length transfer price.

As a consequence, almost any transfer price is potentially exposed to uncertainty as to whether it is assessed arm's length or not and, if not, to what extent the income from such related-party business will be adjusted by tax authorities. This tax uncertainty is even more striking since the feedback from the tax authority as to whether a transfer price is arm's length often comes several years after the transaction between related parties took place. Also, cross-country differences in accounting and tax provisions often trigger transfer pricing as a *game of dice* for the taxpayer and the tax authorities, instead of a predictable governance: Whether a transfer of economic value needs to be priced or not depends upon the interpretation of country-specific provisions and case law. MNCs and tax authorities have controversial positions about – or are often not fully aware of – which kinds of value transfer need to be priced and which do not. Consequently, many such interpretations are done by courts rather than, in the first place, by the taxpayer.[4] Since much related-party business is outside any pricing mechanism at all (Ernst & Young, 2003), today's tax bases of multinationals are generally underestimated, let alone the controversial search for appropriate prices.

6.2.2 Identifying the tax base

Transfer pricing and income allocation in the course of taxing multinationals are primarily driven by the problem of defining and identifying the tax base.[5] To do so, transfer pricing experts, such as internal experts of MNCs as well as consultants and tax authorities, make use of analyses on the basis of so-called functions, risks, and assets to assess transfer prices under the ALP. However, despite these analytical exercises and the use of top-level expertise,[6] transfer pricing can be characterized by vagueness, fuzziness, premature concepts, and lack of transparency. Transfer pricing is still at an early stage of institutionalization and standardization – if compared with classical national tax issues. For example, whether, in principle, a trademark is valuable or not is subject to the business partners' assessment (as long as the relevant accounting principles do not prescribe the valuation and its accounting). The valuation options offer a huge range of possible results. The size of the trademark's value may be even more subject to the business partners' discretion and assessment. The answers to such questions significantly affect whether the cost incurred in developing such a trademark is deductible for tax purposes. So, the amount of the state's corporate income tax revenue depends to a large extent on the view that both the MNC (and its related-party taxpayer) and tax authorities can agree on various items defining the tax base.

An even more challenging problem in setting appropriate transfer prices in accordance with the ALP is related to business restructuring activities and investment issues. Restructuring as an ongoing process of shifting business functions, risks, and assets from one tax jurisdiction to another one – mostly from a high-wage or high-tax jurisdiction into a more preferential one – leads to huge vagueness regarding the tax base. If, for example, in a high-tax country expenses were deducted in the course of developing, say, a production site including patents and manufacturing processes, the MNC may have reason to shift such functions to a low-tax and/or low-wage country at a time when, along the product life cycle, the product starts generating high profits. Such a shift is often realized after the investment has been paid and deducted (depreciation) and the losses carried forward are wiped out. As a consequence of outbound business restructuring at the time of the product life cycle, the tax jurisdiction loses twice: Firstly, through the shift of tax base of future profits and, secondly, when it previously allowed the deduction of expenses (depreciation) to establish this tax base (and in many cases, thirdly, even through tax holidays granted for the investment).

In general, the identification of an MNC's relevant tax base and the allocation of this tax base into the jurisdiction in which the multinational operates is a key problem in corporate income taxation. Some steps to harmonize international or supranational corporate income taxation have already been taken: The dense net of double tax treaties, the OECD Model Tax Convention, and the OECD Transfer Pricing Guidelines, or the initial attempts of the EU tax harmonization process. However, the general institutionalization process in international taxation is still in its infancy and is characterized by a low level of harmonization regarding cross-country procedures.[7]

6.2.3   The role of APAs in taxing multinationals

Several national tax authorities have established Advance Pricing Agreement (APA) programs (for an overview, see Brem, 2005). An APA is an arrangement that determines, ideally in advance of controlled related-party transactions, an appropriate set of criteria for the determination of transfer pricing for those transactions over a fixed period of time (Vögele and Brem, 2003a; Sawyer, 2004). The criteria shaping an APA are, for example, the transfer pricing method(s) used, the possible third-party comparables and appropriate adjustments, and the so-called critical assumptions which define economic indicators as a framework for using TPMs: Ranges of currency fluctuation, market development, economic crises, etc.

6.2.3.1   The OECD perspective on APAs

Normally, an APA is formally initiated by a taxpayer and requires negotiations between the taxpayer, one or more related-party entities, and the tax administration(s) of one or more nation states. APAs are intended to supplement the traditional administrative, judicial, and treaty mechanisms for resolving transfer pricing issues. They may be most useful when traditional mechanisms to allocate income of related-party business within a multinational group fail or are difficult to apply because of a lack of institutionalization and standardization in international taxation aspects, such as transfer pricing and tax base allocation (OECD, 2001b, Paragraph 4.124).

The OECD Transfer Pricing Guidelines describe an APA as having the following characteristics (in reference to the mutual agreement procedures (MAP) of the OECD):

'[. . .] The objectives of an APA process are to facilitate principled, practical and cooperative negotiations, to resolve transfer pricing issues expeditiously and prospectively, to use the resources of the taxpayer and the tax administration more efficiently, and to provide a measure of predictability for the taxpayer.

[. . .] To be successful, the process should be administered in a nonadversarial, efficient and practical fashion, and requires the cooperation of all the participating parties. It is intended to supplement, rather than replace, the traditional administrative, judicial, and treaty mechanisms for resolving transfer pricing issues. Consideration of an APA may be most appropriate when the methodology for applying the arm's length principle gives rise to significant questions of reliability and accuracy, or when the specific circumstances of the transfer pricing issues being considered are unusually complex.

[. . .] One of the key objectives of the MAP APA process is the elimination of potential double taxation.'

(OECD, 2001b, A9–11)

In contrast to the traditional form of tax assessment, which is often an adversarial mechanism imposed by a sovereign tax authority, an APA is a kind of cooperative arrangement between tax authorities (of at least one jurisdiction) and a multinational corporate taxpayer (Ring, 2000; OECD, 2001b, Paragraph 4.135). In addition to classical ex-post binding rulings, an APA serves to resolve, in a cooperative manner before the business has taken place, the potential transfer pricing disputes between these parties. As the OECD points out:

'APAs, including unilateral ones, differ in some ways from more traditional private rulings that some tax administrations issue to taxpayers. An APA generally deals with factual issues, whereas more traditional private rulings tend to be limited to addressing questions of a legal nature based on facts presented by a taxpayer. The facts underlying a private ruling request may not be questioned by the tax administration, whereas in an APA the facts are likely to be thoroughly analyzed and investigated. In addition, an APA usually covers several transactions, several types of transactions on a continuing basis, or all of a taxpayer's international transactions for a given period of time. In contrast, a private ruling request usually is binding only for a particular transaction.'

(OECD, 2001b, Paragraph 4.133)

Advance ruling systems and, in particular, APA programs are increasing in number and are now deployed by many states, particularly OECD member states. However, such states differ in the timing, type, and scope of APAs used for resolving transfer pricing issues. Early forerunners include the USA, Canada, the Netherlands, the UK, France, and Japan. China, Korea, and Mexico, among others, are following such examples.

The most comprehensive study on transfer pricing is the Ernst & Young Global Transfer Pricing Study, which has been published every second year since 1995. The latest available edition is the 2005 Survey (Ernst & Young, 2005). The survey of 2003 (Ernst & Young, 2003) contains information about APAs on over 800 MNC entries, of which 14% of parent companies and 18% of subsidiaries used the APA process to seek a higher level of transfer pricing certainty (p. 23). Of the companies which used APA processes – almost 90% (87% of parents, 89% of subsidiaries) – indicated that they would use the APA process again.

The survey also states (Ernst & Young, 2003, p. 23) that:

'[N]onetheless, if tax administrations want their APA programs to attract taxpayers, they must still overcome the perception that they are not "user friendly". The trend among non-APA using parents to consider use of APAs in the future continued to decline in this survey. Only 33% of parents responded favorably in 2003, down from 38% in 2001 and 45% in 1999. However, this year we find that non-APA using subsidiaries indicate increasing openness to future use of APAs – 47% this year, compared to 34% in 2001 and 41% in 1999.

In general, the preliminary approval of a certain transaction is appropriate in cases where such transactions are rare and would need complex statutory provisions. APAs normally refer to such special cases, namely complex related-party transactions of multinationals for which standard transfer pricing techniques may not apply or might be viewed differently by the parties involved (for example, taxpayers and tax administrations of the countries involved).

In countries that apply the OECD Model Tax Convention and the OECD Transfer Pricing Guidelines, the APA process is designed to produce a formal agreement between the taxpayer and the revenue authority on four basic issues (OECD, 1999; IRS, 2002; Ernst & Young, 2003, p. 22):

- the factual nature of inter-company transactions to which the APA applies
- an appropriate transfer pricing methodology to apply to those transactions
- the expected arm's length range of results from application of the transfer pricing methodology to transactions
- in a bilateral or multilateral APA, in addition to the agreement between the taxpayer and the domestic tax administration (for example, the local revenue authority), a mutual agreement between the competent authorities of participating states.

An APA links the prospective application of agreed transfer pricing methodology to the taxpayer's covered transactions, usually for a period of five years. In addition, such methodology may also apply to all open tax years (years not yet audited) prior to APA years. Such rollback may sometimes cover as many as six or seven years. For bilateral APAs, an MNC can thus achieve certainty on two jurisdictions' treatment of its related-party transactions for a significant period of time. Though it can be a lengthy and somewhat costly process, an APA presents an efficient alternative to the traditional means of resolving a transfer pricing dispute and can provide certainty for a period of over a decade.

6.2.3.2 Implemented programs

The most detailed and widespread APA program is operated by the US IRS, a forerunner implementing a defined 'APA Program' for transfer pricing and international tax issues. Under the US approach, the taxpayer voluntarily submits an application for an APA, together with a user fee as outlined in the respective Rev. Proc. 2004-40 (here: Paragraph 4.12). An APA under jurisdiction of the US-IRS APA Program is in principle a contract between the tax administration and the taxpayer. Given the contractual nature of this agreement under private law, the tax administration enjoys a relatively high degree of flexibility. The contract rules out the key fact pattern of the transfer pricing case as considered later for audit purposes, the determination of the respective transfer pricing method for this business, and the critical assumptions underlying this method. The contract also determines the length of the agreement and, if necessary, the mode of adjustment which applies to any changes in business and/or the critical assumptions.

Table 6.1   Office structure and APA staff of the US IRS APA Program

Director's office

1 director
1 special counsel to the director
1 secretary to the director

Branch 1	Branch 2	Branch 3	Branch 4
1 branch chief	1 acting branch chief	1 branch chief	1 branch chief
1 secretary	(also special counsel)	1 secretary	1 secretary
7 team leaders	1 paralegal	7 team leaders	3 team leaders
	4 economists		1 economist

Source: IRS (2005a, p. 6).

In direct contrast to other countries, such as Germany, the US IRS has established its APA Program with dedicated resources and capabilities (offices, human power, etc.; see Table 6.1). In 2004, the APA office consisted of four branches, with Branches 1 and 3 staffed with APA team leaders and Branch 2 staffed with economists and a paralegal. Branch 4, the APA West Coast branch, is headquartered in Laguna Niguel, California, with an additional office in San Francisco, and is presently staffed with both team leaders and an economist.

The APA Program has responded to the needs of top economic and procedural transfer pricing expertise with established internal training programs for its personnel. The APA office continues to emphasize the priority of training (cf. IRS, 2005a, p. 6) and has developed dedicated training packages. Training sessions address APA-related current developments, new APA office practices and procedures, and international tax law issues. The APA New Hire Training materials are updated throughout the year as necessary. The updated materials are available to the public through the APA Internet site (see http://www.irs.gov/businesses/corporations/article/0,,id=96221,00.html). Though these materials do not constitute an explicit guide on the application of the arm's length standard (IRS, 2005a, p. 6), by making the materials public, it is hoped taxpayers may consider the views of the APA Program on developing, discussing, negotiating, and enforcing APAs. The IRS also seeks to achieve a higher level of mutual understanding of complex transfer pricing issues for the parties and people involved, including tax consultants, foreign tax authorities, and their competent authorities.

The APA process can be broken down into five phases (Sawyer, 2004, p. 46; IRS, 2004, pp. 3–6):

- Application
- Due diligence
- Analysis
- Discussion and agreement
- Drafting, review, and execution.

6.2.3.3   Nonadversarial governance of transfer pricing matters

It is a common understanding among transfer pricing experts that an APA is a mechanism through which the tax authority collaborates with the taxpayer in defining and determining the tax base of selected legal entities of a multinational group (Ring, 2000; OECD, 2001b; European Commission, 2001; Rodemer, 2001; Romano, 2002; Waegenaere et al., 2005). An APA is described as a collaborative governance model that involves state agency flexibility and provisional regulation (IRS, 2000, 2005a) – in contrast to more inelastic, bureaucratic, and quasi-fixed codification of traditional tax base determination.

APAs are conceptually understood to be a nonbureaucratic coordination mechanism between the taxpayer and the tax authorities involved (normally two or more countries) on unique or controversial case facts and their treatment for transfer pricing purposes (Sawyer, 2004, p. 44). Although there is a certain level of international agreement among tax jurisdictions on the type and nature of transfer pricing issues and principles to be applied (for example, the OECD-wide accepted ALP), not all jurisdictions in which the multinational operates (or is sought to be liable for taxation) have the same view on fact patterns and interpretation of legal principles (Rodemer, 2001; Sawyer, 2004). For example, the specific use of transfer pricing methods is causing increasing controversy between taxpayer(s) and their tax administration(s). Also, the increasing relevance of intangible assets (trademarks, patents, or know-how on production processes) determining the performance, profitability, and rentability of modern business organizations regularly causes transfer pricing controversy, and APAs may be used to resolve such disputes.

In general, the APA process is designed to enable taxpayers and tax authorities to agree on proper treatment regarding transfer pricing matters. The most important transfer pricing matters covered by APAs include (cf. IRS, 2005b):

- The identification of functions performed, risks borne, and assets deployed for business with related parties of an MNC.

- The selection of an adequate transfer pricing method (a method to determine the arm's length result) out of a possible set of transfer pricing methods provided by the national transfer pricing regulations of countries involved.
- The definition of transactions covered by the APA and the case-specific design of the transfer pricing methods, including the determination of which (profit level) indicators will be used for comparing the related party's (= tested party's) profit margin with third-party comparables (unrelated companies).
- The definition of so-called 'critical assumptions' which, independent of the filed income statement, are to be met by the taxpayer in order to deem the transfer pricing case in accordance with the terms and conditions of an APA when the tax case is assessed.
- The type and scope of required documentation which the taxpayer has to submit (normally each year) so that the tax administration can assess compliance with the APA provisions.

An APA refers to the relationship between the taxpayer and the tax administration (unilateral APA) in a given country. If more than one tax jurisdiction is involved, the APA is bi- or multilateral, and refers additionally to the relationship between tax authorities of both jurisdictions. In a bilateral or multilateral APA, the contractual arrangement between the jurisdictions is governed by the Mutual Agreement Procedures, if the relevant double-tax treaty between these countries provides for that. The number of parties involved in an APA is not definite but subject to the APA in question. Figure 6.1 illustrates the basic structure of a bilateral APA.

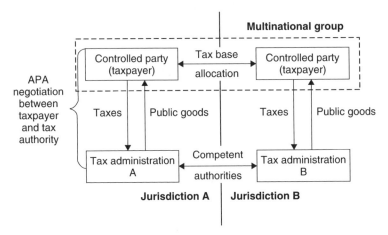

Figure 6.1   Basic structure of bilateral APAs. First published in Vögele, A. and Brem, M. (2003). *Tax Notes International*, 30(4):363–376

6.2.3.4 APAs and binding rulings

Similar to APAs are so-called *binding rulings*. A binding ruling can provide the taxpayer with greater certainty and the tax administration with higher effectiveness of processing tax assessment and auditing than traditional tax measures may achieve (Sawyer, 2004, p. 41). The binding ruling is normally designed to illustrate the tax consequences of a given transaction either before the associated arrangement becomes unconditional, or at least before the tax return is filed and a tax position is taken concerning the arrangement.

In some tax jurisdictions, the terms APA and *binding ruling* refer to the same purpose of ex-ante ruling. In other tax jurisdictions, the term *binding ruling* is referred to as an ex-post procedure to reach an agreement on controversial case facts (hereafter referred to as Binding Ruling Type I), while the term APA is considered explicitly for ex-ante agreements.

Germany, for instance, offers a slightly different type of binding ruling called *Verständigungsverfahren* (hereafter referred to as Binding Ruling Type II) to settle disputes in the tax auditing process (Herzig, 1996; Hahn, 2001). The purpose of the classical *Verständigungsverfahren* is to resolve an ongoing auditing process for a taxpayer and, by doing so, should produce a common understanding between the taxpayer and the tax authorities involved about the same (or similar) fact patterns in future years. While Binding Ruling Type I regularly covers tax cases which have been already started to be realized as business but have not yet been assessed or audited, Binding Ruling Type II deals with cases which are under tax audit. In Germany, Binding Ruling Type II is becoming increasingly important to help resolve transfer pricing controversies of the past and, by finding an agreement between relevant parties, to lay groundwork to avoid such controversies in the future. On October 5, 2006, the Federal Ministry of Finance, Germany, issued its administrative principles on advance pricing agreements which clarify the legal nature and procedural approach regarding advance mutual agreement procedures (and advance pricing agreements) in which Germany is involved.

Romano (2002, p. 486) elaborates on some differences between binding rulings and APAs: Legally, a binding ruling is a unilateral agreement, only affecting the respective tax administration and the taxpayer, while APAs can be unilateral, bilateral, or multilateral. Also, in general, binding rulings are a one-sided statement of the tax administration; The taxpayer can or cannot accept the ruling issued. In the case of an APA, it is an agreement between both (all) parties where the taxpayer at least approves the content (de facto it is an agreement). In a binding ruling procedure, the taxpayer may have a participating role in the initial phases of the process. Finally,

APAs normally bind both the taxpayer and the tax authority, while binding rulings normally bind the tax authority alone. Such binding normally refers to one specific transaction or case pattern, whereas the APA may cover a set of transactions or even a complex transfer pricing structure with various related-party transactions involved.

In the language of governance concepts, the introduction of APA programs in many tax jurisdictions may characterize a shift from bureaucratic taxation to a form of cooperative interaction between the taxpayer and tax authorities. As Lacaille (2002) pointed out, the increasing relevance of APAs may indicate a new direction in administering law, from bureaucracy to negotiation. Given the administrative nature of APAs, and in the light of globalization and the debate on internationalization, the emergence of APAs seems to be an interesting case for the political analysis of shifts in international tax policies. Three aspects of APAs appear to be of special relevance:

- The factors determining the existence of an APA program in a given country
- The nonbureaucratic negotiation between parties in order to reach an APA
- The ex-ante nature of an APA – that is, the APA is normally negotiated and agreed by the parties prior to generation of the income to be taxed.

6.3 From bureaucracy to nonadversarial coordination

6.3.1 Public bureaucracies: Governance choice

To explain why APAs have evolved in the past, we refer to a theory of governance choice, which is based on a concept outlined by transaction cost economics (TCE) as developed by Williamson (1985) and in line with new institutional economics (for an overview on new institutional economics, see also North, 1990; Richter, 2005). We believe that the governance choice model of Williamson (1998) can explain the evolution of APA programs – and their temporary relevance in a period of transition into a globalized world. This model can explain the shift from bureaucratic state administration towards more regulative and hybrid governance in the field of tax base identification and assessment with respect to international taxation. The model of governance choice based on TCE involves issues of internal and external coordination, administrative traditions, actor behavior, as well as institutional design and change.

6.3.1.1 Making use of TCE

TCE structures societal phenomena into discrete choices of coordination which is subject to transaction costs. Allen (1991, p. 3) defines transaction costs as the resources used (and burdens assumed) to establish and maintain property rights.

They include resources used to protect and capture (appropriate without permission) property rights, plus any deadweight costs that result from potential or real protecting and capturing. The need for establishing and maintaining property rights is caused by two basic principles of human behavior: Bounded rationality and opportunism (Williamson, 1985, 1998).

As proposed by Williamson (1999), the concept of governance choice can not only be deployed for the make-or-buy decision, but also for public policy design. In his model (see Figure 6.2), unassisted market (M), unrelieved hybrid (X_U), hybrid contracting (X_C), private firm (F), regulation (R), and public agency (B for bureau) are distinct governance modes for coordinating exchange between transaction partners. In the traditional TCE perspective, M, X_U, and X_C are governance modes of external coordination, whereas F, R, and B refer to internal coordination. TCE poses the question – and seeks to answer – whether a given exchange problem (transaction) should be coordinated in either governance mode. In the case of hierarchical, internal governance, this would be F (within a firm), R (through regulation), or even B (within the public agency), though feasible alternatives of external governance exist and can be described (Williamson, 1999). Features such as forming incentives, administrative control, autonomous behavior, enforcement, and safeguarding against hazards determine the choice of governance.

The basic mechanism of governance choice in TCE can be seen in Figure 6.2. With increasing contractual hazards (h) and the need for contractual safeguards (s),

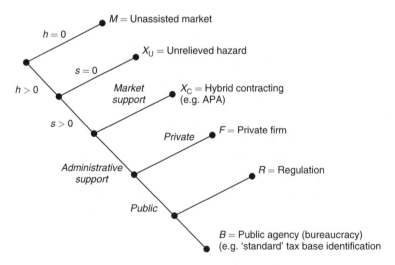

Figure 6.2   Contracting schema extended. Adapted from Williamson, O.E. (1999). Public and Private Bureaucracies: A Transaction Cost Economics Perspective. *Journal of Law, Economics, and Organization*, 15(1):306–342, by permission of Oxford University Press

the transaction cost-efficient governance choice is, instead of M or X_U, a hybrid contracting X_C or, even more transaction cost efficient, an organization-internal coordination (F, R, or B). Among these three options, public agency (mode B) provides the most safeguarding, given high asset specificity and contractual hazards. However, there is a trade-off against lower incentives, high administrative control, and less autonomous behavior. In contrast to private bureaucracy F such as a firm, governance mode B describes the internal organization of transactions. According to Williamson (1999, p. 336), B results in the highest level of bureaucratization, adaptive integrity, and staff security. Also, it provides the lowest level of incentive intensity, adaptive autonomy, executive autonomy, and legalistic dispute settlement.

Williamson (1999, Table 2, p. 336) mentions the following features of public bureaucracy: (a) Very low-powered incentives; (b) Extensive administrative controls and procedures; (c) Appointment and termination of the agency's leadership by a quasi-independent sovereign (for example, president, legislature); (d) An elite staff with considerable social conditioning and security employment. For example:

> '... private bureaucracy (contracting out) [the governance change from public bureaucracy (state government agency) to a private' firm, MB] has the strongest incentives and the least administrative control, the strongest propensity to behave autonomously (display enterprise and be adventurous) and the weakest propensity to behave cooperatively (be compliant), works out a (comparatively) legalistic dispute settlement regime, appoints its own executives, and affords the least degree of security of staff employment. The public bureaucracy is the polar opposite in all of these respects, while regulation (public agency plus private firm) is located in between these two along all dimensions (with the caveat that regulation may have more administrative controls, possibly of a dysfunctional kind).'

> (Williamson, 1999, p. 336)

Given this basic mechanism of governance choice, it may be more efficient for the governance of (domestic) taxation to follow B: The state coordinates the process of generating its revenue by means of bureaucratic organization, and there is a trade-off between highly bureaucratic principles of organization and provisions, low incentives, small space for discretional decision-making, high administrative control, high legalistic dispute settlement, and high job security for personnel. The (bounded) rationale for transaction cost efficiency behind this governance mechanism includes probity, equity, and neutrality. Since the sovereign state may gain most benefit if its main 'budget generation process' (= taxation[8]) is equitable and neutral, *B* might be the most transaction cost-efficient governance structure for taxation.

6.3.1.2 State interacts with taxpayers: Relying on bureaucracy to generate state revenue

In addition to the internal view of a public agency organization, a comprehensive perspective on bureaucratic governance allows a focus on external transactions – that is, how the interaction is organized between the public agency and its external 'transaction partner' (here: Taxpayer). While a public agency may offer external contracts for certain transactions, like for any consumer or firm (spot market purchase of office furniture, hybrid contracting of regularly recurring transactions such as computer purchases associated with frequent maintaining services), it normally resorts to bureaucratic governance for transactions regarding sovereign administrative tasks such as tax base assessment and tax collection. Taxation is an interaction between the taxpayers and the tax authority to generate state budget, and can thus be deemed 'bureaucracy' (mode *B*). Under such TCE perspective, the taxpayer is hierarchically bound to bureaucratic tax mechanisms which the state imposes to safeguard its tax base.

TCE interprets a public bureaucracy 'as a response to extreme conditions of bilateral dependency and information asymmetry' (Williamson, 1999, p. 337). Instead of private ordering, public bureaucracies provide safeguards against contractual hazards beyond *M*, X_U, X_C, or *F*. As mentioned above, factors why – in a world of domestic tax cases – bureaucracy may govern these hazards more efficiently than market-like mechanisms include probity (Williamson, 1999, p. 338) and, in taxation, neutrality of treatment. For example, the sovereign state has incentives to treat taxpayers with neutrality, in accordance with the tax code and its revenue procedures. Otherwise, in a constitutional state, administrative unpredictability could trigger lawsuits against the tax authority and the taxpayer would have incentives to shift his tax base into another tax jurisdiction (tax emigration) or to underperform.

Terms like probity can be paraphrased with concepts such as trust, relational contracting, corporate culture, or influence aspects. What probity has in common with these terms is the impact from transaction cost optimization on the governance of contractual hazards *h*. Because taxation requires a high level of probity, and this level may be best endured through a public agency, equitable and fair taxation may be efficiently coordinated through bureaucratic interaction with the taxpayer: The sovereign state (public agency) generates its budget by means of bureaucratic ex-post money subtraction from the taxpayer's income.[9] If an entity falls under tax liability, given the legal principles in the jurisdiction, the agency assesses ex-post the facts of the tax case, the tax base, methods of taxation, and further circumstances. In addition, under a classic taxation mechanism, parties do not negotiate on the tax case in advance.

As a compromise, the public agency may use the transaction cost-efficient mechanism to establish an exchange process of taxation with a high level of probity and neutrality. In contrast to other governance forms, bureaucratic state revenue collection may provide a climate where the revenue donor (taxpayer) can rely on probity and neutrality.

6.3.2   Taxation: Unilateral asymmetric information

The key for explaining bureaucratic governance as a contractual safeguard for the taxing jurisdiction is asymmetric information. Measurements which are subject to a high level of asset specificity determine a situation where the taxpayer has an information advantage over the tax authority. In tax terms, the transaction attributes have synonyms, such as compliance costs and legal uncertainty, which are subject to two types of asset specificity. One type refers to the jurisdiction's need to generate budget in order to be able to fulfill its tasks to which the sovereign state has committed through its constitution or public policies (provision of public goods such as law-making, legal enforcement, national defense, social programs, etc.). The other type of specificity stems from cross-country discrepancy in tax systems, and the resultant problem identifying the true tax base. The informational advantage on the taxpayer's side is linked to transaction attributes and thus determines whether the state applies 'standard' bureaucratic governance for 'tax base identification and tax collection'. An alternative to the tax base identification model is withholding taxes which simplifies taxation with the effect that tax principles such as neutrality and equity are not necessarily met (Keen and Ligthart, 2005).

Measurement problems (what is the 'true' tax base?) and asset specificity (location specificity of taxpayers, such as individual employees, companies) lead to 'standard' taxation (= bureaucratic) as part of transaction cost-optimal governance. Bounded rationality and opportunism are assumed to be characteristic human behaviors in this situation. The tax authority ex-ante lacks information about the true facts and circumstances on the taxable case, whereas the taxpayer has strong incentives not to disclose all available information about the case. Given a constitutional state with democratic principles, the sovereign tax authority is ex-post legally bound to laws and administrative procedures, around which the taxpayer may design his or her tax strategy. As a consequence of asymmetric information, and to the disadvantage of the tax authority, the state does not negotiate with the taxpayer about the identification of facts and the determination of the tax base. In this asymmetrical situation (hence a hybrid or market governance structure where the tax authority bargains with the taxpayer about the assessment of the tax case), negotiation seems to be less efficient. Because of the high costs of establishing and maintaining probity, an opportunistic (cheating) taxpayer would generate lower revenues for the state agency under a nonbureaucratic governance structure.

Following Hart (1995, p. 20; see also Hart and Moore, 2005), a transaction cost-efficient choice for a governance structure does not reduce asymmetric information per se. Likewise for taxation, public-bureaucratic taxation cannot eliminate the information problem for the public agency (tax authority). Rather, from a TCE point of view, the sovereign's choice to resort to public bureaucracy in generating revenue can be explained as such: Equalizing information is too costly for the state so it has to resort to bureaucratic tax collection.[10]

'Try markets, try hybrids, try firms, try regulation, and resort to public bureaus only when all else fails.'

(Williamson, 1998, p. 47)

6.3.3 Taxing multinationals: Two-sided asymmetric information

In a purely one-jurisdictional situation, taxation may be a transaction which is preferably (efficiently) governed by bureaucracy – with respect to internal coordination as well as regarding external relationships. However, if MNCs are to be taxed, the parties on both sides of taxation face asymmetric information affiliated with measurement and specificity problems: MNC taxpayers lack ex-ante information about the ex-post assessment of its transfer prices; The taxing state lacks – as indicated above – information about the true case facts. In the field of transfer pricing, the taxpayers are not able to foresee whether a tax authority will accept the TPM and the tax base deployed in a given transfer pricing case. They are also unaware if, and to what degree, the filed tax base allocation between the legal entities of the MNC will be adjusted by the authorities in the audit process several years later.

This results in hazards not only for the tax authority, but also for the taxpayer. In the international context of transfer pricing and corporate income tax base allocation, with its underdeveloped institutionalization process and heterogeneous tax systems around the globe, there is a high likelihood that the taxpayer is exposed to double taxation (if at least one jurisdiction adjusts the taxpayer's allocated profit). The choice of a 'correct' transfer pricing approach has not yet been uniformly defined and accepted by the international taxation community. Moreover, the ALP is in itself arbitrary – it cannot provide for the 'true' taxable pie but, if at all, a likely range of arm's length results.

The deficient institutionalization of cross-border taxation provides ground for a governance shift away from an adversarial tax regime (bureaucratic) to a collaborative interaction (hybrid). Not only the authority but also the corporate taxpayer has to cope with asymmetric information, resulting in a mutual information asymmetry (two-sided information asymmetry). Factors such as the inadequacy of the ALP in transfer pricing (Oestreicher, 2000; Rodemer, 2001) and the discrepancy between tax systems (Radaelli, 1997; European Commission, 2001) frequently expose the involved parties to hazards and legal uncertainty. Thus, collaborating on matters such as identifying the correct TPM and determining the tax base can significantly reduce transaction costs accruing in the process of income allocation (taxpayer) and of running a neutral tax system (tax authority).

In contrast to intra-jurisdictional tax base allocation, the relative lack of institutionalization in inter-jurisdictional tax rules requires MNCs to gamble on several choices regarding corporate income tax filing: (a) The critical assumptions underlying basic assumptions of the overall transfer pricing case; (b) Appropriate TPM; (c) The appropriate tax base allocation through arm's length transfer prices (or profits) in accordance with functions performed and risk borne; (d) Due allocation of the tax base into jurisdictions where the legal entities of MNCs are subject to taxation. Such decisions have to be taken by both the taxpayer and the authorities (of all jurisdictions), with a wide range of interpretation, definition, and unpredictability, resulting in legal uncertainty for a potentially long period of time.

These factors may lead to extreme contractual hazards for both the tax administration and the taxpayer in the case of taxing cross-border, related-party business. In the international context of taxation, with vague models of transfer pricing and related-party income tax base allocation, these transactional attributes can be translated as follows: Discrepancy between the different jurisdictions' tax systems can cause high specificity, as neither the tax authority nor the taxpayer can overrule the other jurisdiction's tax system without risking double taxation; They are highly dependent upon the other jurisdiction's tax assessment. Likewise, the investments of the taxpayer are often highly specific to the location and/or time; For this reason, the taxpayer is economically hindered to shift its business unit (function) into a more preferential tax jurisdiction for the short term. Uncertainty in international taxation is high because of the unforeseeable transfer pricing assessment of jurisdictions involved and the unidentified facts of a business case. Finally, differences in accounting standards across countries leave room for companies to design their own annual statement. Again, this results in higher tax base measure costs for the tax authority.[11]

6.3.4 APA as alternative mode for identifying and allocating the tax base

Efforts to rebut the presumption of transfer pricing manipulation and illegal income tax base shifting on the taxpayer's side, as well as double taxation and transfer pricing penalties imposed by the tax administration, will lower both the taxpayer's earnings after taxation and the state's incentive structure to attract international investments. In the light of taxation as a transaction to be governed between the state and the taxpayer, costs of compliance with country-specific regulations and possible losses in earnings after taxation (income adjustments, penalties, foregone business opportunities) can be deemed transaction costs.[12] Given the criterion for economizing transaction costs in 'taxation', the two-sided information asymmetry may trigger the evolution of alternatives in the case of taxing multinationals – in contrast to traditional bureaucratic governance. One of these alternatives, which provides a reduction in contractual hazards, is the APA as an ex-ante collaboration between both parties to reach a mutual understanding of how a given transfer pricing situation should be considered for tax base allocation purposes.

The emergence of APA programs in an increasing number of countries can be explained by mechanisms of governance change in light of TCE: From bureaucracy to hybrid systems (as indicated by a shift from mode B to mode H_C in Williamson, 1999). The collaborative interaction between the corporate entities (taxpayers) and the tax authorities can be understood as a kind of hybrid system (Freeman, 1995, 1997; Williamson, 1996) – or, at least, a nonbureaucratic governance.[13] As opposed to 'standard' taxation and its one-sided information asymmetry, in an APA the tax authority negotiates with the taxpayer on tax facts and circumstances ('What are the critical assumptions?') and on the assessment of the tax base ('What transfer pricing method?' 'What allocation mechanisms?').

6.3.5   Factors explaining the use of APAs

In light of TCE with its basic model of institutions, actors, and governance structures, factors determining the governance choice of tax base identification can be
classified on four analytical levels:

- Institutional framework to establish an APA program
- Institutional framework to work out an individual APA
- Economic conditions and attractiveness
- Actors.

Table 6.2, as derived from Brem (2005), illustrates these levels with respect to
a case comparison on factors determining an APA in Germany and the USA. Data
are from a recent case study.

The overview above provides a preliminary model based on TCE which requires
more empirical investigation. Notwithstanding the incompleteness of the model,
the following factors could be identified for a possible explanation of the evolution
of APA programs and the use of individual APAs:

- Institutional frameworks to establish APA programs: National institutions
  (*statics*) and their history (*dynamics*) appear to matter significantly in the
  development of national APA programs.
  - Federal structures of a national jurisdiction are important if they lead to
    an authoritative structure below the federal level with respect to income
    taxation.
  - Legal and constitutional principles regarding taxation may affect the evo-
    lution of APA programs. The principle of tax assessment (*official investiga-
    tion* vs *self-assessment*) may be one possible distinction. It seems that
    self-assessment supports the establishment of an APA program. No infor-
    mation could be analyzed as to whether tax principles such as 'source-based
    income taxation' vs 'worldwide income taxation' affect the evolution of
    an APA program.
  - Administrative traditions determine the space for discretional power at
    the administrative level. Compared with the 'Weberian' model, it seems
    that the Anglo-American model of administrative tradition shows some
    demand (or susceptibility) for APAs because of the higher degree of discre-
    tional power assigned to administrative units and officers. Also, the organ-
    ization of an administration in a nation state was identified as an important
    factor in the emergence of APAs. For example, in Germany the tax assess-
    ment authority on corporate income tax is assigned to the federal states,

Table 6.2 Factors determining the existence of APAs

Analytical level	Factor	Definition and item description	Germany[a]	USA	Effect
Institutional framework to establish an APA program in a given country					In relative favor of APAs in the USA compared to Germany
Political framework	**Federalism**	Organization of a jurisdiction's tax system (nation level)	Federal income tax, but tax is assessed at federal state level; Under current tax organization principles, federal states have assessment authority and thus coordinate APAs	Federal income tax; Tax assessment authority is allocated at the federal level; APAs are coordinated on a federal level	Yes
	Legislative process	Constitutional procedure for federal tax legislation on introducing APA programs	Complex involvement of federal states (*Bundesrat*) in the case of income taxation (*Zustimmungsgesetze*)	Federal tax legislation without political involvement of the states for issuing an APA program	Yes
Legal	**Principle of assessment**	The type of investigation and assessment of the tax case in a given country	Official Investigation Principle (*Amtsermittlungspflicht*) Consequence: Assessment by tax office normally yields small divergence between assessment and ex-post audit results	Self-Assessment Principle (*Selbstveranlagung*) Consequence: Self-assessment by the taxpayer normally yields higher probability of divergence between the view of the taxpayer and that of the tax authorities (audit)	Yes

				worldwide income	No information
	international income taxation	worldwide income			
Administrative	**Administrative tradition**	Type of administrative system	'Weberian model' on the basis of Roman-Law traditions	Anglo-American system	Yes
	Administrative organization	Organizational type of tax administration	Tax administration governed by the federal states	Federal (national) tax administration in the field of federal corporate income taxation (transfer pricing)	Yes
Judicial	**Tax courts**	Relative importance of tax courts to trigger institutional change	High relevance of Federal Tax Court and regional tax courts; APA cases have not yet been brought to the court	High relevance of the competent tax courts	Indifferent
Institutional framework to generate an individual APA					
Administrative	**Legal title**	Nature of legal right to receive an APA	De lege, taxpayer has no legitimate title to receive an APA	De facto, taxpayer has legitimate title to contract an APA	Yes
Legal	**Agreement type**	Nature of agreement between tax authority and taxpayer	'Receiving' an APA from the tax authorities	'Contracting' an APA between the tax authorities and the taxpayer	Yes
	Distortion on legal enforceability	Relative advantage of taxpayers over tax administrations in the courtroom	Taxpayers have won most international tax cases in the courtroom; However, this has been many years after audit	Taxpayers have won most international tax cases in the courtroom; However, this has been many years after audit	Indifferent

(Continued)

Table 6.2 (Continued)

Analytical level	Factor	Definition and item description	Countries compared	Effect
Economic conditions and attractiveness				
Economy	**Economic demand for APAs**	Share of cross-border related-party business (MNC business) to total cross-border business between two countries	Large share	Indifferent
Industry	**Business type**	Type of transaction and business to be covered by the ex-ante APA (possible characteristics: Large profit/loss volatility, high margins, high relevance of intangibles like patents, trademarks, etc.)	Industry type: Computer and electronics manufacturing, aeronautics industry, pharmaceuticals, banking, etc. Transaction type: Sales of tangible and intangible, services, use of intangible, financial loans	Ditto. Cf. IRS statistics (IRS, 1999–2005a)	Indifferent No publicly available statistic in Germany available to compare with US statistics
Economic	**Economic environment**	Degree of economic stability and reliability ('post-industrialized' countries versus 'transition' countries)	Post-industrialized economic environment; Relatively mature tax code system	Post-industrialized economic environment; Relatively mature tax code system	Indifferent
Governance	**Type of audit**	Purpose of audit in the course of corporate	Audit as an administrative step in the course of the	Audit as an essential administrative test to check	Yes

Type of application	income taxation process / Request versus application	tax authorities' taxation process / 'Request' for APA process	for the taxpayer's correctness of self-assessment / 'Application' for APA process	More market-like
Actors					
Taxpayer — **Experience of the taxpayer**	Level of preference and experience with APA processes	New methodology of reducing tax risk for selected transactions	Higher level of knowledge and know-how due to 'experience' and 'expertise'	Yes
Tax administration — **Experience of tax administration**	Dedicated APA resources such as APA personnel, resources, procedures	Low level of experience with advance ruling in the area of 'transfer pricing'; No specialized APA Program and unit with dedicated tax experts and economists	The APA Program explicitly dealing with APAs; The APA unit within the federal tax administration with dedicated tax experts and economists	Yes
Tax consultant — **Experience of tax consultant**	Average number of APA cases per transfer pricing consultant	Small number of cases; No specialized APA consultancy	Large number of cases; Specialized APA consultancy within the 'Big Four' tax consulting firms	Yes
OECD — **Impact from international organization**	Acceptance/Incorporation of international regime principles by national tax administration	Yes; Vice versa, Germany partly has impact on OECD	Partly; Vice versa, USA significantly influences OECD positions on transfer pricing guidelines	Yes

a In Germany, the upcoming constitutional reform of the federal system of legislative approval by the second chamber (Bundesrat) may bring in changes in legislative and executive authority in the field of tax assessment and tax revenue redistribution.

(Bundesländer) of the Federal Republic of Germany preventing the current federal tax administration, including the Federal Ministry of Finance, to launch a fully fledged APA program similar to that in the USA.

- ○ Tax courts and the judicial role in institutionalizing transfer pricing provisions may also impact the evolution of APA programs. However, the analysis could not identify clear information on this factor. Yet, both in the USA and in Germany, highest court decisions and regional court decisions on transfer pricing cases have increased the awareness among the parties to treat controversial issues ex-ante through an APA.
- Institutional frameworks to generate an APA as if an APA program or similar mechanisms are already in place:
  - ○ The legal title of an APA means the tax authority is obliged to accept and process an APA request and this may be part of its relative attractiveness. In some countries (for example, the USA), the taxpayer is entitled to claim an APA, while in other countries the taxpayer may have no such legitimate title.
  - ○ The legal nature of an APA is relevant for cross-country comparisons. In Anglo-American countries, an APA is normally a contract, while under Roman-Law principles the taxpayer receives a legal statement from the tax administration. Another important factor is the 'distorted legal enforceability' power. For example, in Germany, most important tax cases in transfer pricing were finally won by the taxpayer (for example, the seminal Federal Tax Court decision on transfer pricing documentation dated 17 October 2001).
- Economic factors describe the conditions under which an APA is an attractive mechanism to govern the tax base allocation problems behind transfer pricing:
  - ○ Without 'economic demand' for APAs, such nonadversarial mechanisms may not be the most attractive method to resolve transfer pricing cases. There are several upfront costs associated with an APA process – compared with a large, but unknown, range of ex-post cost possibilities because of audit and income adjustments. Economic demand might be measured by the share of cross-border business within multinational groups – measured as business between two countries – to total cross-border business between these two countries.
  - ○ The industry the MNC's transfer pricing case belongs to seems to play a role in relative attractiveness of an APA. As is often the case in high-tech business or in the chemical and pharmaceutical industries, related-party

transactions affiliated with a high level of intangibles are more likely to be candidates for APA solutions than transactions with the involvement of routine functions and standard business processes (for example, contract manufacturing). One reason could be the demand for ex-ante certainty on the appropriate transfer pricing method and pricing principles in such nonroutine transactions (for example, shift of intangibles).

○ The economic environment may provide stable and reliable business conditions or unstable and unforeseeable thresholds which determine a particular transfer pricing policy. As economic and institutional stability in the field of transfer pricing increases, we might hypothesize that transfer pricing controversy may decrease and, hence, the binding ex-ante nature of the APA vehicle may become less favorable to the tax base allocation problem. In stable economic environments, it might be preferable to resolve a particular controversy in a standardized tax world outside APA governance.

○ The governance provided by APA programs also determines the relative attractiveness of APAs. Here, the type of application (for example, 'request' vs. 'application') and the type of audit in a given country may affect the relative preference for an APA.

- Finally, the actors involved in drafting individual APAs and in designing APA programs appear to have explanatory power regarding the existence of APAs:

  ○ The taxpayer's preference for ex-ante mechanisms and information disclosure in the course of an APA process, as well as their experience, is likely to determine whether an APA is considered the preferred solution to allocate the tax base in a given transfer pricing situation.

  ○ The same theory applies for tax administration. Some tax administrations (for example, the US IRS) have dedicated resources for an APA program so the marginal administrative costs (processing, administering, and organization) for each new APA decrease. Other states initially have to invest in start-up activities in order to reorganize resources of the country's tax administration (mainly human resources such as economists and transfer pricing experts) in order to develop an APA process.

  ○ Likewise, tax consultants may or may not have experience with APA processes. Some tax consultants specialize in transfer pricing and APAs, while others may feel that an APA is challenging or even suspicious.

  ○ Finally, the OECD plays the role of rule setter in international taxation. Some countries construct their transfer pricing agreements on the basis of the OECD Transfer Pricing Guidelines (OECD, 1995b) and international regimes, including the guidelines on APAs (OECD, 1999). Other states choose not to use the guidelines, or they take only part of the information. In the case of the USA, the OECD guidelines on APAs are heavily influenced by the US IRS system of APA processes, which suggests that the existence of an APA program may not necessarily follow the relative influence the OECD has on each country, given that the OECD has not had an effective influence over US policies (rather, it is the other way round). It seems that whether a certain nation is a member of the OECD or not does not fully explain the relative influence the OECD can have on national APA programs and individual APAs. Also, other international institutions, such as the WTO, IMF, or UN, do not seem to have a major influence on national decisions regarding APAs.

6.4 Conclusion

The deployment of APAs and the evolution of corresponding national APA programs is an interesting example of a shift in international tax policy. This chapter analyzes taxing multinational companies (MNCs) to illustrate how global business processes may force governance change in international income tax base allocation. The underlying question is: How can we explain changes in the interaction of the sovereign state and the MNC taxpayer regarding the allocation of the tax base related to cross-border income? As globalization and the integration of global business processes within the boundaries of multinationals continue to grow in number and volume, we expect that the question on shifts in international governance of tax base allocation will also substantiate.

The analysis on governance change is illustrated by APAs, a new form of formalized negotiation and cooperation between the main parties involved in transfer pricing and tax base allocation. An APA is featured as a cooperative arrangement between the tax administration and the MNC taxpayer and, if bi/multilateral, between other states' tax administration and the MNC affiliates present in this state. The agreement determines, ideally in advance of controlled related-party transactions within the boundaries of an MNC, an appropriate set of criteria for the determination of transfer pricing for these transactions over a fixed period of time. As the role of transfer pricing between related-party corporations of a multinational group dramatically increases in the globalizing business world, the taxpayer and the tax authorities face complex problems of tax base allocation (OECD, 2001a; European Commission, 2001; Ernst & Young, 2003).

APAs are intended to supplement the traditional administrative, judicial, and treaty mechanisms for resolving transfer pricing issues and tax base allocation. They are assumed to be most useful when traditional mechanisms to allocate income of related-party business within the multinational group fail or are difficult to deploy because of a lack of institutionalization in international taxation and the transfer pricing systematic.

Based on this analysis, we can make some recommendations on governing international taxation in the field of transfer pricing and international tax base allocation: In the long run, state activity such as taxation finds its transaction cost-efficient governance structure – as for private sector transactions. In the case of taxing MNCs, the tax base allocation is in some instances efficiently governed in a nonbureaucratic form (nonhierarchical) as a cooperative mechanism based on principled negotiation. International tax policies should consider that cooperative, nonadversarial mechanisms can be a helpful tool to resolve transfer pricing and tax base controversies which could otherwise not be governed properly, leaving both the taxpayer and the tax authorities involved with deadweight losses.

However, nonbureaucratic governance may not be the most efficient policy design under all circumstances – as the prevalence of bureaucratic taxation mechanisms in almost all tax jurisdictions proves. In international taxation, as international regimes and international organizations begin to provide problem-solving principles, rules, norms, and provisions to both the taxpayer and the tax administration, resolving transfer pricing disputes ex-ante through the APA vehicle is likely to be a temporary mechanism. If, by means of, say, better tools or principles, transfer pricing becomes a standardized mechanism in international tax base allocation, bureaucratic governance may supersede the hybrid APA governance mode. However, such a prospected disappearance of nonbureaucratic governance in the field of international tax base identification and allocation may be accompanied by a shift in some elements of tax sovereignty from the nation state to supranational and/or international jurisdiction.

Acknowledgments

This chapter emerged from a research project on advance pricing agreements at the Department of Political Sciences of the FernUniversität Hagen (Germany), and it was completed during a teaching and research visit of the first author at the Indian Institute of Management, Ahmedabad, India. The research was completed in late 2005. We are grateful to both academic institutes for fruitful seminar discussions and resources provided to launch this paper. Also, we thank Martin Galdia, Rebecca Simmons, and P.S. Seshadri for research assistance.

Notes

1. Irving (2001) reports litigation periods of up to 15 years (also see Walpole, 1999; Erard, 2001).
2. Around four-fifths of parent companies and nearly all subsidiaries consider transfer pricing as the most crucial tax issue nowadays; APAs are understood by around half of multinationals as a potential dispute avoidance mechanism in corporate taxation (cf. Ernst & Young, 2001; See also http://www.legalmediagroup.com/default.asp?Page=1&SID=15032).
3. TPMs are transaction-based methods, such as Comparable Uncontrolled Price (CUP), Cost Plus (C+), Resale Price Minus (R−), Transactional Net Margin Method (TNMM). Examples of profit-based methods are Residual Profit Split Method (RPS), Comparable Profit Method (CPM), and Profit Split Methods (PS). Some countries also consider Formula Apportionment using certain allocation factors (often, assets, sum of wage, turnover) as an appropriate TPM (cf. Eden, 1998).
4. Also, many emerging countries such as China, India, or Brazil lack a sound body of transfer pricing case law — as compared to the USA or many European Union-15 countries.
5. As is often misunderstood in the public debate on tax reforms and tax burdens, the key challenge in both domestic and international taxation is not the size of the tax rate but whether principles such as *tax withholding* vs. *revenue sharing with information exchange* between countries are applied (Keen and Ligthart, 2005). Under the latter case, the determination and identification of the tax base is the core problem. One reason for the misleading discussion on the relevance of (nominal) tax rates on the total tax burden of a taxpayer might be caused by the economic models used for cross-country comparisons of the tax burden. These models normally assume comparable procedures and methods to identify the tax base on which a different tax rate is applied and for what affect it will have on the taxpayer (investment behavior). Often the large variance across countries to define the tax base is not reflected, especially in the field of practiced transfer pricing with its huge dependency upon the definition of expenses and cost in a given jurisdiction of accounting principles. Transfer pricing plays a key role in identifying the tax base, hence constituting a 'hot topic' in international taxation (Eyk, 1995; Bartelsman and Beetsma, 2000; Ernst & Young, 2003).
6. All major tax and business consultancies, including audit units (PricewaterhouseCoopers, Ernst & Young, KPMG, Deloitte & Touche, Transfer Pricing Associates, GlobalTransferPricing Business Solutions), run a global team of top transfer pricing experts providing services to their international clients. Consultancy fees for transfer pricing services are among the highest in the tax consulting service industry segment.
7. This can also be illustrated by the fact that, if a certain tax case enters the process of so-called Mutual Agreement Procedures (MAP), in many countries the Ministry of Foreign Affairs needs to be involved to meet the requirements of such a country to interact internationally.
8. Of course, in addition to the *taxation* mechanism, a sovereign state can also generate budget through nonadministrative activities such as running firms, taking part in capital and currency markets through publicly owned banks and through central banks, imposing tariffs and fees on services, etc.
9. We follow Williamson's (1999, p. 316) *remediableness criterion*, which holds that an extant mode of organization is efficient if no feasible alternative can be described and implemented with expected net gains.
10. For an examination of the distinction between costs of equalizing asymmetric information and costs of apprising an arbiter of the true information condition, see also Williamson (1996,

p. 65). Tanzi and Zee (2000) describe the role of information exchange for taxation in a borderless world.

11. For example, because of shortcomings in traditional tax auditing of MNCs, the German Ministry of Finance released the 'electronic audit' provisions as part of Germany's landmark 2000 Tax Reduction Act. These provisions, having taken effect on 1 January 2002, grant Germany's tax inspectors access rights to taxpayer computer systems for auditing purposes, indicating a measure to lower transaction costs to access information on the tax case. This adversarial tax behavior could be seen as an alternative to APAs, representing a move away from possible governance choices as in opposition to collaborative governance.

12. Erard (2001, pp. 317–335) reports compliance costs of about 2.7% of taxes paid for a weighted fortune in a top 500 Canadian nonfinancial corporations sample in 1995 (average compliance costs C\$507,000), and of about 3.2% for a weighted fortune in a top 500 US corporations sample (average compliance costs US\$2,100,000); Compliance costs increase significantly if foreign affiliated operations are involved. This estimation does not yet reflect costs of income adjustments on the basis of transfer pricing audits, which may exceed the actual tax burden and/or any penalties incurred in transfer pricing documentation provisions.

13. Interestingly, and to our best knowledge, in contrast to other sovereign state activities such as labor contracting, running companies, defense, etc., both the internal governance of taxation and the relation between tax authorities and taxpayers (external governance) have remained bureaucratic over the modern age. As a historical overview of US government contracting reveals (Nagle, 1999), taxation has not been a matter of nonbureaucratic 'contracting' over the past two centuries. We welcome examples that dispute this fact.

References

Allen, D.W. (1991). What are Transaction Costs? *Research in Law and Economics*, 14:1–18.

Bartelsman, E.J. and Beetsma, R.M.W.J. (2000). Why Pay More? Corporate Tax Avoidance Through Transfer Pricing in OECD Countries. *Journal of Public Economics*, 87(9/10): 2225–2228.

Brem, M. (2005). *Advance Pricing Agreements: Shifts in International Tax Policies*. Thesis, Fern University, Hagen.

Brem, M. and Tucha, T. (2006). Transfer Pricing: Conceptual Thoughts on the Nature of the Multinational Firm. *Vikalpa*, 31(2):29–43.

Buckley, P.J. and Casson, M.C. (2000). Models of the Multinational Enterprise. In: *Multinational Firms, Cooperation and Competition in the World Economy* (Buckley, P.J., ed.), pp. 9–43. Macmillan Press, London.

The Economist (2001). Globalisation and Tax. Special Report. *The Economist*, 29 January.

Eden, L. (1998). *Taxing Multinationals: Transfer Pricing and Corporate Income Taxation in North America*. University of Toronto Press, Toronto.

Eden, L. and Kurdle, R.T. (2005). Tax Havens: Renegade States in the International Tax Regime? *Law and Policy*, 27(1):100–127.

Erard, B. (2001). The Income Tax Compliance Burden on Canadian Big Business. In: *Tax Compliance Costs: A Festschrift for Cedric Sandford* (Evans, C., Pope, J. and Hasseldine, J., eds), pp. 317–335. Prospect Media, St Leonards, USA.

Ernst & Young (2001). Transfer Pricing 2001 Global Surveys (www.ey.com).

Ernst & Young (2003). Transfer Pricing 2003 Global Surveys (www.ey.com).

Ernst & Young (2005). 2005–2006 Global Transfer Pricing Surveys (www.ey.com).

European Commission (2001). *Towards an Internal Market without Tax Obstacles.* COM (2001) 582 final, http://europa.eu.int/comm/taxation_customs/publications/official_doc/IP/ip1468/communication_en.pdf. (*Ein Binnenmarkt ohne steuerliche Hindernisse: Strategie zur Schaffung einer konsolidierten Körperschaftssteuer-Bemessungsgrundlage für die grenzüberschreitende Unternehmenstätigkeit in der EU.*) KOM (2001) 582 (23 October 2001).

Eyk, S.C.v. (1995). *The OECD Declaration and Decisions Concerning Multinational Enterprises: An Attempt to Tame the Shrew.* Proefschrift Universiteit Utrecht, Ars Aequi Libri, Nijmegen, The Netherlands.

Feldstein, M., Hines, J.R. and Hubbard G.R. (eds) (1995). *Taxing Multinational Corporations*, pp. 29–38. University of Chicago Press, Chicago.

Freeman, J. (1995). *Cooperative Governance in the Administrative State.* Doctoral Thesis, Harvard Law School, Cambridge, MA.

Freeman, J. (1997). Collaborative Governance in the Administrative State. *UCLA Law Review*, 45(1):1–98.

Garcia, F.J. (2005). Globalization and the Theory of International Law. Research Paper 75, Boston Colleage Law School (www.ssrn.com/abstract=742726).

Hahn, H. (2001). Probleme der verbindlichen Auskunft im Steuerrecht – Überlegungen im Anschluss an den 53. Jahreskongress der IFA in Eilat (Israel). IFSt-Schrift No. 389. Institut Finanzen und Steuern, Bonn.

Hart, O.D. (1995). *Firms, Contracts, and Financial Structure.* Oxford University Press, New York.

Hart, O.D. and Moore, J.H. (2005). On the Design of Hierarchies: Coordination versus Specialization. *Journal of Political Economy*, 113(4):675–702.

Herzig, N. (ed.) (1996). Resümee. *Advance Pricing Agreements (APAs): Ein neues Instrument zur Vermeidung von Verrechnungspreiskonflikten?*, pp. 83–95. Otto-Schmidt-Verlag, Cologne.

IRS (1999, 2000, 2001, 2002, 2003, 2004, 2005a). *Announcement and Report Concerning Advance Pricing Agreements.* Internal Revenue Service, US Department of Treasury (available from http://www.irs.gov/businesses/corporations/).

IRS (2005b). Advance Pricing Agreements. *BNA Tax Management Transfer Pricing Report*, 13(21):1095.

Irving, N. (2001). OECD to Resume Watch on Transfer Pricing Guidelines. *International Tax Review*, April 22 issue.

Keen, M. and Ligthart, J.E. (2005). Coordinating Tariff Reduction and Domestic Tax Reform under Imperfect Competition. *Review of International Economics*, 13(2):385–390.

Lacaille, J. (2002). *Administering Law Through Negotiation: The Example of Advance Pricing Agreements in International Taxation.* Thesis (LL.M.), Harvard Law School, Cambridge, MA.

Lengsfeld, S. (2005). Verrechnungspreise und Organisationsstrukturen in multinationalen Unternehmen – zum Erkenntnisstand formaltheoretischer Analysen. *Betriebswirtschaftliche Forschung und Praxis*, 57(2):137–156.

Messere, K. (1993). *Tax Policy in OECD Countries* (especially Chapter 12). IBFD Publications BV, Amsterdam.

Nagle, J.F. (1999). *A History of Government Contracting*, 2nd edn. George Washington University, Washington, DC.

Neighbour, J. (2002). Transfer Pricing – Keeping it at Arm's Length. *OECD Observer* (http://www. oecdobserver.org/news/fullstory.php/aid/670/Transfer_pricing:_Keeping_it_at_arms_length.html). OECD Centre for Tax Policy and Administration.

North, D.C. (1990). *Institutions, Institutional Change and Economic Performance.* Cambridge University Press, Cambridge, MA.

OECD (1995a). *OECD Model Tax Convention.* OECD, Paris.

OECD (1995b). *Transfer Pricing Guidelines for Multinational Enterprises and Tax Administrations*, Parts I and II. OECD, Paris.

OECD (1999). *Guidelines for Conducting Advance Pricing Arrangements under the Mutual Agreement Procedure.* OECD, Paris.

OECD (2001a). *Measuring Globalization: The Role of Multinationals in OECD Economies.* OECD, Paris.

OECD (2001b). *Transfer Pricing Guidelines for Multinational Enterprises and Tax Administrations.* OECD, Paris.

OECD (2003). *Tax Haven Update.* OECD, Paris.

Oestreicher, A. (2000). *Konzern-Gewinnabgrenzung.* C.H. Beck, Munich.

Owens, J. (1998). Taxation within a Context of Globalization. *Bulletin for International Fiscal Documentation*, 52:290.

Radaelli, C.M. (1997). *The Politics of Corporate Taxation in the European Union – Knowledge and International Policy Agenda.* Routledge, London.

Richter, R. (2005). The New Institutional Economics: Its Start, Its Meaning, Its Prospects. *European Business Organization Law Review*, 6(2):161–200.

Ring, D. (2000). On the Frontier of Procedural Innovation: Advance Pricing Agreements and the Struggle to Allocate Income for Cross Border Taxation. *Michigan Journal of International Law*, 21(2):143–234.

Rodemer, I. (2001). *Advance Pricing Agreements im US-amerikanischen und im deutschen Steuerrecht.* Otto-Schmidt-Verlag, Cologne.

Roin, J. (2002). Taxation without Coordination. *Journal of Legal Studies*, 31:61–94.

Romano, C. (2002). *Advance Tax Rulings and Principles of Law: Towards a European Tax Ruling System?* International Bureau of Fiscal Documentation, Doctoral Series, Vol. 4.

Sawyer, A. (2004). Is an International Tax Organisation an Appropriate Forum for Administering Binding Rulings and APAs? *eJournal of Tax Research*, 2(1):8–70.

Tanzi, V. and Zee, H.H. (2000). Taxation in a Borderless World: The Role of Information Exchange. *Intertax*, 28(29):58–63.

Vögele, A. and Brem, M. (2003a). *Advance Pricing Agreements.* Unpublished manuscript.

Vögele, A. and Brem, M. (2003b). From Bureaucracy to Cooperation? On the Evolution of Hybrid Governance in International Taxation. *Tax Notes International*, 30(4):363–376.

Waegenaere, A.d., Sansing, R.C. and Wielhouwer, J. (2005). Using Bilateral Advance Pricing Agreements to Resolve Tax Transfer Pricing Disputes. Working Paper No. 2005-24, Tuck School of Business at Dartmouth (http://ssrn.com/abstract=766044).

Walpole, M. (1999). Compliance Cost Control by Revenue Authorities in the OECD. In: *Tax Compliance Costs: A Festschrift for Cedric Sandford* (Evans, C., Pope, J., and Hasseldine, J., eds), pp. 369–388. Prospect Media, St Leonards, USA.

Whalley, J. (2001). Puzzles over International Taxation of Cross Border Flows of Capital Income. Working Paper 8662 (http://www.nber.org/papers/w8662). National Bureau of Economic Research, Cambridge, MA.

Wilkinson, I. and Young L. (2002). On Cooperating: Firms, Relations, and Networks. *Journal of Business Research*, 55(2):123–132.

Williamson, O.E. (1985). *The Economic Institutions of Capitalism*. Free Press, New York.

Williamson, O.E. (1996). *The Mechanisms of Governance*. Oxford University Press, Oxford.

Williamson, O.E. (1998). Transaction Cost Economics: How It Works, Where It Is Headed. *De Economist*, 146:23–58.

Williamson, O.E. (1999). Public and Private Bureaucracies: A Transaction Cost Economics Perspective. *Journal of Law, Economics, and Organization*, 15(1):306–342.

Documentation of Transfer Pricing: The Nature of Arm's Length Analysis

Thomas Tucha and Markus Brem

Abstract

Given the arm's length principle as proposed by the OECD Model Tax Convention, the type and structure of arm's length analysis on transfer pricing between related parties of a multinational group depends upon the economic nature of the related-party transactions considered. Many documentation projects for the tax purpose of cross-border income allocation are solely based on a database-driven margin analysis to estimate arm's length transfer prices. However, this type of analysis often does not reflect the economics in the functional pattern of related-party transactions, especially if the functions considered along the value chains of the multinational group of corporate taxpayers vary in complexity, integration, and density. In order to account for the functional complexity, integration, and density in different types of transfer pricing situations, we propose to measure two dimensions of functional scope. The feature 'functional type' makes reference to the economic difference between (a) risk insurable (or insured) and (b) uncertainty managed by the entrepreneur. The feature 'functional density' measures the degree of comparability of a given functional pattern of related parties with an arm's length dealings situation. The chapter shows that a model to characterize the 'function' can improve our approaches on valuation, which is an incremental part of transfer pricing documentation and the arm's length analysis.

7.1 Introduction

Several countries have introduced transfer pricing documentation provisions in the last decade as an enforcement mechanism on the tax jurisdictional level so that tax authorities can audit the taxable income of related-party taxpayers. The international principle underlying such audits is the so-called 'arm's length principle' as proposed in Article 9 of the OECD Model Tax Convention (OECD 1995a, b; Feldstein et al., 1995). A key feature of documentation requirements is the *arm's length analysis* for transactions between related-party taxpayers of multinational corporate groups. Related-party taxpayers are requested to deploy the arm's length analysis in order to establish a traceable reasoning on the nature, appropriateness, and pecuniary value of transfer prices for such related-party transactions. While the factual case documentation is often referred to as 'paperwork', with the notion of providing the tax auditor with relevant documents and descriptions, the arm's length analysis is analytical. However, in practice, the arm's length analysis is often reduced to a simplified model of margin comparisons. Subject to the economic conditions and factual case pattern, however, alternative important features of an arm's length test can be the so-called value chain analysis and/or the budget-actual assessment.

In order to achieve the arm's length analysis, the first step is the characterization of the multinational's functional units regarding their economic nature and activity. The characterization is necessary for the choice of the most appropriate arm's length

149

test model (i.e. price or margin test, value chain analysis, budget-actual analysis). The OECD Guidelines (OECD, 1995b) on transfer pricing and income allocation as well as national provisions and/or tax authority-internal guidelines for documentation – as, for instance, in the USA, Germany, UK, or France – deem the economic nature and activity decisive for the type and model of arm's length analysis. For example, in the prevailing transfer pricing language, whether a function is characterized as 'routine' or 'nonroutine' determines the use of the most suitable transfer pricing method, which itself may have impacts on the arm's length nature, and size, of a given transfer price to be tested.[1]

In this chapter we offer an economic model which structures the arm's length analysis subject to the economic features of the transfer pricing case. Though we illustrate the model in its theoretical dimensions, in practice the model can support transfer pricing decision-makers on questions of what type of transfer pricing case requires what type of arm's length analysis. For characterizing the entrepreneurial units involved in the business process of multinational companies, we distinguish between two dimensions – 'functional type' and 'functional density'. In our model, the attribute 'functional type' measures functional features along the dimension contractible risk versus entrepreneurial uncertainty. The attribute 'functional density' measures along the dimension comparability versus uniqueness. Normatively, we believe – from our own experience – that assessing these two dimensions allows the transfer pricing expert to make substantial and economically sound decisions on suitable arm's length analysis.

The relevance of the question addressed in this article is considerable (cf. Eden, 1998; Owens, 1998; European Commission, 2001; *The Economist*, 2001; OECD, 2001, 2005). Cross-border trade in the OECD region is about US$ 15 trillion. Estimates indicate that, depending upon the two countries considered, up to 80% of such trade between two countries takes place within the boundaries of multinational groups, i.e. between related-party taxpayers. Transfer pricing ranks number one among the tax challenges of multinational taxpayers (Ernst & Young, 2005). To audit the income allocation assessment of such related-party taxpayers, the US approach of using database-driven margin analysis is widespread in the transfer pricing community. On the other hand, litigation has significantly increased in the last decade (Walpole, 1999) and litigation periods of 15 years or more are possible even in well-functioning legal jurisdictions.[2] Besides the tax risk of income adjustment imposed by the tax authorities involved in transfer pricing cases, it is the compliance costs that matter for related parties of a multinational player, especially in the case of mid-sized group companies. Compliance costs increase significantly if foreign affiliated operations are involved (Erard, 2001). For the USA, it was reported that as of September 1992 and again as of June 1994, proposed adjustments for trans-fer pricing cases of large taxpayers (i.e. those with assets over $100 million or more in a year of return) awaiting administrative resolution in appeals or litigation totaled US$14.4 bn (Ring, 2000, p. 171). This figure may also explain why this tax pie is so eagerly advertised by consulting teams specializing in transfer pricing.[3]

To mitigate the shortcomings of the standard approach of the arm's length test, expert groups seek to further develop the model to establish arm's length transfer pricing behavior. As the need for model revisions emerges on the horizon of international taxation, the transfer pricing and documentation provisions in Germany appear to provide an interesting and promising model for future arm's length analysis. Being a laggard regarding documentation provisions in the 1990s, in 2003 Germany introduced its law on documentation requirements in the form of Article 90(3) AO (*Abgabenordnung*; Tax Procedures Act) and GAufzV (*Gewinnabgrenzungsaufzeichnungsverordnung*; Regulations on Documentation of Income Allocation, BR-Drs. 583/03) about a decade later than the USA and later than many other OECD countries.[4] The 2003 documentation law was completed by the very detailed Administrative Principles on Documentation and Procedures (IV B 4 – S 1341 – 1/05)[5] published by the Federal Ministry of Finance on 12 April 2005.[6] Further administrative procedures can be expected soon, such as proce-dures on base shifting, long-term losses,[7] and advance pricing agreements.

Within the European Union, the Administrative Principles on Documentation and Procedures (Administrative Principles 2005) represent some progress towards more economic soundness of the arm's length analysis compared with approaches which explicitly make use of classical margin analysis (cf. Tucha, 2002). On some points, the German provisions even exceed the forerunners in the transfer pricing methodology, for example the provisions in the USA (for a detailed comparison, see Hirsch, 2005).

Diversified global business structures of multinational groups in general, and an economic pushing of the economic concepts in the OECD Guidelines and national documentation provisions (such as in Germany) in particular, have triggered the demand for rethinking the structure and concept of arm's length analysis. A discus-sion on the economic foundation of legal provisions is essential to keep the arm's length principle alive and to enforce transfer pricing documentation as set forth in many economies.

While the Internal Revenue Service of the USA (US IRS) has made use of provi-sions on arm's length analysis in the form of US Regulations 1.482, in Germany the Administrative Principles of 1983 and 2005 introduce to the jurisdiction's tax audi-tors the methodology of arm's length analysis. There, the type of appropriate arm's length test is subject to the economic fact pattern of the transfer pricing case. What is new is that, in addition to deploying external data such as comparable units (so-called "comparables") of price or margin, in most cases the arm's length test is expected to be established on the basis of internal data such as budget-actual analysis and assessment (cf. Paragraph 3.4.12.2 of Administrative Principles 2005). Because transfer prices have the feature that their arm's length nature cannot be audited by means of one single figure but a corridor of plausible results, generally the tax authorities request the taxpayer to demonstrate that transfer prices were considered on the basis of the arm's length principle. In many countries documentation requirements are based on the notion of a legal concept that, while the burden of proof is with the tax authority, the taxpayer is obliged to provide evidence that it believes the appropriateness and the arm's length nature of transfer prices.

Obviously, several ways of documentation approaches can be found. A flowchart on frequently used documentation steps in many countries is provided in Figure 7.1. Transfer prices are primarily documented by means of two dependent packages of information: Documentation of facts and arm's length documentation. The documentation of facts consists of the documentation of the company and the group, as well as the documentation of the business environment. In order to prepare the arm's length analysis, the identification of relevant related-party transactions is necessary. As the circled part of the chart shows, the arm's length analysis itself is based on the function and risk analysis and a choice on the arm's length test approach. Subject to the underlying fact pattern ('routine' yes or no, 'entrepreneur' yes or no), the three alternatives proposed are comparable analysis, planning and adjustment calculation, and value chain analysis. Special related-party business issues (e.g. expatriates, long-term losses, restructuring, and shift of functions and intangibles) may require specific steps (which are not discussed in this paper).

For instance, the Administrative Principles 2005 provide in Paragraph 3.4.10.2 that the appropriateness of margin analysis to test for arm's length transfer prices is limited to simple and repeating business activities (cf. IRS Sections 1.482-3 and 1.482-6). In mainstream transfer pricing language, such business activities are called routine functions. Now, the Administrative Principles 2005 provide that more complex functions with nonroutine and/or entrepreneurial features are not accessible to the traditional margin analyses. Rather, arm's length analysis is more complex using internal data and value chain analysis (on the use of database analyses, see Tucha, 2002; Oestreicher and Vormoor, 2004).

Hence, in order to select the appropriate procedure for arm's length analysis, classification of company types involved in the related-party business is essential. This chapter offers such a classification, together with features to be considered.

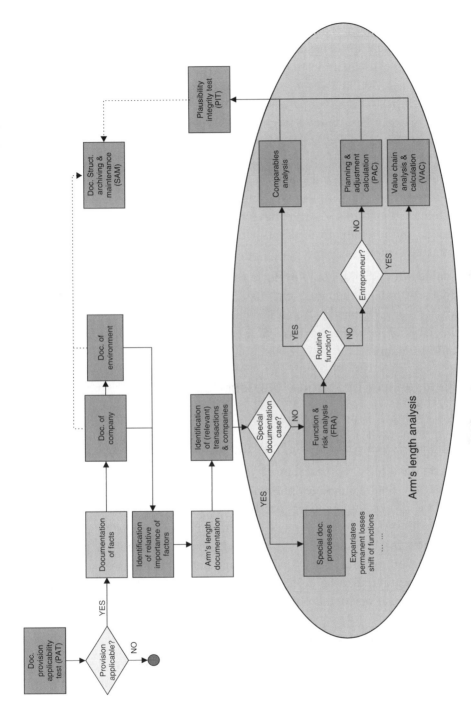

Figure 7.1   Arm's length analysis in the context of transfer pricing documentation

7.2 Company types

Basically, documentation of transfer pricing is referred to as the arm's length comparison, subject to the underlying factual case pattern. The arm's length comparison can be external or internal, subject to data availability, reasonableness, and company type. While data availability and reasonableness are facts which the taxpayer may not determine, the 'company type' is subject to the fact pattern and, hence, can be strategically designed. Generally, the company type is determined by the type of transactional exchange, as well as the features 'functional type' and 'functional density'. Hence, the contractual nature of the related-party exchange determines the company type and the type of economic analysis appropriate to demonstrate arm's length behavior.

In practice, three company types can be distinguished as proposed in the Administrative Principles 2005:

1. Business units which only perform routine functions.
2. Business units which perform material functions in an entrepreneurial way and are responsible for strategy and risk bearing.
3. Business units which perform more than routine functions, yet are not 'entrepreneurs'.

7.2.1 Companies with routine functions

In transfer pricing terminology, business units with routine functions are units (entities or center units) of the multinational group which show a limited scope of functional activity and risk borne. Such units are, for instance, service providers, contract manufacturers, and distributors without marketing responsibility ('low-risk distributor'). Such companies normally do not bear the risk of bad debt loss and market risk. Asset deployment is limited; Investment risk is 'hedged' by means of contracts with suppliers or customers, and strategies are assumed as given. In the absence of economic turbulence, companies with routine functions achieve small but constant profit margins. For transfer pricing analysis purposes, such routine functions (or routine business units) are assigned with gross or net markups as reflected in the Cost Plus Method or Resale Minus Method.

7.2.2 Entrepreneur as strategy unit

In contrast to the routine enterprise, the other pole along the functional scale is the 'entrepreneur unit', often called the 'strategy unit'. Such units are conceived to contribute material tangible and intangible assets to the business. The entrepreneur units are made accountable for the success or failure of the overall organization. They bear strategy risks and uncertainty involved in that business. Decision-makers who decide the strategy of the group, or the value chain considered, are thought to be allocated at the entrepreneurial unit. It is this unit which in transfer pricing terminology is considered to be the residual claimant of a business process along various functional steps, after having remunerated routine functions. With respect to arm's length analysis and documentation, it is economically difficult to determine whether the residual profit of such strategic units is at arm's length or not. Primarily, lack of comparable variables is the reason, owing to the large impact of unique business activity. Hence, the arm's length analysis is performed indirectly through a differential between profit for nonentrepreneur functions and total value chain profit.

7.2.3 Hybrid units

Between the routine type (e.g. low-risk distributor) and nonroutine type (entrepreneur, strategy unit) of company, real-world business offers various hybrid types. Considering the transfer pricing model of function and risk allocation, risk borne and assets deployed at the hybrid functional profile are more than in the routine unit, but less than in an entrepreneurial unit. For documentation purposes, such units frequently lack comparables. Hence, internal budget planning data and actual data are necessary to establish whether transfer prices are at arm's length – as, for example, proposed in Paragraph 3.4.10.3b of the Administrative Principles 2005.

The following classification regarding uncertainty and risk will indicate such hybrid units. Whereas risk involved in the business operation of such units can be assessed, the insurance premium cannot be calculated or insurance coverage is prohibitively high to be provided by the market. Hence, a company corresponding with such a type may internalize risk.

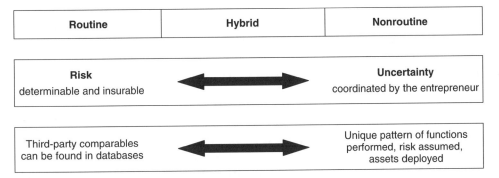

Figure 7.2   Characterization of companies between routine and nonroutine

7.3 Between routine risk and high uncertainty

Regularly, the arm's length analysis requires that the functional pattern of both/all related parties as identified members of the multinational's value chain(s) is investigated by means of function and risk analysis. This ensures an understanding of the arm's length nature of transfer prices, i.e. whether the profit is a markup, a gross margin, or a residual profit. In practice, the related parties of the multinational group are characterized according to their functional pattern, including the risk structure and asset deployment along the dimension 'routine' versus 'nonroutine'. However, this dichotomy in characterizing economic activity appears short-sighted. As a next generation feature of transfer pricing, we propose to differentiate between functional type (risk versus uncertainty) and functional density (comparability versus uniqueness).

7.3.1 Traditional terminology

In classical transfer pricing terminology, functions are differentiated between 'routine' and 'nonroutine'. Nonroutine is often labeled as an entrepreneurial or strategy unit (cf. Paragraph 3.4.10.2b of Administrative Principles 2005). This differentiation helps to assess which related party or which function along a value chain process within the multinational group is engaged in producing unique products and services which, for an economically sound organization, cannot or should not be procured from outside. In classical transfer pricing language, such product or service requires the performance of a kind of nonroutine function(s). The more such units perform as nonroutine, the less the profit–loss result of such unit can be forecasted in advance. In other words, the result of such a unit turns out to be residual after having remunerated the units with routine functions.

Altogether, in traditional transfer pricing the profit type and income level of the organizational units of a multinational group depend upon the pattern of risk and assets assigned to certain functions. In mainstream transfer pricing, the pattern is a routine/nonroutine dichotomy characterized by transfer pricing practitioners on the basis of a more or less undefined catalog of criteria which are supposed to measure the scope of functions and risk.

7.3.2 Distinction between risk and uncertainty

Unfortunately, what the mainstream approach misses is an economically sound distinction between 'risk' and 'uncertainty'. This distinction, however, is important to account for the nature of the firm and the difference between risk insurance and uncertainty safeguards, because it is this that determines the nature of profit. If no direct price comparison is possible, it is this distinction which determines whether the arm's length analysis can be based on margin analysis, budget-actual analysis, or value chain analysis, with allocation of residual profit pies at the nonroutine functions along the value chain.

Transaction cost economics as developed by Williamson (1985, 1996, 1998) distinguishes between risk and uncertainty in order to measure the degree of entrepreneurship. Risk can be governed by insurance contracts. Such insurance costs can be calculated in terms of insurance premiums and/or other measures. The insurance of risk can be group-internal, such as in the course of a sophisticated group risk management model or external in the form of an insurance policy with a third party. Whether it is internal or external is of secondary importance regarding the degree of entrepreneurship of a given functional unit. However, it is of particular relevance regarding the arm's length nature of prices or margins: If a risk is insured internally, the price might be lower compared to a situation where the risk is insured through an external insurer. The reason lies in the principal-agent structure and the information about the true nature of the risk. Likewise, if the risk exposure is not insured but borne by the (related) party A, which transfers its good or service to related party B, the price could be smaller than in a comparable situation where the risk is covered by a third-party insurance contract. Alternatively, risk borne without a damaging occurrence produces higher profit margins compared to a situation where risk hurts through damage.

On the other hand, uncertainty is not governed by means of internal or external insurance. Rather, it is coordinated by means of governance structures different from insurance. Examples are certain mechanisms to search for information on the creditability and/or liability of suppliers, subcontractors, or customers in order to avoid interruptions in the transactional exchange of products and services. Such mechanisms rarely show the nature of 'insurance' rather than 'governance'. Also, the internal uncertainty of a firm (e.g. the hazard of quality misalignment) might be governed by certain mechanisms such as quality assurance systems or even employee motivation programs. These measures are also costly and, in the language of transaction cost economics, to a large extent represent transaction costs. Note that such costs are not insurance costs on risk. Alternatively, uncertainty can be turned into risk if the rate of frequency is sufficiently large.

The difference between risk and uncertainty lies in quantification and calculation. Risk can be quantified and calculated, uncertainty cannot. Risk can be insured, uncertainty usually not. Risk is thought to be susceptible to assessment by using a likelihood, uncertainty not. Uncertainty is observed – and, possibly, moderated – by the coordination skills of the entrepreneur. Hence, the term entrepreneur refers to governance of new, unknown, and uncertain situations. For example, the task to search for new business partners is full of hazards and uncertainty. If the entrepreneur is able to quantify such hazards, it becomes risk. He might insure for that or not.

For example, the consequence of failed strategies is damage or even bankruptcy. Because strategies regularly show the features of innovation and novelty, they are performed under uncertainty rather than risk. The accurate level of risk cannot be determined in situations of novelty and also in instances where there was no occurrence of damage until the present. In such a configuration, the skills of the entrepreneur ensure that the potential for damage does not materialize or, if it does, that it does as little harm as possible.

In our model on function and risk analysis for transfer pricing purposes, an entrepreneur takes into account uncertainty in all decision-making issues. For example, will the product and marketing strategy be successful? Will services find customers? Will the new manufacturing plant abroad function well? Are employees sufficiently trained and motivated? The task of the entrepreneur is to navigate around such potential hazards of the organization. Partially, inherent uncertainties can be assessed ex-ante if a rule of thumb – be it industry- or individual-specific – allows this. Also, the entrepreneur might wish to cover part of that uncertainty by contracting with an insurer (e.g. liability insurances), notwithstanding the lack of an exact risk assessment.

Theoretically, of course, the entrepreneur could safeguard against all risks and uncertainty. However, this would consume large parts of the profitability, or even result in losses, since the insurer would have to provide coverage for risks which cannot be assessed or are assessed at a very high cost of underwriting. Hence, insurance coverage limits the profits of a company if the damage does not occur. It is this aspect that, among other challenges, makes transfer pricing so crucial in terms of comparability of the tested party with similar third parties.

In other words, transactions and the respective coordination, if performed for the first time or very rarely, lack a consistent body of rules of thumb and experience. Transactions of strategy units developing permanent solutions to new problems make transfer pricing difficult in large organizations.

7.3.3 Intermediary results

For the assessment as to whether transfer prices are at arm's length, it is essential to understand the nature of functions performed and risk borne by a certain business unit of the multinational group. The 'entrepreneur' seeks to coordinate uncertainty in such a way that damaging occurrences are averted. An insurance coverage on uncertain damage would sap the company's profit. Hence, internal coordination of uncertainty is preferred over external insurance coverage. The entrepreneur is this unit within the group's value chain who can be characterized with transactional attributes such as uncertainty (instead of risk), low frequency (instead of high), specific asset deployment (instead of nonspecific), and low measurability of effort spent by individuals (instead of easy measurability).

From a business decision-making perspective, the term 'entrepreneur' is closely related to the terms 'investment competence' and 'accountability'. Investment competence means that this business unit within the multinational group is authorized to make investment decisions. This decision-making freedom might be budgeted to a certain level. However, what is different between a 'profit center' and an 'investment center' with investment competence is the authorization of the latter to make such decisions. If the chosen investment strategy fails, it is this unit (and its managers) who will be accountable. This unit's capital is then deployed to meet liability claims. Hence, such a unit performs as a residual claimant, i.e. it receives the residual after having remunerated other factor deployments and other liability claims.

7.4   Classification of companies

With the economics of function and risk analysis in hand, we now shift attention to conducting an economically sound arm's length analysis. The new German Administrative Principles offer an interesting concept which is worth introducing. In Paragraph 3.4.10.2, it is stated that the type of arm's length analysis depends upon the company type with respect to the function and risk profile. Hence, the analysis of the company type precedes the arm's length analysis. For the analysis of company type, we use the term function and risk analysis 'in the broader sense', which is to establish in principle the pattern of functions performed, risks borne, and assets deployed. In contrast, the function and risk analysis 'in the narrow sense' provides an information profile on the adequate size of profit components which are to be allocated to business units (e.g. cost center, profit center, investment center) along the value chains of the multinational group (cf. Paragraph 3.4.11.5; also see Brem and Tucha, 2005). This latter type of function and risk analysis is closely related to valuation aspects where the transfer price, or the profit margin of such a transaction, is to be assessed by its monetary size.

7.4.1 Function and risk analysis in the broader sense

The function and risk analysis in the broader sense – as, for instance, stipulated by Article 4, No. 3a GAufzV (cf. Paragraphs 3.4.11.4 and 3.4.10.2, Administrative Principles 2005) – intends to generate information as to whether a related party (or the business units of it) can be characterized as a business unit with routine functions, entrepreneurial functions, or hybrid functions. It is exactly this distinction between company types which determines the arm's length nature of a business unit's profit (cost plus, resale minus, comparable profit, residual profit) and the level of such profit and transfer prices. However, it is not the label itself but the functional attributes related to tasks, risk/uncertainty, and assets which determine the functional type.

While in mainstream transfer pricing the analysis distinguishes between 'routine' and 'nonroutine', the German Administrative Principles differentiate (in Paragraph 3.4.10.2a–c) the related party units according to the dimensions 'comparability versus uniqueness' and 'risk versus uncertainty'. Hence, by introducing degrees of entrepreneurship with respect to comparability and risk structures, the German provisions appear to go beyond the standard OECD language on 'routine versus nonroutine' at the level of function and risk analysis in international transfer pricing. In principle, the new German provisions represent an economic approach in the field of transfer pricing and international income allocation which can be deemed more consistent with the overall target to link the arm's length principle to real-world economics of multinational group companies, stakeholder governance, and entrepreneurship. The distinction into 'routine', 'hybrid', and 'entrepreneurship' are based on the notion that economic actors choose the governance structure which fits the economic needs to safeguard transactional hazards and to provide for managerial incentives according to the economic risk pattern involved and the assets deployed. This distinction determines the conceptual and procedural nature of arm's length analysis.

Consequently, the function and risk analysis in the broader sense serves as a basis for the selection and design of the arm's length analysis per se. The transfer pricing analyst may have to opt for either the database-driven screening on routine functions, and/or the presentation of planning calculations and budget-actual positions for hybrid companies, and/or the residual profit allocation for entrepreneurial units. Ultimately, it is the function and risk analysis which has to elaborate whether the transaction considered allows a comparable analysis or internal-data analysis.

7.4.2 Selection of the type of arm's length analysis

As stated above, the Administrative Principles 2005 offer two variables, 'functional type' and 'comparability', to select the appropriate arm's length test mechanism. The functional type has the features determinable risk versus coordinated uncertainty, while comparability measures uniqueness and can be assessed between 'yes, comparable' and 'no, not comparable'. Though a given sample of cases may show continuous distribution of observations on these two variables, at present we suggest a dichotomous value type, as provided in Paragraph 3.4.10.2 of Administrative Principles 2005. Figure 7.3 shows the basic types of arm's length analysis subject to functional type and comparability.

7.4.3 Functional type: Risk versus uncertainty

The variable 'functional type' characterizes the organizational unit of a value chain (e.g. related party or center unit) as to whether the risk is determinable and can be quantified or whether it is uncertain and not quantifiable (or not quantified). In this model, the 'prudent businessman' includes risk in a cost calculation (either as cost factor or as insurance coverage cost), while uncertainty is dealt with

		Function type (governing risk)	
		Risk (determinable)	**Uncertainty** (coordinated by entrepreneur)
Comparable activity (functional density, functional scope)	**Yes**	**Routine party** Database-driven arm's length test (e.g. profit margins on basis of C^+, R^- or TNMM) (comp. Tz. 3.4.10.2 a)	**Hybrid party** Cost calculation and budget-actual assessment prior year-end (comp. Tz. 3.4.10.2 c)
	No	**Hybrid party** Cost calculation and budget-actual assessment prior year-end (comp. Tz. 3.4.10.2 c)	**Entrepreneur** Allocation of residual profit to nonroutine functions of the value chain (comp. Tz. 3.4.10.2 b)

Figure 7.3   Basic types of arm's length analysis as proposed by the German Administrative Principles 2005

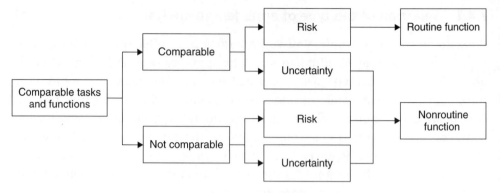

Figure 7.4   Determination of routine and nonroutine functions

as a residual in the company's profit (cf. Paragraph 3.4.10.2a, Administrative Principles 2005).

From a transaction cost economics perspective, a transaction between two parties will be economically feasible if the contract provides both parties with sufficient safeguard against hazards. If, however, the governance of a transaction is too complex because of transactional hazards, opportunism, and/or unforeseeable incentive structures, the transaction might preferably be internalized and, hence, does not take place between two parties – notwithstanding whether they are members of the same multinational group or third parties. This is what transaction cost economics suggests as hierarchical coordination within the same organizational unit (cf. Sansing, 1999; Oestreicher, 2000; Grossman et al., 2003; Brem and Tucha, 2005). Hence, the contractual safeguard deals with the hold-up problem which arises if specific investments are necessary for generating certain goods or services.

From this perspective, it follows that the coordination of goods or services is preferably carried out within the entrepreneurial unit (integration) if, for example, highly specific assets in physical and/or human capital are necessary and the hazards of opportunistic behavior and incentive structure cannot be governed by means of a contract between the two parties. The entrepreneur, hence, seeks to govern the uncertainty by means of hierarchical and internal coordination. A contractual safeguard of such uncertainty is not possible because an insurer cannot be found or insurance is economically not sound because of prohibitively high costs. On the other hand, the transactional relationship between the 'entrepreneurial unit' and another related party (or another business unit) of the same multinational organization is coordinated externally through a contract.[8]

7.4.4   Functional density: Comparability versus uniqueness

The Administrative Principles 2005 assume that some transfer pricing fact patterns will not have comparable data to be used for the arm's length analysis (cf. Paragraphs 3.4.12.2 and 3.4.12.4). The classification into company types according to Paragraph 3.4.10.2 requires an assessment as to whether the multinational's unit (related party or business unit) can be assessed by means of transactional comparisons.

The second dimension on the company type analysis provides a measure for the comparability of the tested party with third parties. Reciprocally, it is a measure of uniqueness. A low degree of comparability indicates a high level of intangible assets used for the value-generation process of the business unit considered. Patents, trademarks, know-how, process, and market knowledge are examples of such intangibles which affect comparability.

In Figure 7.3, the functional scope is measured by means of the variable 'comparability' and its dichotomous values, 'yes' and 'no': Regarding the arm's length principle, a related party with a unique set of functions, risk, and assets will not have comparable data. Such a unit is characterized by either a high level of determinable risk resulting in a hybrid company type (Paragraph 3.4.10.2c) or coordinated uncertainty, deeming it an entrepreneur company type (Paragraph 3.4.10.2b).

In contrast, if the related party can be characterized by a pattern of functions, risks, and assets which may have comparable data in the market, the arm's length analysis can be conducted along the mechanism 'comparability'. A comparable unit with determinable risk structures is a 'routine company' (cf. Paragraph 3.4.10.2a), while one dealing with coordinated uncertainty is a 'hybrid' (cf. Paragraph 3.4.10.2c).

7.5   Arm's length analysis

The function and risk analysis 'in the broader sense' provides the functional type of the company. As indicated earlier, this is the basis of the arm's length analysis per se. Three types of arm's length analysis are proposed by the Administrative Principles 2005: Margin analysis, planning and budget-actual analysis, and value chain analysis with residual profit split (Paragraph 3.4.12.2).

7.5.1   'Routine company' and third-party comparison

If the tested party represents a routine company type, transaction-based transfer pricing methods are deemed appropriate (cf. Paragraph 3.4.10.3a). The underlying assumption is that company units with routine profiles can be compared with third

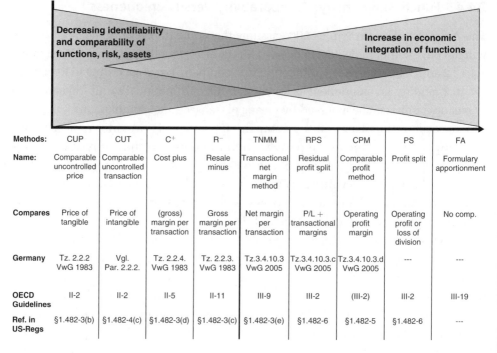

Methods:	CUP	CUT	C⁺	R⁻	TNMM	RPS	CPM	PS	FA
Name:	Comparable uncontrolled price	Comparable uncontrolled transaction	Cost plus	Resale minus	Transactional net margin method	Residual profit split	Comparable profit method	Profit split	Formulary apportionment
Compares	Price of tangible	Price of intangible	(gross) margin per transaction	Gross margin per transaction	Net margin per transaction	P/L + transactional margins	Operating profit margin	Operating profit or loss of division	No comp.
Germany	Tz. 2.2.2 VwG 1983	Vgl. Par. 2.2.2.	Tz. 2.2.4. VwG 1983	Tz. 2.2.3. VwG 1983	Tz.3.4.10.3 VwG 2005	Tz.3.4.10.3.c VwG 2005	Tz.3.4.10.3.d VwG 2005	---	---
OECD Guidelines	II-2	II-2	II-5	II-11	III-9	III-2	(III-2)	III-2	III-19
Ref. in US-Regs	§1.482-3(b)	§1.482-4(c)	§1.482-3(d)	§1.482-3(c)	§1.482-3(e)	§1.482-6	§1.482-5	§1.482-6	---

Figure 7.5   Transfer pricing methods and reference to selected national provisions

parties. Hence, the price for a transaction or, more likely, the profit margin (or an indicator for profitability) of the tested party and the third party can be compared by means of database-driven margin analysis (cf. Brem and Tucha, 2006a).

Transaction-based methods are often called standard methods. While many tax jurisdictions exclusively accept transaction-based methods, others indicate merely a preference allowing also for other methods.

7.5.2   'Hybrids', budget planning, and budget-actual assessment

Given the company type classification, hybrid units (as in Paragraph 3.4.10.2c) may come under two categories: (a) Hybrids with a high level of uncertainty, yet low degree of uniqueness (=comparability) and hence high level of uncertainty; (b) Hybrids with a high level of determinable risk and low degree of uniqueness.[9]

To compile an appropriate arm's length analysis for documentation purposes in jurisdictions such as Germany, it is essential to note that the transactional net margin method is no longer deemed applicable to tested parties with hybrid function features (cf. Paragraph 3.4.10.3b – second dash). The argument there is that the functional and risk profiles differ significantly between the tested-party and third-party companies, which might be considered as comparable quantities. Hence, at best, database-driven margin analysis can support plausibility arguments of arm's length analysis. The Administrative Principles assume (in Paragraph 3.4.10.2c) that the ordinary and prudent businessman of a hybrid company calculates arm's length prices by means of budget planning calculations (Paragraph 3.4.12.6a) and, if the plan is not met during any given financial year on the basis of continuous budget-actual assessments, the prudent businessman is expected to react with internal measures such as sales price adaptation, purchase price renegotiation, cost cutting, etc. The Administrative Principles 2005 do not rule on any standardized approach of arm's length analysis which will be audited by the tax auditor. They rather guide the tax auditor in such a way that classical database-driven margin analysis alone is not sufficient to document arm's length transfer pricing behavior in the case of hybrid company types.

Rather, budget planning combined with budget-actual assessments and profit forecasts (including investment calculations) are the appropriate arm's length analysis for hybrid units (Paragraph 3.4.12.6). In particular, long-term loss situations and restructuring activities require this approach. For example, the taxpayer has to indicate by means of such analysis that a loss in the start-up years or any loss-making period is offset by a total period profit. Transfers of market penetration costs from the sales unit to the manufacturing unit would be arm's length, if the manufacturing unit also benefits at, or after, the break-even point. Hence, what deems a certain transfer pricing situation at arm's length is the demonstration that the businessman seeks to generate profit ('intention to realize profit').

7.5.3 'Entrepreneur' and allocation of residuals

As indicated above, a test on arm's length behavior in transfer pricing is economically weak – not sound – if the tested party represents an 'entrepreneur' unit, especially if such a test is based on comparison with a third party. Rather, the entrepreneurial unit's profit is a residual: The entrepreneur receives the remaining part after meeting the contractual obligations on remuneration. It is this logic which needs to be reflected in the documentation of arm's length profit of entrepreneurial related-party taxpayers.

For arm's length assessment, it is decisive that the residual can be positive or negative. In line with the Administrative Principles 2005, we propose that the documentation of the arm's length nature of a residual profit or loss situation for such entrepreneur units requires quantitative value chain calculation, based on the function and risk analysis in a broader sense.

What this logic also shows is that the indirect arm's length analysis where the profit (and not the transfer price) is tested considers the residual profit allocation at the entrepreneur unit subordinated to margin analysis and budget-actual assessment. Hence, the test on arm's length situations of the entrepreneur unit needs to be part of a value chain analysis. A demonstration of the arm's length situation at other functional units (routine and hybrid units) is a precursor to any assessment of appropriate profit allocation at the entrepreneurial unit. Analytically, we propose three steps to analyze transfer pricing at the entrepreneur unit (cf. Paragraph 3.4.11.5):

- Assessment of functions, risks, and assets subject to the related-party transaction
- Allocation of profit margins to routine and hybrid units of the value chain (for the latter, profit margins are used to support the results of planning and budget-actual assessment)
- Demonstration of the residual profit/loss situation at the entrepreneur unit and if applicable, split among such units along the value chain.

It is worth mentioning that value chain analysis via these three steps regularly allows a lowering of the number of database-driven margin analyses of comparable third-party quantities. Simultaneously, it increases the level of plausibility of such margin analyses.

7.6 Conclusion

The objective of this chapter is to illustrate the conceptual logic of an economically sound model of arm's length analysis for documentation purposes in the area of transfer pricing and income allocation. The message is that the type and procedure of arm's length analysis primarily depends upon the economics of the transfer pricing case, which needs to be investigated by means of a well-conceptualized function and risk analysis in the broader sense. From this function and risk analysis, we can derive whether it is sufficient to base the arm's length test of transfer prices on traditional database-driven searches with third-party margin analysis, more complex planning calculations with continuous budget-actual assessments, or residual profit allocations to entrepreneur units. For that, the function and risk analysis in a broader sense ('in principle') distinguishes between function type (contractible risk versus entrepreneurially coordinated uncertainty) and functional scope (comparability versus uniqueness).

Further work is needed to clarify the approach. In particular, questions on how to eliminate the effects of risk insurance on the revenue and profit indicators have not been discussed. To a large extent, such costs determine the level of risk insurance, uniqueness, and routine.[10] While the risk premiums can be identified in principle and in size in the books of the related-party companies, available data from commercial databases do not provide information for such analysis. Hence, we always lack information on the comparability of the tested party and the 'comparable' third parties. The same effect applies, among others, for the market-based profitability of assets deployed, which in some cases is part of the costs assumed and in other cases not.

The economic analysis of transfer pricing in international taxation is at a far from satisfying level. With respect to the increasing relevance of cross-border business in general, and the large share of such business conducted within multinational group companies in particular, it is valuable to further elaborate on economic models to assess the nature and degree of the arm's length structure of transfer pricing cases. To our mind, topics such as vertical and horizontal profit allocation, function and risk profiles, or role of intangibles will gain relevance. Economic analysis of income allocation for tax purposes is, indeed, in need of greater theoretical and empirical foundation.

Acknowledgments

This chapter has emerged from ongoing discussions on new transfer pricing documentation provisions in Germany. The chapter was conceptualized and drafted during the second author's research and teaching visit to the Indian Institute of Management, Ahmedabad. The usual disclaimers apply.

Notes

1. Transfer pricing methods are transaction-based methods such as Comparable Uncontrolled Price Method (CUP), Cost Plus Method (C+), Resale Minus Method (R−), Transactional Net Margin Method (TNMM). Examples of profit-based methods are Comparable Profit Method (CPM) and Profit Split Methods (PS), including the Residual Profit Split Method (RPS). Some countries also consider Formula Apportionment using certain allocation factors (e.g. assets, sum of wage, turnover) as an appropriate transfer pricing method (TPM).
2. In emerging countries such as India, significantly longer litigation periods are possible.
3. To our knowledge, the largest transfer pricing dispute in 2006 was GlaxoSmithKline against US IRS which was finally settled at a US$3.1 billion additional tax change – the largest ever single payment to the IRS (International Tax Review, 2006).

4. The 2003 documentation law of Germany was triggered by the Highest Tax Court (*Bundesfinanzhof*) decision in 2001 (BFH v. 17.03.2001, I R 103/00; BStBl 2004 II, 171), which ruled that Article 92(2) of the Tax Procedures Act was not a sufficient legal basis for the tax administration to request special documentation from the taxpayer on cross-border transfer pricing issues.

5. Administrative Principles are called *Verwaltungsgrundsätze* or *BMF-Schreiben*. The German title is: 'Grundsätze für die Prüfung der Einkunftsabgrenzung zwischen nahestehenden Personen mit grenzüberschreitenden Geschäftsbeziehungen in Bezug auf Ermittlungs- und Mitwirkungsp-flichten, Berichtigungen sowie auf Verständigungs- und EU-Schiedsverfahren' (abbreviation: Verwaltungsgrundsätze Dokumentation und Verfahren).

6. Recently, the administrative principles on advance pricing agreements were published on October 5, 2006.

7. Given a 2005 decision of the Highest Tax Court (BFH v. 06.04.2005, I R 22/04; IStR 2005, 598), some experts opine whether further administrative provisions on dealing with long-term losses in the context of related-party business are necessary at all.

8. In transaction cost economics, the choice of governance structures is determined by transactional attributes (cf. Williamson, 1985; Oestreicher, 2000). Transactional attributes can be used as variables to characterize the functional pattern of related-party business units. The following transactional attributes are typically deployed: Uncertainty, frequency of coordination, specificity of assets deployed (among others, human specificity, physical specificity, time specificity, dedicated speci-ficity), measurability of effort contributed by stakeholders (cf. Brem and Tucha, 2006b).

9. We expect that, subject to the thresholds applied, most tested parties follow the company type 'hybrid'. It is a matter of presentation in the course of the transfer pricing analysis to demon-strate if a related party is structured into legal, operative, or hierarchical group structures (cf. Brem and Tucha, 2006a).

10. We hypothize that for income allocation purposes and demonstrating arm's length behavior towards tax authorities, the analytical problem of cost allocation and cost design over the related parties of a group (including the problem of differences in cross-country accounting principles) plays a greater role than the question of assigning a certain profit margin (as a percentage) to the respective functions. The reason is that the basis of any percentage margin is the cost. So, designing – or manipulating – the cost basis can have a significantly larger impact than turning the margin screw, especially if that function is allocated in a high-tax jurisdiction in which in practice stable but small cost plus markups may be assigned to "satisfy" the revenue service.

References

Brem, M. and Tucha, T. (2005). The Organization of the Multinational Firm: Perspectives on Global Transfer Pricing. *BNA Tax Planning International – Transfer Pricing*, 6(12):6–10.

Brem, M and Tucha, T. (2006a). Transfer Pricing: Conceptual Thoughts on the Nature of the Multinational Firm. *Vikalpa*, 31(2):29–43.

Brem, M. and Tucha, T. (2006b). Transfer Pricing in Related-party Value Chains: Value Chain Pricing, Related-party Organization, Arm's Length Principle, and Tax Risk Management. Conference Paper presented at the International Conference of Logistics, Hamburg University of Technology, 15–16 September 2006.

The Economist (2001). Globalisation and Tax. Special Report, 29 January.

Eden, L. (1998). *Taxing Multinationals: Transfer Pricing and Corporate Income Taxation in North America*. University of Toronto Press, Toronto.

Erard, B. (2001). The Income Tax Compliance Burden on Canadian Big Business. In: *Tax Compliance Costs: A Festschrift for Cedric Sandford* (Evans, C., Pope, J., and Hasseldine, J., eds), pp. 317–335. Prospect Media, St Leonards, USA.

Ernst & Young (2005). 2005–2006 Global Transfer Pricing Surveys (www.ey.com).

European Commission (2001). *Towards an Internal Market without Tax Obstacles*. COM (2001) 582 final, http://europa.eu.int/comm/taxation_customs/publications/official_doc/IP/ip1468/communication_en.pdf. (*Ein Binnenmarkt ohne steuerliche Hindernisse: Strategie zur Schaffung einer konsolidierten Körperschaftssteuer-Bemessungsgrundlage für die grenzüberschreitende Unternehmenstätigkeit in der EU.*) KOM (2001) 582 (23 October 2001).

Feldstein, M, Hines, J.R., and Hubbard, G.R. (eds) (1995). *Taxing Multinational Corporations*, pp. 29–38. University of Chicago Press, Chicago.

Grossman, G.M., Helpman, E., and Szeidl, A. (2003). Optimal Integration Strategies for the Multinational Firm. NBER Working Paper No. W10189, December. Available at SSRN, http://ssrn.com/abstract=482681.

Hirsch, G. (2005). Cost Sharing Agreements: Krauts vs. Yankees – New German Transfer Pricing Rules Compared to their US Counterparts. *BNA Tax Planning International – Transfer Pricing*, 6(10):4–15.

International Tax Review. (2006). *Weekly News*. September 19.

OECD (1995a). *OECD Model Tax Convention*. OECD, Paris.

OECD (1995b). *Transfer Pricing Guidelines for Multinational Enterprises and Tax Administrations*, Parts I and II. OECD, Paris.

OECD (2001). *Measuring Globalization: The Role of Multinationals in OECD Economies*. OECD, Paris.

OECD (2005). *International Trade Report 2005*. OECD, Paris.

Oestreicher, A. (2000). *Konzern-Gewinnabgrenzung*. C.H. Beck, Munich.

Oestreicher, A. and Vormoor, C. (2004). Verrechnungspreise mit Hilfe von Datenbanken – Vergleichbarkeit und Datenlage. *Internationales Steuerrecht*, 2:95–106.

Owens, J. (1998). Taxation within a Context of Globalization. *Bulletin for International Fiscal Documentation*, 52:290.

Ring, D. (2000). On the Frontier of Procedural Innovation: Advance Pricing Agreements and the Struggle to Allocate Income for Cross Border Taxation. *Michigan Journal of International Law*, 21(2):143–234.

Sansing, R. (1999). Relationship-specific Investments and the Transfer Pricing Paradox. *Review of Accounting Studies*, 4(2):119–134.

Tucha, T. (2002). Der Einsatz von Unternehmensdatenbanken bei Verrechnungspreisanalysen. *Internationales Steuerrecht*, 21:745–752.

Walpole, M. (1999). Compliance Cost Control by Revenue Authorities in the OECD. In: *Tax Compliance Costs: A Festschrift for Cedric Sandford* (Evans, C., Pope, J., and Hasseldine, J., eds), pp. 369–388. Prospect Media, St Leonards, USA.

Williamson, O.E. (1985). *The Economic Institutions of Capitalism*. Oxford University Press, Oxford.

Williamson, O.E. (1996). *The Mechanisms of Governance*. Oxford University Press, Oxford.

Williamson, O.E. (1998). Transaction Cost Economics: How It Works, Where It Is Headed. *De Economist*, 146:23–58.

Corporate Tax Competition and Coordination in the European Union: What Do We Know? Where Do We Stand?

Gaëtan Nicodème*

Abstract

This chapter reviews the rationales for and facts about corporate tax coordination in Europe. Although statutory tax rates have dramatically declined, revenues collected from corporate taxation are fairly stable and there is so far no evidence of a race to the bottom. Nevertheless, welfare gains can be expected from tax coordination, though the ambiguous results from economic tax theory and the institutional setting may have prevented the EU from taking policy action in the area of tax competition. Following its 2001 Communication, the European Commission is currently working with Member States to define a common consolidated corporate tax base for European companies.

8.1   Introduction

The issue of corporate tax competition and coordination has gained importance in the European Union. In a world where economies are increasingly integrated and capital increasingly mobile, the current trend of declining statutory corporate tax rates has led to fears of a race to the bottom. Tax competition is, however, a complex phenomenon that can materialize through multiple channels, and whose effects on real economic activity and on governments' tax revenues are often ambiguous. This chapter reviews the recent theoretical and empirical economic literature and discusses recent European policies to remove tax obstacles to the full implementation of a European Single Market.

8.2   The European Union as a global power

With more than 460 million inhabitants and a Gross Domestic Product of above €11,000 billion (US$13,300 billion), the European Union is a major economic player in the world. Starting with six founding members in 1958, the European Union has undergone five enlargements to reach 25 Member States in 2004. The process of economic and political integration over the last half century has been rather impressive. Building on the original Customs Union – that is, a free trade area and a common external tariff – in 1987 the EU Member States signed the Single

---

* This article was written by Gaëtan Nicodème, The Directorate-General for Economic and Financial Affairs, B-1049 Brussels, Belgium. © European Communities, 2006. The views expressed in this article are those of the author and do not necessarily reflect the official position of the European Commission.

European Act, a piece of legislation which provided that the European Community (as it was called at the time) would take measures to establish an internal market before the end of 1992 by removing remaining tariff and nontariff barriers between its members. This internal market or 'Single Market' was based on what is known as the four basic freedoms, i.e. freedom of movement for goods, services, labor, and capital. Another important step was reached in 1999 with the creation of the Economic and Monetary Union and the introduction in most Member States of the euro as a common currency.

In parallel to economic integration, the EU's institutions and decision-making process have become politically more integrated. EU policymaking rests on three main institutions. The European Commission, representing the community-wide interest, is the only body that can make legislative proposals; It also plays a role as 'Guardian of the Treaties' by launching court procedures against Member States that fail to transpose (or inappropriately transpose) EU legislation into their national laws or breach the rules of the Treaty. Secondly, the Council, comprised of the 25 governments, votes (with different weights for different countries) to adopt, amend, or reject the proposed European legislation. Finally, the European Parliament, having increasingly gained power over time, is now fully part of the legislative process in what is known as the 'co-decision procedure' with the Council. Besides these three main institutions, the European Court of Justice (ECJ) has been a growing force for European integration, notably through its action in applying and interpreting European legislation, as well as fighting discrimination. The European Economic and Social Committee, representing social and economic interest groups, and the Committee of the Regions, representing the regions of Europe, have played a role in the dialog with stakeholders by giving opinions (with advisory, not binding, status) on proposed EU legislation. Important economic policies have been transferred to European level, notably monetary policy (which is in the hands of an independent European Central Bank), competition policy (whose most important legislation and control functions are in the hands of the European Commission), and trade policy (for which the European Commission receives a mandate to negotiate on behalf of the European Union and its Member States).

8.3 The institutional design of and rationale for taxation

Interestingly enough, the powers of the European Union in direct taxation are limited. Member States jealously retain most tax powers and concede only limited prerogatives to the EU. Opponents of increasing the EU's powers regarding direct taxation have both economic and political arguments why redistribution and sta- bilization (and the assignment of tax powers to achieve this) should in their view remain in national hands:

1. Some consider that because they are not directly elected (with the excep- tion of the European Parliament), EU institutions may lack the democratic legitimacy – or rather, they claim that whatever legitimacy they do have is indirect at best – that is needed to have tax-raising powers, since some Member States have adopted the motto 'no taxation without representation'. This argument seems highly debatable since the European Commission derives its legitimacy from the fact that its members are appointed by dem- ocratically elected governments and approved by the directly elected mem- bers of the European Parliament. In addition, powers to raise and manage taxes could be vested in the Council or the European Parliament themselves, as is done in any other federation.
2. Member States vary widely in the extent of their preference for redistribution policies, and citizens may well be much less concerned about the income/ poverty levels of those living in other EU Member States than the situation in their home country.
3. There is still much more that could be done by national budgetary policies to achieve stabilization, and there would be considerable problems in design- ing an effective stabilization fund at EU level, due to the difficulty in iden- tifying in real time the source, scale, and duration of economic shocks which could lead to lags in the disbursement of funds. The economic rationale for assigning to the EU public policies that need large-scale public expen- diture has been weak for the same reasons: The financing of EU policies can easily be arranged on an ad hoc basis.
4. The scale of cross-border externalities requiring centralized 'corrective' tax interventions may be relatively small, although further economic integration may increase the number and amplitude of cases.[1]

This, however, is not to argue that there is no economic rationale for any EU involvement in tax policy matters whatsoever. There may be some cases when some degree of EU involvement is warranted:

1. Increased economic integration and mobility of factors of production may lead to a situation in which, on the one hand, Member States develop 'harmful' strategies to attract or retain mobile tax bases and, on the other

hand, taxation is increasingly shifted to the immobile factor, labor. In this case, coordinated action at the EU level could be needed. This was the rationale behind the 1996 informal ECOFIN Council in Verona, which led to the 1997 fiscal package (see Aujean, 2005).

2. There are tax obstacles to the implementation of the Single Market and common action is required to tackle them because action at national level could lead to an inefficient allocation of resources.

3. There are tax externalities that can be better tackled at the EU level.

4. Even though the delimitation of the EU's powers limits its role in stabilization and redistribution, cooperation at the EU level may actually help Member States to preserve the resources needed to achieve these policies at the domestic level by coordinating their tax policies.

5. Because of the existence of a common monetary policy, there may be a need for multilateral surveillance on the impact of taxes on economic output and stability.

The EU involvement in taxation issues is somewhat limited. This is reflected in the Treaty and in particular the subsidiarity principle. The Treaty delimits the scope of action of the EU in tax matters, restricting it mainly to issues of multilateral surveillance, the proper functioning of the Single Market, competition issues in tax state aid, tax discrimination, and ad hoc tax measures to attain specific objectives of the Union (e.g. environmental or social objectives). Article 5 of the EC Treaty introduces the concepts of subsidiarity, which limits the range of action of the European Commission in regard to fiscal issues by stating that:

> 'In areas which do not fall within its exclusive competence, the Community shall take action, in accordance with the principle of subsidiarity, only if and insofar as the objectives of the proposed action cannot be sufficiently achieved by the Member States and can therefore, by reason of the scale and effects of the proposed action, be better achieved by the Community.'

As taxation is not an exclusive competence of the Community, both principles of scale of action and proportionality contained in subsidiarity apply. This reduces the European Commission proposals to the minimum necessity to remove distortions. Furthermore, harmonization generally takes place by means of directives, which, pursuant to Article 249 of the EC Treaty, are only binding as to the result to be achieved (as opposed to regulations which are binding in their entirety), thus leaving a certain amount of leeway for the Member States when they transpose them into national law. These restrictions, and the political difficulties linked to the fact that any EU decisions on tax matters still require unanimity among all

Member States, reflect the clear desire from (at least some) Member States to retain full control of their tax policies. The main areas of EU intervention can be summarized as follows:

- *The EU role in taxes is mainly limited to indirect taxation and tax state aid.* Articles 90–93 EC deal specifically with tax provisions. However, the scope of these articles is limited as they only allow the European Commission to work on '*provisions for the harmonization of legislation concerning turnover taxes, excise duties and other forms of indirect taxation to the extent that such harmonization is necessary to ensure the establishment and the functioning of the internal market within the time-limit laid down in Article 14*'. Article 87 EC on State aid provides another rationale for intervening when a tax distorts competition by favoring certain undertakings or the production of certain goods and affects trade between Member States. Despite its strict formulation, this article has been widely used by the European Commission to remove harmful tax measures.
- *Nondiscrimination is increasingly used as a basis for intervention.* Article 12 EC enshrines this principle. The use of this article to tackle differences in taxation between residents and nonresidents is nevertheless difficult. Indeed, the principle of nondiscrimination only applies as long as the person invoking it lies within the scope of the Treaty. A resident citizen cannot ask for anything other than the application of the law of her/his own State. Therefore, a resident cannot use this article to contest the nontaxation of a nonresident since the only provisions she/he can use would be the regime applicable to residents. However, both the ECJ and the European Commission have used a broad interpretation of this article to act against some tax measures considered detrimental to the Single Market.
- *Tax obstacles to the Single Market remain the first ground for intervention in direct taxation.* Article 94 EC has been the principal legal basis on which the European Commission has acted when issuing proposals for directives in fiscal matters. It states that '*the Council shall, acting unanimously on a proposal from the European Commission and after consulting the European Parliament and the Economic and Social Committee, issue directives for the approximation of such laws, regulations or administrative provisions of the Member States as directly affect the establishment or functioning of the common market*'. Indeed, differences of treatment in terms of accounting and fiscal rules both constitute a distortion that directly affects the functioning of the markets for goods and financial services and prevents full integration in

these areas. The unanimity in the Council on fiscal issues required by the article, however, makes it difficult to reach a compromise and slows down the process of removing tax distortions. It has, however, served as the basis for proposals such as those to coordinate corporate taxation.

- *Multilateral surveillance role of the European Commission.* Article 99 EC assigns the European Commission the role of conducting multilateral surveillance. The Broad Economic Policy Guidelines and the Employment Guidelines are typical examples of this task. However, both sets of guidelines have so far been relatively shy when it comes to discussing taxation issues.
- *Targeted actions.* Finally, Articles 136 and 137 EC assign the European Commission the role of supporting and complementing the actions of the Member States in various domains, such as social protection and the environment. Taxation may be used as a tool to achieve those aims.

In consequence of these strictly delimited competences, European tax legislation has been – mainly – limited to the harmonization of the value-added tax base (one of the main resources for the European budget), the exemption or taxation at a low level of new capital raised by companies (Directive 69/335/EEC), issues of mutual assistance between tax administrations (Directive 77/799/EEC), several ad hoc pieces of legislation in the areas of taxation of savings and tax obstacles to the Single Market (see below), and multilateral surveillance.

8.4 The evolution of tax receipts in the European Union

Aggregated at the EU level, total taxes collected today represent just under 40% of GDP (compared to just under 30% for the USA and Japan). The total tax burden gradually increased between 1970 and the end of the century, probably reflecting both the need to collect revenues to finance increasingly desired public policies and the post-oil-shock adverse economic situation (Figure 8.1).

Since the end of the 1990s, we observe an unprecedented several-year decrease of the total tax burden, which seems to have leveled off in the last three years. This of course hides a considerable diversity in levels and trends across Member States, as well as the influence of the economic cycle. There is also no indication that total tax burdens are converging within the European Union. Changes in the tax-to-GDP ratios of individual countries in fact reveal that most changes – either increases or decreases – have occurred in countries with a below-average total tax burden.

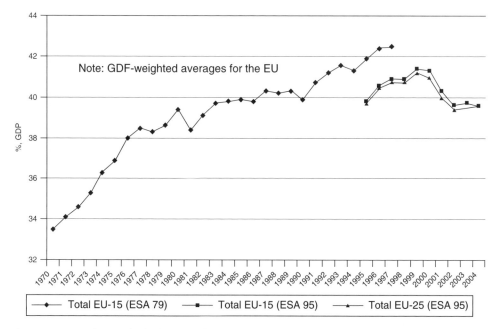

Figure 8.1 Total taxes (including social security contributions) as percentage of GDP in the EU. Note the statistical break due to a change in classification at Eurostat. *Source*: European Commission (2006a)

When we decompose the tax-to-GDP ratios into the three main economic functions, we observe that the recent slight decline in total-tax-to-GDP ratios is largely due to a decline in the collection of taxes on labor income relative to GDP. The trends indicate both a slight decrease in labor taxes collected as a share of GDP and an increase in capital taxes collected as a share of GDP in the EU-15 (see Figure 8.2).[2]

8.5 Corporate tax competition in the European Union: Theory and empirical evidence

8.5.1 Tax competition and the underprovision of public goods

'The result of tax competition may well be a tendency towards less than efficient levels of output of local services. In attempting to keep taxes low to attract business investment, local officials may hold spending below those levels for which marginal benefits equal marginal costs . . .'

(Oates, 1972)

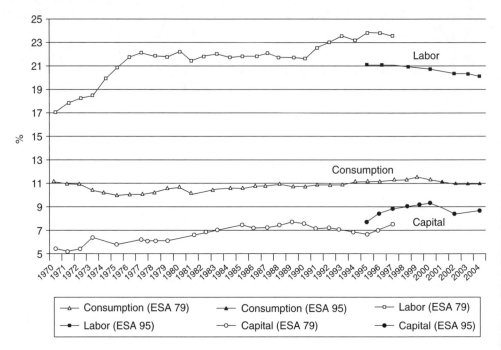

Figure 8.2 Taxes (including social security contributions) as percentage of GDP by economic function in the EU-15. Note the statistical break due to a change in classification at Eurostat. *Source*: European Commission (2006a)

Tax competition – broadly defined as noncooperative tax setting by independent governments competing for a mobile tax base – has attracted growing attention as economic integration progresses and factors of production and some taxpayers become increasingly mobile. The debate is not a new one and the tax competition literature as far back as the 1950s (Tiebout, 1956) already mentioned the possibility for voters to 'vote with their feet' so as to choose their preferred combination of tax contribution and provision of local public services across competing local jurisdictions. In the mid-1980s, both Zodrow and Mieszkowski (1986) and Wilson (1986) derived in a formal way the dynamics and the consequences of tax competition in what have come to be known as the basic models of tax competition. In their models, tax competition for mobile tax bases leads to a 'race to the bottom' in tax rates and leaves the competing jurisdictions with too little revenue to be able to provide public services at a socially optimal level. This basic result has also led to the fundamental question whether capital taxation – and for that matter corporate taxation – can survive in the long run (Gordon, 1992; Mintz, 1994; Weichenrieder, 2005).

8.5.2 What do theories of tax competition tell us?

Notwithstanding the findings of the basic models mentioned above, the consequences of tax competition depend on a complex range of features (for a complete discussion, see Wilson, 1999; Krogstrup, 2003; Zodrow, 2003; Wilson and Wildasin, 2004). Over the last 20 years, economic research has attempted to remove the strict assumptions of the basic models of tax competition[3] and has come up with a more finely contrasted picture, which suggests that tax competition does not necessarily lead to a 'race to the bottom', and that any calculation of the potential consequences needs to take into account the public expenditure side of the problem, as well as various other characteristics, for example the availability of corrective mechanisms across jurisdictions such as subsidies that can substitute for the need to compete for capital (Wildasin, 1989) or the capacity of tax policy to influence the after-tax rate of return on capital (Wildasin, 1988). The degree of (a)symmetry in the size of countries (Bucovetsky, 1991) or asymmetries in endowment of factors (Wilson, 1991; Kanbur and Keen, 1993) between jurisdictions will also influence the outcome of tax competition. Geographical location and the extent of concentration of production may lead to different optimal levels of taxation between regions, for example in a core-periphery model (Kind et al., 2000; Baldwin and Krugman, 2004). In addition, the existence of trade between the members of a union (Wilson, 1987) or with the rest of the world (Janeba and Wilson, 1999) may lead to specialization and hence different equilibrium levels of taxation. The availability of multiple tax instruments besides capital taxation (Bucovetsky and Wilson, 1991), the existence of economies of scale in public service provision (Wilson, 1995), international spillovers in public goods (Bjorvatn and Schjelderup, 2002), and the possibility for the public sector to provide public input goods that will either reduce the private cost of production (Keen and Marchand, 1997) or reduce income uncertainty via redistribution (Wilson, 1995) are also elements that will influence the effects of tax competition. Obviously, the degree of mobility of the factor(s) of production (Lee, 1997; Brueckner, 2000; Wildasin, 2003), the complementarities between mobile and immobile factors (Lee, 1997), a possible home bias in investment (Ogura, 2006), the degree of citizens' demand for social insurance (Persson and Tabellini, 1992), the presence of cross-border loss offset (Gérard and Weiner, 2003), and the possibility to export the tax burden to foreigners (Mintz, 1994; Huizinga and Nielsen, 1997, 2002;

Wildasin, 2003) are further features that will determine the equilibrium effect of tax competition.

Finally, there is an unresolved debate in the economic literature about the merits and demerits of tax competition, with the so-called Leviathan models finding a useful role for tax competition in curbing the tendency of governments to overextend the size of the public sector (Brennan and Buchanan, 1980; Edwards and Keen, 1996).

8.5.3   How well does the European Union fit the theory?

Very few papers have sought to assess which of the features of tax competition models described above best fit the European Union. Zodrow (2003, p. 660) underlined the basic difficulty of assessing the combined effect of some of these features since the economic literature 'typically focus[es] on only one or two of the economic effects of tax competition'. Such an assessment is therefore highly speculative at this stage and more research on this issue is badly needed.[4] Assuming that Member States do in fact compete over corporate taxes, some broad predictions can be made.

On the one hand, some features of the EU may theoretically mitigate the adverse effects of corporate tax competition on the provision of public goods and the race to the bottom predicted by the basic models, thus decreasing the need for policy coordination. The existence of a core-periphery model with some agglomeration forces, for example, is one element that may explain why large core countries may sustain a higher tax rate than small countries at the periphery. One can also assume that there are economies of scale in the provision of public goods and that hence the problems of underprovision decrease with the size of the population. The large differences in preferences across Europe coupled with a relative home bias in investment and an increasing (albeit still small) mobility of labor are other European characteristics that may also play a role.

On the other hand, the absence of large-scale redistribution policies at the EU level,[5] and hence of corrective subsidies, a relatively widespread European taste for social protection, the general absence of a consolidated tax base for pan-European companies, and the increased mobility of capital are possible reasons why tax coordination would be desirable. The existence of trade has ambiguous effects. On the one hand, trade between Member States may lead to specialization patterns and reinforce the inefficiency costs of tax competition but, on the other, the existence of trade with the rest of the world allows for an elastic supply of capital and mitigates these costs.

Two other features of the European Union are also interesting in this debate. First, it has a mix of large and small Member States. Theory predicts that, in equilibrium, large Member States choose higher taxes on the mobile factor (capital) than small ones. This is mainly because, while taxation increases the required pre-tax rate of return on capital, capital outflows will have a negative impact on the world after-tax rate of return on capital and, in states that are large enough for these outflows to be substantial, the second effect will mitigate the first. Large countries therefore face a lower elasticity of capital than small countries. This prediction is empirically confirmed by Huizinga and Nicodème (2006), whose regressions show a significant and robust positive relationship between the tax burden faced by companies and the size of their residence country measured by the logarithm of GDP, although Euroframe (2005) did not find strong evidence of this. In addition, the possibility of exporting the tax burden to foreign owners may also influence the pattern of corporate taxation in the European Union. Sørensen (2000) evaluated the potential gains from international tax policy coordination using a simulation model characterized by partial foreign ownership and an absence of residence-based capital income taxes. His sensitivity analysis showed that reducing foreign ownership from 25% to zero lowers the uncoordinated and coordinated average capital income tax rates from 33.8% to 23% and from 46.5% to 41% respectively. However, he did not consider the opposite case. Huizinga and Nicodème (2006) used firm-level financial data for 21 European countries for the period 1996–2000. They found that in 2000 foreign ownership in Europe stood at about 21.5%. They investigated the effects of foreign ownership on the tax burden of companies, using simultaneously a firm-level and a macro-level foreign ownership variable, alongside a wide range of controls. They found a strong and robust positive relationship between the macro-level foreign ownership variable and the tax burden. Their benchmark results suggested that an increase in the foreign ownership share by 1% would lead to an increase in the average corporate income tax rate by between 0.5% and 1%.[6] This suggests that company tax policies in Europe are in part motivated by the desire to export corporate tax burdens. In the decades to come, foreign ownership can be expected to increase in the European Union and thus might mitigate any 'race to the bottom' in corporate tax burdens.

Finally, the question of 'Leviathan' behavior by European governments remains unsolved. Although the effect of Leviathans is potentially larger in a European Union, there has been very little research in Europe on whether such behavior has been at play. One of the main difficulties is that tax competition leads to a reduction in the size of the government in both the Zodrow–Mieszkowski model and the Leviathan model, making them difficult to distinguish from an empirical perspective (Wilson and Wildasin, 2004).

8.5.4   Do European Member States compete on tax rates?

A more basic question is whether EU Member States compete over corporate taxes at all. Over the last 25 years, Europe has experienced declining statutory tax rates for both mobile bases and less mobile ones. As documented in Table 8.1, statutory corporate tax rates have sharply declined in most of the 25 EU Member

Table 8.1   Statutory corporate tax rates (including local taxes and surcharges)

Statutory corporate tax rates (including local taxes and surcharges)	1980	1990	1995	2000	2005
Austria	55	39	34	34	25
Belgium	48	41	40.17	40.17	33.99
Cyprus	n.a.	42.5	25	29	10
Czech Republic	n.a.	n.a.	41	31	26
Denmark	n.a.	40	34	32	30
Estonia	n.a.	n.a.	26	26	24
Finland	59	41	25	29	26
France	50	37	36.67	36.67	34.93
Germany	52.8	57.7	56.8	51.63	38.29
Greece	43.4	46	40	40	35
Hungary	n.a.	50	19.64	19.64	17.68
Ireland	45	43	40	24	12.5
Italy	36.3	41.8	52.2	41.25	37.25
Latvia	n.a.	n.a.	25	25	15
Lithuania	n.a.	35	29	24	15
Luxembourg	n.a.	39.4	40.9	37.45	30.38
Malta	n.a.	32.5	35	35	35
Netherlands	48	35	35	35	31.5
Poland	n.a.	40	40	30	19
Portugal	n.a.	36.5	39.6	35.2	27.5
Slovak Rep.	n.a.	n.a.	40	29	19
Slovenia	n.a.	n.a.	25	25	25
Spain	33	35	35	35	35
Sweden	n.a.	40	28	28	28
UK	52	34	33	30	30
EU-15 average	n.a.	40.4	38.0	35.3	30.4
New Member States-10 average	n.a.	n.a.	30.6	24.8	18.2

Source: IBFD (2005) and own calculations. Estonia: 0% on retained earnings.

States and so have tax rates on interest income and financial wealth (Schjelderup, 2002; Huizinga and Nicodème, 2004). The issue of a 'race to the bottom', putting pressure on the financing of the welfare state and leading to a shift of the tax burden from capital to labor, has been taken very seriously at both the EU and the OECD levels. In the European Union, the issue was discussed at the informal ECOFIN Council in Verona in April 1996 and led to the publication in 1999 of a code of conduct for business taxation based on the work of a group of national experts led by Dawn Primarolo of the UK Treasury. The report (Primarolo, 1999) – based on a nonbinding peer-review exercise – identified 66 tax measures with harmful features which Member States agreed to revise or replace. However, while specific regimes were targeted, the report did not consider low statutory rates 'harmful'.[7]

One important question is of course whether the decline in corporate tax rates is the result of tax competition and whether there is a 'race to the bottom' under way. Since the seminal work of Case et al. (1993) and in the context of evolving estimating and modeling techniques (Brueckner, 2003), several authors have tried to estimate whether jurisdictions of various natures were setting taxes in an inter-dependent fashion. In particular, Devereux et al. (2003) and Redoano (2004) found some evidence of strategic interaction in corporate tax setting for the OECD between 1992 and 2002 and for the EU-25 from 1980 to 1995. Looking at the issue of capital mobility, Krogstrup (2003) found a positive relationship between an index of capital mobility and the tax burden in 13 European countries. The effect of capital mobility seems to be confirmed by Besley et al. (2001), who used tax reaction functions for five different taxes in the OECD between 1965 and 1997, finding that tax setting was generally interdependent and became more so with a more mobile tax base. In particular, they found more interdependence amongst EU countries than between EU and non-EU countries.

There is, however, no strong evidence in the literature of the reason for this interaction – that is, whether it is the result of tax competition to attract mobile tax bases, yardstick tax competition in which countries try to mimic each other's tax policy to seek the votes of informed voters (Besley and Case, 1995), or simply convergence across countries in economic structures and/or dominant economic thinking (Slemrod, 2004). In addition, with the exception of Besley et al. (2001), all studies used statutory or forward-looking effective tax rates[8] (themselves very dependent on statutory rates). These results were recently challenged by Stewart and Webb (2006), who looked at the evolution of corporate tax burdens – measured as corporate tax collected on GDP and on total taxes – in the OECD countries between 1950 and 1999. Based on both a descriptive and a cointegration analysis, the authors found no evidence of a race to the bottom and little evidence of a

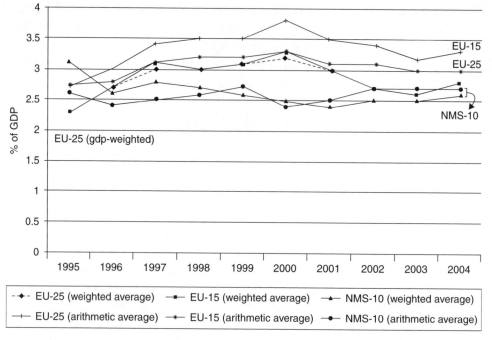

Figure 8.3   Taxes on incomes of corporations as percentage of GDP (1995–2004).
Source: Structures of Taxation Systems. DG TAXUD

harmonization of the tax burden. We are therefore left with the finding already made by Slemrod (2004) of a negative association between measures of openness and statutory rates, but not revenues collected. This is apparent from the evolution of corporate tax collected on GDP, which is relatively stable at around 3%. It may reflect the fact that tax competition decreases the rate of taxation per unit of investment, but also allows countries to attract a large corporate tax base (Lassen and Sørensen, 2002). It certainly also reflects a general trend towards lower statutory rates – a trend currently also noticeable in personal income taxes – but counterbalanced by a widening of corporate tax bases.[9] There is in fact no obvious relationship between the cuts in corporate statutory tax rates between 1995 and 2004, and the evolution of revenues collected from this tax. Figure 8.4 indeed suggests that – broadly speaking – the new Member States that have cut their rates have lost corporate tax revenues as a percentage of GDP, while most EU-15 countries that have done likewise have seen their revenue grow.

To conclude, both the theoretical and the empirical literature are rather inconclusive on the effects and the extent of corporate tax competition in the European

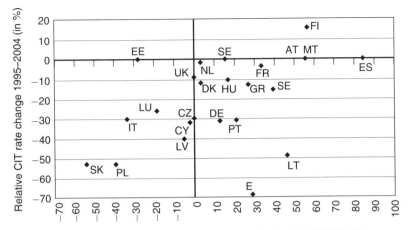

Figure 8.4   Evolution of corporate tax rates and revenue as percentage of GDP (1995–2004).
Source: European Commission and own calculations

Union. This ambiguity has of course translated into the political debate and is reflected in the tax proposals made by the European Commission.

8.6   The corporate taxation debate in the European Union: The early proposals

The debate over EU corporate tax harmonization is not new. One should keep in mind that a similar debate was previously held on taxation of capital (interest and dividend payments) with parallel arguments and that the first formal proposals to harmonize or coordinate corporate tax systems in Europe date from as far back as the early 1960s, when the fiscal and financial committee set up by the Commission and chaired by Professor Fritz Neumark proposed in July 1962 – after two years of work – to gradually harmonize tax systems in Europe, starting with turnover taxes and then doing the same with direct taxes with a split-rate system. However, the proposal was not followed by policy action. In 1970, another committee chaired by Professor Van den Tempel analyzed the various tax systems in place in the Member States and recommended that all adopt the classical system.[10] This proposal came shortly after the Werner Report on economic and monetary union in Europe, which stressed that tax harmonization should accompany the creation of a monetary union. Two Council resolutions followed in 1971 and 1972 which agreed that it was necessary to proceed with fiscal harmonization. Driven by this momentum, the European Commission proposed in 1975 to harmonize the corporate tax rates between 45% and 55% (Radaelli and Kraemer, 2005).[11] Interestingly, this proposal was challenged in 1979 by the European Parliament, whose agenda (as set out in the Nyborg Report) was to harmonize tax bases before tax rates. Measures to do just that were incorporated in a 1988 proposal by the European Commission but, because of the strong opposition of some Member States, it was never formally sent to the Council. According to Radaelli (1997), the harmonization of corporate taxation in Europe slowed down from 1989, when Commissioner Christiane Scrivener took the taxation portfolio, as she preferred to focus on fighting double taxation – notably in cross-border operations of companies and in taxation of savings – and stressed the need for subsidiarity. The 1975 proposal was withdrawn in 1990. The next step took place in 1992, when another committee, this time chaired by Onno Ruding, was given a mandate to look at whether differences in corporate taxes distorted investment decisions. The committee proposed some minimum standards in corporate tax bases and a band for tax rates of between 30% and 40% (Ruding Report, 1992). However, once again, this proposal was also not translated into political action.

During all these years, the European Commission was battling on two fronts (Radaelli and Kraemer, 2005). First, it had to solve the problem of tax evasion, not only to low-tax third countries, but also and foremost within the European Union, where savings of nonresident European were generally untaxed. Second, it had to overcome the problem of tax obstacles to the Single Market. These concerns led to proposals on the taxation of savings and on the taxation of various cross-border operations.

8.7 The corporate taxation debate in the European Union: The 2001 Communication

The prospects for more coordination in corporate taxation were revived in 2001, when the European Commission issued a communication on company taxation in the Single Market (European Commission, 2001a). The communication was accompanied by a study on the level, dispersion, and determinants of corporate effective tax rates in the EU-15, and itself made concrete policy proposals based on the identification of a series of tax obstacles to the completion of the Single Market, the presence of excessive tax administrative costs, double-taxation problems and other tax-related difficulties for companies doing business on a Europe-wide basis.

8.7.1   Comprehensive and targeted solutions

The study used forward-looking marginal and average effective corporate tax rates for domestic and cross-border investment in 1999 and 2001 (to analyze the effect of the 2000 German tax reform). It found a wide dispersion of these rates in Europe as the average effective tax rate varies, for example from 10.5% in Ireland to 34.9% in Germany. The report did not study the impact of this dispersion on investment patterns in Europe, nor did it assess the welfare effects. However, it provided static simulations of the effect of policy changes on the dispersion of the effective rates. Its main conclusion was that effective rates are mainly influenced by statutory rates and that harmonizing the latter would significantly reduce dispersion. In contrast, several of the policy changes in the tax base it looked at would have little effect in harmonizing effective tax rates and would even increase their dispersion – if, for example, Home State Taxation or the Common Consolidated Corporate Tax Base (see below) were implemented.

The European Commission's policy recommendation was a two-track approach to tackle the tax obstacles to cross-border economic activity in the Internal Market (for an insightful presentation and discussion of the report, see Devereux, 2004). First, some so-called targeted solutions aimed to refresh some pieces of EU legislation in order to deal with specific situations not foreseen by the legislator or to widen their scope of action. For example, the new European Company Statute was integrated into the 1990 Parent–Subsidiary Directive and the 1990 Merger Directive.[12] Second, the Commission put on the table four so-called comprehensive solutions for harmonizing corporate tax bases in Europe:

(a)   An EU corporate income tax (with full harmonization of rates and bases).
(b)   A compulsory harmonized method to compute the tax base.
(c)   The same harmonized method to compute tax bases but made optional (Common Corporate Consolidated Tax Base, hereafter CCCTB).
(d)   The system of Home State Taxation (whereby subsidiaries follow the same rules as their parent company, wherever they are located).

At the ECOFIN Meeting in September 2004, a large majority of Member States agreed that it would be useful to progress towards a common base, with an emphasis on reducing the administrative burden resulting from the existence of 25 systems. It was decided that a working party, chaired by the European Commission, would be created to look at the issue of harmonization of the tax bases (i.e. solution c).[13] It is now doing so and, depending on the support of Member States, hopes to come up with a legislative proposal in 2008. It should also be noted that, despite the well-known reluctance of some Member States, no Member State actually declined the invitation to participate in the working party. The prospects for harmonizing the tax bases will depend on the success of this work and of course the political willingness of Member States to apply its results. At this stage, no one can predict the outcome and all options remain open: A comprehensive agreement, a solution adopted through enhanced cooperation, or no agreement at all.[14]

The comprehensive solutions seek to tackle particular tax obstacles to cross-border activities, to reduce the compliance cost of dealing with 25 different tax systems, and to improve the competitiveness of European companies while preserving the public finances of the Member States. Two particular tax obstacles were widely reviewed in the 2001 report of the European Commission, leading to policy intervention: Cross-border loss relief and transfer pricing.

8.7.2 Cross-border loss relief in the European Union

As documented in Table 8.2, there are wide variations in the treatment of intragroup losses across Europe. Several Member States (Belgium, Czech Republic, Estonia, Greece, Hungary, Lithuania, Slovak Republic) do not offer any possibility to offset losses occurring in one member of a group against the profit of another domestic member of the same group. Other countries offer this possibility, either by specifically allowing group loss relief or by organizing tax consolidation. However, the applicable holding thresholds vary from 50% to 100% and some countries offer the possibility to offset foreign losses while others totally preclude it. These differences may presumably influence corporate location and create a home bias in investment, as domestic losses may be easier to offset than foreign ones.

A consolidated corporate tax base, such as the CCCTB, would take care of this problem. However, as we have seen above, designing such a base takes time and energy. It is not surprising that, in the meantime, the business community has legally challenged the difference of treatment between domestic and foreign loss relief. In December 2005, a decision by the European Court of Justice, ruling on a case brought by the retail company Marks & Spencer against the UK tax authorities (case C-446/03), stated that the fact that Marks & Spencer was not allowed to offset the losses of its Belgian, German, and French subsidiaries against its profit in the UK was not compatible with Articles 43 EC and 48 EC (which enshrine the concept of the EU as a single market), insofar as the subsidiaries had exhausted

Table 8.2   Fiscal consolidation in European Member States, 2005

Countries	Rules for fiscal consolidation of subsidiaries
Austria	Fiscal consolidation if holding 50%
Belgium	No fiscal consolidation
Cyprus	No fiscal consolidation but group losses relief if holding 75%
Czech Republic	No fiscal consolidation
Denmark	Fiscal consolidation if holding 50% + one vote, extendable to foreign subsidiaries
Estonia	No fiscal consolidation
Finland	Fiscal consolidation if holding 90%
France	Fiscal consolidation if holding 50%, extendable to foreign subsidiaries
Germany	Domestic fiscal consolidation if holding 50%
Greece	No fiscal consolidation
Hungary	No fiscal consolidation
Ireland	No fiscal consolidation but group losses relief possible if holding 75%
Italy	Domestic and worldwide fiscal consolidation if holding 50%
Latvia	No fiscal consolidation but domestic and EU-wide (or treaty partners) group losses relief possible if holding 90%
Lithuania	No fiscal consolidation
Luxembourg	Fiscal consolidation if holding 95%
Malta	No fiscal consolidation but group loss relief possible if holding 51%.
The Netherlands	Fiscal consolidation if holding 95%, extendable to foreign companies under conditions
Poland	Fiscal consolidation if holding 95%
Portugal	Fiscal consolidation if holding 90%
Slovak Republic	No fiscal consolidation
Slovenia	Fiscal consolidation if holding 90%
Spain	Fiscal consolidation if holding 75%
Sweden	Fiscal consolidation if holding 90%
UK	No fiscal consolidation but group loss relief possible if holding 75%

Source: IBFD (2005). Note that all fiscal consolidation schemes are optional.

all possibilities available in their respective state of residence to deduct losses and no possibilities remained for those losses to be taken into account in the future, either by the subsidiary or by a third party. Although the ruling does not go as far as allowing companies to freely practice cross-border loss offsetting, the decision is a step towards ending discrimination.

The absence of cross-border consolidation is a major problem in the European Union. Implementing cross-border loss relief could, as shown by Gérard and Weiner (2003), improve the situation by mitigating tax competition. The 1991 proposal for a directive on this issue (European Commission, 1991) received favorable opinion from the European Parliament but was never discussed by the European Council. It was withdrawn by the European Commission in December 2001 because it was thought that some technicalities needed revision and that a more comprehensive proposal would be desirable.

8.7.3 Transfer pricing and profit shifting in the European Union

Transfer pricing is the second issue tackled by the European Commission (2001a). The report stressed the increasing differences between the transfer prices calculated for tax purposes and the underlying commercial rationale. It also pointed to the high compliance costs imposed by the Member States in the form of documentation requirements, the differences and uncertainty of the treatment of those operations by national tax authorities, the lack of use of the arbitration convention (90/436/EEC), and the subsequent double taxation. The report estimated that '*medium-sized multinational enterprises spend approximately €1–2 million a year on complying with transfer pricing rules*' and that '*large multinational enterprises incur compliance costs related to transfer pricing of approximately €4 up to 5.5 million a year. These figures do not include the costs and risks of double taxation due to transfer pricing disputes*' (European Commission, 2001a, p. 343). To overcome these difficulties, the European Commission has proposed to establish a Code of Conduct to standardize the documentation that companies must provide to tax authorities on their pricing of cross-border intra-group transactions (European Commission, 2004a). This is a first result of the work of the EU Joint Transfer Pricing Forum, which brings together business and tax administration representatives. The Code was adopted by the Member States in December 2004, and also stipulates time limits for dealing with complaints and the suspension of tax collection during the dispute resolution. The Code effectively and coherently implements across Member States the EU's Arbitration Convention, which was originally proposed in 1976 and signed in July 1990 (European Commission, 1990).

Devereux (2004) rightly pointed out the dichotomy between the European Commission's 2001 report, which is concerned with double taxation and compliance costs for companies, and the economic literature, which considers the issue rather in terms of profit shifting across jurisdictions and the subsequent tax revenue losses.[15] Profit shifting can take several forms. First, companies can decide to locate their production – and therefore their profit – in low-tax jurisdictions. Gérard (2005) showed that multinationals' decisions both on location and on whether to opt for a foreign subsidiary or a foreign permanent establishment will severely impact the total tax burden. It is well known from the economic literature that taxes do affect business location decisions, although they may be only a second-order determinant (Devereux and Griffith, 1998b; Grubert, 2003; Devereux and Lockwood, 2006), as well as the location of foreign direct investment.

Empirically, de Mooij and Everdeen (2003) carried out a meta-analysis based on a sample of 371 estimates taken from 25 studies in the economic literature. They reported a median value of −3.3 and an average value of −2.4 for the tax semi-elasticity of FDI.[16] For new plants and plant extensions, the average semi-elasticity jumps to −5.7. There is wide variation in estimates across studies. This is due to different choices in terms of both the tax variable and the variable chosen to depict FDI or capital flows. This uncertainty led Devereux and Griffith (2002) to conclude that *the existing literature provides little by way of policy-relevant insights.*

The second broad category of profit shifting consists of the manipulation of the pricing of cross-border intra-group transactions. This tax avoidance practice is of course easier in the absence of reference prices, as is the case for a large range of intangible assets such as patents. The effects of exploiting this asymmetry of infor-mation have been examined by several authors. In particular, Clausing (1993, 2003) and Swenson (2001) both found evidence in the USA of tax-motivated income shifting behavior through the manipulation of intra-group transaction prices. Barteslman and Beetsma (2003) found similar evidence, using sectoral value-added data for 22 OECD countries between 1979 and 1997.

The third broad channel of profit shifting is linked to debt shifting within groups. In most countries, interest payments are tax deductible. Further, these payments are subject to light, often zero, withholding tax rates and benefit from an exemption or a tax credit system in the country of the company receiving the interest payment. There is strong evidence that taxation affects companies' financial policy (MacKie-Mason, 1990; Weichenrieder, 1996; Alworth and Arachi, 2001; Gordon and Lee, 2001; Altshuler and Grubert, 2003; Ramb and Weichenrieder, 2005). Using firm-level data for companies and their subsidiaries located in 31 European countries for the period 1999–2004, Huizinga et al. (2006) found that corporate debt policy reflects national tax features and international differ-ences in taxes, suggesting that debt shifting is an important phenomenon in Europe. To counteract this practice, several Member States have implemented thin capitalization rules that prevent companies from overloading their foreign affili-ates with debt. The characteristics of these rules vary widely across countries and there is, up to now, very little research on whether these rules have had a significant effect on reported profit.

These international profit-shifting practices lead to a negative relationship between reported profit and the tax burden, which is confirmed by multiple studies (Grubert and Mutti, 1991; Hines and Rice, 1994; Grubert and Slemrod, 1998; Bartelsman and Beetsma, 2003, among others). Interestingly, Grubert (1993) reported that the reactivity of reported profit to taxes has been unchanged despite the globalization trends in the 1980s. Profit shifting presumably leads to tax revenue losses because of lower reported taxable income. At the same time, the economic literature has mentioned two mitigating effects. Mintz and Smart (2004) showed that income shifting may decrease the responsiveness of real investment to taxes. In other words, because the tax burden can be decreased via profit shifting, companies do not feel so much pressure to relocate their activities and thus keep their headquarters and jobs in the high-tax country. The same idea is developed by Gordon and MacKie-Mason (1995), for whom income shifting, both cross-border (through transfer pricing) and domestic (through the decision to incorporate or not), softens the race to the bottom predicted by economic theory. The total net effect is, however, certainly a decrease in tax revenues – as the last two effects only mitigate and do not reverse the tax minimization strategy – though its size is uncertain.

8.7.4   How should the comprehensive solutions be implemented?

Several implementation issues were discussed in the 2001 Communication. Here, we look at three that may have a significant impact on the design of a possible common consolidated tax base. The first one refers to the scope of companies to which the common tax base would apply. One question that arose was therefore whether the new European Company Statute (Societas Europaea, SE) could serve as a pilot for the implementation of a new tax base. The SE is a long-awaited legal form available for companies that merge or create a holding or joint subsidiary. It should facilitate cross-border EU restructuring. However, it does not as yet contain provisions regarding taxation, other than national ones. Although the 2001 report indicates that the SE could be a suitable vehicle for a pilot or test case, the most recent discussions have not taken up the issue further.

A second point concerns the use of the International Financial Reporting Standards (IFRS, formerly International Accounting Standards, or IAS). The IAS Regulation requires listed companies to prepare their consolidated accounts in accordance with these standards from 2005 onwards (see European Commission,

2003a). Because it consists of some form of harmonization of accounting standards, some scholars have wondered whether the IFRS could usefully serve as a level playing field for harmonizing tax bases. CEPS (2005) provides a detailed study of the extent to which IFRS are compatible with tax principles and, despite mentioning some difficulties with some fair value accounting practices for some assets and liabilities, the CEPS report concludes that there is broad compatibility.[17] The European Commission (2001a, 2005b) is more cautious, in that it views IFRS as a tool to guide discussions and definitions but does not want to be bound by rules that are primarily designed for reporting purposes and may constantly be changing.

Finally, a last point regarding the implementation of the comprehensive solutions is the need to allocate profit across jurisdictions. Probably one of the most difficult and important issues is that of formula apportionment, namely the question of how to allocate a common tax base – once it has been defined – across the various jurisdictions that will then apply different tax rates to their share of the base, with consequences on companies' tax liability and hence countries' tax revenues. The USA, Canada, Germany, and Switzerland are examples of federations that have implemented such systems. For example, the formula in the USA is based on property, payroll, and sales, but each state has the freedom to change the tax rates, the weights of each factor, and the definition of taxable profit. However, this leads to many complexities and difficulties (see McLure and Weiner, 2000; Weiner, 2002a, 2006; Hallerstein and McLure, 2004). The trick is to find a formula whose factors cannot be manipulated by companies or the States but that still reflects the factors that generated the profit. Several problems arise with formula apportionment (see Weiner, 2002b). First, it can be demonstrated that the system tends to transform corporate income tax into a tax on the factors included in the formula. Second, if the factors are firm-specific, formula apportionment distorts firms' decisions. In addition, states have an incentive to manipulate the formula. For example, they can decrease the weight of labor to attract labor-intensive activities. This means that tax competition on the location of both real activities and profit remains. Furthermore, as long as an activity is profitable when aggregated for all locations, States can also try to attract activities – even though they would be nonprofitable in their territory – just to increase their share of the global tax base. The formula apportionment mechanism therefore acts as an insurance or risk-sharing mechanism (Buettner, 2002; Gérard and Weiner, 2003). Finally, distortions to investment location are still present with formula apportionment whether it is applied to a common consolidated corporate tax base or to home state taxation (Mintz and Weiner, 2003). All this suggests that the system requires a large degree of harmonization of the tax base, but that even this may not be sufficient to solve all problems. Using value-added tax for formula apportionment is not problem-free either, because a workable system seems to require an origin-based VAT system to include exports (Weiner, 2002a, b), something the European Union has not (yet) implemented.

8.8   What are the gains from coordination?

The bottom line of our review of the theoretical and empirical literature on tax competition and tax coordination is that it is a complex and multifaceted topic, and one that is difficult to analyze in a comprehensive framework. Nevertheless, the effects of tax coordination need to be quantified. Various attempts to do so – albeit with different focuses – have been made in the literature. The European Commission (2001a) used the Tax Analyzer Model to assess the effects of harmonization of tax rates and/or bases on the dispersion of effective tax rates and found that a significant decrease in this dispersion is only achieved in the tax rate harmonization scenario. Several recent attempts have been made with models that try to capture the essence of the complex setting. Mendoza and Tesar (2003a, b, 2005) used a dynamic[18] two-region (UK and Continental Europe, calibrated as France, Germany, and Italy) model with perfect mobility of financial capital and the presence of several types of externalities of national tax policy (i.e. impact on terms of trade, on capital accumulation, and on tax base erosion). The authors simulated capital tax competition, which triggers an adjustment of either labor or consumption taxes to adjust the budgets. The respective net welfare gains of tax coordination in these two simulations are respectively equal to 0.26% and 0.04% of lifetime consumption (Mendoza and Tesar, 2005).

Sørensen (2000, 2001, 2004a, b) used a static (i.e. describing a stationary long-run equilibrium) model of tax competition for the Member States of the EU-15 with – inter alia – countries of different sizes, different earnings across individuals, partial foreign ownership, the presence of lump-sum transfers, imperfect capital mobility, and aggregated national welfare functions that incorporate both the level of domestic citizens' welfare and some degree of social preference for redistribution. His simulations showed EU-average welfare gains from tax coordination ranging from 0.18% to 0.94% of GDP. This potential gain from coordinating corporate taxes in Europe increases to 1.42% of GDP for the scenario where the marginal public revenue is spent on public goods and not on transfers. In addition, the above-mentioned welfare gains are those of the median voter, but the simulations showed that the gains for the poorest quintile are actually much higher.

Parry (2003) used a model to assess the welfare losses of tax competition and introduced, as additional scenarios, possibilities of capital flight from the EU, a Leviathan behavior with large states capable of influencing the after-tax rate of return on capital, and noncompetitive governments (i.e. governments that are less likely to cut taxes, knowing that others may imitate them). He set the value of welfare costs of tax competition that he considered 'significant' at 5% of capital tax revenues (corresponding to about 0.25–0.75% of GDP). His benchmark result showed that this value is reached for a tax elasticity of capital between 0.3 and 0.9. He then unlocked the capital supply elasticity at the EU level and allowed it to increase to 0.5 and 1 (i.e. capital can progressively flee the EU). These scenarios respectively reduce the welfare gains of coordination by about 25% and 50%. The 'Leviathan' scenario unsurprisingly reduced the welfare gains (although capital taxation may be too low or too high depending on the parameters of the model). The same applied for the scenario of noncompetitive governments. The magnitude of these results was broadly confirmed by a study commissioned by the European Commission from Copenhagen Economics (2004), in which the various scenarios of full harmoniza-tion, and harmonization of the bases with or without a minimum rate and/or equal-yield constraints delivered welfare gains between 0.02% and 0.21% of GDP. Potential positive gains were also found by Beltendorf et al. (2006) and van der Horst et al. (2006) in two joint studies looking respectively at tax rates harmonization and consolidation and formula apportionment.

The gains may appear relatively small at first sight – and have been depicted as such by several authors – but they are actually positive (meaning that there are potential welfare gains in coordinating corporate taxes) and are as large as those expected from some other important EU policies. A 0.5% welfare gain as a mean value from Sørensen (2001) compares well with the 0.6–0.7% gain expected from the removal of all obstacles to the free movements of services stemming from the full implementation of the services directive (Copenhagen Economics, 2005a) and with the 0.5% GDP increase[19] expected from EU enlargement (European commission, 2001b). It also corresponds to more than one-fourth of the GDP increase (1.8%) attrib-utable to 10 years of the implementation of the Single Market Programme as esti-mated by the European Commission (2003b) (in line with the 1.1–1.5% GDP increase estimated for the effect of the SMP until 1994 (European Commission, 1996)).[20] This result includes the liberalization of network industries whose own effect is estimated at about 0.6% of GDP (although Copenhagen Economics (2005b) estimates the total EU welfare gain of liberalization of network industries at 1.9% of GDP).

Finally, it should be noted that these models are by definition a simplification of reality and do not capture a number of complicating factors (see Parry (2003) for a discussion of some of these). One important point, in light of the 2001 report from the European Commission, is that the models do not capture the welfare gains linked to the decrease in tax compliance and administrative burden that arise from the harmonization of the tax bases. Several factors, for example profit-shifting issues, are usually left out of the analysis. Huizinga and Laeven (2005), however, estimated that profit-shifting activities are substantial in Europe,[21] with Germany being the main loser as about one-third of the true profit is shifted out of Germany. The aggregate loss in tax collected for European governments represents as much as US$2.7 billion a year. Several other distortions, such as location, financial distortions, and income shifting, and their consequences on tax revenues, have also been reviewed by de Mooij (2005) in relation to the Dutch economy. The absence of cross-border loss offset and the transfer pricing issues have also not (yet) attracted the full attention of modelers.

8.9 Conclusion

Policy actions in corporate taxation at the EU level are relatively infrequent. This reflects both an institutional design that promotes subsidiarity in tax matters and rather ambiguous results as to both the existence and the likely effects of corporate tax competition in Europe. Although statutory rates have fallen over the last few decades, revenues collected from corporate income taxation have been remarkably stable as a percentage of GDP.

This does not, however, suggest that there is no need at all for any EU initiative. Several tax obstacles to the implementation of a truly integrated European market have been identified and there is empirical evidence of varying degrees of tax avoidance activities through relocation, the manipulation of transfer pricing, or profit shifting via thin capitalization. Among the comprehensive measures designed to tackle tax obstacles to cross-border activities in Europe, the European Commission (2001a) proposed a comprehensive agenda to work out an optional common consolidated corporate tax base for companies doing business in Europe.

The proposal presents several important technical difficulties that are currently being dealt with by a working group of national and European experts. It nevertheless promises a quite substantial potential welfare gain for the European Union, thanks to both the coordination of corporate tax policies and the reduced tax compliance costs that a common tax base would bring. Provided it is well designed, it would also bring additional benefits via cross-border fiscal consolidation and better transfer pricing resolutions, two aspects that are costly for both businesses and tax authorities. In addition, the proposal leaves untouched tax rates and hence tax competition – or possibly even reinforces it by making the tax base more transparent.

Ideally, designing a common consolidated corporate tax base offers the possibility to rethink the way we tax companies. Current systems in place in the European Union often lack desirable features. It is important that the European Union reflects on sound economic principles, such as neutrality across investors and sources of financing, equity across firms, simplicity, enforceability, and stability of revenues (Gorter and de Mooij, 2001; European Commission, 2004b; CEPS, 2005), and at the same time, reflect on how best to collect taxes (source-based versus residence-based taxation) and how best to integrate corporate taxation with personal income taxation. Obviously, there is as yet no obvious way to alleviate all distortions, since governments are faced with trade-offs in multiple dimensions. There are several alternative corporate tax systems with their merits and demerits (cashflow taxation, Allowance for Corporate Equity, Comprehensive Business Income Tax, Dual Income Tax, etc.) which deserve to be debated (for a discussion, see Cnossen, 2001; Devereux and Sørensen, 2005). The European Union may also want to reflect on profit-shifting issues, notably the size of the problem and possible remedies, such as thin capitalization rules (the CCCTB working group may start reviewing the issue in early 2007).

Finally, the European Union may also want to examine whether the absence of bilateral tax treaties between some Member States creates double-taxation problems and whether the current systems discriminate between domestic and nonresident investors when dividends are paid. This could potentially lead to an EU model tax convention or an EU multilateral treaty, which could also cover additional issues that create tax barriers but are not reviewed in this article – for instance, the taxation of workers having activity in several countries. In any case, the European Commission has announced that it will issue a Communication in 2006 to explain its strategy in this field. And important as these issues may be, they should not overshadow the overriding goal: To bring the work on a common consolidated tax base to fruition.

Acknowledgments

I thank Michel Aujean, Sophie Bland, Declan Costello, Marco Fantini, and Jean-Pierre De Laet for helpful comments. Remaining errors or omissions and the interpretations are those of the author only.

Notes

1. There may also be the feeling within Member States that, having lost monetary policy instruments, fiscal policy – although constrained by the 3% deficit rule of the Stability and Growth Pact – is one of the few macroeconomic policy tools, along with supply-side policies, left at their disposal.

2. Note that different levels of tax-to-GDP ratios are due to the different proportions of each economic function in GDP and hence do not necessarily reflect a higher taxation of labor. When reported as a share of their own tax base (instead of GDP), the same trends emerge, although in less pronounced form (the ratio for labor, for example, does not diminish as fast). In addition, the implicit rates on labor and on capital appear much closer. These rates are called the backward-looking macro-effective tax rates (or sometimes implicit tax rates).

3. Including large and homogeneous jurisdictions, perfectly competitive markets, jurisdictions that take as fixed the after-tax rate of return on capital and the tax rates in the other jurisdictions, fixed populations and land, identical preferences and incomes for all residents in each jurisdiction, fixed aggregate level of capital stock which is mobile, a single good produced by the capital and land factors, publicly provided private goods with no spillover effects, two local tax instruments, and maximization of welfare of identical residents (see Zodrow, 2003).

4. Note that the assessment becomes even more complicated if one takes into account the results of the tax literature on vertical tax competition (when, for example, the EU level would compete with Member States on the same tax base) and/or on partial tax coordination (as countries may also compete on other noncoordinated tax bases, for example mobile labor).

5. The annual EU 2006 budget amounts to €112 billion (1.01% of the Gross National Income (GNI) of the enlarged EU). About 40% of the budget goes to the Common Agricultural Policy and about another 40% goes to the poorer regions of the Union, to fishing communities, and to regions facing particular problems of high unemployment and industrial decline (European Commission, 2006b).

6. In addition, validating previous theoretical findings (in particular, Wildasin, 2003), their results indicate that this positive relationship between tax burden and foreign ownership is strongest for more mature economies and for sectors with less mobile companies.

7. Instead, the criteria for identifying potentially harmful measures include a significantly lower level of effective taxation than the general level in the country concerned, tax advantages reserved for nonresidents only, tax incentives for activities isolated from the domestic economy, nontraditional rules of taxation for multinational companies, and/or a lack of transparency.

8. This methodology uses the King–Fullerton methodology of taxation of a hypothetical investment using a mix of sources of finance. The method was further developed by Devereux and Griffith (1998a) and is different from backward-looking effective tax rates that use real-life data to compute ratios of tax paid on the tax base. For the respective merits and demerits of both methods, see Nicodème (2001).

9. Other studies point to the effects of tax exporting (Huizinga and Nicodème, 2006) and larger incorporation (Gordon and MacKie-Mason, 1997; Goolsbee, 1998, 2004; Fuest and Weichenrieder, 2002; de Mooij and Nicodème, 2006). It could also be possible that the tax yield is insensitive to the tax rates, possibly because profit-shifting strategies are so efficient and widespread that profit is already reported in low-tax jurisdictions.

10. That is, with taxation at both the corporate and shareholder levels without tax relief.

11. Following the 1971 Resolution from the Council asking the European Commission to propose measures regarding the harmonization of certain types of taxes which may have an influence on capital movements within the Community, the European Commission launched in 1975 a proposal for a directive that concerned both the harmonization of corporate taxation and withholding taxes on dividends. In particular, the Commission proposed a single corporate tax rate on all distributed and nondistributed profits, set at between 45% and 55%, and called for a 25% withholding tax on dividends.

12. In addition, the holding threshold from which the Parent–Subsidiary Directive applies was lowered from 25% to 10% and the Merger Directive was changed to cover the conversion of permanent establishments into subsidiaries.

13. The European Commission favors a consolidated and optional method (European Commission, 2006c). Note also that Home State Taxation (solution d) is proposed for SMEs, as this solution is politically easy to implement and just requires mutual recognition (European Commission, 2005a). However, several Member States are reluctant as this solution carries potential economic and technical problems.

14. In particular, it seems that some Member States fear that harmonization of the tax base will be done in such a way that the agreement would lead to small tax bases, forcing these countries to raise their rates to keep revenues constant. However, it is clear that for efficiency reasons the best option is a broad tax base. In addition, the level of taxation has not been, and will not be, part of the discussions. The European Commission has no plan to harmonize rates or impose a minimum statutory corporate tax rate. These elements are recognized in European Commission (2006c), which can be consulted for further information on recent developments in working out a CCCTB.

15. It is important to note, however, that the first preoccupation does not preclude the second, and that the profit-shifting issues are taken into consideration in the works of the CCCTB.

16. That is, a 1% increase in the host-country tax rate decreases FDI by 3.3% and 2.4% respectively. For the USA, Hines (1999) reported a 'consensus' elasticity of -0.6. In the case of Europe, Gorter and de Mooij (2001) found that intra-EU investment is more responsive to taxes than investment between the USA and Europe. Bénassy-Quéré et al. (2005) found nonlinearities in the impact of tax differentials as only positive tax differentials matter (i.e. disincentives) and, whilst exemption systems result in a linear reaction to tax differentials, credit systems provoke nonlinear reactions. Finally, Desai et al. (2004) and Buettner and Wamser (2006) showed that FDI is also very sensitive to other taxes faced by multinationals, including indirect taxes.

17. Several studies showed that the effect of adopting IFRS will be a broadening of the tax base (European Commission, 2001a, b; Haverals, 2005; Jacobs et al., 2005).

18. In the sense that they represent 'levels of lifetime utility', i.e. a long-run equilibrium – but the model does not include dynamic strategic interactions.

19. Conceptually, the welfare gain in percentage of GDP and the GDP gain are different. However, in the absence of a specific estimate for the former, the GDP increase can be used as a proxy.

20. The ex-ante estimates by Cecchini et al. (1988) gave a potential of between 3.2% and 5.7% GDP increase.

21. Their estimated macro semi-elasticity of reported profits with respect to the statutory tax rate is 1.43. Weichenrieder (2006) found similar results for Germany.

References

Altshuler, R. and Grubert, H. (2003). Repatriation Taxes, Repatriation Strategies and Multinational Financial Policy. *Journal of Public Economics*, 87(1):73–107.

Alworth, J. and Arachi, G. (2001). The Effect of Taxes on Corporate Financing Decisions: Evidence from a Panel of Italian Firms. *International Tax and Public Finance*, 8:353–376.

Aujean, M. (2005). Entre Harmonisation, Coordination et Coopération Renforcée: La Politique Fiscale dans l'Union Elargie. Speech delivered at the Conference *Per Una Costituzione Fiscale Europea*, 28–29 October.

Baldwin, R. and Krugman, P. (2004). Agglomeration, Integration and Tax Harmonisation. *European Economic Review*, 48:1–23.

Bartelsman, E.J. and Beetsma, R.M.W.J. (2003). Why Pay More? Corporate Tax Avoidance Through Transfer Pricing in OECD Countries. *Journal of Public Economics*, 87:2225–2252.

Bénassy-Quéré, A., Fontagné, L., and Lahrèche-Révil, A. (2005). How Does FDI React to Corporate Taxation? *International Tax and Public Finance*, 12:583–603.

Besley, T. and Case, A. (1995). Incumbent Behaviour: Vote Seeking, Tax Setting and Yardstick Competition. *American Economic Review*, 85(1):25–45.

Besley, T., Griffith, R., and Klemm, A. (2001). Empirical Evidence on Fiscal Interdependence in OECD Countries. Mimeograph.

Beltendorf, L., Gorter, J., and van der Horst, A. (2006). Who Benefits from Tax Competition in the European Union? CPB Working Paper, June.

Bjorvatn, K. and Schjelderup, G. (2002). Tax Competition and International Public Goods. *International Tax and Public Finance*, 9:111–120.

Brennan, G. and Buchanan, J. (1980). *The Power to Tax: Analytical Foundations of a Fiscal Constitution*. Cambridge University Press.

Brueckner, J.K. (2000). A Tiebout/Tax Competition Model. *Journal of Public Economics*, 77:285–306.

Brueckner, J. K. (2003). Strategic Interactions among Governments: An Overview of Empirical Studies. *International Regional Science Review*, 26(2):175–188.

Bucovetsky, S. (1991). Asymmetric Tax Competition. *Journal of Urban Economics*, 30:67–181.

Bucovetsky, S. and Wilson, J.D. (1991). Tax Competition with Two Tax Instruments. *Regional Science and Urban Economics*, 21:333–350.

Buettner, T. (2002). Fiscal Federalism and Interstate Risk Sharing: Empirical Evidence from Germany. *Economic Letters*, 74(2):195–202.

Buettner, T. and Wamser, G. (2006). The Impact of Non-profit Taxes on Foreign Direct Investment. Mimeograph, University of Munich. Paper presented at the European Tax Policy Forum Conference, *The Impact of Corporation Taxes Across Borders*, London, April.

Case, A., Rosen, H., and Hines, J. (1993). Budget Spillovers and Fiscal Policy Interdependence: Evidence from the States. *Journal of Public Economics*, 52(3):285–307.

Cecchini, P., Catinat, M., and Jacquemin, A. (1988). *The European Challenge 1992: The Benefits of a Single Market*. Wildwood House, Aldershot.

Centre for European Policy Studies (CEPS) (2005). Achieving a Common Consolidated Corporate Tax Base in the EU. In: *Report from the CEPS Task Force* (Gammie, M., Giannini, S., Klemm, A., Oestreicher, A., Parascandolo, P., and Spengel, C., eds). CEPS, Brussels.

Clausing, K.A. (1993). The Impact of Transfer Pricing on Intrafirm Trade. In: *Studies in International Taxation* (Giovannini, A., Hubbard, R.G., and Slemrod, J., eds). University of Chicago Press.

Clausing, K.A. (2003). Tax-motivated Transfer Pricing and US Intrafirm Trade Prices. *Journal of Public Economics*, 87:2207–2223.

Cnossen, S. (2001). *Tax Policy in the European Union: A Review of Issues and Options.* OCFEB, Rotterdam.

Copenhagen Economics (2004). *Economic Effects of Tax Coordination in an Enlarged European Union.*

Copenhagen Economics (2005a). *Economic Assessment of the Barriers to the Internal Market for Services.*

Copenhagen Economics (2005b). *Market Opening in Network Industries.*

De Mooij, R. (2005). Will Corporate Income Taxation Survive? *De Economist*, 153(3):277–301.

De Mooij, R. and Ederveen, S. (2003). Taxation and Foreign Direct Investment: A Synthesis of Empirical Research. *International Tax and Public Finance*, 10(6):673–693.

De Mooij, R. and Nicodème, G. (2006). Corporate Tax Policy, Entrepreneurship and Incorporation in the EU. *European Economy*. European Commission, forthcoming.

Desai, M.A., Foley, C.F., and Hines, J.R. (2004). Foreign Direct Investment in a World of Multiple Taxes. *Journal of Public Economics*, 88:2727–2744.

Devereux, M.P. (2004). Debating Proposed Reforms of the Taxation of Corporate Income in the European Union. *International Tax and Public Finance*, 11:71–89.

Devereux, M. and Griffith, R. (1998a). The Taxation of Discrete Investment Choices. Institute For Fiscal Studies Working Paper.

Devereux, M. and Griffith, R. (1998b). Taxes and the Location of Production: Evidence from a Panel of US Multinationals. *Journal of Public Economics*, 68:335–367.

Devereux, M. and Griffith, R. (2002). The Impact of Corporate Taxation on the Location of Capital: A Review. *Swedish Economic Policy Review*, 9:11–33.

Devereux, M.P. and Lockwood, B. (2006). Taxes and the Size of the Foreign-owned Capital Stock: Which Tax Rates Matter? Mimeograph, University of Warwick. Paper presented at the European Tax Policy Forum Conference, *The Impact of Corporation Taxes Across Borders*, London, April.

Devereux, M.P. and Sørensen, P.B. (2005). The Corporate Income Tax: International Trends and Options for Fundamental Reform. *EPRU Analysis*, No. 24, University of Copenhagen.

Devereux, M.P., Lockwood, B., and Redoano, M. (2003). Do Countries Compete over Corporate Tax Rates? CEPR Discussion Papers, 3400.

Edwards, J. and Keen, M. (1996). Tax competition and Leviathan. *European Economic Review*, 40:113–134.

Euroframe (2005). Economic Assessment of the Euro Area: Forecast and Policy Analysis. Special Policy Issue on The Future of Corporate Taxation in the EU. Autumn Report 2005.

European Commission (1990). Convention 90/436/EEC on the Elimination of Double Taxation in Connection with the Adjustment of Profits of Associated Enterprises. Official Journal, L 225, 20 August, p. 10.

European Commission (1991). Proposal for a Directive Concerning Arrangements for the Taking into Account by Enterprises of the Losses of their Permanent Establishment and Subsidiaries Situated in Other Member States. COM (1990) 595. Official Journal, C 53, 28 February, p. 30.

European Commission (1996). Economic Evaluation of the Internal Market. European Economy, 4.

European Commission (2001a). Company Taxation in the Internal Market. COM (2001) 582.

European Commission (2001b). The Economic Impact of Enlargement. Enlargement Papers, 4. DG for Economic and Financial Affairs.

European Commission (2003a). Commission Regulation (EC) No. 1725/2003, 29 September 2003, Adopting Certain International Accounting Standards in Accordance with Regulation (EC) No. 1606/2002 of the European Parliament and of the Council. Official Journal, L 261, 13 October, pp. 1–420.

European Commission (2003b). The Internal Market: Ten Years Without Frontiers, http://europa.eu.int/comm/internal_market/10years/docs/workingdoc/workingdoc_en.pdf.

European Commission (2004a). Communication from the Commission to the Council, the European Parliament and the European Economic and Social Committee on the Work of the EU Joint Transfer Pricing Forum in the Field of Business Taxation from October 2002 to December 2003 and on a Proposal for a Code of Conduct for the Effective Implementation of the Arbitration Convention (90/436/EEC, 23 July 1990). COM (2004) 297 final.

European Commission (2004b). Common Consolidated Corporate Tax Base Working Group: General Tax Principles. Working Document, November.

European Commission (2005a). Tackling the Corporation Tax Obstacles of Small and Medium-sized Enterprises in the Internal Market – Outline of a Possible Home State Taxation Pilot Scheme. COM (2005) 702.

European Commission (2005b). Common Consolidated Corporate Tax Base Working Group: Progress to Date and Future Plans for the CCCTB. Working Document, November.

European Commission (2006a). Structures of Taxation Systems in the European Union, forthcoming.

European Commission (2006b). Financial Programming and Budget. http://europa.eu.int/comm/budget/index_en.htm.

European Commission (2006c). Implementing the Community Lisbon Programme: Progress to Date and Next Steps Towards a Common Consolidated Corporate Tax Base (CCCTB). COM (2006) 157 final.

Fuest, C. and Weichenrieder, A. (2002). Tax Competition and Profit Shifting: On the Relationship between Personal and Corporate Tax Rates. *Ifo Studien: Zeitschrift fur Empirische Wirtshaftsforschung*, 48:611–632.

Gérard, M. (2005). Multijurisdictional Firms and Governments' Strategies under Alternative Tax Designs, CESifo WP 1527.

Gérard, M. and Weiner, J.M. (2003). Cross-border Loss Offset and Formulary Apportionment: How Do They Affect Multijurisdictional Firm Investment Spending and Interjurisdictional Tax Competition? CESifo Working Paper, No. 1004.

Goolsbee, A. (1998). Taxes, Organizational Form and the Deadweight Loss of the Corporate Income Tax. *Journal of Public Economics*, 69:143–152.

Goolsbee, A. (2004). The Impact of Corporate Income Tax: Evidence from State Organizational Form Data. *Journal of Public Economics*, 88:2283–2299.

Gordon, R.H. (1992). Can Capital Income Taxes Survive in Open Economies? *Journal of Finance*, 47:1159–1180.

Gordon, R.H. and Lee, Y. (2001). Do Taxes Affect Corporate Debt Policy? Evidence from US Corporate Tax Return Data. *Journal of Public Economics*, 82:195–224.

Gordon, R.H. and MacKie-Mason, J.K. (1995). Why is There Corporate Taxation in a Small Open Economy? In: *The Effects of Taxation on Multinational Corporations* (Feldstein, M., Hines, J.R., and Hubbard, G., eds). University of Chicago Press.

Gordon, R.H. and MacKie-Mason, J.K. (1997). How Much Do Taxes Discourage Incorporation? *Journal of Finance*, 52(2):477–505.

Gorter, J. and de Mooij, R. (2001). *Capital Income Taxation in the European Union: Trends and Trade-offs*. Sdu Publishers, The Hague.

Grubert, H. (1993). Tax Planning by Companies and Tax Competition by Governments: Is There Evidence of Changes in Behavior? In: *Studies in International Taxation* (Giovannini, A., Hubbard, R.G., and Slemrod, J., eds). University of Chicago Press.

Grubert, H. (2003). Intangible Income, Intercompany Transactions, Income Shifting, and the Choice of Location. *National Tax Journal*, 56(1):221–241.

Grubert, H. and Mutti, J. (1991). Taxes, Tariffs and Transfer Pricing in Multinational Corporation Decision Making. *Review of Economics and Statistics*, 33(2):285–293.

Grubert, H. and Slemrod, J. (1998). The Effect of Taxes on Investment and Income Shifting to Puerto Rico. *Review of Economics and Statistics*, 80(3):365–373.

Hallerstein, W. and McLure, C.E. (2004). The European Commission's Report on Company Income Taxation: What the EU Can Learn from the Experience of the US States. *International Tax and Public Finance*, 11:199–220.

Haverals, J. (2005). IAS/IFRS in Belgium: Quantitative Analysis on the Impact on the Tax Burden of Companies. ZEW Discussion Paper 05-38.

Hines, J.R. (1999). Lessons from Behavioral Responses to International Taxation. *National Tax Journal*, 52(2):305–322.

Hines, J.R. and Rice, E.M. (1994). Fiscal Paradise: Foreign Tax Havens and American Business. *Quarterly Journal of Economics*, 109:149–182.

Huizinga, H. and Laeven, L. (2005). International Profit Shifting within European Multinationals. Mimeograph, University of Tilburg.

Huizinga, H. and Nicodème, G. (2004). Are International Deposits Tax-driven? *Journal of Public Economics*, 88(6):1093–1118.

Huizinga, H. and Nicodème, G. (2006). Foreign Ownership and Corporate Income Taxation: An Empirical Evaluation. *European Economic Review*, 50(5):1223–1244.

Huizinga, H. and Nielsen, S.B. (1997). Capital Income and Profit Taxation with Foreign Ownership of Firms. *Journal of International Economics*, 42:149–165.

Huizinga, H. and Nielsen, S.B. (2002). The Coordination of Capital Income and Profit Taxation with Cross-ownership of Firms. *Regional Science and Urban Economics*, 32:1–26.

Huizinga, H., Laeven, L., and Nicodème, G. (2006). Capital Structure and International Debt Shifting in Europe. Mimeograph, University of Tilburg. Paper presented at the European Tax Policy Forum Conference, *The Impact of Corporation Taxes Across Borders*, London, April.

International Bureau for Fiscal Documentation (IBFD) (2005). *European Tax Handbook*.

Jacobs, O.H., Spengel, C., Stetter, T., and Wendt, C. (2005). EU Company Taxation in Case of a Common Tax Base. ZEW Discussion Paper 05-37.

Janeba, E. and Wilson, J.D. (1999). Tax Competition and Trade Protection. *FinanzArchiv*, 56:459–480.

Kanbur, R. and Keen, M. (1993). Jeux sans Frontières: Tax Competition and Tax Coordination when Countries Differ in Size. *American Economic Review*, 83:877–892.

Keen, M. and Marchand, M. (1997). Fiscal Competition and the Pattern of Public Spending. *Journal of Public Economics*, 63:33–53.

Kind, H., Midelfart-Knarvik, K.H., and Schjelderup, G. (2000). Competing for Capital in a Lumpy World. *Journal of Public Economics*, 78(3):253–274.

Krogstrup, S. (2003). Are Capital Taxes Racing to the Bottom in the European Union? HEI Working Paper 2003/1.

Lassen, D.D. and Sørensen, P.B. (2002). Financing the Nordic Welfare States: The Challenge of Globalization to Taxation in the Nordic Countries. Report for the Nordic Council of Ministers.

Lee, K. (1997). Tax Competition with Imperfectly Mobile Capital. *Journal of Urban Economics*, 42:222–242.

MacKie-Mason, J.K. (1990). Do Taxes Affect Corporate Financing Decisions? *Journal of Finance*, 45:1471–1493.

McLure, C.E. and Weiner, J. (2000). Deciding Whether the European Union Should Adopt Formula Apportionment of Company Income. In: *Taxing Capital Income in the European Union: Issues and Options for Reform* (Cnossen, S., ed.). Oxford University Press.

Mendoza, E.G. and Tesar, L.L. (2003a). Winners and Losers of Tax Competition in the European Union. NBER Working Paper 10050.

Mendoza, E.G. and Tesar, L.L. (2003b). The International Macroeconomics of Taxation and the Case against European Tax Harmonization. In: *Economic Policy in the International Economy* (Helpman, E. and Sadka, E., eds). Cambridge University Press.

Mendoza, E.G. and Tesar, L.L. (2005). Why Hasn't Tax Competition Triggered a Race to the Bottom? Some Quantitative Lessons from the EU. *Journal of Monetary Economics*, 52:163–204.

Mintz, J.M. (1994). Is There a Future for Capital Income Taxation? *Canadian Tax Journal*, 42: 1469–1503.

Mintz, J.M. and Smart, M. (2004). Income Shifting, Investment, and Tax Competition: Theory and Evidence from Provincial Taxation in Canada. *Journal of Public Economics*, 88:1149–1168.

Mintz, J.M. and Weiner, J. (2003). Exploring Formula Allocation for the European Union. *International Tax and Public Finance*, 10:695–711.

Nicodème, G. (2001). Computing Effective Corporate Tax Rates: Comparisons and Results. Economic Paper 153. European Commission.

Oates, W. (1972). *Fiscal Federalism*. Harcourt Brace Jovanovich, New York.

Ogura, L.M. (2006). A Note on Tax Competition, Attachment to Home, and Underprovision of Public Goods. *Journal of Urban Economics*, 59(2):252–258.

Parry, I.W.H. (2003). How Large are the Welfare Costs of Tax Competition? *Journal of Urban Economics*, 54:39–60.

Persson, T and Tabellini, G. (1992). The Politics of 1992: Fiscal Policy and European Integration. *Review of Economic Studies*, 59(4):689–701.

Primarolo, D. (1999). Code of Conduct (Business Taxation), http://europa.eu.int/comm/ taxation_customs/resources/documents/primarolo_en.pdf.

Radaelli, C. (1997). *The Politics of Corporate Taxation in the European Union*. Routledge, London.

Radaelli, C. and Kraemer, U. (2005). The Rise and Fall of Governance's Legitimacy: The Case of International Direct Taxation. Mimeograph, University of Exeter.

Ramb, F. and Wiechenrieder, A. (2005). Taxes and The Financial Structure of German Inward. *Weltwirtschaftliches Archiv*, 141(4):670–692.

Redoano, M. (2004). Fiscal Interactions among EU Countries. University of Warwick Discussion Papers 680.

Ruding Report (1992). Report of the Committee of Independent Experts on Company Taxation. Commission of the European Communities, March.

Schjelderup, G. (2002). International Capital Mobility and the Taxation of Portfolio Investments. *Swedish Economic Policy Review*, 9(1):111–140.

Slemrod, J. (2004). Are Corporate Tax Rates, or Countries, Converging? *Journal of Public Economics*, 88(6):1169–1186.

Sørensen, P.B. (2000). The Case for International Tax Co-ordination Reconsidered. *Economic Policy*, 31:431–461.

Sørensen, P.B. (2001). Tax Coordination in the European Union: What are the Issues? *Swedish Economic Policy Review*, 8(1):143–196.

Sørensen, P.B. (2004a). Company Tax Reform in the European Union. *International Tax and Public Finance*, 11(1):91–115.

Sørensen, P.B. (2004b). International Tax Coordination: Regionalism Versus Globalism. *Journal of Public Economics*, 88(6):1187–1214.

Stewart, K. and Webb, M. (2006). International Competition in Corporate Taxation: Evidence from the OECD Time Series. *Economic Policy*, 21(45):153–201.

Swenson, D.L. (2001). Tax Reforms and Evidence of Transfer Pricing. *National Tax Journal*, 54(1):7–26.

Tiebout, C. (1956). A Pure Theory of Local Expenditure. *Journal of Political Economy*, 64:416–424.

Van der Horst, A., Beltendorf, L., and Rojas-Romagosa, H. (2006). Consolidation and Formula Apportionment in the European Union. CPB Working Paper, November.

Weichenrieder, A. (1996). Fighting International Tax Avoidance: The Case of Germany. *Fiscal Studies*, 17(1):37–58.

Weichenrieder, A. (2005). (Why) Do We Need Corporate Taxation? CESifo Working Paper No. 1495.

Weichenrieder, A. (2006). Profit Shifting Within the EU: Evidence from Germany. Mimeograph, University of Frankfurt. Paper presented at the European Tax Policy Forum Conference, *The Impact of Corporation Taxes Across Borders*, London, April.

Weiner, J. (2002a). Formulary Apportionment and the Future of Company Taxation in the European Union. *CESifo Forum*, Spring 2002, pp. 10–20.

Weiner, J. (2002b). Would Introducing Formula Apportionment in the European Union Be a Dream Come True or the EU's Worst Nightmare? *Ifo Studien*, 48(4):519–532.

Weiner, J. (2006). *Company Tax Reform in The European Union (Guidance from the United States and Canada on Implementing Formulary Apportionment in the EU)*. Springer.

Wildasin, D. (1988). Nash Equilibria in Models of Fiscal Competition. *Journal of Public Economics*, 35(2):229–240.

Wildasin, D. (1989). Interjurisdictional Capital Mobility: Fiscal Externality and a Corrective Subsidy. *Journal of Urban Economics*, 25:193–212.

Wildasin, D. (2003). Fiscal Competition in Space and Time. *Journal of Public Economics*, 87:2571–2588.

Wilson, J.D. (1986). A Theory of Interregional Tax Competition. *Journal of Urban Economics*, 19:296–315.

Wilson, J.D. (1987). Trade, Capital Mobility and Tax Competition. *Journal of Political Economy*, 95:835–856.

Wilson, J.D. (1991). Tax Competition with Interregional Differences in Factor Endowments. *Regional Science and Urban Economics*, 21:423–452.

Wilson, J.D. (1995). Mobile Labor, Multiple Tax Instruments, and Tax Competition. *Journal of Urban Economics*, 38:333–356.

Wilson, J.D. (1999). Theories of Tax Competition. *National Tax Journal*, 52(2):269–304.

Wilson, J.D. and Wildasin, D. (2004). Capital Tax Competition: Bane or Boon. *Journal of Public Economics*, 88(6):1065–1091.

Zodrow, G.R. (2003). Tax Competition and Tax Coordination in the European Union. *International Tax and Public Finance*, 10:651–671.

Zodrow, G.R. and Mieszkowski, P. (1986). Pigou, Tiebout, Property Taxation, and the Underprovision of Local Public Goods. *Journal of Urban Economics*, 19:356–370.

Corporate Taxation in Europe: Competitive Pressure and Cooperative Targets

Carlo Garbarino and Paolo M. Panteghini

Abstract

In this chapter we focus on corporation tax in the European Union. Our aim is twofold. We first analyze the dynamics of tax rates within the EU, then we analyze two forces that could lead to coordination. The first top-down factor is the European Commission's aim of eliminating excessive competition. The second bottom-up factor is the circulation of models that are crucial determinants for the evolution of tax systems. In particular, we find that, within the EU, full tax convergence is limited to tax policy issues ruled by EU Directives. Moreover, there is partial convergence for corporate tax rates and models, although domestic tax mechanisms still vary in certain respects. We conclude that, at present, the only feasible matching point of these cooperative forces is the Home State Taxation option, proposed by the Commission of the European Communities in the Communication COM (2001) 582 final.

9.1 Introduction

The creation of a single European market with its subsequent increased factor mobility has increased the profile of the concept of tax competition. European countries are indeed torn between the short-term need to stimulate their own economy even at the cost of subtracting resources from their partners, and the middle- to long-term objective of coordination. In this chapter we use the term *tax competition* in two different respects: Economically, where the term is used to indicate competition on effective and statutory tax rates, and legally as the evolutionary selection of tax models competing against one another (for further details on economic and legal evolution, see Hirshleifer, 1978, 1982; Clark, 1981; Hovenkamp, 1985; Hodgson, 1993). Moreover, we deal with *tax convergence* from two different points of view: Economically there is some convergence if effective and statutory tax rates are closer within EU countries. We will show that tax rates show a downward trend, although heterogeneity is still high.

Legally there is convergence if corporate tax models circulate among EU countries and make tax systems more similar, at least in some respects. We will show that full tax convergence is limited to tax policy issues ruled by EU Directives. Moreover, there is partial convergence for corporate tax rates and models, although domestic tax mechanisms still vary in certain respects. In such a context, convergence cannot be improved exclusively by a top-down approach (by means of Directives or other EU law sources), but must also be the result of an evolutionary process of EU countries' tax systems from the bottom up. The joint effect of both the top-down and bottom-up forces can lead to a higher degree of coordination. In particular, we will argue that, given the high propensity of national governments to maintain freedom of maneuver, the only feasible matching point of top-down and bottom-up forces is the Home State Taxation (HST) option, proposed by the Commission of the European Communities in the Communication COM (2001) 582 final. A detailed analysis of costs and benefits of HST will then be provided.

The structure of the article is as follows. Section 9.2 analyzes the dynamics of both statutory and effective tax rates in the EU. Section 9.3 discusses the main determinants of super-national coordination. Sections 9.4 and 9.5 focus on tax convergence and coordination. In particular, section 9.4 analyzes the evolution of EU corporate tax models, while section 9.5 deals with their circulation. Section 9.6 discusses the 'Home State Taxation' option as a feasible meeting point between top-down and bottom-up forces. Section 9.7 concludes.

9.2 The push towards tax competition in the EU

In this section we present evidence of the dynamics of both statutory and effective tax rates over the last decade in the European Union. Table 9.1 shows the statutory tax rates of both the old EU partners (EU-15) and the new members that entered in 2004 (EU-10). As can be seen, both the EU-15 and EU-10 groups have decreasing average statutory tax rates.

Over the last decade, the EU-15 countries have cut their tax rates, so that the average tax rate has decreased by almost 8%. The most dramatic tax cut was implemented by Ireland, in the second half of the 1990s, and allowed this country to boost its economy and attract a huge amount of foreign direct investment.

With regard to the EU-10 group of countries, most Eastern European countries have also substantially reduced their overall tax rate. In 1994, Estonia moved first by adopting a flat tax of 26% and exempting retained profits.[1] The other two Baltic nations imposed flat taxes in the mid-1990s, with Latvia and Lithuania setting rates of 25% and 33% respectively.[2] Analogously, Slovakia introduced a rate of 19% and the Czech Republic has further cut its rate by 2% at the beginning of 2006 (24%). For the other EU-10 countries, Cyprus cut its tax rate to 10% in 2005, while only Malta and Slovenia kept their rates unchanged over the entire period.

If we compare the dynamics of EU-15 and EU-10 average tax rates, we can see that the tax rate differential is increasing: In 1995 it was 7.4%, while in 2005 it was nearly 10%. This makes the EU-10 countries even more attractive. It is worth noting that, for both groups, standard deviation decreased between 1995 and 2001, and then began to rise again. Such an increase is due to the fact that, while some countries have cut their tax rates further over the last five years, the others

Table 9.1   Statutory tax rates (%) in the EU (1995–2005)

	1995	1996	1997	1998	1999	2000	2001	2002	2003	2004	2005	Change in 1995–2005
EU-15												
Austria	34.0	34.0	34.0	34.0	34.0	34.0	34.0	34.0	34.0	34.0	25.0	−9.0
Belgium	40.2	40.2	40.2	40.2	40.2	40.2	40.2	40.2	34.0	34.0	34.0	−6.2
Denmark	34.0	34.0	34.0	34.0	32.0	32.0	30.0	30.0	30.0	30.0	28.0	−6.0
Finland	25.0	28.0	28.0	28.0	28.0	29.0	29.0	29.0	29.0	29.0	26.0	1.0
France	36.7	36.7	36.7	41.7	40.0	36.7	36.4	35.4	35.4	35.4	34.0	−2.7
Germany	56.8	56.7	56.7	56.0	51.6	51.6	38.3	38.3	39.6	38.3	39.4	−17.4
Greece	40.0	40.0	40.0	40.0	40.0	40.0	37.5	35.0	35.0	35.0	32.0	−8.0
Ireland	40.0	38.0	36.0	32.0	28.0	24.0	20.0	16.0	12.5	12.5	12.5	−27.5
Italy	52.2	53.2	53.2	41.3	41.3	41.3	40.3	40.3	38.3	37.3	37.3	−14.9
Luxembourg	40.9	40.9	39.3	37.5	37.5	37.5	37.5	30.4	30.4	30.4	30.4	−10.5
Netherlands	35.0	35.0	35.0	35.0	35.0	35.0	35.0	34.5	34.5	34.5	31.5	−3.5
Portugal	39.6	39.6	39.6	37.4	37.4	35.2	35.2	33.0	33.0	27.5	27.5	−12.1
Spain	35.0	35.0	35.0	35.0	35.0	35.0	35.0	35.0	35.0	35.0	39.9	4.9
Sweden	28.0	28.0	28.0	28.0	28.0	28.0	28.0	28.0	28.0	28.0	28.0	0.0
UK	33.0	33.0	31.0	31.0	30.0	30.0	30.0	30.0	30.0	30.0	30.0	−3.0
EU-15 average	38.0	38.2	37.8	36.7	35.9	35.3	33.8	32.6	31.9	31.4	30.4	−7.7
S.D. in EU-15	8.1	7.9	8.0	6.9	6.4	6.6	5.5	6.0	6.3	6.2	6.7	−1.4
EU-10												
Cyprus	25.0	25.0	25.0	25.0	25.0	29.0	28.0	28.0	15.0	15.0	10.0	−15.0
Czech Republic	41.0	39.0	39.0	35.0	35.0	31.0	31.0	31.0	31.0	28.0	28.0	−13.0
Estonia	26.0	26.0	26.0	26.0	26.0	26.0	26.0	26.0	26.0	26.0	24.0	−2.0
Hungary	19.6	19.6	19.6	19.6	19.6	19.6	19.6	19.6	19.6	17.7	17.7	−1.9
Latvia	25.0	25.0	25.0	25.0	25.0	25.0	25.0	22.0	19.0	15.0	15.0	−10.0
Lituania	29.0	29.0	29.0	29.0	29.0	24.0	24.0	15.0	15.0	15.0	15.0	−14.0
Malta	35.0	35.0	35.0	35.0	35.0	35.0	35.0	35.0	35.0	35.0	35.0	0.0
Poland	40.0	40.0	38.0	36.0	34.0	30.0	28.0	28.0	27.0	19.0	19.0	−21.0
Slovakia	40.0	40.0	40.0	40.0	40.0	29.0	29.0	25.0	25.0	19.0	19.0	−21.0
Slovenia	25.0	25.0	25.0	25.0	25.0	25.0	25.0	25.0	25.0	25.0	25.0	0.0
EU-10 average	30.6	30.4	30.2	29.6	29.4	27.4	27.1	25.5	23.8	21.5	20.8	−9.8
S.D. in EU-10	7.8	7.5	7.2	6.5	6.3	4.3	4.2	5.7	6.6	6.8	7.3	−0.5
EU-25 average	35.0	35.0	34.7	33.9	33.3	32.1	31.1	29.7	28.7	27.4	26.5	−8.5
S.D. in EU-25	8.7	8.5	8.5	7.5	7.0	7.0	5.9	6.8	7.5	8.0	8.3	−0.3

Source: IBFD.
S.D., standard deviation.

kept their rates unchanged. Increased standard deviation could be a signal for further decreases in tax rates implemented by these late movers.

It is well known that governments use not only the tax rate but also the tax base to determine corporate taxation. For this reason we also look at the forward-looking average effective tax rates that take into account both the legal rate and the width of the tax base. As shown by Overesch (2005), average effective tax rates decreased over the last decade. Despite this generalized 'race to the bottom' (in line with statutory tax rate cuts), high heterogeneity still holds. Table 9.2 compares the 2005 average effective tax rates computed by Overesch (2005), according to the methodology developed by Devereux and Griffith (1999, 2001). As can be seen, within each group, the standard deviation of effective tax rates is very high. Indeed, for

Table 9.2 Effective tax rates (%) in the EU (2005)

EU-15		EU-10	
Austria	23.1	Cyprus	9.7
Belgium	29.7	Czech Republic	22.9
Denmark	25.2	Estonia	21.8
Finland	24.6	Hungary	17.9
France	34.8	Latvia	14.4
Germany	36.0	Lituania	12.8
Greece	28.0	Malta	32.8
Ireland	14.7	Poland	17.0
Italy	32.0	Slovakia	16.7
Luxembourg	26.7	Slovenia	21.6
Netherlands	28.5		
Portugal	24.7	EU-10 average	18.8
Spain	36.1	S.D. in EU-10	6.5
Sweden	24.8	EU-25	
UK	28.9	EU-25 average	24.2
EU-15 average	27.9	S.D. in EU-25	7.4
S.D. in EU-15	5.6		

Source: Overesch (2005). Hypotheses: (1) Investment in real assets (industrial buildings, intangibles, machinery, financial assets, inventories at equal weights); (2) Source of finance: Equity, retained profits, and debt (at equal weights); (3) The economic depreciation rates are 3.1% for industrial buildings, 15.35% for intangibles, 17.5% for machinery; (4) The inflation rate is 2%; (5) The overall rate of return is 20%; (6) The real interest rate is 5%. S.D., standard deviation.

the UE-15 countries average effective rates oscillate between 14.7% (Ireland), 36% (Germany), and 36.1% (Spain). The EU-10 countries' effective tax rates range from 9.7% (Cyprus) to 32.8% (Malta). Such heterogeneity confirms the fact that there is room for further changes, especially in high-tax countries.

Although there are some possible country-specific determinants of tax rate decreases, the most convincing reason for such a generalized 'race to the bottom' is tax competition. This phenomenon is becoming ever more important as the world is integrating and production factors (in particular capital) are becoming increasingly mobile. The argument for capital mobility was clearly shown by Gordon (1986). In his model, he assumed the existence of both mobile (e.g. capital) and immobile factors (such as labor). Moreover, he observed that, in the absence of market imperfections, capital flow would be such as to level returns throughout the world. Therefore, if a country introduced source-based capital taxation, it would experience a flight of capital and would face a welfare loss. Other competing countries would have no interest in taxing their capital. Indeed, if they exempted capital income, they would import the capital in flight from the country that had introduced capital income tax, thereby enjoying a welfare improvement. The policy implication of Gordon's model is that each country, interested in attracting capital income and at the same time aiming to raise tax revenues, should tax immobile labor and ensure full exemption to capital.

Evidence has supported Gordon's forecast of a significant reduction in capital income taxation. For instance, Lee and Gordon (2005) found that in 1980–1989, the average top corporate tax rate was 41.3% (with standard deviation of 8.2%). In the period 1990–1997, it decreased to 34.8% (with a standard deviation of 6.5%). Moreover, Devereux et al. (2004) showed that countries compete both over the statutory tax rate and the tax base, and that tax competition is positively related to the openness of countries. In line with Rodrik (1997), moreover, they showed that the relaxation of capital controls stimulates tax competition and thus reduces both statutory and effective tax rates.

9.3 Tax coordination 'from the top' in the EU

Are big tax cuts likely to occur in the future? As we have seen, many countries have dramatically cut tax rates. Moreover, high tax rate heterogeneity supports the forecast that further tax cuts are not unlikely: In particular, it is not impossible that those members that did not initially implement significant tax cuts could be stimulated to follow the first movers. Despite this downward trend, full exemption of capital income is an improbable event, since there are four main factors that could stop such a race to the bottom.[3] The first factor is capital mobility: In a subsequent article, Gordon (2000) added that capital is not perfectly mobile and therefore its 'flight' from taxation is costly. The second factor is the relationship between corporate taxation and personal taxation. As pointed out by Gordon and MacKie-Mason (1995), corporate taxation serves as a backstop to labor taxes to discourage individuals from converting their labor income into (otherwise untaxed) corporate income: Therefore, the tax rate differential cannot be too big. The evidence supports the 'backstop hypothesis': As shown by Slemrod (2004), there is a strongly positive correlation between the top personal rate (levied on labor) and the top statutory corporate tax rate (levied on capital). This means that corporate taxes reduce benefits arising from the reclassification of labor into corporate income, and thus offset tax avoiding practices.

The third factor is related to the package of Maastricht rules. Further tax rate decreases are harder given the EMU members' urge of keeping public budgets in line with the Stability and Growth Pact. Although interpretation of the Maastricht rules is now much less strict than at first, such constraints are generally binding and may prevent countries from further tax cuts. A good example is provided by Germany. Before the political elections in 2005, both competing coalitions claimed the need for lower corporate tax rates. However, the plan to cut tax rates failed as the ruling coalition and the opposition did not agree on how to finance such reform.[4]

The Stability and Growth Pact also affects the fiscal policies of non-EMU countries, as long as they aim to enter the Monetary Union in the near future. These countries are indeed trying to keep public budgets under control even with increasing difficulties and in some cases pre-commit themselves. An interesting example of pre-commitment to enter the EMU is article 216 of the Polish Constitution, which states that, in line with Maastricht rules, it is 'neither permissible to contract loans nor provide guarantees and financial sureties that would engender a national public debt exceeding three-fifths of the value of the annual Gross Domestic Product'.

The fourth, and to some extent decisive, factor is the role played by the European Commission. Article 2 of the EU Institutional Treaty outlines that community objectives (such as economic development, environmental care, improvement of living standards, economic and social solidarity) should come about 'by the establishment of a common market and economic and monetary union'. However, this Treaty does not assign any general competence for tax matters to the EU. This means that, at present, a federal tax system cannot be implemented and that the

EU's objective is to ensure that states' tax regimes do not contain discriminatory rules that might distort the allocation of resources and the movement of people within the EU. In other words, the EU should coordinate members' tax systems.

What are the EU countries' feelings on coordination? As mentioned earlier, European countries are torn between the middle- to long-term objective of coordination and the need in the shorter term to stimulate their own economy, even at the cost of taking resources from its own partners. On the one hand, most countries are aware that tax competition taken to the extreme could excessively reduce revenue, thereby leading to an under-provision of public goods. For this reason many EU members (in particular, most of the older members) are willing to cooperate and set a minimum tax rate on mobile factors. On the other hand, countries are still reluctant to lose control over fiscal tools by delegating part of their power to the EU. To give an idea of this mixed and even contradictory feeling, let us look at Italy's White Paper for Reform of the Tax System (Italy's Council of Ministers, 2001). The White Paper claims the will to coordinate Italy's system with a so-called 'European tax model'. In particular, it states that 'the reform has one principal objective: To harmonize our tax system with the most efficient ones, implemented by industrialized countries, in particular the members of the European Union'. Quite surprisingly, however, the paper also expresses the will to pursue its objectives in the 'logic of tax competition'.

With regard to the EU's attempts to coordinate direct taxation, the 1980s saw the failure to introduce a single fiscal system for the whole Community. Only in 1990 were three important Directives introduced: The first concerning mergers and acquisitions (90/434/CEE), the second on double taxation of distributed income between parent corporations and their foreign subsidiaries located in other states (90/435/CEE), and the third (adopted as a convention) aimed at eliminating double taxation on dividends (90/436/CEE). These laws could become the pillars upon which a EU federal tax system could be founded. However, much has to be done to ensure a coordinated environment.

The European Commission is aware of members' mixed feelings about competition and coordination. However, it forcibly points out that the fact that companies must conform to 25 or more different tax regimes remains the present cause for most existing tax problems in the internal market, as well as high compliance costs. In Communication COM (2001) 582 final, the European Commission stressed the need for more corporate tax coordination. This communication did not give any quantitative evaluation of the benefits that could arise from increased coordination.[5] On the contrary, it rationalized such reform on negative terms, observing that the strong mobility of capital could cause *excessive* competition in the Union, thus producing considerable welfare losses. Such losses may be due to:

1. The difficulty in calculating correct transfer prices to define the value of transactions made within the same industrial group, by entities operating from countries outside the EU.
2. The double-tax burden that is generated when both the resident country and the source country tax the same income.
3. The existence of significant tax burdens for extraordinary operations (such as, for example, mergers and reorganizations).[6]

In Communication COM (2001) 582 final, the European Commission assumed an intermediary position between coordination and competition. Indeed, on the one hand, it stressed the need to offer a common legal base; On the other, it implicitly accepted the existence of a reasonable degree of tax competition as long as this encouraged Member States to become more efficient in managing their resources.

To pursue its objectives, the European Commission has placed much hope in the work of the European Court of Justice (ECJ), which is significantly contributing to the coordination of tax rules by eliminating causes of tax discrimination within the EU. However, it is quite clear that the ECJ per se cannot guarantee a coordinated system. For this reason the ratification of the Treaty of Nice (G.U.C.E C80, 10 March 2001) is another important pillar for future European strategy. According to Article 43 of the Treaty, a group of at least eight countries can start reinforced cooperation, as long as certain requisites are respected. In particular, this cooperation must be aimed at promoting Union and Community objectives, protecting and serving their interest, and reinforcing the integration process. Furthermore, cooperation must not be an obstacle or discrimination for commercial exchange between Member States.

The Treaty of Nice implicitly allows EU members to go ahead with a *two-speed Europe*, in which each country could choose immediately to opt for coordination, or would be free to keep its own system unchanged. Even if a unified solution between all states would probably be preferable, the possibility of reinforced cooperation should not be a point of contention for at least two reasons.

Firstly, there are varying degrees of integration between EU members that can justify adopting tax and fiscal standards over different periods. Secondly, the very fact that reinforced cooperation can be accomplished might paradoxically help the definition of a coordinated system shared by all Member States. As Bordignon and Brusco (2006) pointed out, each state is aware that late adhesion is generally more burdensome than immediate adhesion of reinforced cooperation. The reason for this is simple: The content of any reinforced cooperation is coordinated among the countries that opt for immediate inclusion. Therefore, the agreement will not take into consideration the specific interests of countries that decide to adhere later. If, in the future, these countries were to decide to cooperate, they might be constrained to adhere to cooperation that is based on unfavorable conditions that have already been established by other states. Of course, the new entrant could try to renegotiate the basic conditions of coordination. However, there is no guarantee that this would be successful, and therefore late adhesion might turn out to be an expensive option. For this reason, Bordignon and Brusco (2006) argued that if the costs of late entry are high enough, then unanimous and simultaneous adhesion would be the optimal strategy for EU countries.

9.4 Tax coordination from the bottom: Evolution of EU corporate tax models

So far we have analyzed coordination from a supranational perspective. However, a higher degree of coordination can also be achieved by means of the circulation of tax models among countries. This phenomenon is related to 'policy learning', which has been dealt with in the political science literature: The idea underlying this concept is that many countries have followed fundamental tax reforms in the USA and the UK, and adjusted their systems to these two models (for further details, see, for instance, Radaelli, 1997; Swank, 2004). This imitative behavior, which entails a sort of endogenous coordination, might also explain the recent wave of tax reforms introduced in Europe. Here, we apply a diagnostic approach where corporate *tax problems* are considered as policy issues, and EU countries' *tax mechanisms* are analyzed with respect to their *structural elements*. These definitions are then included in a comparative theory of the evolution of corporate tax models (for a detailed analysis of the methodological issues applied here, see Garbarino, 2006).

In general, a 'problem', as defined by the Oxford Dictionary, is 'a matter needing to be dealt with' and an agent is faced with a *practical* problem when there is some doubt about what to do. A 'tax problem' is therefore 'a *tax* matter needing to be dealt with' and therefore is a *practical problem*, because the policymaker confronted with a tax problem must decide a specific course of action using a set of rules. In this diagnostic approach, tax policy decisions concerning corporate taxes are solutions to tax problems (on the political economy of taxation, see, for instance, Farber and Frickey, 1991; Breton, 1996; Hettich and Winer, 1999).

Once it is clarified what we mean by tax problem, we can distinguish three different levels of evolutionary comparative analysis:

- At the first level, there is a common core of corporate tax systems of EU countries in relation to basic *tax problems.*
- At the second level, there is circulation of *tax models* among different EU countries.
- At the third level, there is regulatory articulation of domestic corporate *tax mechanisms*, which are meant as a set of rules aiming to solve corporate tax problems.

In this section we will discuss these three levels.

9.4.1   The first level: Basic tax problems

We can identify a core of four corporate tax problems that are common to EU countries:[7]

1. *Tax treatment of corporate distributions.* Each EU country has to decide how (and to what extent) to avoid double dividend taxation caused by the overlapping of personal and corporate income taxes.
2. *Limitation on the deduction of interest expenses.* Each EU country has to decide whether (and to what extent) interest payments and other financial costs can be deducted.
3. *Tax treatment of corporate reorganizations.* Each EU country has to decide whether (and to what extent) gains/losses, resulting from transactions relating to assets or entities, trigger the recognition of taxable capital gains or deductible capital losses.
4. *Consolidated corporate taxation.* Each EU country has to decide whether (and to what extent) profits/losses of companies can be offset with profits/losses of companies belonging to the same group.

Despite the fact that EU members share these basic features and form a single EU *corporate tax family,*[8] the solutions so far adopted by each country have led to remarkable differences.

9.4.2   The second level: The emergence of tax models

The second level of evolutionary comparative taxation is the development of tax models as responses to policy problems (as regards the emerging stream of literature dealing with comparative taxation, see, for instance, Thuronyi, 2000, 2003; Ault and Arnold, 2004). At this level there is a selection of partially different and alternative policy choices by EU countries aimed at solving common problems concerning the treatment of corporate income. Therefore, while at the first level (common core) we can identify a single common EU tax family, at least for the EU-15 countries, at the second level different EU corporate tax models emerge. The main EU corporate tax models can be referred to the basic corporate tax problems listed at the beginning of this section.[9]

In relation to the tax treatment of corporate distributions, these models are:

1. The classical system, which can be divided into two sub-models: The unmodified classical system (which does not provide relief for personal income tax on dividends) and the modified classical system, or shareholder relief (which provides shareholder relief of various kinds for personal income tax on dividends unconnected with corporate income tax paid on distributions).
2. The imputation system, which can also be divided into two sub-models: The partial imputation system (according to which partial credit is given for a shareholder's personal income tax liability in respect to corporate income tax paid on distributed dividends) and the full imputation system (according to which full credit is given for a shareholder's personal income tax liability in respect to corporate income tax paid on dividends).
3. Reduced taxation of distributed profits.[10]
4. Participation exemption, which provides zero or reduced taxation on dividends and/or gains from sales of qualified participations.

In relation to the *limitation to the deduction on interest*, the EU tax models are:

1. The fixed debt/equity ratio (or tax treatment of thin capitalization), which entails that if the debt/equity ratio exceeds a given threshold, the exceeding interest remuneration is deemed as constructive dividends. In this case, the debtor cannot deduct interest paid on loans granted by qualified shareholders and/or related parties.
2. The recharacterization of interest as nondeductible expenses, according to which interest is recharacterized as nondeductible expenses in so far as the underlying financial source meets crucial requirements of equity rather than of debt.
3. The 'arm's length' approach, which entails the nondeductibility of interest paid between affiliated companies which is in excess of what would be

paid between unconnected parties dealing at arm's length, on terms that would have been agreed between unconnected parties.

4. The assets dilution ratio, according to which certain expenses related to acquisition of participations generating nontaxable income (capital gains or dividend) are not deductible for the acquiring company, either by way of a ratio between taxable and nontaxable income or by a ratio between financial and nonfinancial assets.

In relation to *tax treatment of corporate reorganizations*, the tax models emerging at the EU level basically are:

1. Transactions in which either assets or participations are sold.
2. Reorganizations of entities.

For *transactions of assets*, we can identify three different sub-models: Full taxation of gains/losses, and the rollover relief at a financial value model or at tax value. With reference to transactions on participations, in addition to these sub-models, there is also the participation exemption sub-model, in which gains are exempt and losses are not deductible. In *reorganizations of entities*, it is possible to identify two basic sub-models: the Taxation model and the rollover relief (neutrality) model. EU countries that follow a taxation model recognize taxable capital gains and deductible capital losses resulting from cross-border (or internal) corporate reorganizations, while those countries that follow a neutrality model do not recognize taxable capital gains and deductible capital losses resulting from reorganization.

Finally, in relation to *consolidated corporate taxation*, the tax models emerging at EU level are:

1. Domestic tax consolidation (or fiscal unity), according to which a group of companies that are resident in the same EU country is regarded for tax purposes as a single taxpayer, so that the profits and losses of the participating companies can be offset against each other.
2. Trans-border tax consolidation, which entails that the profits and losses of a group of companies resident or not resident in the same EU country can be offset against each other.
3. Group contribution, according to which each company belonging to a group continues to file its own tax return and to pay its own taxes, but is allowed to make a contribution to a company with losses. Such a contribution is deductible for tax purposes in the hands of the former company and taxable in the hands of the latter company, so that profits and losses can be offset.[11]

4. Group relief, according to which tax losses and other qualified tax attributes may be surrendered by one member of a group to another member of the same group.

9.4.3 The third level: From tax models to domestic tax mechanisms

The third level of comparative analysis deals with the evolution of domestic corporate tax mechanisms in various EU countries. There is evolution of a tax mechanism if, at any given time, one or more of its elements are modified in respect to a previous arrangement of the same tax mechanism.

In order to deal with the third level, we introduce a methodological tool, which will be applied in section 9.5.[12] Let us thus start with the three basic processes for corporate tax evolution:

1. Intra-system evolution.
2. EU inter-system transplantation.
3. EU inter-system evolution.

Intra-system evolution takes place when an element of a corporate tax mechanism is modified within a single EU country if such an element is innovative, namely if it serves a new function in respect of the previous arrangement.

EU inter-system transplantation occurs between different EU countries when an element of a corporate tax mechanism modified within country A has a common origin with respect to the same element found in a tax mechanism of country B.[13] *EU inter-system evolution* occurs between different EU countries when an element of a tax mechanism in country A has the same function as the element of the similar tax mechanism in country B, without actually being transplanted. In such a case, the elements have a common function but not a common origin and there is innovation of the tax mechanism of country B which does not amount to importation of this element.[14]

In the EU, corporate tax mechanisms do not change exclusively through domestic internal processes (intra-system evolution); They also do so through importation of tax mechanism elements (EU inter-system transplant) as well as legal innovations inspired by foreign tax mechanisms (EU inter-system evolution). In the latter two cases, we therefore have the *circulation of models*. The outcomes of such circulation can be summarized as follows:

- Full tax convergence
- Partial tax convergence (divergence)
- Full tax divergence.

Full tax convergence entails that the development of new corporate tax mechanisms is blocked in EU countries, while the generally adopted tax model prevails and generates very similar tax mechanisms, which do not have major differences from the initial tax model. We will show that full convergence is limited only to specific areas covered by EU tax Directives.

Partial tax convergence can occur at the level of either (i) corporate tax mechanisms or (ii) corporate tax models. At the level of corporate tax mechanisms, partial EU tax convergence entails that while the tax models are common, domestic tax mechanisms compete over certain specific features of such a model – for example, a certain domestic tax mechanism of participation exemption may be more attractive than another in respect to exemption requirements.[15]

Finally, *full tax divergence* occurs mainly at the level of corporate tax models and entails the predominance of a given corporate tax model over all others: A typical example is the widespread diffusion of tax havens, which have radically different corporate tax features from other countries. However, we can say that full tax divergence of corporate tax models does not occur, at least among the EU-15 countries, since their models belong to the same tax family.

9.5 Tax coordination from the bottom: Convergence and circulation of tax models

In this section we focus on the four basic tax problems listed above (tax treatment of corporate distributions, limitation of deductions on interest, tax treatment of corporate reorganizations, and consolidated corporate taxation), and show how circulation of models has modified tax systems and can enhance coordination from the bottom.

For *tax treatment of corporate distributions*, we can say that over the last decade inter-system legal transplants (and therefore circulation of models), within the EU-15 group, has led to the coexistence of the classical system, the imputation system, and the participation exemption. In particular, the imputation system was originally widespread in the EU-15 as a result of previous intra-system evolution based on domestic change of imputation tax mechanisms (showing relevant variations). Currently, EU-15 countries (except Spain and the UK, which still adopt the imputation system) adopt (see Table 9.3):

1. The classical system (in an unmodified or modified form) for individual and portfolio corporate shareholders, generally providing 'rough and ready' relief of double taxation.
2. Participation exemption for corporate shareholders.

Table 9.3 Tax treatment of company distributions in EU-15 countries (2005)

	Classical system (unmodified – modified)	Imputation system (partial – full)	Participation exemption
Austria	*Individuals and portfolio corporate shareholders:* A final withholding tax is imposed on the gross distribution.		*Substantial corporate shareholders:* 100%.
Belgium	*Individuals:* Dividends are taxable in the name of the individual shareholders.		*Corporate shareholders:* 95%.
Denmark	*Resident portfolio shareholders and individual shareholders on dividends:* Reduced income tax rates.		*Resident substantial corporate shareholders:* 100%.
Finland	*Individuals:* If a listed company distributes dividends, 70% (57% in 2005) of the total amount of the dividend is considered as capital income, while the rest is tax exempt. Nonlisted companies may distribute tax-exempt dividends in an amount corresponding to 9% annual yield on the net worth of the company.		*Corporate shareholders:* 100%.
France	*Individuals:* Dividends paid to resident individuals from 1 January 2005 (and assessed to tax in 2006) no longer carry an imputation credit. Instead, the dividends are assessed to income tax, but only for 50% of their amount. *Minority shareholders with generally under 5% shareholdings:* Pure classical system.		*Parent companies with at least 5% shareholdings:* 95%.

Table 9.3 (Continued)

	Classical system (unmodified – modified)	Imputation system (partial – full)	Participation exemption
Germany	*Individuals:* Taxed 50% of the dividend received.		*Corporate shareholders:* 95%.
Greece			*All kinds of shareholders:* 100%.
Ireland	*Individuals:* Dividends are generally liable to income tax at the individual's marginal income tax rate; Credit is given for the dividend withholding tax paid on these dividends and a refund of the withholding will be made to the extent it exceeds the income tax liability thereon.		*Corporate shareholders:* 100%.
Italy	*Qualified individuals and individuals who hold the participation in a business capacity:* 60% exemption. *Other individuals:* Final withholding tax at a rate of 12.5%.		*Corporate shareholders:* 95%.
Luxembourg	*Individuals and minority shareholders:* 50% of dividends and other profit distributions are exempt.		*Majority corporate shareholders:* 100%.
Netherlands	*Individual substantial shareholding:* Flat rate of 25%. *Individuals who hold the participation in a business capacity and portfolio corporate shareholders:* Taxed at progressive rates up to 52%. *Other individuals:* Annual fixed yield of 4% of the average economic value of the investment. This fixed yield is taxed at a flat rate of 30%.		*Substantial corporate shareholders:* 100%.

Portugal	*Individual shareholders and portfolio corporate shareholders:* Partial participation exemption – 50%. *Substantial corporate shareholders:* 100%.
Spain	*Individuals and portfolio corporate shareholders:* Partial imputation system. *Substantial corporate shareholders:* Full imputation system.
Sweden	*Individual shareholders:* Unless distributed profits are eligible for the exemption. Individual shareholders of unlisted Swedish and nonresident companies are exempt from tax on dividends received, up to an amount corresponding to 70% of the interest rate on government borrowing, multiplied by the acquisition value of the shares, plus, under certain circumstances, part of the payroll. The distributing company must not have held, directly or indirectly, 10% or more of the voting power or the capital of a listed Swedish or nonresident company at any time during the preceding four financial years. *Corporate shareholders:* 100%.
UK	*Individuals and corporate shareholders:* Partial imputation system.

Source: IBFD.

With respect to dividend taxation, there is full tax convergence, at least for those issues covered by Directive 435/90, which has implemented the participation exemption model only for intra-group qualified corporate distributions. Since the beginning of the 2000s, many countries have abandoned the full imputation system and switched to classical and participation exemption models. These reforms are the joint result of top-down pressure and of bottom-down circulation of models. On the one hand, in Saint-Gobain ZN, case C-307/97, 21 September 1999, the ECJ declared that Germany's full imputation system was discriminatory as it granted a tax credit to resident shareholders only, thereby placing a restriction on the free movement of capital within the EU. This ruling, as well as subsequent ones regarding other Member States, forced Germany and other countries to switch to partial exemption.[16] On the other hand, the treatment of shareholding has been overshadowed by the treatment of the income of the underlying companies. This phenomenon is related to the increased number of foreign shareholders. In such a context, full imputation is informationally very demanding and thus less manageable.

It is finally worth noting that if we compare the EU-15 group with the EU-10, we can say that so far there is divergence, since, as pointed out in section 9.2, most of the new EU members have applied flat taxation.

Problems relating to *limitations on the deduction of interest* have evolved over the last decade through EU inter-system legal transplants and therefore by circulation of the fixed debt/equity ratio model. On the contrary, the models of recharacterization of interest as nondeductible expenses and asset dilution ratio have evolved nationally (intra-system evolution), with adjustments that have occurred either at a statutory level or administratively and/or as judicial guidelines.[17] Both recharacterization of interest and the asset dilution ratio have developed by intra-system evolution, leading to country-specific tax mechanisms, while the 'arm's length' approach has been introduced as a model due to OECD guidelines. As shown in Table 9.4, several EU countries have adopted the fixed debt/equity ratio with limited variation of the structural elements of the specific domestic tax mechanisms, but with significant variation on the ratio itself (which ranges from 1:1 to 4:1). As can be seen, the fixed debt/equity ratio is now predominating, although it coexists with recharacterization of interest and the 'arm's length' model. On the contrary, the recharacterization and assets dilution approach is only marginally applied.

As regards the *tax treatment of corporate reorganizations*, EU countries have originally developed their tax rules autonomously at a domestic level, so that EU legal inter-system evolution was initially quite limited. Subsequently, the introduction of common effective rules (namely, rules that are apparently different in their structure but similar in their effects) has been developed through inter-system

	Arm's length approach	Hidden profit approach	Fixed ratio approach (debt/equity)	No revenue protection
EU-15				
Austria	X		3:1	
Belgium	X		1:1 if loans granted by managers, by shareholders, or by manager of foreign societies; 7:1 if granted by not taxed or undertaxed corporations	
Denmark	X		4:1	
Finland	X			
France	X		1.5:1	
Germany	X		1.5:1 (€250,000)	
Greece	X			
Ireland	X	X		
Italy	X		4:1	
Luxembourg	X	X	85:15	
		Interest on loans granted by shareholders or their affiliates at excessively high rates may be deemed to constitute a hidden profit distribution.		
Netherlands	X		3:1 (€500,000)	
Portugal	X		2:1	
Spain	X		3:1	
Sweden	X			
UK	X		1:1	

(Continued)

Table 9.4 (Continued)

	Arm's length approach	Hidden profit approach	Fixed ratio approach (debt/equity)	No revenue protection
EU-10[a]				
Cyprus	X			No thin capitalization rules
Czech Republic	X		4:1	
Estonia	X			No thin capitalization rules
Hungary	X		4:1	
Latvia	X		1:1	
Lithuania	X		1:1	
Malta	X			General anti-avoidance rule (according to OECD guidelines)
Poland	X		3:1	
Slovakia	X			No thin capitalization rules (since 1 January 2004)
Slovenia	X		Deductibility of interest rates applied by the inter-banking market	Not specified thin capitalization rules

Source: IBFD and Di Gregorio et al. (2005).
[a] This part of the table gives an initial indication of the process of circulation of corporate tax models in the EU-10 group.

evolution, in which the principles of tax neutrality, rollover relief, and nonrecognition of gains/losses of qualified transactions have predominated. Tax convergence has been favored by the EC Merger Directive (90/434/EEC), which provided harmonized tax rules for cross-border corporate reorganizations based on the tax neutrality model. However, the implementation of the Merger Directive has generated various domestic tax mechanisms which were partially different from the model. For this reason, two new EC Directives (Directive 19/2005/CE amending Directive 90/434/EEC and Directive 2005/56/CE on cross-border mergers of limited liability companies) have been introduced to fill the gap. At present, however, both Directives still have to be implemented by EU countries.

The problems relating to *consolidated corporate taxation* have traditionally evolved nationally (intra-system evolution). Such an evolution has created four different models (fiscal unity, trans-border tax consolidation, group contribution, group relief) that still share the common function of offsetting profit and loss.

As shown in Table 9.5, there is partial convergence towards fiscal unity and group relief. However, there are still three sources of heterogeneity regarding

Table 9.5   Domestic group taxation in the EU (2005)

No group relief	Intra-group loss transfer	'Pooling' of result of a group	Full tax consolidation
• Belgium	**'Group relief'**	• Denmark	• 'Fiscale eenheid' in
• Czech Republic	• Ireland	• Germany	the Netherlands
• Greece	• Cyprus	• Spain	
• Lithuania	• Malta	• France	
• Slovakia	• UK	• Italy	
• (Estonia)	**'Intra-group contribution'**	• Luxembourg	
	• Latvia	• Austria	
	• Finland	• Poland	
	• Sweden	• Portugal	
		• Slovenia	
No loss compensation available, namely a group of companies is disregarded for tax purposes.	Every group member is taxed separately; Losses may be transferred on a definitive basis from one group member to another.	Each group member determines its tax base, which is then pooled at the level of the parent company.	Legal personality of each group member is disregarded for tax purposes; Profits/losses of subsidiaries are treated as if realized by the parent company.

Source: Commission of the European Communities (2005).

group taxation. Firstly, seven countries do not provide any group relief. Secondly, participation thresholds range from 50% to 95%.[18] Thirdly, only three countries (Denmark, France, and Italy) provide trans-border tax consolidation.[19]

9.6 Coordination from the top and from the bottom: A feasible meeting point

Quite interestingly, the current situation reveals, on the one hand, a fairly partial convergence of models, and on the other a full convergence of common core tax problems. For this reason, we think there is room for further coordination, at least in terms of tax consolidation. However, there are several elements of the consolidation model that need to be addressed in order to improve convergence: (a) Domestic tax consolidation; (b) Trans-national elements of domestic tax consolidation (including relief of double taxation on income of the resident-controlling company and nonresident-controlled companies); (c) Effects of the exercise of election[20] and reporting requirements for entities participating in tax consolidation; (d) Interruption of domestic tax consolidation; (e) Tax liability of controlling and controlled companies.

Convergence of these structural elements of domestic consolidation rules (either by legal transplants or by inter-system evolution of similar effective rules) is a prerequisite for multilateral reciprocity. If this happens, then there is room for reinforced cooperation, in line with the Treaty of Nice. In particular, multilateral reciprocity and reinforced cooperation could lead to the implementation of the Home State Taxation (HST) model, proposed by the Commission of the European Communities in the Communication COM (2001) 582 final.[21] Under HST, the member states (or even only a subgroup of these) would agree that corporations operating in the EU could calculate their income according to the laws in which their parent company is located. This system would be voluntary and would also allow the individual states to set their own tax rate (for further details on the HST proposal, see, for instance, Lodin and Gammie, 2001).

We are aware that the high flexibility of HST may be its Achilles' heel in at least four respects (for further details on EU corporate taxation, see Martens-Weiner, 2006). Firstly, the Commission itself noted that with the lack of a central authority, HST requires that countries agree about the control system to use for companies operating in more than one state. Secondly, applying HST could favor large corporations that operate in more than one state.[22] Thirdly, HST would risk reducing control over the taxpayer with the probable negative effect of reducing EU revenue.[23]

Many experts (e.g Cnossen, 2003) and the European Commission itself agree that HST might cause an increase in tax competition. However, there is no agreement on whether increased competition might be considered as a negative effect (in line, for instance, with Sørensen, 2001) or a positive one. The Commission's feeling on this point is quite mixed as well. As pointed out in section 9.3, in Communication COM (2001) 582 final, the Commission complained about the danger of excessive competition. Further details are provided in the Commission Staff Working Paper SEC (2001) 1681 (Commission of the European Communities, 2001b). In a more recent document (SEC (2005) 1785, p. 9; Commission of the European Communities, 2005), however, it states that 'the HST scheme increases competition in *host* Member States. This should lead to global productivity gains and improvement in the allocation of resources ...'.

Despite the above limits, and the EC's contradictory feeling, in the medium-term HST is the only feasible option for improving coordination. First of all, HST is based on existing laws and therefore on experience and knowledge that has already been acquired. Thus, HST does not need fully harmonized accounting and fiscal laws. Another interesting feature of tax consolidation based on HST is that once there is convergence of domestic rules on tax consolidation by EU countries participating in 'reinforced cooperation', the other three basic corporate tax problems outlined in section 9.4 (tax treatment of corporate distributions, limitation of interest deduction, tax treatment of corporate reorganizations) are neutralized at the group level, as long as corporate distributions are exempt, interest payments are freely deductible, and intra-group reorganizations are tax neutral. Finally, given HST's characteristics, national governments would maintain a wide freedom of maneuver. This would make this option acceptable for domestic policymakers, who are usually worried about losing power.

9.7 Conclusion

In this article we analyzed the dynamics of both statutory and effective tax rates, and then focused on the circulation of models within the EU. In particular, we showed that tax rates have dramatically decreased over the period 1995–2005, although the standard deviation has risen since 2002. This higher heterogeneity is due to the fact that while some countries have further cut their tax rates over the last five years, the others have kept them unchanged. It is therefore not unlikely that further tax decreases will be implemented in the near future. As we pointed out, however, full exemption of capital income is still an improbable event.

233

In the past, EU corporate tax systems have evolved through domestic policy, while now EU corporate tax systems have tended to evolve by means of a more rapid international circulation of models. At this stage, therefore, such a circulation is a major feature of the current evolution of EU corporate tax systems.

Existing EU corporate tax mechanisms apparently vary greatly and are the result of complex evolutionary processes. This would suggest a lack of coordination. However, we have shown that there is widespread inter-system legal transplantation with partial convergence of corporate tax models. Moreover, the areas covered by EU Directives are characterized by full tax convergence. In such a context, evolutionary pressures indicate that the procedure of reinforced cooperation could be suitable to foster *partial convergence*, leading to the introduction of the HST model, which could represent a solution to the four basic problems outlined in section 9.4 (tax treatment of corporate distributions, limitation of deductions on interest, tax treatment of corporate reorganizations, consolidated corporate taxation). As pointed out, there would be no need to harmonize nominal rates or rules on the taxable base, especially with the constant convergence of effective corporate tax rates.

In the next future, one of the tasks of domestic policymakers is to assess evolutionary pressures, rather than to impose isolated domestic solutions that might be ineffective or even lead to tax discrimination. At the same time, the EU is faced with the task of finding a practical approach to make European corporation tax applicable.

Acknowledgments

We would like to thank Francesco Cohen and Elena Iscandri for helpful research assistance.

Notes

1. Estonia must change its tax regime to comply with the EU standards imposed by the Parent–Subsidiary Directive by December 2008.
2. It is worth noting that this 'race to the bottom' has also involved many non-EU Eastern European countries. Following the example of the Baltic countries, Serbia (with a 14% tax rate), Romania (16%), Georgia (12%), and Russia (13%) introduced flat tax rates. For further details, see Mitchell (2005).
3. Other factors (such as the so-called 'treasury transfer effect' and the taxation of country-specific rents) are surveyed by Zodrow (2006).
4. After the German elections, the new ruling coalition is still looking for a financial solution to implement tax cuts.

5. It is worth noting, however, that Sørensen's (2000, 2001) simulations showed that tax coordination in the EU would lead to a significant welfare improvement.

6. These burdens can indeed discourage groups to restructure even if this restructuring could guarantee considerable improvement in terms of efficiency.

7. Much research is devoted to the policy reasons underlying corporate taxation and to its alternatives – see, for instance, Bird (2002) and Mintz (1995).

8. One of the main areas of comparative legal studies is the determination of *families*, namely a group of countries forming a homogeneous area in respect to regulatory issues. Mattei (1997) provides helpful details on this topic.

9. Notice that EU tax models consist of various structural elements: Each element serves to solve a specific regulatory problem, while all elements combined together can solve the tax problem of the model implemented. For example, the structural elements of each of the various models for tax treatment of corporate distributions are: (i) The definition of the participating and participated (or distributing) entity; (ii) The notion and the requirement of dividends; (iii) The amount of relief (exemption, credit, or modified corporate taxation). For a comparative analysis of these elements, see Garbarino (2006).

10. A good example of reduced taxation is provided by Germany's split-rate system, according to which, until 2000, retained profits were taxed at 40%, whereas dividends were taxed at 30%. This system was abandoned in 2001.

11. Tax groups usually have no minimum period of existence, though in most cases tax benefits are enjoyed only if the necessary holding was achieved in the previous tax year.

12. This third level of convergence/divergence of corporate tax mechanisms shows that comparative analysis is meaningful only when aimed at finding, from an evolutionary approach, which elements of a given corporate tax mechanism have a common origin with those of another country (circulation of models) and which elements have a common function (domestic evolution of mechanisms).

13. A variation of EU inter-system transplantation occurs when an element of a tax mechanism, once imported by a country, subsequently develops a new function in the tax system of destination.

14. For example, the effective rule of asset dilution ratio can be implemented in a given country without adopting a fixed ratio, but adopting an administrative guideline.

15. Competition among institutional alternatives is analyzed by North (1990), Komesar (1994), and Posner (1996). On competition among legal rules, further details can be found in Mattei and Pulitini (1991), and Mattei (1997). Finally, the emergence of rules is dealt with by Ullmann-Margalit (1977) and Axelrod (1984).

16. In order to prevent revenue losses, none of these countries decided to extend full imputation to nonresident shareholders.

17. For example, in certain cases, deduction is limited by an explicit statutory ratio, while in other cases ad hoc guidelines determine whether interest is related to exempted income and therefore not deductible.

18. As shown in the Commission Staff Working Document, SEC (2005) 1785, the minimum participation thresholds are: Austria 50%, Cyprus 75%, Denmark 100%, Germany 50%, Finland 90%, France 95%, Ireland 75%, Italy 50%, Latvia 90%, Luxembourg 95%, Malta 51%, Netherlands 95%, Poland 95%, Portugal 90%, Slovenia 90%, Spain 75%, Sweden 90%, UK 75%.

19. It is not unlikely that trans-border tax consolidation will be implemented after the ECJ's ruling on Case C-446/03, regarding Marks & Spencer. Indeed, in December 2005, the Court held that

restricting the availability of group relief to UK companies constitutes a restriction on the freedom of establishment in that it applies different tax treatment to losses incurred by a resident subsidiary and losses incurred by a nonresident subsidiary.

20. In particular, with reference to the effects of the exercise of election, the following structural elements should be regulated uniformly or in a pattern of convergence: (i) Computation of global comprehensive income; (ii) 'Consolidation adjustments'; (iii) Access to domestic and foreign tax losses and tax attributes; (iv) Tax treatment of intra-group transactions.

21. In this respect, the Commission of the European Communities (2001b), in the document *Company Taxation in the Internal Market* (and in the subsequent 2002 document), stated that the pivotal element for the effectiveness of the HST model is multilateral reciprocity. For further details on the four options proposed by the European Commission, see Cnossen (2004).

22. While small firms, operating only nationally, should apply domestic laws, large corporations could opt for the most convenient system and therefore enjoy a tax benefit.

23. If the fiscal controls were made by individual national authorities, these authorities would, at least in theory, need to know and apply the laws from each of the 25 nations of the EU. Obviously this would be almost impossible. It would therefore be natural to assign a controlling role to the national authority where the company has its headquarters. As Giannini (2002) pointed out, however, this would abolish the controlling authority of each of the national administrations, and this would risk reducing control over taxpayers, with the likely negative effect of reducing EU revenue.

References

Ault, H.L. and Arnold, B.J. (2004). *Comparative Income Taxation. A Structural Analysis.* Kluwer, The Hague.

Axelrod, R.M. (1984) *The Evolution of Cooperation.* Basic Books, New York.

Bird, R.M. (2002). Why Tax Corporations? *Bulletin for International Fiscal Documentation,* 56(5):194–203.

Bordignon, M. and Brusco, S. (2006). On Enhanced Cooperation. *Journal of Public Economics,* 90(10–11):2063–2090.

Breton, A. (1996). *Competitive Governments: An Economic Theory of Politics and Public Finance.* Cambridge University Press, Cambridge.

Clark, R.C. (1981). The Interdisciplinary Study of 'Legal Evolution'. *Yale Law Journal,* 90(5): 1238–1274.

Cnossen, S. (2003). How Much Tax Coordination in the European Union? *International Tax and Public Finance,* 10(6):625–649.

Cnossen, S. (2004). Reform and Coordination of Corporate Taxes in the European Union: An Alternative Agenda. *Bulletin for International Fiscal Documentation,* 58(4):134–150.

Commission of the European Communities (2001a). *Towards an Internal Market without Tax Obstacles.* Communication COM (2001) 582 final, Brussels.

Commission of the European Communities (2001b). *Company Taxation in the Internal Market.* Commission Staff Working Paper SEC (2001) 1681, Brussels.

Commission of the European Communities (2002). *Company Taxation in the Internal Market.* Office of Official Publications for the European Communities, Brussels.

Commission of the European Communities (2005). Annex to the Communication from the Commission to the Council, the European Parliament and the Economic and Social Committee. *Tackling the Corporation Tax Obstacles of Small and Medium-Sized Enterprises in the Internal Market – Outline of a Possible Home State Taxation Pilot Scheme.* Commission Staff Working Document, SEC (2005) 1785, Brussels.

Council of Ministers (2001). *Relazione al Disegno di Legge Delega per la Riforma del Sistema Fiscale.* Rome.

Devereux, M.P. and Griffith, R. (1999). The Taxation of Discrete Investment Choices. IFS Working Papers W98/16.

Devereux, M.P. and Griffith, R. (2001). Summary of the 'Devereux and Griffith' Economic Model and Measures of Effective Tax Rates, Annex A of European Commission. *Company Taxation in the Internal Market.* COM (2001). 582 final, Brussels, Belgium.

Devereux, M.P., Lockwood, B., and Redoano, M. (2004). Do Countries Compete over Corporate Tax Rates? Mimeograph.

Di Gregorio, C., Mainolfi, G., and Scazzeri, G. (2005). *L'Imposta sulle Società nell'Unione Europea.* Il Sole 24 Ore, Milan.

Farber, D. and Frickey, P. (1991). *Law and Public Choice: A Critical Introduction.* University of Chicago Press, Chicago.

Garbarino, C. (2006). Comparative Corporate Taxation and Circulation of Models. Mimeograph.

Giannini, S. (2002). Home State Taxation versus Common Base Taxation. *CESifo Forum: Company Taxation and the Internal Market*, Spring, pp. 24–30.

Gordon, R.H. (1986). Taxation of Investment and Savings in a World Economy. *American Economic Review*, 76(5):1086–1102.

Gordon, R.H. (2000). Taxation of Capital Income vs. Labour Income: An Overview. In: *Taxing Capital Income in the European Union, Issues and Options for Reform* (Cnossen, S., ed.). Oxford University Press, Oxford.

Gordon, R.H. and MacKie-Mason, J.K. (1995). Why is There Corporate Taxation in a Small Open Country? In: *The Effects of Taxation on Multinational Corporations* (Feldstein, M. et al., eds). University of Chicago Press, Chicago.

Hettich, W. and Winer, S.L. (1999) *Democratic Choice and Taxation.* Cambridge University Press, Cambridge.

Hirshleifer, J. (1978). Natural Economy versus Political Economy. *Journal of Social and Biological Structures*, 1(4):319–337.

Hirshleifer, J. (1982). Evolutionary Models in Economics and the Law: Cooperation versus Conflict Strategies. *Research in Law and Economics*, 4:1–60.

Hodgson, G.M. (1993). *Economics and Evolution: Bringing Life Back to Economics.* Polity Press, Cambridge.

Hovenkamp, H. (1985). Evolutionary Models in Jurisprudence. *Texas Law Review*, 64(4):645–685.

Komesar, N.K. (1994). *Imperfect Alternatives: Choosing Institutions in Law, Economics, and Public Policy.* Chicago University Press, Chicago.

Lee, Y. and, Gordon, R.H. (2005). Tax Structure and Economic Growth. *Journal of Public Economics*, 89(5–6):1027–1043.

Lodin, S.-O. and Gammie, M. (2001). *Home State Taxation.* IBFD Publications, Amsterdam.

Martens-Weiner, J. (2006). *Company Tax Reform in the European Union.* Springer, New York.

Mattei, U. (1997). *Comparative Law and Economics*. Michigan University Press, Ann Arbor, MI.

Mattei, U. and Pulitini, F. (1991). A Competitive Model of Legal Rules. In: *The Competitive State* (Breton, A., ed.). Kluwer, The Hague.

Mintz, J. (1995). The Corporation Tax: A Survey. *Fiscal Studies*, 16(4): 23–68.

Mitchell, D.J. (2005). Eastern Europe's Flat Tax Revolution. *Tax Notes International*, 14 March:989–990.

North, D. (1990) *Institutions, Institutional Change and Economic Performance*. Cambridge University Press, Cambridge.

Overesch, M. (2005). The Effective Tax Burden of Companies in Europe. *CESifo DICE Report*, 4/2005:56–63.

Posner, E.A. (1996). Law, Economics and Inefficient Norms. *University of Pennsylvania Law Review*, 144(5):1697–1744.

Radaelli, C.M. (1997). *The Politics of Corporate Taxation in the European Union*. Routledge, New York.

Rodrik, D. (1997). *Has Globalization Gone Too Far?* Institute for International Economics, Washington, DC.

Slemrod, J. (2004). Are Corporate Tax Rates, or Countries, Converging? *Journal of Public Economics*, 88(6):1169–1186.

Sørensen, P.B. (2000). The Case for International Tax Coordination Reconsidered. *Economic Policy*, 31:429–472.

Sørensen, P.B. (2001). Do We Need Tax Co-ordination? *Contribution to the Liber Amicorum in honour of Sijbren Cnossen*. Kluwer, Dordrecht.

Swank, D. (2004). Tax Policy in an Era of Internationalization: An Assessment of a Conditional Diffusion Model of the Spread of Neoliberalism. Mimeograph.

Thuronyi, V. (2000). *Tax Law Design and Drafting*. Kluwer, The Hague.

Thuronyi, V. (2003). *Comparative Tax Law*. Kluwer, The Hague.

Ullmann-Margalit, E. (1977). *The Emergence of Norms*. Clarendon Press, Oxford.

Zodrow, G. (2006). Capital Mobility and Source-based Taxation of Capital Income in Small Open Economies. *International Tax and Public Finance*, 13(2–3):269–294.

10

The Economics of Taxing Cross-border Savings Income: An Application to the EU Savings Tax

Jenny E. Ligthart

Abstract

The deepening globalization and increased capital mobility, facilitated by advancements in technology and the elimination of exchange controls, have affected countries' ability to effectively tax cross-border savings deposits and more generally portfolio investments. Due to the ready access to foreign financial markets – often located in offshore financial centers levying no or low tax rates – investors can more easily than before conceal capital income from their domestic tax authorities. While the literature has paid much attention to the institutional arrangements and practicalities of tax information sharing, the economics of the issue has hardly been analyzed. Many questions arise. Why would source countries (that is, those in which the savings income arises) voluntarily choose to provide information to residence countries and thereby make themselves less attractive places to foreign investors? Does self-interest induce countries to provide an appropriate amount of information? Why is it – as the experience in the European Union has been – that small countries prefer to levy withholding taxes, whereas (relatively) large countries favor information sharing? This overview article presents what is known about these questions with a view to provide insights into the economics of tax information exchange.

10.1   Introduction

The increased mobility of capital flows, facilitated by advancements in technology and the elimination of foreign exchange controls, has negatively affected countries' ability to tax income from cross-border savings.[1] Due to the ready access to foreign financial markets – often located in tax havens, levying little or no tax[2] – private investors can easily conceal capital income from their domestic tax authorities. As a result, tax authorities of the investor's country of residence are faced with an increasing number of 'disappearing' taxpayers. No reliable estimates exist of the scope of international tax evasion. Evidently, if we could measure it, we could tax it too! Nevertheless, most experts agree that the tax evasion problem is substantial and growing rapidly. Indeed, external bank deposits of nonbank investors for a group of 24 countries[3] have grown on average by 123% during 1995–2004. It is likely that part of this sizeable growth is attributable to increased noncompliance with national tax laws. Consequently, national governments are losing public revenue at a time when their public finances are already overstretched[4] and their banking sectors are suffering from (unfair) foreign competition.

One way of helping tax authorities to combat international tax evasion is to improve the cross-border exchange of taxpayer-specific information, which has emerged in recent years as one of the key issues in international tax policy discussions (applying a withholding tax is another instrument – see below for a detailed discussion). Information exchange is at the heart of the EU's savings tax directive, which has been in effect since July 2005. The EU savings tax directive prescribes that 22 of 25 Member States share automatically between each other tax information on residents' cross-border interest income. However, three of the smaller EU Member States – Austria, Belgium, and Luxembourg – are allowed instead to levy a withholding tax on the savings income of residents of other Member States. To prevent capital flight, the European Commission has negotiated 'equivalent measures' with five non-EU countries and a group of dependent and associated (DA) territories of EU countries. Information sharing also features prominently in the OECD's controversial 'Harmful Tax Practices' project (OECD, 1998), which began by identifying, in June 2000, 35 noncooperative tax havens for further analysis and dialog. In the policy debate, this country list is often referred to as the 'OECD blacklist'. Listed jurisdictions were asked to enter into commitments to put in place effective information sharing and transparent tax practices.

Given the strong focus of recent policy initiatives on tax information sharing, it is of importance to understand its economics. While the literature has paid much attention to the institutional arrangements and practicalities of tax information sharing, the economics of the issue has not been extensively analyzed. The theoretical academic literature – which typically employs two-country, game-theoretic models – is relatively small (key contributions are those of Bacchetta and Espinosa, 1995, 2000; Eggert and Kolmar, 2002a, b, 2004; Huizinga and Nielsen, 2003; Makris, 2003; Keen and Ligthart, 2005, 2006b). Tanzi and Zee (1999, 2001) provide an informal analysis of incentive issues in information sharing, while Keen and Ligthart (2006a) give a comprehensive overview of information sharing issues on which this paper partly draws. When analyzing the information sharing issue, many policy-relevant questions arise. Why would source countries (that is, those in which the savings income arises) voluntarily choose to provide tax information to residence countries (that is, those in which the private investor resides), thereby making themselves less attractive locations to foreign investors? Does the unbridled pursuit of self-interest induce countries to provide an optimal amount of information? Why is it – as the experience with the EU savings tax has been – that relatively small countries prefer to levy withholding taxes at source, whereas large countries favor information sharing? This chapter presents what is known about these questions to provide insight into the economics of information sharing. More specifically, it employs these insights to analyze the workings and effectiveness of the EU savings tax directive as a case in point.

The chapter is organized as follows. Section 10.2 sets out the general principles underlying the taxation of cross-border savings income. Section 10.3 discusses the economics of information sharing, studies alternative instruments to tax cross-border capital income, and touches upon the 'third country' issue. Section 10.4 analyzes the EU savings tax directive. Finally, Section 10.5 summarizes and concludes.

10.2 General principles of information sharing

10.2.1 The fundamental need for information

The need for taxpayer-specific information on capital income taxes arises from the universal use of the residence principle in the taxation of cross-border savings (the source principle – see below – is used in the taxation of income from foreign direct (or active) investment). Under the residence principle, income tax is ultimately payable to the country in which a taxpayer (that is, a natural person or company) resides, perhaps with some credit or exemption for taxes paid in the country of source.[5] If effectively enforced, the residence principle ensures capital-export neutrality because pre-tax rates of return on capital are equalized across jurisdictions. In other words, it does not discriminate between financial capital according to where it is located (because otherwise output could be increased by shifting capital from where its marginal return is low to where it is high). Consequently, the residence principle yields global production efficiency in the Diamond and Mirrlees (1971) sense. In contrast, the source principle – under which income tax is payable to the country in which the income is generated – yields differing pre-tax rates of return on capital, potentially giving rise to tax competition among countries (for a comprehensive overview of tax competition studies, see Wilson, 1999). Consequently, investment will be distorted in favor of locations with low tax rates.

In practice, the conditions underlying the Diamond–Mirrlees theorem are far from trivial. It requires that an economy's pure profits be fully taxed away. Even more stringent conditions need to be imposed in an international setting. On the latter, Keen and Wildasin (2004) demonstrated that when countries cannot make lump-sum transfers between each other, production inefficiencies (in the form of source-based taxes) may need to be introduced to move around the world's second-best utility frontier.

The merits of the residence principle are of interest here only because it provides a welfare-theoretic underpinning of information sharing.[6] To enforce residence taxation, countries must have information on their residents' capital income (and potentially assets) abroad. Many countries legally require taxpayers to disclose details of such income to the tax authorities of their country of residence, but the possibility of fraudulent or no declaration is all too evident.[7]

To address this, countries may wish to have access to alternative sources of information in the country of source, requiring the participation of the foreign tax authority (and third parties such as commercial banks). Implementing full information sharing and eliminating any existing creditable source tax yields an 'ideal' tax system in the sense of being socially optimal, which is to be preferred over a pure source tax.

10.2.2   Basic principles of information sharing

Generally, tax authorities of countries employ three ways to share case-specific tax information with each other. The most common form is information exchange upon request, where a country passes information in response to a specific request related to a taxpayer. The second form concerns automatic exchange – typically being the largest in volume – which mainly pertains to information about routine, periodic payments, such as interest and dividends paid to nonresidents. The third type, spontaneous exchange of information, often occurs in the course of an audit when one tax authority uncovers details that it thinks may be of interest to its counterpart in the taxpayer's country of residence. Noncase-specific information is also regularly exchanged between tax authorities. For example, tax authorities may – under the heading of administrative assistance – wish to share their auditing experiences in a particular sector.

Most countries have laws that protect the confidentiality of information that tax authorities have gathered about a particular taxpayer. As a result, a country cannot provide information about a taxpayer to another country without a legal instrument permitting such disclosure. Information exchange has been carried out under three types of treaties: (i) Bilateral double-income taxation treaties, which include an information-sharing clause modeled after Article 26 of the OECD model tax convention; (ii) Bilateral information-sharing treaties such as those concluded between the USA and various Caribbean jurisdictions; (iii) Multilateral mutual assistance or information-sharing treaties such as the Mutual Assistance directive.[8] Under those treaties, countries are expected to rely on their domestic sources before making a specific request to a treaty partner. Such requests have to be precise; They should include details about the taxpayer in question, the fiscal year, the transaction(s) under scrutiny, and the relevance of the information being sought. All of these requirements are designed to prevent countries from overburdening each other with demands, and to ensure that taxpayer information is disclosed only when necessary.

Tax authorities are typically not compensated for the ordinary costs of information provision, because information sharing is viewed as a matter of reciprocity.

The desire to maintain equity in the net benefit allocation across countries could potentially explain this practice.[9] Since tax authorities do not receive any direct compensation, they have little incentive to give priority to foreign information requests,[10] reducing its timeliness value. In addition, no formal (financial) penalties exist to punish noncomplying countries. Instead, countries could punish each other by not reciprocating future information requests by the noncomplying country or by not cooperating with that country on other policy issues (so-called issue linkage).

10.3   The theoretical literature

The key challenge is to explain why any capital-importing country may choose to provide voluntarily tax information to capital-exporting countries. By supplying tax information, the capital-importing country helps the capital-exporting country to enforce its capital income tax law, thereby making itself a less attractive place to foreign portfolio investors. As a result, information-supplying countries will lose banking business – and the associated banking profits – and, if they operate a nonresident withholding tax, also experience a loss of public revenue. Furthermore, the capital-importing country incurs administrative costs related to information gathering and transmission for which it does not receive any financial compensation from the information-requesting country. Trade in tax information is thus a form of gift exchange between countries. Accordingly, small, tax haven jurisdictions – typically, net capital importers, reflecting their low capital-income tax rates – would be net exporters of information and thus have least to gain. By the same token, there is a presumption that tax information will be under-supplied in a decentralized equilibrium.

10.3.1   Reasons for information sharing

The theoretical literature uses small game-theoretic models – of a partial equilibrium nature – to study tax information and revenue sharing between countries. Table 10.1 summarizes the main model characteristics. In general terms, the frameworks differ by assumptions made on the number of countries included, the size of countries (symmetric versus asymmetric), the game structure (one-shot versus infinitely repeated games), and the presence of tax restrictions (whether a full range of taxes can be optimized). The literature identifies four circumstances under which countries may indeed find it in their interest to supply tax

Table 10.1 Theoretical studies on tax information sharing

Study	Builds on:	Model characteristics			
		Number of countries, size, and symmetry	Game structure	Tax setting	Other
Bacchetta and Espinosa (1995)	Zodrow and Mieszkowski (1986)	Two, large (symmetric)	Two stage	Restricted (resident tax is fixed in benchmark)	
Bacchetta and Espinosa (2000)	Bacchetta and Espinosa (1995)	Two, large (asymmetric)	Infinitely repeated	Restricted (resident tax is fixed in benchmark)	Focus on sustainability of tax treaties
Eggert and Kolmar (2002a)	Bucovetsky and Wilson (1991)	Two, large (asymmetric)	Two stage	Unrestricted	
Eggert and Kolmar (2002b)	Bucovetsky and Wilson (1991)	Two, small (symmetric)	Two stage	Unrestricted	Inclusion of banking sector
Huizinga and Nielsen (2003)	Gros (1990)	Two and three, small (symmetric and asymmetric)	Infinitely repeated	Restricted (resident tax is fixed)	Inclusion of banking sector
Makris (2003)	Bacchetta and Espinosa (1995)	Two, small (symmetric)	Two stage	Unrestricted	
Eggert and Kolmar (2004)	Zodrow and Mieszkowski (1986) Bucovetsky and Wilson (1991)	Two, small (symmetric)	Three stage	Un- and restricted	Inclusion of banking sector
Keen and Ligthart (2005)	Gros (1990) Kanbur and Keen (1993)	Two, small (asymmetric)	Two stage	Residents and nonresidents taxed at the same rate	Focus on revenue sharing (exogenous IE)[a]
Keen and Ligthart (2006b)	Huizinga and Nielsen (2003)	Two, small (asymmetric)	Two stage	Restricted (resident tax is fixed)	Focus on revenue sharing (exogenous IE)[a]

air donator information exchange

information: (i) Beneficial strategic effects; (ii) Revenue sharing; (iii) Reputation effects; (iv) Unrestricted tax setting.

In the first case, set out in the key contribution of Bacchetta and Espinosa (1995), countries commit to tax information sharing prior to the noncooperative setting of nonresident income tax rates. This mimics the important feature of international tax negotiations, in which countries are more willing to agree on tax information-sharing treaties (which are long-term in nature) than on key tax income tax rates and bases (which may be changed more easily). In such a setting, country A may benefit unilaterally by providing some information to country B because it induces this country to set a higher nonresident income tax rate (reflecting the reduced threat of capital flight). In turn, country B's response allows country A to set a higher nonresident tax rate too. This beneficial strategic effect, however, must be weighed against the direct effect of information provision at unchanged tax rates. If the former is strong enough, however, countries may choose to provide full information. As Keen and Ligthart (2006b) showed, large countries always benefit. But for very small countries, the strategic tax rate effect of information sharing may not be large enough to compensate the information-providing country for the direct harm from its reduced attractiveness to foreign investors.

A second reason for countries to be motivated to engage in information sharing is the presence of revenue-sharing schemes. As a carrot rather than a stick, some of the additional revenues collected as a consequence of information sharing can be transferred from the residence to the source country to induce the latter to share information. Keen and Ligthart (2005, 2006b) analyzed the incentive effects of such transfers in a setting in which the tax authority can and cannot discriminate between residents and nonresidents. There is nothing inherent in the Diamond–Mirrlees (1971) efficiency argument for residence taxation that requires all collected revenue on cross-border investment to accrue to the residence country. Although the efficiency argument for such transfers is weak, the positive distributional effects may have a useful role to play in inducing small, low-tax countries to participate in information-sharing agreements. In this way, it may resolve the conflict of interest between small and large countries (as set out in Keen and Ligthart, 2006b). A practical problem with such revenue-sharing schemes is that the information-providing country does not know exactly – and has no way to verify – how much additional revenue the residence country actually collects as a result of the information passed to it. Consequently, the residence country has an incentive to underreport the true amount in an attempt to reduce its transfers to the source country. This probably explains why the OECD and European Union have not looked into revenue sharing under a regime of information sharing yet.

The third case concerns the reputation effect associated with repeated interaction between countries over time. Some multilateral cooperation may be sustained if the choice of nonresident tax rates is viewed as an infinitely repeated (noncooperative) game. Each country must then weigh the benefits from continued cooperation against the cost of defection by the other country. Generally, the latter implies more aggressive competition on capital income tax rates and no provision of information at all. The temptation of defecting turns out to be greater the more impatient policymakers are (because continued cooperation will get a lower weight), the more imbalanced capital flows are (because the greater will be the advantages to the capital-importing country of not providing information), and, for the same reason, the more sensitive are capital flows to their effective tax treatment.

Finally, various authors – see Eggert and Kolmar (2002a, b, 2004) and Makris (2003) – have studied information sharing in a setting in which governments can optimize over a full set of tax instruments (that is, nonresident withholding taxes, resident capital income taxes, and labor income taxes). In contrast, Huizinga and Nielsen (2003) and Keen and Ligthart (2006b) assume an exogenously given nonresident withholding tax. In a world of no impediments to capital mobility, the Diamond–Mirrlees theorem implies that they choose a zero nonresident withholding tax. But, given that collecting revenue from nonresidents is the prime reason for countries not to exchange information, source countries do not see any disadvantages in not passing full information to residence countries (this assumes the absence of profits from banking business). Full information sharing is not the only equilibrium of the game, however; Zero information sharing is also an equilibrium. The policy problem in such a setting of multiple equilibria is how to shift the world to the Pareto superior outcome of full information sharing.

10.3.2 Outside tax havens

A proper treatment of 'third countries' or outside tax havens – that is, those countries that feature a sizeable financial sector, but are outside an information-sharing agreement – is important in the context of tackling international tax evasion. Outside tax havens exert downward pressure on nonresident tax rates and reduce the gains to any subset of countries participating in an information exchange agreement. This raises the question of the optimal size of the grand coalition of information-sharing jurisdictions. Gordon and Hines (2002) argued that international tax evasion cannot be fully stemmed; As long as there is one tax haven outside the grand coalition, all funds could (in theory) be diverted to that sole remaining tax haven.

Complete country coverage is unlikely to be an economically meaningful outcome because both governments and investors will conduct a dynamic cost-benefit analysis. Foreign investors will factor in security concerns; The risk of losing their funds through bank default makes it less attractive for tax evaders to deposit funds in financial centers without a proven track record. Investors' transactions costs – for example, travel and communication costs – are also a determinant in such cost-benefit analysis. Tax evaders are therefore less inclined to deposit funds at larger distances. In addition to the factors mentioned in section 10.3.1, governments may refrain from joining an information-sharing agreement because of bank secrecy rules. For information exchange to be effective, however, it is important that key financial centers and tax havens participate in an agreement. The EU savings tax directive, therefore, has concluded 'equivalent measures' with five outside tax havens (see section 10.4.2).

10.3.3 Alternative instruments

It was argued above that tax information sharing buttresses the enforcement of the residence principle. What other instruments are available to tax cross-border savings income? How do they compare in terms of efficiency and equity?

Nonresident withholding taxes are a widely used and administratively simple way of taxing cross-border income flows. Under withholding, taxes on interest income (set by the source country) are collected by financial institutions (commercial banks, insurance and trust companies, etc.) rather than being determined through self-assessment by individual taxpayers. But, unless all countries impose the same withholding tax rate, withholding suffers from the disadvantage of distorting investments in favor of locations with low effective tax rates. Taxation through withholding at source typically makes tax competition more aggressive, tending to lead to Nash equilibrium tax rates below the socially efficient level. Indeed, as shown by Huizinga and Nicodème (2004), the average (statutory) withholding tax imposed on nonresidents for a group of 19 OECD countries has fallen gradually from 0.40% in 1992 to 0.18% in 2000.

A second feature of withholding taxes is that they allocate revenue – in the opposite direction of the residence principle – to the country in which the income is generated, which is not a source of inefficiency in itself but runs counter to apparently widely held notions of inter-nation equity. Note that crediting of withholding taxes under the residence principle generates an *implicit* revenue transfer from the residence to the source country. In the knife-edge case of a foreign withholding tax rate equal to the income tax rate on residents, the residence country does not collect any revenue at all! And, the revenue transferred in this way is not unimportant. Keen and Wildasin (2004) discussed the case of the USA, in which implicit transfers to foreign countries exceed the amount of explicit US foreign aid (averaging about 0.2% of GDP during recent years).[11]

If countries, however, could sign a treaty specifying the socially efficient withholding tax rates and required revenue transfers, an efficient and equitable outcome in line with pure residence-based taxation would be obtained. But the underlying conflict of interest between countries evidently prevents this from happening. Countries with no or a low tax rate fear losing out from a harmonized withholding tax rate at some minimum level (because these countries are net importers of capital). In this political game, an international tax agency – coined the World Tax Organization (WTO) by Tanzi (1999) – could have a meaningful role to play (of course, the WTO could also play a useful role in negotiating information-sharing treaties).

Recent literature (e.g. Keen and Ligthart, 2006b) shows that information exchange is more efficient than withholding taxes in the sense of generating larger global revenues. Intuitively, information sharing brings additional taxpayers into the tax net by their home country, and these taxpayers are typically taxed at (income tax) rates exceeding the nonresident withholding tax rates paid abroad. The size of this effect is larger the greater the difference between the rates of the resident income tax and the foreign withholding tax, the larger the probability of the evader being caught by the foreign authorities, and the larger the imposed fines. Moreover, information exchange has the further advantage that it may also help tax authorities uncover tax evasion in other tax categories (for example, wage or social security taxes)[12] or provide leads in detecting criminal activities, including money laundering. Indeed, evasion of the capital income tax is not the only motive to deposit money abroad; It is likely that some share of the funds is earned in the underground economy or is generated by criminal activities, and therefore must be concealed.

If all countries were identical, one would expect information sharing to emerge as the preferred outcome. Once allowance is made for asymmetries in country size, it is not immediately evident what kind of taxation regime would result. Very small countries – often operating as tax havens (section 10.4.2) – may prefer to levy nonresident withholding taxes. Moreover, this would allow small countries to maintain their bank secrecy legislation or tradition (if any is applicable). As was argued above, by passing some of the additional revenue collected as a consequence of information shared to the jurisdiction that provided it, small countries may be induced to opt for information exchange.

10.4   The EU savings tax

This section provides a brief historical background of the EU savings tax directive, analyzes its key features, and studies its effectiveness in taxing cross-border savings income.

10.4.1   Brief historical background

Since the late 1980s, there have been efforts in the European Union to coordinate the taxation of residents' cross-border savings income. Table 10.2 provides an overview of the key elements of the various proposals. In 1989, the European Commission submitted a proposal for a Council directive, which envisaged a community-wide minimum withholding tax of 15% on cross-border savings income of EU residents. The proposal was heavily criticized on two accounts: (i) For not covering key outside tax havens, potentially generating capital outflows to these jurisdictions; (ii) For intervening with a country's sovereignty to set its own tax rates.

Faced with these political hurdles, attention turned to the alternative strategy of encouraging source countries to pass to the tax authorities of the residence country sufficient information for the latter to bring all the capital income of their residents into the tax net, so at least preserving countries' sovereignty in tax rate setting. It is important to note that tax information sharing is not an entirely new instrument because various treaties exist that provide some authority for the sharing of information on income taxes between EU countries (the most commonly known are bilateral double-taxation treaties between EU Member States and the EU Mutual Assistance directive). The main problem with the current legal framework is that it allows Member States to refuse furnishing information under certain conditions (for example, if it is contrary to their domestic laws or requires efforts beyond normal administrative practice). Furthermore, the existing legal frameworks do not incorporate common rules concerning the details of the information to be provided and frequency of exchanges.

In view of the bank secrecy tradition in Austria, Belgium, and Luxembourg, a uniform information-sharing regime turned out to be politically unfeasible.[13] A new proposal for a directive was presented in 1998, taking into account bank secrecy. The so-called coexistence model allowed each Member State the choice

Table 10.2 Historical background of the EU savings tax

Name	Date of proposal	Key elements	Source
Withholding model	1989	Minimum withholding tax of 15%	European Commission (1989)
Coexistence model	1998	Member States have a choice between: (a) Automatic information sharing, or (b) Minimum withholding tax of 20%	European Commission (1998)
Feira agreement	June 2000	(a) 12 Member States exchange information automatically (b) Austria, Belgium, and Luxembourg operate a withholding tax during 7 years transition period (15% during years 1–3 and 20% during years 4–7). Revenues are shared (c) Equivalent measures in third countries and DA territories[a]	
Modified Feira agreement	2001	(a) 12 Member States exchange information automatically (b) Austria, Belgium, and Luxembourg operate a withholding tax during transition period (15% during years 1–3, 20% during years 4–7, and 35% thereafter). Sharing of withholding tax revenues (c) Equivalent measures in six third countries and DA territories	European Commission (2001)
Final agreement	January 2003 to July 2003[b]	(a) 22 Member States exchange information automatically[c] (b) Austria, Belgium, and Luxembourg operate a withholding tax during transition period at modified Feira rate schedule. Revenues are shared (c) Equivalent measures in five third countries and DA territories	European Commission (2003)

[a] DA stands for dependent and associated.
[b] Date on which the final text was determined.
[c] Includes 10 new Member States that entered into the European Union on 1 May 2004.

of either providing tax information or applying a nonresident withholding tax at a minimum rate of 20%. Member States opting for a withholding tax were to retain all revenue from taxing nonresident savings income. The distributional effects of the directive were a sticking point in the negotiations between the European Commission and its Member States. The UK and its AD territories would lose, whereas France and Germany would gain.

The Feira agreement of June 2000 modified the 1998 proposal by requiring Member States (except for the three bank secrecy jurisdictions) to automatically exchange tax information. The three bank secrecy jurisdictions would be allowed to operate a withholding tax regime during a seven-year transition period. A withholding tax rate of 15% would apply during the first three years and a rate of 20% during the remaining four years. In July 2001, the European Commission issued a revised proposed directive, which formed the basis of a political agreement in January 2003.

10.4.2 General principles

In January 2003, the EU Council reached political agreement on a proposed savings tax directive, the final text of which was determined in June 2003. The savings tax was supposed to take effect in January 2005. After half a year delay, on 1 July 2005, two taxation regimes became effective. The first regime consists of 22 EU Member States (The 12 old Member States that have committed to information sharing and 10 new EU Member States that joined in May 2004) that exchange tax information automatically – that is, without the need for any specific request from the residence country – to all other Member States about the cross-border interest payments to individuals within the European Union. Interest for that purpose means interest income from debt claims of every kind, such as savings deposits, corporate and government bonds, other negotiable debt securities, and income from investment funds (as long as the portfolio share of bonds exceeds 40%). The information[14] is collected from interest-paying financial institutions, typically commercial banks, and passed to the domestic fiscal authority. The latter in turn transmits it to the foreign fiscal authorities (at least once a year), which allows the residence country to charge the domestic tax on the foreign savings income of its residents, giving, if applicable, a credit for nonresident withholding tax paid abroad. Under the EU savings tax, information is thus collected on interest income (a flow), so that the directive does not touch upon the individual's savings position (a stock).

In the second taxation regime, the three EU countries with a bank secrecy tradition (Austria, Belgium, and Luxembourg) apply a nonresident withholding tax.[15] They levy tax according to a graduated rate schedule: A rate of 15% during the first three years (July 2005–June 2008), 20% for the subsequent three years (July 2008–June 2011), and 35% from July 2011 onwards. The 35% tax rate corresponds to the current Swiss withholding tax on interest and dividends, which, contrary to that of most EU countries, applies to both residents and nonresidents equally.

The first innovative feature of the EU savings tax involves the coverage of non-EU countries and DA territories of EU countries. To mitigate capital flight from the European Union, five non-EU jurisdictions – that is, Andorra, Liechtenstein, Monaco, San Marino, and Switzerland – have implemented 'equivalent measures', which implies that they apply a withholding tax under the same arrangements as the three EU countries in the transition regime (this tax is also referred to as the 'retention tax', which is just another name for the withholding tax). Time and again, the European Commission has talked with the USA in its third-country negotiations. The USA, however, has not accepted the savings tax directive and, consequently, neither provides information automatically to EU countries nor does it impose a withholding tax on EU capital income. However, the Internal Revenue Service (IRS) of the USA does receive information on US citizens' and its alien residents' interest on bank accounts through its network of qualified intermediaries (QIs) abroad.[16] This information-gathering role of QIs reduced the pressure on the USA to participate in the EU savings tax.

Three further characteristics of the withholding regime are noteworthy. First, withholding taxes are, in theory, not imposed on EU residents that have opted to disclose information on their savings income to their home tax authorities. In practice, the effective availability of this choice depends on whether the foreign financial institutions are willing to incur the additional administrative costs. Second, in cases of tax fraud,[17] the five non-EU countries will provide information upon request of the EU tax authorities. Finally, the transitional regime ends when the five third countries and the USA agree to exchange information on request in civil tax matters, and/or the three EU countries with a bank secrecy tradition elect to switch to automatic information sharing.

The European Commission has negotiated 'similar measures' with DA territories of the Netherlands and the UK (10 in total) (Table 10.3), which are obvious targets for tax evaders given their EU dependency. Four jurisdictions exchange information automatically, whereas the remaining six levy a nonresident withholding tax along the lines of Austria, Belgium, and Luxembourg. Seven DA territories have entered into a reciprocal agreement in which they receive from EU countries tax information or, if applicable, receive withholding tax revenues on interest income of their residents that have invested in participating EU countries

Table 10.3 Overview of jurisdictions participating in the EU savings tax

Jurisdiction[a,b]	Status[c]	Population (in thousands)	GDP per capita (in US$)	Area (square kilometers)
		Automatic information sharing		
Anguilla	DU	12.0	10,810.5	96
Aruba	DD	98.2	21,131.0	193
Cayman Islands	DU	44.1	38,594.2	264
Cyprus	MS	825.9	18,562.2	9251
Czech Republic	MS	10,229.0	10,461.9	78,866
Denmark	MS	5414.2	44,593.5	43,094
Estonia	MS	1335.1	8227.3	45,100
Finland	MS	5235.2	35,515.2	338,145
France	MS	60,256.8	33,966.9	551,500
Germany	MS	82,645.3	32,707.5	357,022
Greece	MS	11,098.3	18,491.5	131,957
Hungary	MS	10,124.1	9908.4	93,032
Ireland	MS	4079.6	44,521.2	70,273
Italy	MS	58,032.7	28,913.1	301,318
Latvia	MS	2318.5	64,600.0	5876
Lithuania	MS	3443.3	6391.0	65,200
Malta	MS	399.8	14,074.0	316
Montserrat	DU	4.2	12,032.2	102
Netherlands	MS	16,226.2	35,683.3	41,526
Poland	MS	38,559.4	6265.4	323,250
Portugal	MS	10,441.4	16,063.3	91,982
Slovakia	MS	5401.5	7607.5	49,012
Slovenia	MS	1967.2	16,358.9	20,250
Spain	MS	42,646.4	24,385.9	505,992
Sweden	MS	9007.8	38,456.9	449,964
UK	MS	59,479.3	35,717.7	242,900
Average		16,897.1	24,386.2	146,788
		Withholding taxes		
Andorra	TC	66.9	25,786.0	468
Austria	MS	8171.1	35,777.4	83,859
Belgium	MS	10,399.7	33,878.5	30,528
British Virgin Islands	DU	21.7	43,366.3	151
Guernsey	DU	65.2	2781.2	78

(Continued)

Table 10.3 (Continued)

Jurisdiction[a,b]	Status[c]	Population (in thousands)	GDP per capita (in US$)	Area (square kilometers)
Isle of Man	DU	76.7	2929.9	572
Jersey	DU	90.8	5311.6	116
Liechtenstein	TC	34.2	101,653.8	160
Luxembourg	MS	459.0	69,423.0	2586
Monaco	TC	34.9	32,984.1	1
Netherlands Antilles	DD	180.9	5376.1	800
San Marino	TC	27.9	44,607.3	61
Switzerland	TC	7239.7	49,366.6	41,284
Turks and Caicos Islands	DU	25.2	9923.7	430
Average		1921.0	33,083.3	11,507

Sources: UNCTAD (2006) database and European Commission (2005).
[a] Based on 2004 data.
[b] The United States is not included because it neither shares information with the EU nor does it impose a withholding tax. Gibraltar is counted as part of the UK and Madeira as part of Portugal. Bermuda (UK independent territory) was accidentally missed out by the EU.
[c] The following labels are used: EU member state (MS), Third country (TC), Dutch dependency (DD), and UK dependency (DU).

(because third countries are not part of the European Union, no reciprocal agreement applies). Not all DA territories consider this of particular importance; Three DA territories – that is, Anguilla, Cayman Islands, and Turks and Caicos Islands – do not have a reciprocal effect because residents' savings income is not taxed.

The second innovative feature of the savings tax directive concerns the revenue-sharing rule: Jurisdictions operating a withholding tax will transfer 75% of the revenue that they collect to the investor's country of residence. Besides being able to keep 25% of the revenue, those jurisdictions will get valuable information from EU partners on their residents' foreign savings income. This applies to all three EU countries in the transitional regime and DA territories that apply a withholding tax combined with a reciprocity agreement. The rationale for the revenue-sharing rule is the notion that the 'rights' to the revenue – after subtraction of a compensation for the administrative and collection costs – should, in line with the residence principle, accrue to the residence country.

Table 10.3 shows the 40 jurisdictions participating in the EU savings tax classified by the regime of savings taxation. Information sharing is the dominant regime; 26 jurisdictions (65 percent) share tax information automatically and 14 apply a withholding tax and share its revenues. It can be seen that relatively large countries (in terms of population size or surface area) have opted to operate an information-sharing regime. The average population size of information-sharing countries is 17 million against 1.9 million for the jurisdictions levying a withholding tax. If the three EU Member States in the transition regime are excluded, the average population size of countries with a withholding regime drops to 0.7 million. Removing Switzerland reduces the average population size to 62,400. These countries are thus dot sized. Similarly, in terms of square kilometers found, the average size of information sharing jurisdictions is 147,000 square kilometers versus 11,500 square kilometers in the withholding regime. Bigger countries are not necessarily wealthier if measured by GDP per capita. A small country like Liechtenstein has, with US$101,600, the highest GDP per capita of all savings tax jurisdictions, which is substantially above the average of US$27,430 for all savings tax jurisdictions. It is noteworthy that countries in the withholding regime – which are on average smaller – feature a higher per capita GDP than countries in the information-sharing regime.

10.4.3 Effectiveness of the EU savings tax

The most obvious way for EU residents to avoid[18] the EU savings tax is to relocate their funds to source countries not participating in the EU savings tax or to relocate themselves to residence countries not participating in the savings tax. Of course, emigration involves high transactions and emotional costs to tax evaders, which, on the margin, are unlikely to outweigh the benefits. A more profitable strategy for EU residents is to masquerade as nonresidents (in some cases, if need be, by round-tripping their funds through intermediaries abroad),[19] which amounts to outright tax evasion. Evidently, the tax elasticity of bank deposits and financial capital more generally is larger than that of labor, and therefore the focus is on the former in the following discussion.

Some observers in policy circles claim that important financial centers such as Canada, Hong Kong SAR, Japan, and Singapore should be added to the list of countries participating in the EU savings tax to make the arrangement effective (see Weiner, 2002). To investigate this claim, Table 10.4 has been constructed.[20] Column 4 calculates the GDP share of external deposits of nonbank investors for 39 jurisdictions as reported by the BIS. In the sample, on average, external deposits amount to 12.9% of GDP. Of 39 cases, nine jurisdictions have an external deposits-to-GDP share exceeding 100%, being an indicator of their position as key financial centers.

Table 10.4 External deposits of nonbank investors by country, 2004

Jurisdiction[a]	1995 (US$, billions)	2004 (US$, billions)[b]	Percentage change	2004 shares		List coverage	
				Percent of GDP	Share of total[c]	EU savings tax[d]	On original OECD list[e]
Total	0.0	4566.3	—[f]	12.9	28.8	21	9
Cayman Islands	172.3	480.7	179.0	28,241.2	55.5	WT	X
Jersey	—	102.2	—	1924.1	47.7	WT	X
Bahamas	65.3	82.8	26.8	1720.3	30.7		X
Guernsey	—	45.2	—	1625.2	43.3	WT	X
Isle of Man	—	38.7	—	1471.5	92.8	WT	X
Singapore	80.6	150.4	86.6	601.6	32.5		
Luxembourg	167.7	180.5	7.6	566.4	36.5	WT	
Netherlands Antilles	1.9	11.3	494.7	364.0	43.3	WT	X
Bahrain	15.6	26.1	67.3	237.8	27.0		X
Ireland	13.3	133.1	900.8	73.3	24.3	IE	X
Bermuda	—	2.5	—	60.4	78.1		X
Belgium	57.8	169.8	193.8	48.2	32.9	WT	
Hong Kong SAR	65.1	79.2	21.7	48.1	26.9		
UK	328.2	977.5	197.8	46.0	27.5	IE	
Panama	—	5.9	—	43.5	58.4		X
Netherlands	56.5	131.9	133.5	22.8	22.0	IE	
Switzerland	439.7	354.1	-19.5	16.7	42.8	WT	
Germany	150.9	423.1	180.4	15.7	34.0	IE	
Portugal	—	24.1	—	14.4	15.0	IE	
Spain	40.9	130.5	219.1	12.5	29.8	IE	
Greece	—	23.9	—	11.6	46.8	IE	

Taiwan China	–	24.7	–	8.1	48.0	
Denmark	7.5	18.8	150.7	7.8	14.4	IE
Austria	11.6	20.3	75.0	6.9	18.8	WT
USA	93.2	597.6	541.2	5.1	27.9	
France	56.8	101.1	78.0	4.9	10.0	IE
India	–	32.7	–	4.8	78.0	
Canada	29.7	41.6	40.1	4.2	28.7	
Sweden	8.1	13.3	64.2	3.8	8.6	IE
Australia	–	22.1	–	3.5	26.2	
Finland	0.7	4.6	557.1	2.5	10.7	IE
Italy	12.8	36.3	183.6	2.2	7.6	IE
Turkey	–	5.9	–	2.0	26.0	
Norway	2.1	4.7	123.8	1.9	13.9	
Chile	–	1.4	–	1.5	23.7	
Japan	20.6	65.6	218.4	1.4	11.5	
Brazil	–	1.8	–	0.3	9.1	
Mexico	–	0.3	–	0.0	15.8	

Sources: BIS (2006), Tables 3A–B of the *Locational Statistics*, and statistical agencies of Guernsey, Isle of Man, and Jersey. Nominal GDP is taken from the UNCTAD database (2006).

[a] Country coverage is determined by the availability of statistics for these countries.

[b] Stock of external deposits as of December 2004.

[c] Total external deposits of nonresident investors (the denominator) consist of inter-bank deposits and deposits made by nonbanks (numerator). The latter include deposits made by individuals, businesses, and nonbank financial institutions.

[d] WT and IE denote withholding tax and information sharing respectively.

[e] Countries on the June 2000 OECD list of noncooperative tax havens.

[f] The totals cannot be compared due to the smaller country coverage (24 countries in 1995 versus 39 in 2004).

The nine jurisdictions (in order of size) are: the Cayman Islands, Jersey, the Bahamas, Guernsey, Isle of Man, Singapore, Luxembourg, Netherlands Antilles, and Bahrain. Column 5 of the table shows that all jurisdictions (except Bahrain) have an above average share of nonresident deposits in total external (including inter-bank) deposits, suggesting that attracting nonresident, nonbank deposits is an important economic activity. Six of the nine (offshore) financial centers operate a withholding tax under the EU savings tax (column 6). Of the 19 countries with an external deposit-to-GDP share exceeding the average, six are not covered by the EU savings tax: The Bahamas, Bahrain, Bermuda, Hong Kong SAR, Panama, and Singapore (Bermuda – a dependent territory of the UK – seems to have been accidently left out by the European Union). In absolute terms, Singapore, the Bahamas, and Hong Kong SAR are the three most important financial centers on this list. Four of the six noncovered jurisdictions – that is, the Bahamas, Bahrain, Bermuda, and Panama – are on the original (June 2000) OECD list of uncooperative tax havens. In sum, the country coverage of the EU savings tax is far from complete, which is hardly a surprising conclusion. Canada and Japan – which were put forward by Weiner (2002) in the discussion of country coverage – do not seem to feature prominently on the list of offshore financial centers.

Gnaedinger and Radziejewska (2003) have raised doubts about the EU savings tax's ability to raise public revenue because people may have nontax motives for holding cross-border deposits. Individuals may, for example, be holding foreign bank accounts for convenience during vacations or business trips abroad. Evidently, no information is available to substantiate this claim. But there can be little doubt that tax motives for holding foreign bank accounts do play a role for wealthy individuals, just as they do in companies' location decisions.

The EU savings taxation directive only applies to individuals' savings and not those of corporations and other legal entities (such as partnerships, limited partnerships, foundations, and many trusts), reflecting the reduced likelihood of tax evasion by corporations as compared to individuals (due to annual filing requirements and regular audits of corporations, tax evasion by corporations is smaller than by individuals). Such differential treatment entails the risk that truly wealthy Europeans incorporate their cross-border savings to evade taxation, giving rise to undesirable distributional effects. The incentives to incorporate are likely to be small in countries with high corporate income taxes, since corporate profits are generally taxed as high as personal income. But many of the smaller jurisdictions covered by the EU savings tax do not have corporate income taxes (that is, Anguilla, the British Virgin Islands, the Cayman Islands, and Turks and Caicos Islands), making them excellent business locations.

The range of savings instruments covered by the savings tax is incomplete. It does not apply to shares, income from insurance and pension products, dividends, interest payments on certain grandfathered bonds, and income from investment funds (with a bond share of less than 40%).[21] The incomplete coverage and high substitutability between assets induces risk-neutral investors to convert their savings deposits and bonds into shares and to increase their share of assets held in investment funds.[22] Ideally, income from shares should be treated in the same way as interest income. Covering shares is problematic because the measurement of capital gains associated with trade in shares involves substantial administrative costs.

Very little is known about how extensive information is shared under established agreements and how effectively information is used.[23] This makes it hard to foresee what are the key hurdles that EU tax authorities may be experiencing under the savings tax. For information exchange to be effective, tax information needs to be provided in a timely fashion; The EU savings tax guarantees information sharing at least once a year. To some degree, of course, it is not only the actual use made of the information received which matters, but also the use that investors believe will be made. In the long run, however, one would expect these perceptions to come to match reality. Perceptions are likely to be influenced by information about the tax authority's capabilities to match information received with a country's own records on the taxpayer. Without a common taxpayer number, such a matching exercise will be a nontrivial exercise. Moreover, Tanzi and Zee (2001) pointed out that problems may arise due to differences in definition of tax bases, interpretation of legal provisions, and linguistic barriers.

Finally, due to bank secrecy restrictions, tax authorities may be denied access to bank information on interest income, which is the case in a minority of OECD countries, including well-known financial centers such as Switzerland and Luxembourg. The latter jurisdictions are required to operate a (second-best) withholding tax to prevent loopholes in the savings tax system.

10.5 Conclusion

To stem the rapidly growing incidence of international tax evasion, recent policy initiatives of the EU and OECD have focused on the exchange of taxpayer-specific information. The EU has committed 26 jurisdictions to implement tax information sharing on EU residents' cross-border savings income. In addition, 14 jurisdictions have -committed themselves to levy a withholding tax combined with revenue sharing.

In comparison with the small number of signatories of existing information-sharing treaties (typically less than 25), the EU savings tax directive has been quite successful in achieving multilateral commitments to information exchange.

The savings tax features a number of loopholes, which could potentially harm its effectiveness in addressing international tax evasion. First, not all the important financial centers (for example, Singapore and Hong Kong) are included. Even smaller ones that are obvious candidates, such as the Bahamas and Bermuda, are not covered. Second, asset coverage is incomplete, which is likely to give rise to substitution away from bonds and bank deposits to shares. Third, truly wealthy individuals may incorporate themselves to avoid savings taxation, thereby shifting the distribution of income in favor of wealthy individuals. Finally, differences in the interpretation of legal provisions and the absence of a uniform taxpayer identification number may reduce the usefulness of received information.

The EU savings tax aims for a regime in which all participating jurisdictions share information eventually. Nevertheless, it is clear that a number of countries with a bank secrecy tradition – notably Switzerland and Luxembourg – are reluctant to commit themselves to information sharing of the kind that others seek. This legal hurdle and the weaknesses identified above will lessen the effectiveness of the EU savings tax. Not much is known about the effectiveness of the EU savings tax and other information-sharing arrangements, which is not surprising given the confidentiality with which data on information sharing is treated. It is therefore unlikely that information sharing will put an end to discussions on the coordination of underlying income tax systems themselves.

Notes

1. Note that the terms cross-border savings, deposits, and investments will be used interchangeably to refer to passive (portfolio) investments abroad.
2. Following Hines and Rice (1994), tax havens are defined as locations that: (i) Levy low or negligible corporate or personal tax rates; (ii) Feature legislation that supports banking secrecy; (iii) Employ advanced communications facilities; (iv) Promote themselves as financial centers. Others, for example the OECD (1998), employ slightly different definitions.
3. Based on a group of countries (see Table 10.3 for a country list) for which the Bank for International Settlements (BIS) has data available.
4. Many EU governments have to cut public spending to meet the ceilings on their fiscal deficit and debt (of 3% and 60% of GDP respectively) imposed by the Stability and Growth Pact.
5. The aim of a tax-crediting system is to prevent double taxation in the residence country of taxed foreign source income of its residents. Typically, the credit is capped by the tax liability in the residence country, implying that residence countries do not refund excess tax to the beneficial

owner. Due to tax crediting, the power of taxation of cross-border income is effectively shared between the residence and source countries.

6. As Keen and Ligthart (2006a) pointed out, the Diamond–Mirrlees theorem is silent on equity issues. It does not specify whether the revenue from the residence tax should accrue to the source or residence country.

7. It is safe – and common practice in the literature – to assume that residents do not report their income to the tax authorities at all, turning the residence system (without information sharing) into effectively a pure source tax system.

8. The Mutual Assistance directive (concluded in 1977) is a multilateral instrument providing for the sharing of information on direct and indirect taxes among EU authorities. See Keen and Ligthart (2006a) for further details.

9. In an overview on the economics of reciprocity, Fehr and Gächter (2000) concluded that there is some disagreement about its determinants. Generally, three determinants are important: Equity motives, boundedly rational behavior, and the reward to kind intentions.

10. A solution is to let the information-providing country share in the additional revenue obtained by the information receiving (or residence) country (see section 10.3.1).

11. In a world in which *explicit* revenue transfers are feasible, which in practice is difficult though not infeasible (see section 10.4.2), the residence country may want to claim back (part of) the tax credit from the source country.

12. This requires that the tax categories under consideration are administered by a single tax administration or, if administered by different administrations, assumes a great deal of cooperation between them.

13. Luxembourg and Austria have bank secrecy regulations, which are moderately strong in the case of Austria. In Belgium, bank secrecy is not explicitly written down, but is observed as a tradition.

14. The minimum amount of information typically consists of: Interest income earned, account number, identity and residence of the beneficial owner, and contact information of the paying agent. Under the 'know-your-customer' rules of anti-money laundering legislation, commercial banks have already collected the identity and residence of their customers.

15. In addition to these two pure regimes, a third regime is theoretically possible (but nonexistent in practice) in which a Member State applies a combination of automatic information sharing and a (source-type) withholding tax on interest paid to nonresidents.

16. QIs levy a withholding tax provided by the tax treaty between the USA and the respective country of source and transfer the proceeds to the IRS. In this case, the withholding tax rate is determined by the residence country and revenue-sharing amounts to 100% (rather than the 75% specified by the EU savings tax). Gérard (2005) proposed a QI-like system as an alternative to the EU savings tax.

17. Tax fraud (a criminal tax matter) is loosely defined to include the intentional violation of a legal requirement concerning the accurate reporting, determination, or collection of tax. The definition of tax fraud varies by country. Switzerland, for example, employs a much narrower definition than that employed in the average EU country (see OECD, 2000).

18. Tax avoidance – reducing one's tax liability within the boundaries of the law – should be distinguished from tax evasion, which involves illegal behavior.

19. Masquerading as nonresidents will not be that easy, although there is evidence that it is a relevant concern in the design of tax policy (Keen and Ligthart, 2005). An individual who claims to

be living in a country different than that listed in his or her passport has to present a certificate of residency issued by the third country.

20. The country list is determined by the availability of data on external deposits of nonbanks and therefore cannot be exhaustive. Note that it covers nine of the 35 tax havens on the OECD blacklist and 14 on the list of tax havens compiled by Hines and Rice (1994). Nevertheless, the sample is big enough to support the case of less than complete country coverage of the EU savings tax.

21. Information sharing applies only to bonds issued after March 2001 with a view to protect London's eurobond market.

22. No estimates are available on the size of these substitution effects. The European Commission, however, is committed to extend the scope of the directive if these effects were to turn out large.

23. A notable exception is Huizinga and Nicodème (2004), who investigated whether information exchange has had a negative effect on international depositing patterns. They cannot find a significant effect, however, raising doubts about the effectiveness of information sharing. Note, however, that their analysis may have been affected by a simultaneity problem. Information sharing itself is likely to be a function of capital flows.

References

Bacchetta, P. and Espinosa, M.P. (1995). Information Sharing and Tax Competition Among Governments. *Journal of International Economics*, 39:103–121.

Bacchetta, P. and Espinosa, M.P. (2000). Exchange-of-information Clauses in International Tax Treaties. *International Tax and Public Finance*, 7:275–293.

Bank for International Settlements (BIS) (2006). *Locational Statistics*, Tables 3A-B. Internet: http://www.bis.org/statistics/bankstats.html.

Bucovetsky, S. and Wilson, J.D. (1991). Tax Competition with Two Tax Instruments. *Regional Science and Urban Economics*, 21:333–350.

Diamond, P. and Mirrlees, J.A. (1971). Optimal Taxation and Public Production. II: Tax Rules. *American Economic Review*, 61:261–278.

Eggert, W. and Kolmar, M. (2002a). Information Sharing, Multiple Nash Equilibria, and Asymmetric Capital-tax Competition. EPRU Working Paper Series No. 02-01. EPRU, Copenhagen.

Eggert, W. and Kolmar, M. (2002b). Residence-based Capital Taxation in a Small Open Economy: Why Information is Voluntarily Exchanged and Why it is Not. *International Tax and Public Finance*, 9:465–482.

Eggert, W. and Kolmar, M. (2004). The Taxation of Financial Capital Under Asymmetric Information and the Tax Competition Paradox. *Scandinavian Journal of Economics*, 106:83–105.

European Commission (1989). Tax Measures to be Adopted by the Community in Connection with the Liberalization of Capital Movements: Proposal for a Council Directive on a Common System of Withholding Tax on Interest Income, COM (89) 295 final. European Commission, Brussels.

European Commission (1998). Proposal for a Council Directive to Ensure a Minimum of Effective Taxation of Savings Income in the Form of Interest Payments Within the Community, COM (98) 295 final. European Commission, Brussels.

European Commission (2001). Proposal for a Council Directive to Ensure Effective Taxation of Savings Income in the Form of Interest Payments within the Community, COM (01) 400. European Commission, Brussels.

European Commission (2003). Council Directive 2003/48/EC on Taxation of Savings Income in the Form of Interest Payments. *Official Journal of the European Communities*, L157:38–46.

Fehr, E. and Gächter, S. (2000). Fairness and Retaliation: The Economics of Reciprocity. *Journal of Economic Perspectives*, 14:159–181.

Gérard, M. (2005). The US Qualified Intermediaries and some EU Tax Innovations: Stones to Build Up a New System of International Savings Taxation. *Proceedings of the 97th Annual Conference of the National Tax Association*, pp. 215–220.

Gnaedinger, C. and Radziejewska, N. (2003). EU Achieves Savings Tax Breakthrough. *Tax Notes International*, January:343–345.

Gordon, R.H. and Hines, J.R. (2002). International Taxation. In: *Handbook of Public Economics* IV (Auerbach, A.J. and Feldstein, M., eds). Elsevier Science, Amsterdam.

Gros, D. (1990). Tax Evasion and Offshore Centres. In: *Reforming Capital Income Taxation* (Siebert, H., ed.), pp. 113–127. Mohr (P. Siebeck), Tübingen.

Hines, J.R. and Rice, E.M. (1994). Fiscal Paradise: Foreign Tax Havens and American Business. *Quarterly Journal of Economics*, 109:149–182.

Huizinga, H. and Nielsen, S.B. (2003). Withholding Taxes or Information Exchange: The Taxation of International Interest Flows. *Journal of Public Economics*, 87:39–72.

Huizinga, H. and Nicodème, G. (2004). Are International Deposits Tax Driven? *Journal of Public Economics*, 88:1093–1118.

Kanbur, R. and Keen, M. (1993). Jeux Sans Frontières: Tax Competition and Tax Coordination when Countries Differ in Size. *American Economic Review*, 83:877–892.

Keen, M. and Ligthart, J.E. (2005). Information Exchange under Non-Discriminatory Taxation. CentER Discussion Paper No. 2005-69. Tilburg University, Tilburg.

Keen, M. and Ligthart, J.E. (2006a). Information Sharing and International Taxation: A Primer. *International Tax and Public Finance*, 13:81–110.

Keen, M. and Ligthart, J.E. (2006b). Incentives and Information Exchange in International Taxation. *International Tax and Public Finance*, 13:163–180.

Keen, M. and Wildasin, D.E. (2004). Pareto-efficient International Taxation. *American Economic Review*, 94:259–275.

Makris, M. (2003). International Tax Competition: There is No Need for Cooperation in Information Sharing. *Review of International Economics*, 11:555–567.

OECD (1998). *Harmful Tax Competition: An Emerging Global Issue*. OECD, Paris.

OECD (2000). *Improving Access to Bank Information for Tax Purposes*. OECD, Paris.

Tanzi, V. (1999). Is There a Need for a World Tax Organization? In: *The Economics of Globalization: Policy Perspectives from Public Economics* (Razin, A. and Sadka, E., eds). Cambridge University Press, Cambridge.

Tanzi, V. and Zee, H.H. (1999). Taxation in a Borderless World: The Role of Information Exchange. In: *International Studies in Taxation: Law and Economics* (Lindencrona, G., Lodin, S-O., and Wiman, B., eds). Kluwer Law International, UK.

Tanzi, V. and Zee, H.H. (2001). Can Information Exchange be Effective in Taxing Cross-border Income Flows? In: *Modern Issues in the Law of International Taxation* (Andersson, K., Melz, P., and Silfverberg, C., eds). Kluwer Law International, Stockholm.

UNCTAD (2006). Statistics Online. Internet: http://www.unctad.org.

Weiner, J.M. (2002). EU Savings Tax Collapses at ECOFIN Meeting. *Tax Notes International*, December:959–961.

Wilson, J.D. (1999). Theories of Tax Competition. *National Tax Journal*, 52:269–304.

Zodrow, G. and Miezkowski, P. (1986). Pigou, Tiebout, Property Taxation and the Underprovision of Local Public Goods. *Journal of Urban Economics*, 19:356–370.

11

Tax Misery and Tax Happiness: A Comparative Study of Selected Asian Countries

Robert W. McGee

Abstract

This article examines the relative tax burden of selected Asian economies from a micro-economic perspective. It employs data from the Tax Misery Index and the Index of Economic Freedom to compare the tax burden of selected Asian economies to that of some European and North American economies. It then creates a hybrid index, which provides another, more representative, look at relative tax burdens from an investor's perspective.

11.1 Introduction

Investing in a given economy must balance profit opportunities with any tax burden that partially or totally offsets these profit opportunities. Financial transparency, corporate governance, and public finance must also be weighted. It does not matter how profitable an investment might be if some government takes most of the profits. What matters in the final analysis is how much is left after taxes have been paid. However, most studies of taxation and public finance take a macro approach. They look at factors like government expenditures or taxes as a percentage of Gross Domestic Product (GDP) or some other macro variables. One problem with this approach, especially in transition or developing economies, is that the statistics may not be accurate, for a number of reasons. Because transition and developing economies often have a large unrecorded sector (unofficial economy), it is not possible to know what the actual GDP might be. Some Asian economies may be classified as transition or developing economies, whereas others already have a strong, vibrant private sector.

This study departs from the typical macro study. It takes a micro approach to public finance by examining certain aspects of taxation and public finance from the perspective of corporations and individuals – those who actually pay the taxes. Using the *Forbes* Tax Misery Index and Global Happiness Index, comparisons are made between selected Asian economies and some developed Western economies to determine how competitive Asian economies are in the area of public finance. The 2006 Index of Economic Freedom is also consulted. A comparison is then made between the two studies, which present a somewhat different view of public finance. A third approach is recommended that incorporates components of the Tax Misery Index and the Index of Economic Freedom to form a new index that better measures the relative competitiveness of Asian economies in the area of public finance.

11.2 Tax misery

Each year, *Forbes* magazine publishes a study on tax misery. The *Forbes* Global Misery and Reform Index is a proxy for evaluating whether tax policy attracts or repels capital and talent. It is computed by adding the top marginal tax rate for the corporate income tax, individual income tax, wealth tax, employer's and employee's social security tax, and value added tax (VAT). The higher the total, the more the misery. Some taxes are omitted, such as the real and personal property tax and excise taxes. The 2005 Index was used for this study, which uses 2004 data. Fifty-six countries are ranked. Table 11.1 contains all the Asian countries that were included in the Index, as well as selected developed and developing countries for comparison purposes. All of the top 10 countries are included for information purposes.

As can be seen, the range of misery varies widely. French taxpayers have to endure more than twice the misery of taxpayers in India, Thailand, or Taiwan, and nearly 10 times as much misery as the taxpayers of the United Arab Emirates. Luxembourg is at the midpoint in 28th place with a score of 108.1. Three of the 12 Asian economies (China, Japan, and Turkey) have higher than average scores. Nine Asian economies (South Korea, Australia, Indonesia, Malaysia, India, Thailand, Taiwan, Singapore, and Hong Kong) have below average scores. Australia is included in the Asian country category because its economy is tied in to the economies of several Asian countries and it is in physical proximity to several Asian nations. Furthermore, many immigrants who now live in Australia were born in an Asian country.

From Table 11.1, one may tentatively conclude that the Asian economies are generally more competitive than the average developed market economy. But this conclusion can only be tentative, as we shall see later, because there is more to consider.

Anderson (2005) pointed out that over the prior 12-month period more countries have reduced their tax rates than have increased them and that there is a move to the flat tax, both for individuals and corporations. This increasing popularity of the flat tax has occurred mostly in Europe, especially in transition economies. Although American economists have been advocating the flat tax for decades (Hall and Rabushka, 1985), the concept has not yet caught on in the USA. Part of the hesitancy is because of the perception in some quarters that the rich need to pay higher taxes than the poor for moral reasons (McCaffery, 2002). However, the case for the graduated income tax, which Marx and Engels (1848) advocated as a means of destroying the capitalist system in their Communist Manifesto, has been demolished on both utilitarian economic grounds (Blum and Kalven, 1953) and ethical grounds (deJouvenel, 1952; McGee, 1998a, b, 2004).

Table 11.1 Tax misery for selected countries, 2005

Rank	Country	Corp. inc. tax	Indiv. inc. tax	Wealth tax	Employer soc. sec. tax	Employee soc. sec. tax	VAT	Misery 2005
1	France	34.4	59	1.8	45	15	19.6	174.8
2	China	33	45	0	44.5	20.5	17	160.0
3	Belgium	34	53.5	0	34.5	13.1	21	156.1
4	Sweden	28	56	1.5	32.5	7	25	150.0
5	Italy	37.3	43	0.7	35	10	20	146.0
6	Austria	25	50	0	31.2	18.2	20	144.4
7	Poland	19	50	0	20.0	27.0	22	138.0
8	Spain	35	45	2.5	30.6	6.4	16	135.5
9	Argentina	35	35	0	27	17	21	135.0
10	Greece	32	40	0	28.1	16	18	134.1
14	Netherlands	31.5	52	0	17.6	7.1	19	127.2
15	Brazil	34	27.5	0	28.8	11	25	126.3
16	Hungary	16	38	0	33.5	12.5	25	125.0
17	Czech Republic	26	32	0	35	12.5	19	124.5
18	Japan	39.5	50	0	14.9	13.9	5	123.3
21	Turkey	30	36.8	0	19.5	14	18	118.3
23	USA (New York City)	46	47	0	7.7	7.7	8.4	116.7
24	Romania	16	16	0	46.75	17	19	114.8
26	UK	30	40	0	12.8	11	17.5	111.3
28	Luxembourg	30.4	39	0.5	11.5	11.8	15	108.1
31	Switzerland (Zurich)	33	40	1	12.6	12.6	7.6	106.7
33	Germany	19	42	0	13	13	16	103.0
34	South Korea	29.7	39.6	0	14	7.5	10	100.8

(*Continued*)

Table 11.1 (Continued)

Rank	Country	Corp. inc. tax	Indiv. inc. tax	Wealth tax	Employer soc. sec. tax	Employee soc. sec. tax	VAT	Misery 2005
36	Australia	30	47	0	9	1.5	10	97.5
40	Ukraine	25	13	0	37	0	17.5	92.5
42	Ireland	12.5	42	0	10.8	4	21	90.3
43	Indonesia	30	35	0	12	2	10	89.0
44	Malaysia	28	28	0	12	11	10	89.0
47	India	37	34	1	0	0	12	84.0
48	Thailand	30	37	0	5	5	7	84.0
49	Taiwan	25	40	0	9.4	2.7	5	82.1
50	Russia	24	13	0	26	0	18	81.0
52	Singapore	20	21	0	13	20	5	79.0
55	Hong Kong	17.5	16	0	5	5	0	43.5
56	UAE	0	0	0	5	13	0	18.0

Table 11.2 measures relative tax misery for the Asian economies that were included in the *Forbes* study. The figures are computed by dividing the Tax Misery Index of the individual country by 108, which is the approximate median for the 56 countries in the survey. Countries scoring above 1.00 are experiencing greater than average misery.

Figure 11.1 illustrates the relative degree of tax misery for the 12 Asian countries included in this study.

Table 11.2 Relative tax misery, Asian economies, 2005 (1.0 = average misery)

Greater than average misery	
China	1.48
Japan	1.14
Turkey	1.10
Less than average misery	
South Korea	0.93
Australia	0.90
Indonesia	0.82
Malaysia	0.82
India	0.78
Thailand	0.78
Taiwan	0.76
Singapore	0.73
Hong Kong	0.40

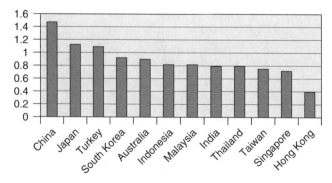

Figure 11.1   Relative tax misery

11.3   Tax reform

Table 11.3 measures the increase or decrease in tax misery from 2000 to 2005 for the Asian economies that were included in the *Forbes* data. However, the numbers do not provide a good direct comparison. For example, the increase for China is for the period 2001–2005, which includes just five years rather than six. Some other Asian economies were included in the index only after 2000. Table 11.3 shows whether the various Asian economies have increased or reduced their tax pain over time.

11.4   Happiness Index

Another micro approach to public finance is to compare the gross to net salaries that employees in various income categories earn. *Forbes* calls this measurement the Happiness Index.

Table 11.4 shows the relationship of gross to net salary for married employees with two children who earn €50,000. The net salary is what employees receive after income tax and the employee share of social security taxes are deducted. The higher the figure, the happier the employee. The table includes all the Asian economies that were included in the *Forbes* data plus a selection of developed countries for comparison purposes. Since the tax system in the USA is at three

Table 11.3   Change in tax misery 2000–2005, Asian economies

Rank	Country	Tax misery						Incr. (decr.)
		2005	2004	2003	2002	2001	2000	2000–2005
2	China	160.0	160.0	160.0	154.5	156.0		4.0
18	Japan	123.3	121.5	124.9	117.3	117.2	123.6	(0.3)
21	Turkey	118.3	126.5	124.5				(6.2)
34	South Korea	100.8	100.7	99.8	102.5	103.0		(2.2)
36	Australia	97.5	88.5	90.0	88.5			9.0
43	Indonesia	89.0	89.0	80.7	80.7			8.3
44	Malaysia	89.0	89.0	89.0				0
47	India	84.0	80.0	79.3	79.3	79.0		5.0
48	Thailand	84.0	83.0	83.0				1.0
49	Taiwan	82.1	82.1	81.7				0.4
52	Singapore	79.0	80.0	87.0	93.5			(14.5)
55	Hong Kong	43.5	43.0	43.0	41.0			2.5

Table 11.4 Happiness Index, married with two children earning €50,000

Rank	Country	Net to gross salary (%)
Above average happiness		
1	UAE	95.00
4	Hong Kong	92.20
6	Russia	87.00
7	Ukraine	86.57
10	Taiwan	84.13
11	Singapore	83.96
14	Japan	82.75
15	Switzerland (Zurich)	82.36
16	South Korea	81.64
19	Ireland	80.24
22	Thailand	77.91
23	USA (New York)	77.28
24	China	76.54
25	Spain	75.85
26	Brazil	75.25
27	France	74.71
Below average happiness		
30	UK	73.03
32	Germany (Berlin)	71.95
36	Argentina	70.38
39	Indonesia	69.99
40	Netherlands	69.48
41	Malaysia	69.04
42	Australia	68.57
43	Turkey	68.26
44	Czech Republic	67.76
45	India	67.70
46	Poland	66.76
48	Austria	63.36
50	Greece	63.12
52	Belgium	62.88
53	Italy	60.36
54	Sweden	57.76
55	Hungary	55.26

levels – federal, state, and local – and since each state has a different tax structure, statistics will vary by state. New York was chosen to represent the USA, since it was one of the statistics that *Forbes* included in its study. There were 56 jurisdictions in the *Forbes* study. The top 28 countries are classified as having above average happiness.

One interesting finding is that, of the 12 Asian economies in the study, seven were above average in terms of happiness (Hong Kong, Taiwan, Singapore, Japan, South Korea, Thailand, and China) and five were below average (Indonesia, Malaysia, Australia, Turkey, and India), which means there was a more or less even distribution among Asian economies.

Countries that have progressive tax structures make a conscious effort to take a larger portion of marginal income from the rich than from the poor and middle class. Whether they are successful in doing so depends on a variety of factors. Merely having a graduated income tax does not automatically result in more taxes being extracted from the rich. The effect of graduated tax rates may be reduced if exceptions, exclusions, and deductions creep into the system. The actual tax bite as one climbs the income ladder may be less dramatic than the graduated nature of the tax structure suggests.

One way to measure the actual tax bite is to look at the after-tax income taxpayers receive as their income increases. The Happiness Index can be used to see what the actual relationship of income earned to income kept is as income levels increase. Table 11.5 gives the data for workers who are married with two children who earn €100,000 per year, for the same countries that were examined in Table 11.4.

Table 11.5 shows that, of the 12 Asian economies in the study, seven were above average in terms of tax happiness at the €100,000 level, compared to only seven at the €50,000 level, while only five were below average at the €100,000 level, compared to five at the €50,000 level. In other words, the ratio of above average happiness to below average happiness remained the same as income increased from €50,000 to €100,000.

One way to measure the degree of tax envy in a society is to see how much it takes from the rich. The more it takes from the rich compared to the poor, in percentage terms, the more envious the society is of the rich.

Tax envy is a bad thing. Not only does it sew social discontent within the society, but it also dampens the incentive for the relatively rich people in the society to produce and invest in the country. The reason Michael Caine became a US citizen is because he felt he was overtaxed by Prime Minister Harold Wilson's administration. Numerous celebrities, rock stars, and other high earners have changed countries to avoid excessive taxation by their governments. Corporations

Table 11.5 Happiness Index, married with two children earning €100,000

Rank	Country	Net to gross salary (%)
Above average happiness		
1	UAE	95.00
5	Russia	87.00
6	Ukraine	86.79
7	Hong Kong	86.10
8	Singapore	84.19
12	Taiwan	77.87
14	Japan	77.54
16	Switzerland (Zurich)	75.95
19	Brazil	73.87
20	South Korea	73.25
22	Thailand	72.73
25	China	71.18
26	France	70.68
27	USA (New York)	70.19
Below average happiness		
29	Ireland	68.01
30	Germany (Berlin)	67.83
31	India	67.02
32	Argentina	66.96
33	Indonesia	66.75
34	Turkey	66.63
35	UK	66.49
36	Spain	66.24
38	Malaysia	65.06
41	Czech Republic	63.63
43	Poland	62.28
45	Austria	60.77
46	Greece	60.45
47	Australia	60.04
48	Netherlands	58.97
50	Hungary	56.13
52	Italy	55.25
54	Belgium	51.60
55	Sweden	50.95

also tend to leave, or to never enter, a country that has a relatively unattractive tax structure.

Table 11.6 shows the percentage of gross income that married individuals with two children earning €200,000 get to take home. The higher the percentage, the lower the degree of exploitation and tax envy.

Table 11.6 shows that Asian economies do not exploit their rich any more than do other economies. Nine of the 12 Asian economies included in the study (Hong Kong, Singapore, Taiwan, Thailand, Japan, South Korea, India, Turkey, and Indonesia) had above average happiness scores, while three (China, Malaysia, and Australia) had below average happiness scores.

Table 11.7 shows the degree of tax happiness as one progresses up the income scale. Since the *Forbes* data included statistics on 56 jurisdictions, ranks of 28 or less were above average in terms of tax happiness and those with ranks higher than 28 were less than average in terms of happiness.

Table 11.6   Happiness Index, married with two children earning €200,000

Rank	Country	Net to gross salary (%)
Above average happiness		
1	UAE	95.00
4	Russia	87.00
5	Ukraine	86.89
6	Hong Kong	84.00
8	Singapore	82.49
13	Brazil	73.19
19	Taiwan	69.01
20	Thailand	67.86
21	Japan	67.25
22	South Korea	67.07
23	India	66.68
24	Switzerland (Zurich)	66.46
26	Argentina	65.98
27	Turkey	65.82
28	Indonesia	65.13

(Continued)

Table 11.6   (Continued)

Rank	Country	Net to gross salary (%)
Below average happiness		
31	China	63.39
32	Malaysia	63.03
33	UK	62.74
35	France	62.31
36	USA (New York)	62.17
37	Germany (Berlin)	62.03
38	Ireland	61.97
39	Czech Republic	61.56
40	Spain	60.62
41	Greece	60.47
42	Poland	60.04
44	Austria	58.53
46	Hungary	56.57
47	Australia	55.77
50	Netherlands	53.49
51	Italy	52.80
53	Sweden	47.48
55	Belgium	46.02

Table 11.7   Comparison of tax happiness by income level selected Asian countries

	€50,000		€100,000		€200,000	
	Rank	Income retained (%)	Rank	Income retained (%)	Rank	Income retained (%)
Hong Kong	4	92.20	7	86.10	6	84.00
Taiwan	10	84.13	12	77.87	19	69.01
Singapore	11	83.96	8	84.19	8	82.49
Japan	14	82.75	14	77.54	21	67.25
South Korea	16	81.64	20	73.25	22	67.07
Thailand	22	77.91	22	72.73	20	67.86
China	24	76.54	25	71.18	31	63.39
Indonesia	39	60.99	33	66.75	28	65.13
Malaysia	41	69.04	38	65.06	32	63.03
Australia	42	68.57	47	60.04	47	55.77
Turkey	43	68.26	34	66.63	27	65.82
India	45	67.70	31	67.02	23	66.68

11.5   Country analysis

Table 11.7 shows the ranking of all the Asian economies that were in the *Forbes* study, as well as the percentage of income retained at the three income levels. At the €50,000 level, seven of the 12 Asian economies had above average tax happiness, since they ranked in the top 28 of a sample population of 56. That number remained at seven at the €100,000 level, then increased to nine at €200,000. Thus, more than half were above average in terms of tax happiness. However, some countries scored significantly better than others.

The rankings also shifted somewhat as the income level increased. Table 11.8 shows the shift in relative ranking.

The relative ranking of Hong Kong became only marginally worse as income increased, going from 4 at €50,000, then rising to 7 at the €100,000 level, then dropping to 6 at the €200,000 level. Taiwan got consistently worse as the income level rose, as did Japan, South Korea, China, and Australia. Singapore, Thailand, Indonesia, Malaysia, Turkey, and India saw their ranking improve as the income level rose.

China barely made it into the above average tax happiness category for the first two income levels, ranking 24th and 25th respectively, and slid into the less than average rankings at the highest income level, in 31st place.

Table 11.8   Shift in tax happiness as income level increases

	Rank €50,000	Rank €100,000	Rank €200,000
Hong Kong	4	7	6
Taiwan	10	12	19
Singapore	11	8	8
Japan	14	14	21
South Korea	16	20	22
Thailand	22	22	20
China	24	25	31
Indonesia	39	33	28
Malaysia	41	38	32
Australia	42	47	47
Turkey	43	34	27
India	45	31	23

Figure 11.2 shows the shift in tax happiness as income level rises.

Flannery (2005) provided some insight about China's long-term public finance problem. Although it has a booming economy and relatively cheap labor costs, its high payroll taxes put it at a competitive disadvantage. High taxes, rising wages, and a pension funding system that can only get worse will cause China to be increasingly less competitive as the years pass. Its population is aging and its pension system is basically a pay as you go system, which means that people who are still working will have to pay for the pensions of people who are retired. Local officials who must find the cash to pay retirees are under pressure to take funds out of individual accounts, which increases unfunded liabilities. Flannery speculates that it will be mostly the foreign corporations that invest in China that will pay this tax, which is up to 45% of payroll. This rate is higher than even some of the bloated welfare states in Western Europe.

Other Asian countries also face long-term pension funding problems as their population ages while birth rates decline. One way to reduce the pressure on the pension system is immigration. Allowing a flood of young immigrants into the country would increase the pool of people paying into the pension system. However, loosening immigration requirements might cause other problems, depending on the facts and circumstances.

Another way to eliminate the problem would be to privatize the pension system. Privatization would end the redistributive aspects of government-managed pension funds as individuals would take responsibility for their own retirement funding. But privatization would not solve the transition problems, since the pensions of current retirees would still have to be funded.

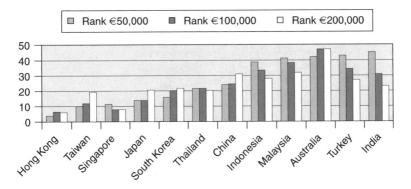

Figure 11.2   Shift in tax happiness

11.6   Index of Economic Freedom

Another way to compare the public finance systems of various countries is to compare their top marginal individual and corporate income tax rates and their year-to-year change in government expenditures as a percentage of GDP. These are the variables used to compute the fiscal burden scores for 161 countries in the Index of Economic Freedom (2006), an annual study that is commissioned by the *Wall Street Journal* and the Heritage Foundation. Each variable in this study was assigned a grade of 1 to 5, where 1 was the lightest burden and 5 was the heaviest burden. The scores for each of the three individual variables were then weighted to arrive at the final score. The corporate income tax was assigned a weight of 50% and the other two variables were weighted 25% each.

One advantage of the Index of Economic Freedom is that it includes more countries than does the Tax Misery Index, 161 versus 56. Another advantage is that it includes more Asian economies. One disadvantage is that it omits some taxes from the burden calculation.

Table 11.9 shows the relative fiscal burden for the 12 Asian countries plus selected other countries. Some of the 161 countries in the study could not be ranked because of unreliable data. The table is subdivided into quadrants – top quarter, second quarter, third quarter, and lowest quarter.

Figure 11.3 shows the relative fiscal burden ranking for the 12 Asian countries included in the present study.

Table 11.9   Ranking of relative fiscal burden (1 = lightest, 5 = heaviest)

Rank (out of 161)	Country	Score
Top quarter (1–40)		
1	UAE	1.3
8	Hong Kong	1.8
9	Romania	1.9
14	Singapore	2.1
16	Ireland	2.3
22	Hungary	2.4
22	Poland	2.4
28	Czech Republic	2.5
28	Russia	2.5
39	Brazil	2.8

(*Continued*)

Table 11.9 (Continued)

Rank (out of 161)	Country	Score
Second quarter (41–80)		
44	Switzerland	2.9
44	Ukraine	2.9
56	Germany	3.1
56	Turkey	3.1
58	Taiwan	3.3
58	Korea	3.3
58	Malaysia	3.3
66	Thailand	3.4
74	Austria	3.5
Third quarter (81–120)		
83	Sweden	3.6
83	Japan	3.6
101	UK	3.9
101	Australia	3.9
101	USA	3.9
101	China	3.9
101	India	3.9
114	Netherlands	4.0
114	Italy	4.0
114	Greece	4.0
114	Argentina	4.0
Lowest quarter (121–161)		
127	Belgium	4.1
127	France	4.1
127	Indonesia	4.1
141	Spain	4.3

Table 11.9 reveals several interesting things about the relative ranking of the various economies. The top quarter, which represents the lightest fiscal burden, has a high percentage of transition economies. The only two Asian economies in this quadrant are Hong Kong and Singapore. The second quadrant includes five Asian countries (Turkey, Taiwan, South Korea, Malaysia, and Thailand). The third quadrant includes Japan, Australia, China, and India. The only Asian country in the fourth quadrant is Indonesia, with a score of 4.1.

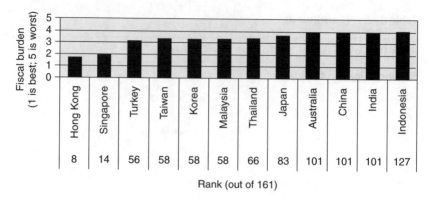

Figure 11.3   Ranking of fiscal burden

Table 11.10   Asian economies' fiscal burden, ranked by relative position

Quarter	Number of Asian economies	%
1	2	16.7
2	5	41.7
3	4	33.3
4	1	8.3
Total	12	100.0

Table 11.10 summarizes the relative fiscal burden rankings of the Asian economies. Two, or 16.7%, were in the top quarter, followed by five countries, or 41.7%, in the second quarter. In other words, 58.4% of the Asian economies in the present study ranked in the top half.

This finding is somewhat different from that found when the Tax Misery Index is used to make comparisons. In that index, a higher percentage of Asian economies were above average in terms of happiness.

Another difference that can be seen by making a comparison of the various ranking of each country is that some countries did better or worse using the Index of Economic Freedom data. This difference can be explained by the differences in the components of the two indexes. The Tax Misery Index included the employer and employee payments for social security, the value added tax, and the wealth tax, which the Economic Freedom Index did not. The Economic Freedom Index included government spending, which the Tax Misery Index did not.

Which index is a better measure of public finance competitiveness? When one speaks of competitiveness, one usually thinks of the attractiveness of investing or starting a business in a particular country. Thus, the corporate income tax is an important component of reaching that decision. The Index of Economic Freedom gives the corporate income tax a double weighting, 50%, compared to 25% for the other two variables. The Tax Misery Index also includes the corporate income tax but does not give it any extra weight.

But corporate income tax is not the only measure that investors and corporate officials look at when deciding where to invest. They look at other costs of doing business, such as employee payroll taxes. The Tax Misery Index includes these taxes, whereas the Index of Economic Freedom does not. But the Tax Misery Index also includes some taxes that do not directly affect a corporation's cost of doing business, such as the wealth tax and the individual income tax.

Perhaps a better index to use would be to include the corporate income tax, the employer portion of social security taxes, and the VAT. Those are the taxes that most directly affect the cost of doing business. The other taxes cause pain, but not to employers. If the goal is to choose which countries in which to conduct one's business, perhaps only the taxes that affect the cost of doing business should be included in the index. But the Tax Misery Index perhaps provides better information for policymaking purposes.

One area for further research would be to develop an index that includes just the taxes that corporate employers pay directly. Table 11.11 does that, but only for the countries that were included in Table 11.1. It includes data for 34 countries, 12 Asian economies and 22 developed or transition economies. The midpoint is 17, which is represented by Turkey. The countries ranked 1–17 include only two Asian countries (China and Turkey). These countries impose the highest tax burden on employers. The 17 countries in the bottom half impose the lightest tax burden on employers. This group includes 10 of the 12 Asian economies. Thus, the vast majority of Asian countries included in the present study – 10 out of 12 – impose lower than average tax burdens on corporations.

Based on the figures in Table 11.11, it appears that Hong Kong is the best Asian economy to do business in, at least in terms of relatively light tax burden. Its score of 22.5 places it in a very competitive position. Interestingly enough, China is the worst Asian country to do business in, in terms of tax rates. Its score of 94.5 places it in second position, behind France. Its corporate income tax is relatively high (33%) and so is its employer share of social security taxes (44.5%). Only France (45%) and Romania (46.75%) have higher social security taxes imposed on employers.

Table 11.11 Tax misery for employers, 2005 (selected countries)

Rank	Country	Corp. inc. tax	Employer soc. sec. tax	VAT	Misery 2005
Above average misery					
1	France	34.4	45	19.6	99.0
2	China	33	44.5	17	94.5
3	Belgium	34	34.5	21	89.5
4	Brazil	34	28.8	25	87.8
5	Sweden	28	32.5	25	85.5
6	Argentina	35	27	21	83.0
7	Romania	16	46.75	19	81.75
8	Spain	35	30.6	16	81.6
9	Czech Republic	26	35	19	80.0
10	Ukraine	25	37	17.5	79.5
11	Greece	32	28.1	18	78.1
12	Austria	25	31.2	20	76.2
13	Hungary	16	33.5	25	74.5
14	Italy	37.3	35	20	74.3
15	Netherlands	31.5	17.6	19	68.1
16	Russia	24	26	18	68.0
17	Turkey	30	19.5	18	67.5
Below average misery					
18	USA (New York City)	46	7.7	8.4	62.1
19	Poland	19	20.0	22	61.0
20	UK	30	12.8	17.5	60.3
21	Japan	39.5	14.9	5	59.4
22	South Korea	29.7	14	10	53.7
23	Switzerland (Zurich)	33	12.6	7.6	53.2
24	Indonesia	30	12	10	52.0
25	Malaysia	28	12	10	50.0
26	India	37	0	12	49.0
26	Australia	30	9	10	49.0
28	Germany	19	13	16	48.0
29	Ireland	12.5	10.8	21	44.3
30	Thailand	30	5	7	42.0
31	Taiwan	25	9.4	5	39.4
32	Singapore	20	13	5	38.0
33	Hong Kong	17.5	5	0	22.5
34	UAE	0	5	0	5.0

11.7   Conclusion

Most of the Asian countries selected for inclusion in this study are average to better than average competitors in the area of public finance. The Tax Misery Index shows them to be above average competitors, in the sense that nine of the 12 Asian countries included in the study were ranked above average in terms of tax happiness (or below average in terms of tax misery). The Index of Economic Freedom shows that many of the Asian countries included in the study are in the top half, in terms of lightness of fiscal burden, which might lead one to conclude that they are, on average, stronger competitors than the more developed market economies.

Of course, there are many other factors that investors and corporations need to consider before deciding whether to invest in a transition economy. A strong rule of law is very important, which includes strong protection of property rights and enforcement of contracts. Corruption and the extent of the underground economy, monetary policy, trade policy, and the level of education of the workforce are also important factors.

References

Anderson, J. (2005). The Tax World Gets Flat and Happy. *Forbes Global*, 23 May, online edition.

Blum, W.J. and Kalven, H. Jr (1953). *The Uneasy Case for Progressive Taxation*. University of Chicago Press, Chicago.

deJouvenel, B. (1952). *The Ethics of Redistribution*. Cambridge University Press, Cambridge.

Flannery, R. (2005). Time Bomb. *Forbes Global*, 23 May, online edition.

Hall, R.E. and Rabushka, A. (1985). *The Flat Tax*. Hoover Institution Press, Stanford, CA.

Index of Economic Freedom (2006). The Heritage Foundation, Washington, DC and the *Wall Street Journal*, New York. Also available at www.heritage.org.

Marx, K. and Engels, F. (1848). *Manifesto of the Communist Party*.

McCaffery, E. J. (2002). *Fair Not Flat: How To Make the Tax System Better and Simpler*. University of Chicago Press, Chicago.

McGee, R.W. (1998a). Is the Ability to Pay Principle Ethically Bankrupt? *Journal of Accounting, Ethics and Public Policy*, 1(3):503–511.

McGee, R.W. (1998b). Are Discriminatory Tax Rates Ethically Justifiable? *Journal of Accounting, Ethics and Public Policy*, 1(4):527–534.

McGee, R.W. (2004). *The Philosophy of Taxation and Public Finance*. Kluwer Academic, Boston.

Tax Misery and Reform Index (2005). *Forbes Global*, 23 May, online edition.

Part 3

Global Challenges and Global Innovations

The Ethics of Tax Evasion:
Lessons for Transitional
Economies

Irina Nasadyuk and Robert W. McGee

Abstract

Transitional economies are unable to rely on the innovation of taxation taken for granted in developed economies. One such innovation is the expectation of tax compliance. The ethics of tax evasion has been discussed sporadically in the theological and philosophical literature for at least 500 years. Martin Crowe wrote a doctoral thesis that reviewed much of that literature in 1944. This chapter begins with a review of such literature and identifies the main issues and summarizes the three main viewpoints that have emerged over the centuries. It then reports on the results of a survey of Ukrainian law students who were asked their opinions on the ethics of tax evasion. The survey consisted of 18 statements, representing the 15 issues and three viewpoints that have emerged over the centuries, plus three statements representing more recent issues. Participants were asked to signify the extent of their agreement with each statement by placing a number from 0 to 6 in the space provided. The data were then analyzed to determine which of the three viewpoints was dominant among the sample population. The tax regime in Ukraine has much in common with the tax regimes in other transition economies. Thus, the lessons learned from this study have application to other transition economies.

12.1   Introduction

Most studies of tax evasion take an economic or public finance perspective. Not much has been written from a philosophical or ethical viewpoint. That is probably because most economists are utilitarians and most lawyers are legalists. However, there is a small body of literature that addresses tax evasion issues from a philosophical or theological perspective. The present study is intended to summarize that small body of literature while forming a bridge to the public finance literature as well. The authors developed a survey instrument that included 18 statements incorporating the three major views on the ethics of tax evasion that have emerged in the literature over the last 500 years. The survey was distributed to a group of law students in Odessa, Ukraine. This chapter reports on the results and the statistical validity of that survey.

12.2   Review of the literature

A review of the literature on the ethics of tax evasion reveals that three major views have evolved over the last 500 years. One view takes the position that tax evasion is always or almost always unethical, either because there is a duty to God to pay taxes, or there is a duty to some community or to society. Another view is that there is never or almost never a duty to pay taxes because the government is a thief, nothing more than a band of organized criminals, and there is no duty to give anything to criminals. The third view is that there is some ethical obligation to support the government of the country where you live but that duty is less than absolute.

One of the most comprehensive analyses of the ethics of tax evasion was done by Martin Crowe (1944), who examined the theological and philosophical literature of the last 500 years. Much of this literature took the *always unethical* or *sometimes unethical* positions. McGee (1994) discussed and summarized the Crowe study. A more recent work by McGee (1998a) included the opinions of more than 20 scholars who, collectively, espouse all three viewpoints. The Torgler (2003) study is also comprehensive, although Torgler looked at both ethical and public finance aspects of the issue.

A number of studies have been done that examine tax evasion in a particular country. Vaguine (1998) examined Russia, as did Preobragenskaya and McGee (2004) to a lesser extent. Smatrakalev (1998) discussed the ethics of tax evasion in Bulgaria. Ballas and Tsoukas (1998) discussed the views of Greek taxpayers. McGee (1999e) conducted a series of interviews to determine how people in Armenia think about tax evasion. McGee and Maranjyan (2006) did a follow-up empirical study to determine the views of economics and theology students on the ethics of tax evasion. Surveys have also been conducted of Chinese business and economics students (McGee and Yuhua, 2006), Chinese law, business and philosophy students (McGee and Guo, 2006), and accounting, business and economics students in Hong Kong (McGee and Ho, 2006), as well as international business professors (McGee, 2005a), Romanian business students (McGee, 2005b), and Guatemalan business and law students (McGee and Lingle, 2005). Morales (1998) discussed the viewpoint of Mexican workers. Most of these studies found that taxpayers do not have an ethical problem with evading taxes because their governments are corrupt and they feel that they have no ethical duty to pay taxes to a corrupt government. Morales concluded that a Mexican worker's duty to his family is sometimes more important than his duty to the state.

A number of studies have discussed the ethics of tax evasion from a practitioner perspective. Such studies tend to focus on the accounting profession's ethical code rather than any philosophical concepts. Two studies that take a practitioner's perspective were those of Armstrong and Robison (1998) and Oliva (1998).

If the articles by Cohn (1998) and Tamari (1998) are representative of the Jewish view, one may say that the Jewish view is near absolutist. Because Cohn is an Orthodox rabbi and Tamari is a well-known and highly respected Jewish scholar, one must concede that the viewpoints expressed in their articles at least represent some segment of Jewish thought on the issue.

The Baha'i position is also near absolutist (DeMoville, 1998). The literature of this religion espouses the view that people have a duty to obey the laws of the country in which they live, which is the main justification for their position.

Some Christian groups also take this view – that individuals are morally bound to obey the laws of the country in which they live. There are passages in the Christian Bible that support this absolutist view (Romans, 13:1–2), although another passage is less absolutist, holding that people must give to the state the things that are the state's and to God the things that are God's (Matthew, 22:17, 21). The literature of the Church of Jesus Christ of Latter-Day Saints (Mormons) espouses the absolutist view that people have a duty to obey the laws of the country in which they live (Smith and Kimball, 1998).

But other Christians are not so absolutist. Gronbacher (1998) reviewed the Christian literature and found passages that allow for a less than absolutist view. Basically, he takes the position that there are limits to the duty one owes to the state to pay taxes. Schansberg (1998) reviewed the Biblical literature and arrived at the same conclusion. Much of the literature Crowe (1944) discussed also takes this position. Pennock (1998), another Christian writer, views evasion as ethical when tax funds are used to support an unjust war.

Angelus of Clavisio (1494) took the position that there is no ethical obligation to pay taxes if the government does not use the revenues collected to provide for the common good, at least as long as neither lying nor perjury are involved. Berardi (1898) took the position that there is probably no moral duty to pay a tax even if lying or perjury are involved, since the Prince merely dictates what is owed. Taxpayers never enter into a contract with the Prince, and thus are not bound to pay anything. Genicot (1927) stated that partial evasion is justified on the grounds that the government does not have the right to the full amount and that it would be unfair to impose heavier taxes on conscientious men while wicked men usually pay less. Crolly (1877) took the position that there is no duty to pay taxes unless evasion would result in violence.

Lehmkuhl (1902) took the position that it is unethical to evade taxes when the result is that nonevaders have to pay more. In other words, there is some moral duty to other taxpayers even if there is no moral duty to the government. But Davis (1938) took the position that it would be unfair to require honest taxpayers to take up the slack and pay higher taxes to make up for the evasions of others.

The Islamic position on the ethics of tax evasion is also mixed. McGee (1997, 1998b) reviewed Islamic business ethics literature and concluded that tax evasion might be justified in certain cases, such as when the tax causes prices to increase (tariffs and sales taxes) and where the tax is on income, which destroys incentives. But conversations with some Islamic scholars reject this interpretation of the Quran, the Muslim holy book. Murtuza and Ghazanfar (1998) also discussed the Muslim view on paying taxes but they confined their discussion to *zakat*, the duty to come to the aid of the poor. They did not discuss the relationship between the taxpayer and the state.

McGee critiques the various Christian views (1998c) and various religious views (1999a). Leiker (1998) examined the work of Rousseau and speculated as to what Rousseau's view on the ethics of tax evasion might be.

Not much has been written about the view that people have no duty to pay taxes. Although anarchists take this position, they generally do not focus on tax evasion issues. They tend to discuss the general relationship between the individual and the state. Lysander Spooner, a nineteenth century American lawyer and anarchist, is a case in point. He took the position that the state is always and everywhere illegitimate and that individuals therefore have absolutely no duty to obey any laws (1870). Spooner totally rejected the social contract theories of Locke (1689), Rousseau (1762), and Hobbes (1651).

Block (1989, 1993) examined the public finance literature and could not find any adequate justification for taxation, although he conceded that such justification might exist. It just did not exist in the public finance literature. Public finance writers start with the assumption that taxation is legitimate and go forward from there. They never examine the underlying philosophical foundation of taxation.

A few studies have applied ethical theory to various taxes to determine whether they may be justified on ethical grounds. If one begins with the premise that the state has an obligation to provide services in exchange for tax revenue, the estate tax is on shaky ground, since estate taxes are paid out of the assets of dead people (McGee, 1999b) and the state cannot provide any services to this subgroup of the population. Individuals are being used as means rather than ends in themselves, which violates Kantian ethics (Kant, 1952a, b, c, 1983). The 'fair share' argument also violates Kantian ethics for the same reason. McGee (1999c) examined this issue.

Tariffs might also be an ethically suspect form of taxation if the main purpose is to protect domestic producers at the expense of the general public, which is the main use of tariffs today (McGee, 1999d). Arguing that there is an ethical duty to pay a tax that benefits a special interest at the expense of the general public (general welfare) is an uphill battle.

The capital gains tax might also be challenged on ethical grounds, especially when it is not indexed for inflation (McGee, 1999f). Depending on the facts and circumstances, this tax might actually exceed 100% of income, in cases where the asset has been held a long time and there has been inflation.

Arguing that there is an ethical duty to pay the social security tax has also been subjected to challenge (McGee, 1999g), at least in the case of the social security tax in the USA, which is highly inefficient, therefore violating utilitarian ethics. It also violates Kantian ethics, since one group (workers) is being exploited by nonworkers (retired people). Some authors have said that tax evasion defrauds the government (Cowell, 1990), while other authors have said that the government defrauds the taxpayer (Chodorov, 1954; Gross, 1995; Shlaes, 1999).

12.3 Methodology

A survey instrument was developed to solicit the views of Ukrainian law students on the ethics of tax evasion. The survey consisted of 18 statements that include the major arguments Crowe (1944) discussed, plus three more modern arguments. Each statement generally began with the phrase 'Tax evasion is ethical if . . .'. Respondents were instructed to insert a number from 0 to 6 in the space provided to reflect the extent of their agreement or disagreement with each of the 18 statements. A score of zero (0) represented strong disagreement with the statement, while a score of six (6) represented strong agreement.

The survey was translated into Russian and distributed to students majoring in law at Odessa National Law Academy. Ninety-nine usable responses were collected. The following hypotheses were made:

H1: The prevalent view is that tax evasion is sometimes ethical. This hypothesis will be accepted if average scores are more than 1 but less than 5 for at least 12 of the 18 statements.

H2: Tax evasion will be most acceptable if the system is perceived as being unfair. This hypothesis will be accepted if the scores for the statements regarding fairness (S1, S3, and S14) are higher than the scores for the other statements.

H3: The second strongest reason to justify tax evasion is when the government is perceived as being corrupt. This hypothesis will be accepted if the score for the corruption statement (S11) is higher than the score for all other statements except the statements referring to unfairness.

H4: The third strongest reason to justify tax evasion is when the government engages in human rights abuses. This hypothesis will be accepted if the scores for the human rights abuse statements (S16–S18) are higher than the scores for other statements except those that relate to unfairness or government corruption.

H5: Tax evasion will be least acceptable where the motive for evasion is a selfish motive. This hypothesis will be accepted if the scores for statements in this category receive the lowest scores. Statements in this category include S2, S5, S7–S12, and S15.

H6: Females are more firmly opposed to tax evasion than are males. This hypothesis will be accepted if the female scores are significantly lower than the male scores for at least 12 of the 18 statements.

12.4 Findings

H1: Accepted.

As can be seen from Table 12.1, all 18 scores are more than 1 and less than 5, which indicates the average respondent believes tax evasion to be ethical sometimes. Figure 12.1 shows the relative strength or weakness of each of the 18 statements.

Table 12.2 ranks the statements from strongest to weakest. The strongest statement in favor of tax evasion was the statement that tax rates are too high (S1), which was one of the three fairness statements. The other fairness statements ranked 3 (S3) and 6 (S14). Figure 12.2 shows the range of scores.

Wilcoxon tests were conducted to determine if the differences in the scores were significant. The Wilcoxon test was chosen because it is a nonparametric test and does not assume a normal distribution. The results are given in Table 12.3.

At a 5% significance level the hypothesis is accepted for statements S11 (corrupt government), S17, and S18 (human rights abuses). In all other cases it is rejected. At a 10% significance level the hypothesis could be rejected for statement S4.

H2: The three fairness statements (S1, S3, and 14) ranked 1, 3 and 6, placing them in the top third. The Wilcoxon test determined these scores to be significantly different from the scores for the other statements.

H3: This hypothesis will be accepted if the score for the corruption statement (S11) is higher than the score for all other statements except the statements referring to unfairness. Table 12.4 shows the results.

We cannot reject for S1 (unfair), S3 (unfair), S14 (unfair), S17, and S18 (human rights).

H4: This hypothesis will be accepted if the scores for the human rights abuse statements (S16–S18) are higher than the scores for other statements except those

Table 12.1   Combined scores (0 = strongly disagree, 6 = strongly agree)

S no.	Statement	Score
1	Tax evasion is ethical if tax rates are too high.	4.24
2	Tax evasion is ethical even if tax rates are not too high.	1.36
3	Tax evasion is ethical if the tax system is unfair.	4.00
4	Tax evasion is ethical if a large portion of the money collected is wasted.	3.12
5	Tax evasion is ethical even if most of the money collected is spent wisely.	1.36
6	Tax evasion is ethical if a large portion of the money collected is spent on projects that I morally disapprove of.	2.19
7	Tax evasion is ethical even if a large portion of the money collected is spent on worthy projects.	1.18
8	Tax evasion is ethical if a large portion of the money collected is spent on projects that do not benefit me.	1.99
9	Tax evasion is ethical even if a large portion of the money collected is spent on projects that do benefit me.	1.23
10	Tax evasion is ethical if everyone is doing it.	1.47
11	Tax evasion is ethical if a significant portion of the money collected winds up in the pockets of corrupt politicians or their families and friends.	3.94
12	Tax evasion is ethical if the probability of getting caught is low.	1.69
13	Tax evasion is ethical if some of the proceeds go to support a war that I consider to be unjust.	2.79
14	Tax evasion is ethical if I can't afford to pay.	3.61
15	Tax evasion is ethical even if it means that if I pay less, others will have to pay more.	1.48
16	Tax evasion would be ethical if I were a Jew living in Nazi Germany in 1940.	2.87
17	Tax evasion is ethical if the government discriminates against me because of my religion, race, or ethnic background.	3.75
18	Tax evasion is ethical if the government imprisons people for their political opinions.	4.08

that relate to unfairness or government corruption. Table 12.5 shows the results. At the 5% level, the hypothesis is rejected in 11 of 45 cases. At the 10% level of significance, the hypothesis is rejected in nine of 45 cases.

H5: This hypothesis will be accepted if the scores for statements in this category receive the lowest scores. Statements in this category include S2, S5, S7–S12, and S15. While it can be said that the selfish motive statements are generally weaker than the statements for the other categories, it is not always the case. Thus, we

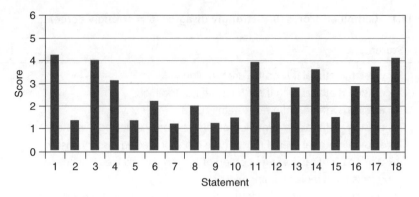

Figure 12.1   Strength of arguments

may say with a fair degree of confidence that selfish motive arguments generally are not as strong as arguments in the other categories.

H6: This hypothesis will be accepted if the female scores are significantly lower than the male scores for at least 12 of the 18 statements. H6 is rejected.

Table 12.6 shows the male and female scores for each statement and also the Wilcoxon p-value. There were 39 male responses and 59 female responses. One respondent did not identify gender.

As can be seen from Table 12.6, male scores were higher than female scores for 13 of the 18 statements, which might lead one to conclude that males are more open to tax evasion than are females. However, such a conclusion would be premature, because the differences might not be significant. Wilcoxon tests were performed to determine the level of significance for each statement. Those scores are reported in the last column.

If significance is defined as $p \leq 0.05$, then none of the scores are significantly different. If significance is defined at the 10% level ($p \leq 0.10$), then the difference is significant only for statements S1 and S2. In either case, it can be concluded that the male and female scores are not significantly different overall.

Several other tax evasion studies have compared male and female responses. The results of those studies are summarized in Table 12.7.

Numerous studies have compared male and female scores on a variety of ethical issues in an attempt to determine whether one gender is more ethical than the other. The results have been mixed. Some studies have found females to be more ethical than males (Baird, 1980; Chonko and Hunt, 1985; Akaah, 1989), while others have found no statistical difference (Fritzsche, 1988; McCuddy and Peery, 1996;

Table 12.2   Ranking of the arguments from strongest to weakest supporting tax evasion (0 = strongly disagree, 6 = strongly agree)

Rank	Statement	Score
1	Tax evasion is ethical if tax rates are too high. (S1)	4.24
2	Tax evasion is ethical if the government imprisons people for their political opinions. (S18)	4.08
3	Tax evasion is ethical if the tax system is unfair. (S3)	4.00
4	Tax evasion is ethical if a significant portion of the money collected winds up in the pockets of corrupt politicians or their families and friends. (S11)	3.94
5	Tax evasion is ethical if the government discriminates against me because of my religion, race or ethnic background. (S17)	3.75
6	Tax evasion is ethical if I can't afford to pay. (S14)	3.61
7	Tax evasion is ethical if a large portion of the money collected is wasted. (S4)	3.12
8	Tax evasion would be ethical if I were a Jew living in Nazi Germany in 1940. (S16)	2.87
9	Tax evasion is ethical if some of the proceeds go to support a war that I consider to be unjust. (S13)	2.79
10	Tax evasion is ethical if a large portion of the money collected is spent on projects that I morally disapprove of. (S6)	2.19
11	Tax evasion is ethical if a large portion of the money collected is spent on projects that do not benefit me. (S8)	1.99
12	Tax evasion is ethical if the probability of getting caught is low. (S12)	1.69
13	Tax evasion is ethical even if it means that if I pay less, others will have to pay more. (S15)	1.48
14	Tax evasion is ethical if everyone is doing it. (S10)	1.47
15	Tax evasion is ethical even if most of the money collected is spent wisely. (S5)	1.36
15	Tax evasion is ethical even if tax rates are not too high. (S2)	1.36
17	Tax evasion is ethical even if a large portion of the money collected is spent on projects that do benefit me. (S9)	1.23
18	Tax evasion is ethical even if a large portion of the money collected is spent on worthy projects. (S7)	1.18

McDonald and Kan, 1997). At least one study found males to be more ethical than females (Barnett and Karson, 1987).

These studies do not make for a good comparison to the present study, however, since those other studies began with the premise that certain acts were ethical or

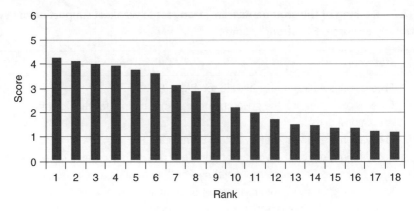

Figure 12.2 Range of scores

Table 12.3 Wilcoxon test of significance for S1, S3, and S14

S no.	Wilcoxon p-value for		
	S1	S3	S14
1		0.4568	0.06588
2	3.167e-20	2.232e-16	1.01e-12
3	0.4568		0.2935
4	0.000274	0.005123	0.08056
5	3.168e-19	8.518e-16	1.409e-12
6	1.146e-11	6.068e-09	3.154e-06
7	5.763e-20	6.132e-17	3.684e-14
8	4.188e-13	3.417e-10	2.601e-07
9	4.691e-19	3.849e-16	1.931e-13
10	3.103e-16	1.223e-13	3.286e-11
11	0.4812	0.9377	0.2713
12	3.474e-16	5.712e-13	8.8e-10
13	4.508e-07	5.958e-05	0.004987
14	0.06588	0.2935	
15	7.332e-19	3.464e-15	9.481e-12
16	0.0002268	0.0028	0.02684
17	0.2601	0.686	0.612
18	0.8176	0.3928	0.09629

Table 12.4　Wilcoxon test of significance for S11

S no.	Wilcoxon p-value for S11
1	0.4812
2	5.733e-16
3	0.9377
4	0.005243
5	2.702e-15
6	1.008e-08
7	3.432e-17
8	6.043e-10
9	9.144e-16
10	2.434e-13
11	
12	1.335e-12
13	7.615e-05
14	0.2713
15	9.264e-15
16	0.002437
17	0.5836
18	0.4991

Table 12.5　Wilcoxon test of significance for S16–S18

S no.	Wilcoxon p-value for		
	S16	S17	S18
1	0.0002268	0.2601	0.8176
2	0.0001469	1.486e-12	2.812e-15
3	0.0028	0.686	0.3928
4	0.4858	0.03447	0.001364
5	7.537e-05	1.977e-12	5.043e-15
6	0.08406	1.423e-06	5.429e-09
7	2.358e-06	4.856e-14	2.119e-16
8	0.02896	1.577e-07	6.385e-10
9	1.291e-05	2.434e-13	1.498e-15
10	0.0001949	2.446e-11	1.447e-13
11	0.002437	0.5836	0.4991
12	0.00256	6.589e-10	1.761e-12
13	0.922	0.002457	2.829e-05
14	0.02684	0.612	0.09629
15	0.0003806	1.292e-11	2.585e-14

Table 12.6 Comparison of male and female scores (0 = strongly disagree, 6 = strongly agree)

S no.	Statement	Male (39)	Female (59)	Score larger by		p-value
				Male	Female	
1	Tax evasion is ethical if tax rates are too high.	4.49	4.07	0.42		0.09151
2	Tax evasion is ethical even if tax rates are not too high.	1.77	1.12	0.65		0.08808
3	Tax evasion is ethical if the tax system is unfair.	4.08	3.92	0.16		0.7035
4	Tax evasion is ethical if a large portion of the money collected is wasted.	3.26	2.98	0.28		0.5640
5	Tax evasion is ethical even if most of the money collected is spent wisely.	1.59	1.24	0.35		0.3898
6	Tax evasion is ethical if a large portion of the money collected is spent on projects that I morally disapprove of.	2.49	1.93	0.56		0.1865
7	Tax evasion is ethical even if a large portion of the money collected is spent on worthy projects.	1.23	1.17	0.06		0.6924
8	Tax evasion is ethical if a large portion of the money collected is spent on projects that do not benefit me.	2.41	1.75	0.66		0.1549
9	Tax evasion is ethical even if a large portion of the money collected is spent on projects that do benefit me.	1.23	1.25		0.02	0.7939
10	Tax evasion is ethical if everyone is doing it.	1.74	1.32	0.42		0.3510
11	Tax evasion is ethical if a significant portion of the money collected winds up in the pockets of corrupt politicians or their families and friends.	3.90	3.93		0.03	0.7799
12	Tax evasion is ethical if the probability of getting caught is low.	2.00	2.44		0.44	0.2926
13	Tax evasion is ethical if some of the proceeds go to support a war that I consider to be unjust.	3.10	2.52	0.58		0.1482
14	Tax evasion is ethical if I can't afford to pay.	3.87	3.42	0.45		0.3779
15	Tax evasion is ethical even if it means that if I pay less, others will have to pay more.	1.82	1.28	0.54		0.3351
16	Tax evasion would be ethical if I were a Jew living in Nazi Germany in 1940.	2.79	2.88		0.09	0.7826
17	Tax evasion is ethical if the government discriminates against me because of my religion, race or ethnic background.	3.46	3.88		0.42	0.4398
18	Tax evasion is ethical if the government imprisons people for their political opinions.	4.08	4.07	0.01		0.8888

Table 12.7   Views by gender: The ethics of tax evasion

	Males more strongly against	Females more strongly against	No difference
Argentina business and law students (McGee and Rossi, 2006)			X
China business and economics students (McGee and Yuhua, 2006)			X
China business, law, and philosophy students (McGee and Guo, 2006)		X	
Hong Kong accounting, business, and economics students (McGee and Ho, 2006)			X
Guatemala business and law students (McGee and Lingle, 2005)		X	
International business professors (McGee, 2005c)		X	
Poland business students (McGee and Bernal, 2006)			X
Romania business students (McGee, 2005b)	X		
Ukraine law students (present study)			X

unethical. The present study does not begin with that premise, but rather attempts to determine whether, and under what circumstances, tax evasion can be considered ethical behavior. Thus, one cannot conclude in the present study that males and females are equally ethical. One can only conclude that their views on the ethics of tax evasion are not statistically different, for the most part.

12.5   Conclusion

The present study has several findings. One of the main findings is that law student respondents in Ukraine consider tax evasion to be ethical in some cases. This finding confirms the findings of several other studies.

Another finding is that some arguments supporting the ethics of tax evasion are stronger than others. The strongest arguments supporting the view that tax evasion can be ethical involve questions of fairness. Evading taxes might be considered ethical if the system is perceived to be unfair. This finding differs from the findings of some other studies, which found corruption to be the strongest argument supporting the view that tax evasion can be ethical.

Corruption was the second strongest argument to support the view that tax evasion can be ethical. As was previously mentioned, some other studies ranked corruption as the strongest argument to support tax evasion on ethical grounds.

The third strongest argument had to do with human rights abuses. This finding also differs from the findings in some other studies, which found human rights abuses to be either the strongest or second strongest argument to support the justification of tax evasion on ethical grounds.

The findings of the present study confirm the findings of other studies, which found that statements involving a selfish motive were the weakest arguments. The present study found no significant difference between the views of males and females, which confirms the findings of some studies and differs from the findings of other studies.

Numerous other studies could be conducted on this topic. Different groups may have different views on the various statements. Business students, law students, philosophy students, or students in other disciplines might have views that diverge. Additional country studies could be made to determine how views differ by country. Additional studies could be done to determine why male and female views are similar in some cases and different in others.

Acknowledgments

We would like to thank Diana Fatkullina for her assistance.

References

Akaah, I.P. (1989). Differences in Research Ethics Judgments Between Male and Female Marketing Professionals. *Journal of Business Ethics*, 8(5):375–381.

Angelus of Clavisio (1494). *Summa Angelica*, as cited in Crowe, M.T. (1944). *The Moral Obligation of Paying Just Taxes*, The Catholic University of America Studies in Sacred Theology No. 84, p. 29.

Armstrong, M.B. and Robison, J. (1998). Ethics in Taxation. *Journal of Accounting, Ethics and Public Policy*, 1(4):535–557. Reprinted in McGee, R.W. (ed.) (1998). *The Ethics of Tax Evasion*, pp. 330–348. The Dumont Institute for Public Policy Research, Dumont, NJ.

Baird, J.S. (1980). Current Trends in College Cheating. *Psychology in the Schools*, 17(4):515–522.

Ballas, A.A. and Tsoukas, H. (1998). Consequences of Distrust: The Vicious Circle of Tax Evasion in Greece. *Journal of Accounting, Ethics and Public Policy*, 1(4):572–596. Reprinted in McGee, R.W.

(ed.) (1998). *The Ethics of Tax Evasion*, pp. 284–304. The Dumont Institute for Public Policy Research, Dumont, NJ.

Barnett, J.H. and Karson, M.J. (1987). Personal Values and Business Decisions: An Exploratory Investigation. *Journal of Business Ethics*, 6(5):371–382.

Berardi, A. (1898). *Praxis Confessariorum II*, as cited in Crowe, M.T. (1944). *The Moral Obligation of Paying Just Taxes*, The Catholic University of America Studies in Sacred Theology No. 84, p. 35.

Block, W. (1989). The Justification of Taxation in the Public Finance Literature: A Critique. *Journal of Public Finance and Public Choice*, 3:141–158.

Block, W. (1993). Public Finance Texts Cannot Justify Government Taxation: A Critique. *Canadian Public Administration/Administration Publique du Canada*, 36(2):225–262. Reprinted in revised form under the title 'The Justification for Taxation in the Economics Literature' in McGee, R.W. (ed.) (1998). *The Ethics of Tax Evasion*, pp. 36–88. The Dumont Institute for Public Policy Research, Dumont, NJ.

Chodorov, F. (1954). *The Income Tax: Root of All Evil*. Devin-Adair, Old Greenwich.

Chonko, L.B. and Hunt, S.D. (1985). Ethics and Marketing Management: An Empirical Investigation. *Journal of Business Research*, 13(4):339–359.

Cohn, G. (1998). The Jewish View on Paying Taxes. *Journal of Accounting, Ethics and Public Policy*, 1(2):109–120. Reprinted in McGee, R.W. (ed.) (1998). *The Ethics of Tax Evasion*, pp. 180–189. The Dumont Institute for Public Policy Research, Dumont, NJ.

Cowell, F.A. (1990). *Cheating the Government: The Economics of Evasion*. MIT Press, Cambridge, MA.

Crolly, G. (1877). *Disputationes Theologicae de Justitia et Jure III*, pp. 1001ff, as cited in Crowe, M.T. (1944). *The Moral Obligation of Paying Just Taxes*, The Catholic University of America Studies in Sacred Theology No. 84, p. 38.

Crowe, M.T. (1944). *The Moral Obligation of Paying Just Taxes*, The Catholic University of America Studies in Sacred Theology No. 84.

Davis, H. (1938). *Moral and Pastoral Theology*, p. 339, as cited in Crowe, M.T. (1944). *The Moral Obligation of Paying Just Taxes*, The Catholic University of America Studies in Sacred Theology No. 84, p. 40.

DeMoville, W. (1998). The Ethics of Tax Evasion: A Baha'i Perspective. *Journal of Accounting, Ethics and Public Policy*, 1(3):356–368. Reprinted in McGee, R.W. (ed.) (1998). *The Ethics of Tax Evasion*, pp. 230–240. The Dumont Institute for Public Policy Research, Dumont, NJ.

Fritzsche, D. J. (1988). An Examination of Marketing Ethics: Role of the Decision Maker, Consequences of the Decision, Management Position, and Sex of the Respondent. *Journal of Macromarketing*, 8(2):29–39.

Genicot, E. (1927). *Institutiones Theologiae Moralis I*, as cited in Crowe, M.T. (1944). *The Moral Obligation of Paying Just Taxes*, The Catholic University of America Studies in Sacred Theology No. 84, p. 37.

Gronbacher, G. M.A. (1998). Taxation: Catholic Social Thought and Classical Liberalism. *Journal of Accounting, Ethics and Public Policy*, 1(1):91–100. Reprinted in McGee, R.W. (ed.) (1998). *The Ethics of Tax Evasion*, pp. 158–167. The Dumont Institute for Public Policy Research, Dumont, NJ.

Gross, M.L. (1995). *The Tax Racket: Government Extortion from A to Z*. Ballantine Books, New York.

Hobbes, T. (1651). *Leviathan*.

Kant, I. (1952a). *Fundamental Principles of the Metaphysics of Morals. Great Books of the Western World*, Vol. 42, pp. 251–287. Encyclopedia Britannica, Chicago.

Kant, I. (1952b). *General Introduction to the Metaphysics of Morals. Great Books of the Western World*, Vol. 42, pp. 381–394. Encyclopedia Britannica, Chicago.

Kant, I. (1952c). *Preface and Introduction to the Metaphysical Elements of Ethics. Great Books of the Western World*, Vol. 42, pp. 363–379. Encyclopedia Britannica, Chicago.

Kant, I. (1983). *Ethical Philosophy* (Ellington, J.W., trans.). Hackett, Indianapolis.

Lehmkuhl, A. (1902). *Theologia Moralis I*, as cited in Crowe, M.T. (1944). *The Moral Obligation of Paying Just Taxes*, The Catholic University of America Studies in Sacred Theology No. 84, p. 76.

Leiker, B. H. (1998). Rousseau and the Legitimacy of Tax Evasion. *Journal of Accounting, Ethics and Public Policy*, 1(1):45–57. Reprinted in McGee, R.W. (ed.) (1998). *The Ethics of Tax Evasion*, pp. 89–101. The Dumont Institute for Public Policy Research, Dumont, NJ.

Locke, J. (1689). *Two Treatises on Government*.

McCuddy, M.K. and Peery, B.L. (1996). Selected Individual Differences and Collegian's Ethical Beliefs. *Journal of Business Ethics*, 15(3):261–272.

McDonald, G.M. and Kan, P.C. (1997). Ethical Perceptions of Expatriate and Local Managers in Hong Kong. *Journal of Business Ethics*, 16(15):1605–1623.

McGee, R.W. (1994). Is Tax Evasion Unethical? *University of Kansas Law Review*, 42(2):411–435. Reprinted at http://ssrn.com/abstract= 74420.

McGee, R.W. (1997). The Ethics of Tax Evasion and Trade Protectionism from an Islamic Perspective. *Commentaries on Law and Public Policy*, 1:250–262. Reprinted at http://ssrn.com/abstract=461397.

McGee, R.W. (ed.). (1998a). *The Ethics of Tax Evasion*. The Dumont Institute for Public Policy Research, Dumont, NJ.

McGee, R.W. (1998b). The Ethics of Tax Evasion in Islam: A Comment. *Journal of Accounting, Ethics and Public Policy*, 1(2):162–168. Reprinted in McGee, R.W. (ed.) (1998). *The Ethics of Tax Evasion*, pp. 214–219. The Dumont Institute for Public Policy Research, Dumont, NJ.

McGee, R.W. (1998c). Christian Views on the Ethics of Tax Evasion. *Journal of Accounting, Ethics and Public Policy* 1(2):210–225. Reprinted at http://ssrn.com/abstract=461398.

McGee, R.W. (1999a). Is It Unethical to Evade Taxes in an Evil or Corrupt State? A Look at Jewish, Christian, Muslim, Mormon and Baha'i Perspectives. *Journal of Accounting, Ethics and Public Policy*, 2(1):149–181. Reprinted at http://ssrn.com/abstract=251469.

McGee, R.W. (1999b). Is It Unethical to Evade the Estate Tax? *Journal of Accounting, Ethics and Public Policy*, 2(2):266–285. Reprinted at http://ssrn.com/abstract=242536.

McGee, R.W. (1999c). An Ethical Look at Paying Your 'Fair Share' of Taxes. *Journal of Accounting, Ethics and Public Policy*, 2(2):318–328. Reprinted at http://ssrn.com/abstract=242549.

McGee, R.W. (1999d). Tariffs as a Form of Taxation: Is Evasion Unethical? *Journal of Accounting, Ethics and Public Policy*, 2(2):376–385. Reprinted at http://ssrn.com/abstract=242565.

McGee, R.W. (1999e). Why People Evade Taxes in Armenia: A Look at an Ethical Issue Based on a Summary of Interviews. *Journal of Accounting, Ethics and Public Policy*, 2(2):408–416. Reprinted at http://ssrn.com/abstract=242568.

McGee, R.W. (1999f). Is It Unethical to Evade the Capital Gains Tax? *Journal of Accounting, Ethics and Public Policy*, 2(3):567–581. Reprinted at http://ssrn.com/abstract=251491.

McGee, R.W. (1999g). Is It Unethical to Evade the Social Security Tax? *Journal of Accounting, Ethics and Public Policy*, 2(3):585–596. Reprinted at http://ssrn.com/abstract=242507.

McGee, R.W. (2005a). The Ethics of Tax Evasion: A Survey of International Business Academics. Presented at the 60th International Atlantic Economic Conference, New York, 6–9 October. Also available at www.ssrn.com.

McGee, R.W. (2005b). The Ethics of Tax Evasion: A Survey of Romanian Business Students and Faculty, Andreas School of Business Working Paper Series, Barry University, Miami Shores, FL, September. Available at www.ssrn.com. Reprinted in McGee, R.W. and Preobragenskaya, G.G. (2006). *Accounting and Financial System Reform in Eastern Europe and Asia.* Springer, New York.

McGee, R.W. (2005c). The Ethics of Tax Evasion: A Survey of International Business Academics. Presented at the 60th International Atlantic Economic Conference, New York, 6–9 October. Also available at www.ssrn.com.

McGee, R.W. and Bernal, A. (2006). The Ethics of Tax Evasion: A Survey of Business Students in Poland. Sixth Annual International Business Research Conference, co-sponsored by the Coggin College of Business, University of North Florida and the School of Management, Warsaw University, 10–11 February, Jacksonville, FL. Reprinted at www.ssrn.com.

McGee, R.W. and Guo, Z. (2006). The Ethics of Tax Evasion: A Survey of Law, Business and Philosophy Students in China. Published in the Proceedings of the International Academy of Business and Public Administration Disciplines (IABPAD), 2006 Winter Conference, Orlando, FL, 3–6 January. Reprinted at www.ssrn.com.

McGee, R.W. and Ho, S.S.M. (2006). The Ethics of Tax Evasion: A Survey of Accounting, Business and Economics Students in Hong Kong. Published in the Proceedings of the International Academy of Business and Public Administration Disciplines (IABPAD), 2006 Winter Conference, Orlando, FL, 3–6 January. Reprinted at www.ssrn.com.

McGee, R.W. and Lingle, C. (2005). The Ethics of Tax Evasion: A Survey of Guatemalan Opinion. Presented at the 60th International Atlantic Economic Conference, New York, 6–9 October 2005. Also available at www.ssrn.com.

McGee, R.W. and Maranjyan, T.B. (2006). Tax Evasion in Armenia: An Empirical Study. Presented at the 4th Annual Armenian International Public Research Group Conference, Washington, DC, 14–15 January.

McGee, R.W. and Rossi, M.J. (2006). The Ethics of Tax Evasion: A Survey of Law and Business Students in Argentina. Sixth Annual International Business Research Conference, co-sponsored by the Coggin College of Business, University of North Florida and the School of Management, Warsaw University, 10–11 February, Jacksonville, FL. Reprinted at www.ssrn.com.

McGee, R.W. and Yuhua, A. (2006). The Ethics of Tax Evasion: A Survey of Chinese Business and Economics Students. Published in the Proceedings of the International Academy of Business and Public Administration Disciplines (IABPAD), 2006 Winter Conference, Orlando, FL, 3–6 January. Reprinted at www.ssrn.com.

Morales, A. (1998). Income Tax Compliance and Alternative Views of Ethics and Human Nature. *Journal of Accounting, Ethics and Public Policy*, 1(3):380–399. Reprinted in McGee, R.W. (ed.) (1998). *The Ethics of Tax Evasion*, pp. 242–258. The Dumont Institute for Public Policy Research, Dumont, NJ.

Murtuza, A. and Ghazanfar, S.M. (1998). Taxation as a Form of Worship: Exploring the Nature of Zakat. *Journal of Accounting, Ethics and Public Policy*, 1(2):134–161. Reprinted in McGee, R.W. (ed.) (1998). *The Ethics of Tax Evasion*, pp. 190–212. The Dumont Institute for Public Policy Research, Dumont, NJ.

Oliva, R.R. (1998). The Schism between Tax Practitioners' Ethical and Legal Obligations: Recommendations for the Fusion of Law and Ethics. *Journal of Accounting, Ethics and Public Policy*, 1(4):603–628. Reprinted in McGee, R.W. (ed.) (1998). *The Ethics of Tax Evasion*, pp. 350–371. The Dumont Institute for Public Policy Research, Dumont, NJ.

Pennock, R.T. (1998). Death and Taxes: On the Justice of Conscientious War Tax Resistance. *Journal of Accounting, Ethics and Public Policy*, 1(1):58–76. Reprinted in McGee, R.W. (ed.) (1998). *The Ethics of Tax Evasion*, pp. 124–142. The Dumont Institute for Public Policy Research, Dumont, NJ.

Preobragenskaya, G.G. and McGee, R.W. (2004). Taxation and Public Finance in a Transition Economy: A Case Study of Russia. In: *Business Research Yearbook: Global Business Perspectives* (Gardner, C., Biberman, J., and Alkhafaji, A., eds), Vol. XI, pp. 254–258. McNaughton & Gunn, Saline, MI. A longer version, which was presented at the 16th Annual Conference of the International Academy of Business Disciplines in San Antonio, 25–28 March 2004, is available at http://ssrn.com/abstract=480862.

Rousseau, J.J. (1762). *The Social Contract*.

Schansberg, D.E. (1998). The Ethics of Tax Evasion within Biblical Christianity: Are There Limits to 'Rendering Unto Caesar'? *Journal of Accounting, Ethics and Public Policy*, 1(1):77–90. Reprinted in McGee, R.W. (ed.) (1998). *The Ethics of Tax Evasion*, pp. 144–157. The Dumont Institute for Public Policy Research, Dumont, NJ.

Shlaes, A. (1999). *The Greedy Hand: How Taxes Drive Americans Crazy and What To Do About It*. Random House, New York.

Smatrakalev, G. (1998). Walking on the Edge: Bulgaria and the Transition to a Market Economy. In: *The Ethics of Tax Evasion* (McGee, R.W., ed.), pp. 316–329. The Dumont Institute for Public Policy Research, Dumont, NJ.

Smith, S.R. and Kimball, K.C. (1998). Tax Evasion and Ethics: A Perspective from Members of The Church of Jesus Christ of Latter-Day Saints. *Journal of Accounting, Ethics and Public Policy*, 1(3):337–348. Reprinted in McGee, R.W. (ed.) (1998). *The Ethics of Tax Evasion*, pp. 220–229. The Dumont Institute for Public Policy Research, Dumont, NJ.

Spooner, L. (1870). *No Treason: The Constitution of No Authority*. Originally self-published by Spooner in Boston in 1870, reprinted by Rampart College in 1965, 1966 and 1971, and by Ralph Myles Publisher, Colorado Springs, CO in 1973.

Tamari, M. (1998). Ethical Issues in Tax Evasion: A Jewish Perspective. *Journal of Accounting, Ethics and Public Policy*, 1(2):121–132. Reprinted in McGee, R.W. (ed.) (1998). *The Ethics of Tax Evasion*, pp. 168–178. The Dumont Institute for Public Policy Research, Dumont, NJ.

Torgler, B. (2003). Tax Morale: Theory and Empirical Analysis of Tax Compliance. Dissertation der Universität Basel zur Erlangung der Würde eines Doktors der Staatswissenschaften.

Vaguine, V.V. (1998). The 'Shadow Economy' and Tax Evasion in Russia. In: *The Ethics of Tax Evasion* (McGee, R.W., ed.), pp. 306–314. The Dumont Institute for Public Policy Research, Dumont, NJ.

13

Money Laundering: Every Financial Transaction Leaves a Paper Trail

Greg N. Gregoriou, Gino Vita, and Paul U. Ali

Abstract

In this chapter we will review what is considered money laundering, why it is so wide-spread, the different stages, its global impact, and the effects it has on the economy, the general population, and why we should all be concerned. We will finally review how countries throughout the world have banded together in their fight against money laundering.

13.1   Introduction

As commonly understood, money laundering is inextricably associated with drug trafficking and the attempts to disguise the criminal character of the funds derived from that activity. When a money-laundering scheme has been successfully implemented, the profits of trafficking will be made to appear legitimate and the persons involved in the trafficking (invariably the directing minds rather than the actual perpetrators) can freely and openly utilize those profits.

While drug trafficking remains, by far, the principal source of the illegal proceeds deployed in money-laundering schemes, money laundering plays an integral role in other criminal activities, in particular those where the overarching motivation is the generation of profits (FATF, 1996, 1997; Trehan, 2004). Financial crimes – primarily bank, credit card and investment fraud, bankruptcy fraud, extortion, illegal gambling, loan sharking, and the smuggling of alcohol, firearms and tobacco – now constitute the second largest source worldwide of illegal proceeds for money-laundering schemes (FATF, 1996, 1997). More recently, trafficking in human beings and illegal migration have emerged as significant generators of illegal proceeds (FATF, 2005).

Money laundering, however, reaches far beyond profit-driven criminal activities. Many other forms of criminal activity (particularly those involving a significant element of premeditation as opposed to opportunistic crimes, such as street muggings, and so-called 'crimes of passion') require funding for their design and implementation. Here the money-laundering techniques developed to sanitize the proceeds of drug trafficking are equally useful in concealing the sources of funds for criminal enterprises. Money laundering has now been identified as a key facilitator of what may be described as not-for-profit criminal activities, such as acts of terrorism, where the motivating factor is not profit but a political or ideological goal (Bell, 2003; FATF, 2003, 2004, 2005).

Nor is money laundering confined to criminal activities. It is possible to categorize the funds that are the subject of money-laundering schemes into 'hot money', 'gray money', and 'dirty money', with only the latter being concerned exclusively with the proceeds of crime (Savla, 2001).

Hot money usually involves the cross-border transfer of funds, where the impetus for the transfer has been an adverse change in the economic, political, or social conditions prevailing in the country of origin of the funds (Savla, 2001). This hot money may represent bribes, the proceeds of embezzlement or other corruption-related proceeds (Chamberlain, 2002), but it also encompasses the legitimate, personal assets (that is, 'flight capital') of the politically vulnerable members of the originating country's socio-economic elites and middle classes. While hot money may be tainted by having been derived from a criminal act, gray money encompasses funds that are legal in origin but have become criminally tainted due to their use in a money-laundering scheme (Savla, 2001). A prime example is the use of alternative remittance systems, such as *hawala*, by migrant communities and guest workers to evade currency controls (Trehan, 2004; FATF, 2005).

Another feature of gray money is what can be described as the increasing retailization of money laundering. Through the seemingly countless books and articles published in local and international business magazines, otherwise honest citizens have been able to educate themselves about and gain knowledge of the procedures to open offshore accounts, settle offshore trusts, and incorporate offshore corporations (see, for example, Cornez, 2000; Starchild, 2001; Vernazza et al., 2001). In many instances, these publications actively encourage their readers to consider using offshore jurisdictions to shelter their assets from spousal claims and creditors, and minimize taxation liability. Governments and, in particular, the revenue authorities have become aware of the negative impact posed by the laundering of gray money on domestic economies and have taken steps to curb these activities. Greater controls have been imposed by many governments on the movements of substantial amounts of cash offshore by individuals and, in many countries, the filing of tax returns requires specific disclosure to be made of income or payments sourced from tax havens.

Money laundering can inflict great harm on a country's economy, in both financial costs and in the erosion of the principles of voluntary tax compliance – for instance, increased volatility in exchange and interest rates, and a marked rise of inflation. Through this hidden economy, billions of dollars in revenue are lost every year by governments, which may affect the stability of their regimes and impact negatively on the global economy (Trehan, 2004; Brittain-Catlin, 2005). Moreover, despite the measures introduced to combat money laundering, whether of criminal proceeds or gray money, many of the critical service providers – including money transfer businesses, offshore incorporation agencies, accountants, tax advisers, and estate planners – find it hard to resist the fees that can be generated from facilitating the sheltering of assets and the recharacterization of cashflows. One example is the offshore credit cards issued by the offshore branches of reputable financial institutions. In some cases, these branches are prepared to open accounts and issue cards for customers under assumed or unverified names, or in the names of offshore corporations or trusts established by them for their customers.

In order to launder funds, those funds must necessarily be placed in a money-laundering scheme. As such, a critical element of many money-laundering schemes is the wire transfer. Wire transfers are a cheap and fast means of moving funds within countries and across borders, and multiple transfers can be readily and cheaply executed to obscure the passage of funds within a money-laundering scheme (FATF, 2004). However, wire transfers create a 'paper trail' and even the interposition of multiple intermediaries, such as offshore dummy corporations, or the structuring of transfers in low-value amounts below disclosable thresholds may not be sufficient to escape detection.

13.2 The authorities are on the lookout

The revenue authorities (for example, the US Internal Revenue Service and the Canada Revenue Authority) are empowered under the anti-avoidance provisions of their taxation laws to demand bank account and credit card files, and complete transaction histories of taxpayers suspected of using money-laundering schemes to evade taxation. While, for example, it is not illegal for individuals to have off-shore credit cards, the use of such cards to evade paying taxes is illegal, and exposes the user to civil and criminal penalties. The US Internal Revenue Service has, on several occasions, obtained orders from US courts requiring American Express, MasterCard, and Visa to provide records on transactions to enable the identification of the holders of credit cards issuing by banks in tax havens (IRS Offshore Credit Card Program, www.irs.gov).

Evidence of money laundering is easier to obtain than may be commonly perceived. The US and Canadian authorities have been able to bring criminal proceedings against investment companies, financial institutions and brokerage houses for participation in money-laundering schemes thanks to the contacts that they have within the financial sectors of the major offshore jurisdictions. Individuals taking frequent trips to tax havens in order to shelter assets or recycle cash also leave paper trails of their travels with the airline companies. On demand, the airline companies will furnish to the US and Canadian authorities the lists of their frequent flyers to those tax havens.

The major industrialized countries, members of G7 (as it then was), created the Financial Action Task Force on Money Laundering (FATF), an intergovernmental body, in 1989. The FATF's purpose is to examine money-laundering techniques and trends, and to develop and promote, both at national and international levels, measures to combat money laundering and terrorist financing (FATF, 2006a). The FATF makes recommendations regarding anti-money-laundering measures and monitors its 31 member countries with respect to their progress in implementing those measures. It also encourages other countries to take similar measures and, through the publication of its list of noncooperative countries, has had considerable success in having such measures adopted by tax havens, emerging markets, and less developed countries.

Many countries have also set up specialized financial intelligence units (for example, the US Financial Crimes Enforcement Network and FINTRAC in Canada). These units, as part of the Egmont Group established in 1995, exchange financial intelligence amongst themselves and cooperate to combat money laundering and terrorist financing. The units will also refer financial intelligence to their national authorities for appropriate enforcement actions to be taken.

13.3 Directions

Individuals may seek to hide their financial gains from their governments because of the illegal activities they are involved in or because they wish to avoid paying taxes. The basic components of money laundering are straightforward, although the actual means by which those components are given effect may be very complex. Nonetheless, the steps involved leave paper trails (however disguised) that can be followed for many years.

For example, the transfer of the legitimate profits of an individual or corporation to an offshore jurisdiction is legal, but what is illegal is the concealment of the revenues gained from the placement of those profits offshore. The transfer of illegally obtained funds to an offshore jurisdiction so as to avoid identifying the source of the funds and permit the reuse of those funds as if they were legitimate profits is likewise illegal. In many cases, it is not only the undeclared profits that an individual will not wish to declare to the tax authorities, but the individual will also want to hide the illicit act or acts that generated the funds to be laundered.

There are three basic steps in money laundering (Savla, 2001; Trehan, 2004; See also United Nations Office on Drugs and Crime, www.unodc.org):

- *Placement.* The first step involves placing the funds to be laundered (whether hot, gray, or dirty money) in the financial system.

- *Layering.* This is the transaction or series of transactions designed to conceal the origins of the funds and thus dissociate them from the activities that generated them. Layering involves converting the funds into another form and often creating several layers of financial transactions (for example, the buying and selling of shares, commodities, or property) between the original funds and the eventual form for which they have been exchanged. This second step will be used frequently by money launderers, even after the third step (integration) has been implemented, to further disguise the source of the funds (via this loop).
- *Integration.* The third step involves placing the laundered proceeds back in the economy under a veil of legitimacy. A money launderer will often invest the funds in a legitimate business, permitting the laundering of even more money.

The traditional methods to whitewash funds have included the use of shell corporations, offshore tax shelters, and cash-only transactions, as well as making use of the services offered by banks, money transfer businesses, and others accepting cash deposits (for example, the operators of alternative remittance systems) to reroute the funds (El Rahman and Sheikh, 2003). While wire transfers enable funds to be transferred cheaply and rapidly, a significant amount of money laundering also involves the transport across borders of physical financial instruments (cash, paper bonds, and share certificates) via smuggling, airline travelers, or airfreight. Although the cross-border transport of financial instruments should be declared to customs officials, that is often not done (also by otherwise legitimate travelers), even if it means risking seizure of the instruments and being the subject of a criminal prosecution. In addition, the electronic transfer of funds via the Internet is on the increase and the obvious potential of such transfers for money laundering represents a major challenge for authorities (FATF, 2000, 2001; Trehan, 2004).

13.4 Techniques

While it is practically impossible to generate an exhaustive list of the methods used to launder funds (given the rapid development of new and hybrid methods), the following are amongst the most commonly used techniques:

- *Purchase of important assets.* The trust is one of the principal methods used by launderers to conceal the true ownership of assets (FATF, 2001; Kennedy, 2005). The assets are bought for cash and registered in the name of a nominee or trustee who holds the assets for the benefit of the launderer and deals with the assets (and any income generated by them) in accordance with the wishes of the launderer. In this way, the launderer is able to conceal ownership of the assets while continuing to have full enjoyment of those assets. The trustee may be a friend or relative and is inevitably someone who is trusted by the launderer, does not have a criminal record, and is often in good standing in society. Thus, the trustee's ownership of the assets is unlikely to attract unwelcome attention or raise suspicions. Apart from real property or high-value mobile assets such as cars and yachts, the proceeds to be laundered may be converted into gemstones, gold bullion and other precious metals, artwork, or antiques, which may more readily be transported out of the jurisdiction without being detected (FATF, 2003; Kennedy, 2005).

- *Foreign currency transactions.* The proceeds to be laundered may be converted into another currency, which can then be transferred by wire or even physically across borders.
- *Identity theft.* This is accomplished in such a way that the victims remain unaware of the fact that their identities are being used for criminal purposes. Within a short period of time, the stolen identity will be used to open bank accounts, deposit and transfer monies, including to foreign jurisdictions. The accounts are generally closed after a few months and replaced by new identities.
- *Casinos.* Large quantities of chips may be purchased with a certain amount played and the remaining chips redeemed for a cheque issued by the casino (Leong, 2004; Kennedy, 2005). To prevent the use of chips in this way to launder funds, more and more casinos will only issue cheques for the amount of winnings. Increasingly, money launderers are turning to Internet casinos, which may have no or less strict anti-money-laundering measures than their 'bricks and mortar' counterparts (FATF, 2001).
- *Deposits of less than the reportable threshold.* This is perhaps the most commonly used method to launder money in more developed economies. The launderer may have his or her associates, friends, or relatives convert the proceeds (often small-denominated notes or 'street cash') into larger denominations for amounts less than $10,000 (which is typically the reportable threshold). Transactions below this threshold are not required to be disclosed to the authorities, including the financial intelligence units of that country or other regulatory agencies tasked with combating money laundering.

- *Private banking services.* Money launderers have, in the past, made use of the private banking services offered by reputable financial institutions to conceal their dealings (FATF, 2002). This practice has, however, become less appealing to launderers, since many jurisdictions have introduced policies requiring accounts suspected of being used for money laundering to be disclosed to the anti-money-laundering agencies.
- *Fictitious loans.* The launderer, after transferring the proceeds to a foreign account in the name of a foreign corporation or trust established by the launderer, may remit the proceeds back to the launderer's jurisdiction falsely represented as a legitimate loan from that account holder (Kennedy, 2005).
- *Brokers.* The liquidity and high turnover in the financial markets, coupled with the returns that can be earned from financial instruments, have made the purchase of shares, bonds, and other market-traded financial instruments an important component of many money-laundering schemes (FATF, 2003; Trehan, 2004; Kennedy, 2005). For obvious reasons, many launderers prefer to purchase bearer securities and bearer negotiable instruments (FATF, 2002).

More recently, it appears that launderers have begun to resort increasingly to the insurance and trade sectors to sanitize proceeds. These proceeds may be used to purchase insurance products, thus converting the proceeds into legitimate payments by the insurance company (FATF, 2005). Also, the returns on insurance may be more certain than those of market-traded instruments where, in addition, the capital component of the launderer's investment may be at risk.

Anti-money-laundering measures have typically focused on the movement of laundered proceeds through the financial system and the physical transportation of cash (FATF, 2006b). Unsurprisingly, this has seen a migration of money laundering to the international trade sector. Proceeds are now increasingly being laundered using methods such as over- and under-invoicing of exported/imported goods, multiple invoicing of such goods, over- and under-shipments of goods, and false declarations of traded goods (Trehan, 2004; FATF, 2006b).

13.5   Eyes wide open

Money laundering exists because certain individuals do not want the authorities to be aware of their illicit activities and the financial gains from those activities, or because they wish to shelter legitimate financial gains from taxation liability. However, whatever the means that are used to launder money, the launderers will often leave behind a paper trail (prime examples are wire transfers, travel documents, and offshore credit card records), a trail that will follow them many years after the activities that generated the proceeds that were laundered. In many instances, the actual steps involved in money laundering are not illegal of themselves (Savla, 2001). For example, it is not illegal to own an offshore bank account or be the proprietor of an offshore corporation. What is illegal is the use of those otherwise legitimate steps to conceal the criminal origins of the proceeds. The use of money-laundering schemes to conceal legitimate financial gains from taxation liability may also result in criminal liability.

13.6 Tightly closed eyes

There is also an increasing onus on bankers, brokers, and other providers of the key financial services employed in money-laundering schemes to 'know their customers' and to report any suspicious account activity or unusual transactions. For example, the largest providers of private banking services worldwide have adopted a set of guidelines – the Wolfsberg Principles – requiring customer identification, identification of all beneficial owners of accounts, due diligence to be performed in relation to high-risk customers and their families and close associates, and the monitoring of account activity (FATF, 2002). Willful blindness – where, for example, a banker ignores the fact that a customer has made frequent cash deposits or purchases of bank drafts within a very short period of time in amounts just under the disclosable threshold – is thus no longer a shield to liability for assisting or conspiring with money launderers (Savla, 2001).

13.7 The 'John Doe' method

The US Internal Revenue Service has, as noted above, been able to obtain 'John Doe' orders to go effectively on 'fishing expeditions' to obtain personal information from the major credit card organizations (American Express, MasterCard, and Visa) concerning the holders of credit cards that have been issued by offshore banks. As a result, credit card issuers in over 30 tax havens (including the Bahamas, the Cayman Islands, Guernsey, the Isle of Man, Jersey, and the Netherland Antilles) have been forced to divulge transaction information and customer details relating to US residents holding credit cards issued by them. The use of these credit cards to purchase goods and services necessarily creates a paper trail of payment records that can be traced back via the credit card organization to the individual cardholder.

13.8 Conclusion: Big Brother is watching

Thousands of US and Canadian customers, for example, of offshore banks are becoming aware of the extent and consequences of the paper trails left by their foreign credit and banking cards. The US federal courts have issued orders making available to the US Internal Revenue Service the records held by offshore banks in relation to transactions within the USA by US citizens with mailing addresses in offshore jurisdictions. The US Internal Revenue Service has publicly stated that the average person does not need to hold an offshore credit card and that there is a reasonable basis for believing that such cards are being used to evade paying US taxes (IRS Offshore Credit Card Program, www.irs.gov).

These court orders have been obtained in respect of the three major credit card organizations, American Express, MasterCard, and Visa. Similar court orders have been obtained against Credomatic, a credit card processor based in Florida, that is the major processor of credit card transactions for banks located in the Caribbean tax havens.

In addition, virtually all offshore banks require an account to be opened with them before issuing credit cards. The balance of the account is used to secure the customer's payment obligations under the credit card (deposits in excess of the card limit are routinely required). Also, often when using those cards to make certain purchases (for example, airline tickets, car rentals, cruise fares, and hotel bills), some form of identification will still need to be provided by the cardholder (as is the case for more conventional payment methods). By having to authenticate their identity, the cardholder is leaving a paper trail that will make it easier for the revenue authorities and anti-money-laundering agencies to trace transactions on the credit card to the customer and connect the customer with the offshore bank account in which the hot, gray, or dirty money may have been deposited.

Nor is the Internet as effective a shield to regulatory scrutiny as is commonly thought. The use of online banking, online payment systems, or Internet-based remittance agencies all create paper trails (or, more accurately, electronic footprints) that can lead to the exposure of the would-be launderer. Even the use of masking software and proxy anonymizers may be of little assistance. For instance, the US Securities and Exchange Commission and FBI have been able to trace the proceeds of securities fraud through elaborate online money-laundering schemes and connect those proceeds to the perpetrator of the fraud. In addition, the US Internal Revenue Service has been able to obtain 'John Doe' orders against PayPal, the online payment system, to obtain information about customers that have been using PayPal to evade paying US taxes.

Money laundering has become a more and more risky business. The steps taken to conceal the criminal origins of the funds being laundered or to shelter legitimate funds from taxation liability invariably leave a paper trail that can be used by the authorities to link the persons utilizing the sanitized funds to the original funds and even the criminal activities that may have generated those funds.

References

Bell, R.E. (2003). The Confiscation, Forfeiture and Disruption of Terrorist Finances. *Journal of Money Laundering Control*, 7(2):105–125.

Brittain-Catlin, W. (2005). *Offshore: The Dark Side of the Global Economy*. Farrar, Straus & Giroux, New York.

Chamberlain, K. (2002). Recovering the Proceeds of Corruption. *Journal of Money Laundering Control*, 6(2):157–165.

Cornez, A. (2000). *The Offshore Money Book: How to Move Assets Offshore for Privacy, Protection and Tax Advantage*. Contemporary Books, Chicago.

El Rahman, F. and Sheikh, A. (2003). Money Laundering Through Underground Systems and Non-Financial Institutions. *Journal of Money Laundering Control*, 7(1):9–14.

Financial Action Task Force on Money Laundering (FATF) (1996). *FATF-VII Report on Money Laundering Typologies*, 28 June.

FATF (1997). *1996–1997 Report on Money Laundering Typologies*, February.

FATF (2000). *1999–2000 Report on Money Laundering Typologies*, 3 February.

FATF (2001). *2000–2001 Report on Money Laundering Typologies*, 1 February.

FATF (2002). *2001–2002 Report on Money Laundering Typologies*, 1 February.

FATF (2003). *2002–2003 Report on Money Laundering Typologies*, 14 February.

FATF (2004). *2003–2004 Report on Money Laundering Typologies*, 26 February.

FATF (2005). *Money Laundering and Terrorist Financing Typologies*, 10 June.

FATF (2006a). *Annual Report 2005–2006*, 23 June.

FATF (2006b). *Trade Based Money Laundering*, 23 June.

Kennedy, A. (2005). Dead Fish Across the Trail: Illustrations of Money Laundering Methods. *Journal of Money Laundering Control*, 8(4):305–319.

Leong, A.V.M. (2004). Macau Casinos and Organised Crime. *Journal of Money Laundering Control*, 7(4):298–307.

Starchild, A. (2001). *Using Offshore Havens for Privacy and Profit*. Paladin Press, Boulder, CO.

Savla, S. (2001). *Money Laundering and Financial Intermediaries*. Kluwer Law International, The Hague.

Trehan, J. (2004). *Crime and Money Laundering: The Indian Perspective*. Kluwer Law International, The Hague.

Vernazza, J.B., Bennett, J., Jacobs, V., and LeVine, R. (2001). Protecting and Conserving Assets Using an Overseas Asset Protection Trust. *Journal of Retirement Planning*, 40–50 (Jan–Feb).

14

Tax Effects in the Valuation of Multinational Corporations: The Brazilian Experience

César Augusto Tibúrcio Silva, Jorge Katsumi Niyama, José Antônio de França, and Leonardo Vieira

Abstract

This chapter examines the tax effects on multinational corporation valuations in Brazil. These effects can be observed from the generated cash flow and in the interest rate adopted to discount this flow. However, the cost of taxation for foreign investments differs, as Brazil can differentiate the tax rate according to the business segment where the resources are applied. Furthermore, in some countries, national tax law provides an investment tax credit or other tax incentives. This chapter demonstrates the tax effects in Brazil, where a decrease of taxation under a law referred to as '*juros sobre capital próprio*' (which is similar to the opportunity cost and can be deducted for corporate tax purposes) is possible by investing in certain activities such as agribusiness, where royalties can be repatriated to corporate headquarters by subsidiaries or associated enterprises.

This chapter has two sections: The first part presents the main aspects of tax effects in valuing multinational corporations, the second discusses the Brazilian experience and the specific tax effects.

14.1   Introduction

When a company decides to make a capital investment in another country, it usually requires estimating future cash flows, along with discounting these cashflows at an appropriate rate to maximize share price. The result will represent the cost of financing. Likewise, the estimated future goods and services flow (discounted at some appropriated rate) is usually adopted for the corporate valuation process. This method is known as discounted cash flow (DCF) (see Pereiro, 2002; Ho and Lee, 2004), and other models, such as APV and the residual profit model, perform similar functions. However, we show that well-applied DCF produces the same results (Fernandez, 2002).

Multinational company value typically includes the total value of each subsidiary, according to the principle of additivity. Therefore, subsidiaries increase total company value. Legalities such as tax rules can also impact the potential cash flow of a company. According to Choi and Meek (2004), 'tax considerations strongly influence decisions on where to invest because taxation is, with the possible exception of cost of goods sold, the largest expense of most businesses'.

Numerous studies have been developed over the last few years about how tax obligations influence corporate performance involving investment overseas. Examples include tax policy and its influence on investments (Desai et al., 2002), the different types of taxation adopted (Aizenman and Jinjarak, 2006), the

relationship and interdependence between the financial sector and tax procedures (Gordon and Li, 2005), tax planning (Desai, 2005), the repatriating policy of
income for the host country (Desai et al., 2002), and tax effects on dividends (Poterba
and Summers, 1984).

There is evidence that the design of national tax policy influences the level of
investment, especially in the case of direct investment (Desai et al., 2002; Simmons,
2003). This supports the idea that many governments maintain low corporate tax
rates to encourage investment. Desai et al. (2002) analyzed the impact of indirect
taxation on foreign direct investment in developing countries.

Aizenman and Jinjarak (2006) addressed panel regressions and controlling
structural factors, and concluded that trade openness and financial integration
have a positive relationship with 'hard to collect' taxes (i.e. VAT, income tax, and
sales taxes) and a negative relationship with 'easy to collect' taxes (tariffs and
seigniorage). Effective tax rates can vary considerably from country to country.
In developing countries, however, tax rules between segments of companies
frequently vary as well. Many firms use legal tax avoidance methods, others find
themselves facing very high liabilities.

Gordon and Li (2005) argued that the optimized use of the financial sector
could be the reason for this difference. They note that when firms generate a
paper trail, they facilitate tax enforcement. The authors further discussed the
impact of domestic tax revenue in developing countries on multinational companies. They concluded that if multinational companies sell goods produced by
domestic taxable firms, the tax effect will depend on the relative taxes paid by
the multinationals *vis-à-vis* the domestic firms. In this situation, for example,
multinationals would pay lower taxes. Additionally, restrictions to entry of foreign firms are common in sectors dominated by domestic firms. Should untaxed
firms dominate the economy or sectors, the entry of multinationals would increase
taxes.

Tax planning is another tax regulation approach, whereby legal tax avoidance
by firms is seen as a transfer of value from the state to shareholders (Desai, 2005).
Desai (2005) and Desai et al. (2004) concluded that governance should be an
important determinant of the valuation of corporate tax savings. In strong governance institutions, the net effect on value should be greater and tax avoidance will
be more difficult to measure.

Altshuler et al. (1995) argued that multinationals have an incentive to repatri-
ate more profits from a subsidiary when the tax cost is temporarily relatively
lower than normal. They will have an incentive to retain more profits when the
tax cost of repatriation is higher than normal.

In some countries, to prevent double taxation of foreign income, the law permits multinationals to claim foreign tax credits for income taxes paid to foreign countries (Desai, et al., 2002). However, multinationals must keep in mind the reported location of their taxable profits to avoid high-tax investment locations.

Finally, Poterba and Summers (1984) found that dividend taxes reduce relative valuation by investors.

This study is divided into two parts. The first presents general tax effects and how they impact multinationals. The second uses Brazil as an example to better illustrate the pro forma model developed in the first section.

14.2   Discounted cash flow

According to the DCF model, the value of a company (V) is as follows:

$$V = \sum_{n=1}^{\infty} \frac{CF_n}{(1 + i_n)^n},$$

where n = period, CF_n = after-tax cash flow of period, i_n = adequate discounted tax rate "n" and at period "n".

According to the principle of additivity, the value of a company is:

$$V = \sum_{c=1}^{j} V^c,$$

where V^c = value of a company in country c.

In each country, the total value of the company is as follows:

$$V^c = \sum_{n=1}^{\infty} \left[\frac{CF_n^c}{(1 + i_n^c)^n} \right],$$

where c = country where discounted cash flow n is generated, and i_n^c = adequate discounted tax rate and CF_n^c = the cash flow for period n and country c.

This formula can be simplified as follows assuming a constant and infinite flow (perpetuity):

$$V^c = \frac{CF^c}{i^c}.$$

There are two basic ways to measure DCF. The first is to obtain the equity cash flow, which is the estimated flow of resources in each country (after payments and receipts). In this case, the cost of opportunity, otherwise known as the capital asset pricing model (CAPM), should be adopted. Any benefits obtained from the tax effects should influence the residual value of shareholder flow.

The second way is through use of the 'free cash flow', which is obtained from 'earnings before tax and interest' (EBIT), where the tax paid (on EBIT) is used to identify the net income (without debt). The 'free cash flow' is therefore equal to net income (without debt), plus depreciation, minus fixed assets and working capital (see Fernandez, 2002). Note that free cash flow should be discounted using the weighted average cost of capital (WACC) (including the cost of debt).

The 'free cash flow' provides the value of stockholder equity, but it also illustrates the company's value. The difference between equity cash flow and free cash flow is the value of the debt. The same result could be obtained by discounting the cost of debt from its cash flow.

During the multinational company valuation process, it is important to analyze the tax effects in the countries where the investment will occur. The tax effects will influence the generation of cash flow (CF) or the discount rate (i), according to Reilly and Schweihs (2000).

One of the more traditional ways of studying tax effects in the valuation process is to consider the cost of capital. Financial expenses are usually deductible for tax purposes, so the net cost of debt is the interest reduced by the tax benefit (Pratt, 1998), as follows:

$$k_{dt} = k_d(1 - t),$$

where k_{dt} = the cost of debt adopted for the discount, k_d = the interest rate of the loans, and t = the tax rate (percentage of net income).

Finally, the debt cost value should also be considered when estimating WACC.

Considering that tax is a payment and could influence the WACC, 'any action that can reduce the tax burden on a firm for a given level of operating income will increase value' (Damodaran, 2001, p. 408). Damodaran gives the following example: A multinational company that generates income from different countries may be able to move to a low- or no-tax country using transfer pricing.

In any event, in order to obtain the generated flow of the multinational in a certain country (V^c), it is important to adopt the effective tax rate of each country where the flow is generated. The tax cost of the foreign capital in a given country could be different from this rate because of local legislation, or according to the capital allocation. The tax legislation of a given country could also allow tax benefits for foreign companies, however.

Tax benefits could influence the cash flow (free and equity) and the discount rate (WACC). For the purposes of this study, we adopt the standardized equity cash flow to obtain the multinational company flow in a given country.

We use three examples to illustrate how a given country's tax legislation can reduce tax payments for a firm and consequently increase the value of its generated wealth. In all situations, the decision process is made according to how much the company's value is increased. For a more illustrative example, we consider Brazilian tax legislation.

14.3 *Juros sobre capital próprio*

The corporate income tax rate in Brazil is 34%. In 1995, a Brazilian law referred to as '*juros sobre capital próprio*' (Law 9249/95) was enacted. This mechanism allows the corporate income tax to be decreased. It is similar to a capital opportunity cost and is also tax deductible.

Before making any decisions to invest in Brazil, it is important to calculate the tax effects carefully, to determine whether there are cash flow increases for stockholders (compared to the traditional tax rules calculation). We obtain the Brazilian corporate income tax as follows:

$$T = \text{EBT} \times t,$$

where EBT = net operating income before tax and after interest, and $t = 34\%$ (9% is required for a 'social contribution' and 25% is the 'effective' corporate income tax).

Adopting the '*juros sobre capital próprio*' concept, the effective corporate income tax can be reduced as follows:

$$\text{JSCP} = i \times E_a,$$

where i = the long-term interest rate (TJLP) established by the government and adopted for public marketable securities, and E_a = the adjusted net equity (stockholder equity), according to:

$$E_a = (E - I + D)$$

where E = net equity (stockholder equity), I = net income, and D = dividends and *juros sobre capital próprio*.

The relationship between $-I$ and $+D$ is part of the income that will be retained. According to Brazilian law, it is permissible to reduce only taxable income by using one of the following two alternatives (or whichever yields the largest amount):

$$L_1 = \frac{\text{EBT}}{2}$$

$$L_2 = \frac{(\text{LA} + \text{RL})}{2},$$

where L_1 = limit 1, EBT = income before tax and after interest, L_2 = limit 2, LA = retained earnings, and RL = the income reserve (income reserve is one of the possible destinations of net income, according to the decision of a shareholder meeting).

We obtain the new net operating income before tax and after interest as follows:

$$\text{EBT}^* = \text{EBT} - \text{JSCP}.$$

We obtain the new income corporate tax as:

$$T^* = \text{EBT}^* \times t$$

$$T^* = (\text{EBT} - \text{JSCP}) \times t,$$

The difference between the two incomes (with and without JSCP) is:

$$I - I^* = \text{EBT} \times (1 - t) - \text{EBT}^* \times (1 - t)$$

$$I - I^* = (\text{EBT} - \text{EBT}^*) \times (1 - t)$$

$$I - I^* = \text{JSCP} \times (1 - t).$$

JSCP are thus similar to stockholder dividends. However, they can be tax deductible. On the other hand, if the company does not adopt JSCP,

$$\text{DIV} = d \times I,$$

where DIV = dividends, d = part of the net income available to be distributed, and I = the net income period.

Considering JSCP as part of the net income and thus taxable (at a rate of 15%), the expression $\text{JSCP} = i \times E_a$ is probably different if compared to the decision company payoff paying dividends. In this case, Brazilian law permits the payment of dividends. In order to maintain the same proportion of payments, as if there were no JSCP payments, we calculate the JSCP net of tax effects as follows:

$$\text{JSCP} \times (1 - t^*).$$

The dividends will be paid ($t^* = 15\%$) as follows:

$$DIV^* = d \times I - JSCP \times (1 - t^*).$$

To clarify, consider this example:

Gross operating income = $90,000
Operating expenses = $40,000
Dividends (d) = 60%
TJLP (long-term interest rate) = 12% per year
Income tax (total) = 34%
Net equity (stockholder equity) before income = $170,000 (capital $100,000, income reserves $40,000, and retained earnings $30,000).

Net income, following Brazilian law, is:

$$I = (90,000 - 40,000)(1 - 0.34) = \$33.000$$

$$d = \$33,000 \times 60\% = 19.800$$

$$E = 170,000 + 33,000 - 19,800 = 183,200.$$

The corporate income tax will be R$17,000, or 34% multiplied by (90,000 − 40,000), if the company does not decide to adopt the JSCP. Assuming the JSCP option, the new figures are:

$$JSCP = (183,200 - 13,200) \times 12\% = \$20,400.$$

The two limits are calculated as follows:

$$L_1 = EBT/2 = (90,000 - 40,000)/2 = \$25,000$$

$$L_2 = (LA + RL)/2 = (30,000 + 40,000)/2 = \$35,000.$$

Given that JSCP ($20,400) is lower than the two limits, it can be tax deductible. The net income assuming JSCP is $19,536, or

$$I^* = (90,000 - 40,000 - 20,400) \times (1 - 0.34) = \$19,536.$$

The difference considering the net income ($33,000) is $13,464, or

$$I - I^* = JSCP \times (1 - t) = 20,400 \times (1 - 0.34) = \$13,464.$$

At the end of the period, the stockholder equity will be a dependent variable of the dividend policy of the company. However, considering the same example adopted (rate of 60%), the stockholder equity will be as follows:

Integralized capital	$100,000
Income reserve	$40,000
Retained earnings	$70,000
Net income of the period	$13,200
Stockholder equity	$183,200

Should the company choose to keep the same level of stockholder equity as in the previous situation (e.g. $183,200), it must make an additional distribution of interest for the JSCP situation. Given that the net adjusted income is $19,536, the company will pay an additional $6536 to stockholders.

The net cash flow to the stockholders will be higher when the company adopts the JSCP (more than 20%), as follows:

Original situation = $19,800
JSCP situation = 17,340 + 6336 = 23,676.

14.4 Tax benefits for rural activities (agribusiness)

Brazilian tax law has established different taxation rules according to investment segment. For agribusiness (rural activities), for example, tax benefits are granted through total depreciation of fixed assets, except for the cost of the unused land, in the same year the fixed assets were purchased. In addition, these types of companies enjoy less rigid rules for tax settlement of losses (other types must follow much stricter limits).

For example, for companies not engaged in rural activities, depreciation expenses are based on useful economic life as defined by the Secretaria da Receita Federal (the governmental body responsible for tax rules). Therefore, operating income before tax and depreciation expenses is:

$$EBTDep = EBT + Dep$$

$$T = EBT \times t$$

$$T = (EBTDep - Dep) \times t$$

$$I = EBT - T$$

$$I = (EBTDep - Dep) \times (1 - t),$$

where I = net income, t = rate, Dep = depreciation expense, and T = corporate tax (expense).

For companies engaged in rural activities, the corporate tax to be paid in the first year, T_1^{r}, is shown as:

$$T_1^{\mathrm{r}} = (\mathrm{EBTDep}_1 - Dep \times n) \times t_1,$$

where n = the useful economic life of the asset and $Dep \times n$ = the depreciable asset (or carrying amount).

For the following period (T_2^{r}), all assets will be considered depreciated during the first year:

$$T_2^{\mathrm{r}} = (\mathrm{EBTDep}_2) \times t_2.$$

Thus, for agricultural companies, the tax expense is the total amount of the tax (year 1) until the end of the useful economic life. The difference between agricultural companies and other companies (for the first year) is expressed as:

$$\Delta T_1 = T_1^{\mathrm{r}} - T_1 = (\mathrm{EBTDep}_1 - Dep \times n) \times t_1 - (\mathrm{EBTDep}_1 - Dep) \times t_1$$

$$\Delta T_1 = Dep \times t_1 - Dep \times n \times t_1$$

$$\Delta T_1 = (1 \times n) \times Dep \times t_1$$

where $\Delta T_1 < 0$.

In other words, agricultural companies pay reduced taxes in the first year. However, in the second year, their depreciation expenses cease, resulting in higher taxes owed:

$$\Delta T_2 = T_2^{\mathrm{r}} - T_2 = \mathrm{EBTDep}_2 \times t_2 - (\mathrm{EBTDep}_2 - Dep) \times t_2$$

$$\Delta T_2 = - Dep \times t_2 > 0.$$

Considering the same tax rate for the period, there is no tax difference after the second year as follows (see Demski and Christensen, 2002):

$$\sum_{k=1}^{n} \Delta T_k = 0.$$

However, this tax benefit could be meaningful for multinational companies, given they postpone depreciation payments the first year. Consider the present cash flow as follows:

$$\frac{\Delta T_1}{(1 + i_1)^1} + \frac{\Delta T_2}{(1 + i_2)^2} + \cdots \frac{\Delta T_n}{(1 + i_n)^n},$$

where i = the appropriated discount rate for period 1, 2, ..., n.

Finally, consider the following example with the comparison as shown below:

Net income before tax and depreciation expense (EBTDep) = \$240,000
Depreciable asset = \$200,000
Useful economic life = 5 years
Tax rate = 34%
Discounted tax rate = 15%.

For a company not engaged in rural activities:

$$EBT_1 = EBT_2 = ... = EBT_5 = 240,000 - (200,000/5) = \$200,000$$
$$T_1 = T_2 = ... = T_5 = 34\% \times 200,000 = \$68,000$$
$$I_1 = I_2 = ... = I_5 = 200,000 - 68,000 = 132,000.$$

For a company engaged in rural activities (e.g., the asset will depreciate fully in the first year):

$$EBT_1^n = 240,000 - 200,000 = \$40,000$$
$$T_1 = 34\% \times 40,000 = \$13,600$$
$$I_1 = 40,000 - 13,600 = 26,400.$$

For the other periods:

$$EBT_2 = EBT_3 = EBT_4 = EBT_5 = 240,000 - 0 = \$240,000$$
$$T_2 = T_3 = T_4 = T_5 = 34\% \times 240,000 = 81,600$$
$$I_2 = I_3 = I_4 = I_5 = 240,000 - 81,600 = 158,400.$$

Note that the total tax paid is the same in both situations.

14.5 Tax credits from commodities imports and royalty payments

Contributions are another unique way the Brazilian tax framework requires additional payments from companies. Examples are PIS (the *Programa de Integração Social*[1]), and COFINS (*Contribuição para Financiamento da Seguridade Social*[2]). Payments are based on net income (on a noncumulative basis) or on cumulative gross sales. Both contributions have been adopted to fund a governmental social policy account.

After 2003 and 2004, new rules were implemented in Brazil, including non-cumulative bases of taxation (PIS and COFINS respectively). According to PIS and COFINS, Brazilian and subsidiaries of foreign companies can obtain tax credits by importing commodities if operating expenses are incurred.

The PIS/COFINS rate and expenses that compose the debt tax influence the multinational company's cash flow. Therefore, we calculate the tax as follows:

$$T_1^p = t \times (R - E_d)$$
$$E = E_d + E_n,$$

where T_1^p = PIS/COFINS, t = the PIS/COFINS rate, R = gross sales, E_d = deductible expenses, and E_n = nondeductible expenses. In this case, the tax to be paid is reduced by deductible expenses. The larger the deductible expense, the smaller the tax.

Table 14.1 illustrates this issue in more depth. According to Brazilian law, the PIS rate is 1.65% and the COFINS rate is 7.6%, calculated over the gross sales basis. We suppose that the multinational company opts to purchase commodities on the foreign market.

This example shows that commodity purchases on the foreign market and royalties for companies (foreign residents) do not allow tax credit maximization (a

Table 14.1   PIS/COFINS example

	Income statement	$	PIS	COFINS
A	Gross sales of commodities	100,000	1.650	7.600
B	Service revenue	20,000	330	1.520
C = A + B	**Total**	**120,000**	**1.980**	**9.120**
D	Commodities purchased (internal market)	80,000	1.320	6.080
E	Commodities purchased (foreign market)	45,000	–	–
F	Rent expense for companies	5000	83	380
G	Other rent expenses	2000	–	–
H	Electrical energy expense	800	13	61
I	Consulting services	1500	25	114
J	Royalty for companies (Brazilian residents)	6000	99	456
K	Royalty for companies (foreign residents)	1000	–	–
L	Administrative expenses	500	8	38
M	**Total**	**141,800**	**1.548**	**7.129**
N = C − M	**Income corporate tax**		**432**	**1.991**

value of \$4255, or $(45,000 + 1000) \times (1.65\% + 7.60\%))$. The corporate income tax burden was increased by this procedure and the cash flow deteriorated. Therefore, the relationship between tax and internal additional value also deteriorated.

14.6   Conclusion

The opportunities in Brazil for productive foreign investment under market conditions can be the same as those for Brazilian companies. The tax benefits obtained through JSCP or through total depreciation for agricultural companies are simply governmental fiscal policies aimed at strengthening the financial position of the firms and consolidating the national economy.

On the other hand, companies may face tax benefit constraints when trading directly with a legal entity abroad, or with an individual residing in Brazil and abroad. Therefore, careful tax planning is required so companies can choose the legal alternatives that will optimize earnings.

As the example of Brazil shows, no matter how heavy the tax burden, a continuous prudential tax planning approach may be able to reduce the burden. Legal tax avoidance schemes can result in attractive effective gains through dividends and capital gains.

Notes

1.   Social Integration Program.
2.   Social Security Financing Contribution.

References

Aizenman, J. and Jinjarak, Y. (2006). Globalization and Developing Countries. NBER Working Paper No. 11933, Cambridge, MA.

Altshuler, R., Newton, T.S., and Randolph, W. (1995). Do Repatriation Taxes Matter? Evidence from the Tax Returns of US Multinationals. In: *The Effects of Taxation on Multinational Corporations* (Feldstein, M., Hines, J.R. Jr, and Hubbard, R.G., eds), pp. 253–272. University of Chicago Press, Chicago.

Choi, F. and Meek, G.K. (2004). *International Accounting.* Pearson, Upper Saddle River, NJ.

Damodaran, A. (2001). *The Dark Side of Valuation.* Prentice-Hall & Financial Times, London.

Demski, D. and Christensen, J. (2002). *Accounting Theory.* McGraw-Hill, New York.

Desai, M.A. (2005). Time to Rethink the Corporate Tax System? Interview by Ann Cullen for the Working Knowledge for Business Leaders, Harvard Business School, Cambridge, MA.

Desai, M., Fritz Foley, C., and Hines, J.R. Jr (2002). Foreign Direct Investment in a World of Multiple Taxes. Working Paper, Harvard Business School, Cambridge, MA.

Desai, M.A., Dyck, I.J.A., and Zingales, L. (2004). Theft and Taxes. NBER Working Paper No. W10978, Cambridge, MA.

Fernandez, P. (2002). *Valuation Methods and Shareholder Value Creation*. Academic Press, Amsterdam.

Gordon, R. and Li, W. (2005). Tax Structure in Developing Countries: Many Puzzles and a Possible Explanation. NBER Working Paper No. 11267, Cambridge, MA.

Ho, T. and Lee, S. (2004). *The Oxford Guide to Financial Modeling*. Oxford University Press, Oxford.

Pereiro, L. (2002). *Valuation of Companies in Emerging Markets*. John Wiley, New York.

Poterba, J. and Summers, L. (1984). New Evidence that Taxes Affect the Valuation of Dividends. *Journal of Finance*, 39(5):1297–1415.

Pratt, S. (1998). *Cost of Capital*. John Wiley, New York.

Reilly, R. and Schweihs, R. (2000). *The Handbook of Advanced Business Valuation*. McGraw-Hill, New York.

Simmons, R. (2003). An Empirical Study of the Impact of Corporate Taxation on the Global Allocation of Foreign Direct Investment: A Broad Tax Attractiveness Index Approach. *Journal of International Accounting, Auditing and Taxation*, 12(2):105–120.

The Economic Impacts of Trade Agreements and Tax Reforms in Brazil: Some Implications for Accounting Research

Alexandre B. Cunha, Alexsandro Broedel Lopes, and Arilton Teixeira

Abstract

This chapter uses a general equilibrium model to evaluate the impacts of trade agreements and tax reforms on the Brazilian economy. The model predicts that welfare gains occur whether Argentina reduces the tariffs it places on Brazilian products or the Free Trade Area of the Americas (FTAA) is implemented. However, the FTAA engenders larger welfare gains. These gains will be even larger if the FTAA is implemented simultaneously to a reduction on domestic consumption taxes. These findings suggest that most of the gains come from the reduction of Brazilian tariff and tax rates. They also stress the importance to improve the tax accounting system in emerging markets as a necessary condition to accomplish the potential welfare gains.

15.1   Introduction

In the post-World War II era, commerce of goods and services has increased steadily. At the same time, the world has seen the formation of trade blocks in which a group of countries agree to adopt free trade policies among themselves (some evidence on this is provided by Bergoeing and Kehoe, 2001). Debate has surrounded the formation of each block. This debate is of particular interest in a region like Latin America, where countries have generally followed what is known as import substitution policies. These policies prescribe closure of the internal market, so that domestic firms will be protected from external competition. Simultaneously, domestic producers may also receive subsidies. At a time when the countries of the American continent are discussing the formation of the FTAA (Free Trade Area of the Americas), the importance of studying the consequences of the formation of these blocks on the Brazilian economy speaks for itself. We study the possible gains and consequences from joining the FTAA.

Brazilian entrepreneurs have pointed out some problems in joining the FTAA. They claim that it is difficult to compete with the US economy in a free trade zone, because of the Brazilian tax system, among other things. Brazil heavily taxes labor and also uses a cascading taxation system that increases the cost and prices of Brazilian goods. Brazilian entrepreneurs argue that Brazil should reform its tax system before joining the FTAA.

In this chapter we evaluate the impacts of FTAA and tax reform on the Brazilian economy in a unified framework. We adopt the computational experiment methodology presented in Kydland and Prescott (1996). We then discuss the implications of our results to the accounting practices of emerging economies.

We assess the impact of FTAA and tax reform quantitatively using a computable general equilibrium model. The use of a general equilibrium model to evaluate alternative policies is common practice today. Kehoe and Kehoe (1994a, b) provided a survey on this subject.

Given the size of the USA, to study the consequences of joining the FTAA is basically to study the consequences of implementing a trade agreement with the USA. Therefore, we adopt a four-country (Argentina, Brazil, USA, and Rest of the World) model to evaluate the impacts of trade blocks and tax policies on the Brazilian economy.

We have specified our model at a very basic level. Family units are described by preference relations and budget sets. Firms are described by their production set and profit functions. The advantage of specifying the model at this structural level, instead of describing a set of demand and supply functions, is that we are able to evaluate welfare implications in an unambiguous way.

We should stress some limitations of our model. First, we are considering a static economy. In this case, we are not allowed to say anything about the transition path from one steady-state to another. Second, we are likely underestimating the impacts of the FTAA. As pointed out by, among others, Kim (2000) and Tybout and Westbrook (1995), trade liberalization is often followed by an increment in total factor productivity (TFP). Since our model is static, we cannot capture such an increment. This change in TFP would increase productivity, reduce the prices of consumption goods, and increase trade and the welfare effects of the formation of trade blocks.

We carried out three experiments. In the first we set the bilateral tariffs for the pair Brazil/Argentina equal to zero. We call this experiment Mercosur. The idea behind this experiment is to quantify the impacts of a reduction of the trade barriers that have been raised by the Argentine government in the last few years. In the second experiment, which we call FTAA, we set all import tariffs between Argentina, Brazil, and the USA equal to zero. As we said before, the reason for calling this experiment FTAA is that the impacts on the Brazilian economy of joining the FTAA (all American countries) should be very close to the impact of joining a free trade zone with just the USA. In the last experiment, we combined the previous policy change with a reduction in Brazilian domestic taxes on consumption.

All three experiments point toward welfare gains for the Brazilian economy. These gains are very modest in the first and second cases. However, they are sizeable in the last experiment (2.4% of Brazilian GDP). These results show a small impact of the FTAA on the Brazilian economy in the static environment used here.

Besides the three experiments described above, we also considered the case in which the US import tariffs on Brazilian goods were initially higher than the US weighted average tariff that we computed. The reason to carry out this experiment is that the USA has nontariff barriers (NTBs) in many sectors, such as steel, sugar, and orange juice. Additionally, the US government heavily subsidizes the country's agricultural sector. Therefore, the effective US average tariff on Brazilian goods is higher than the one that we computed. Since we could not compute a tariff adjusted for the NTBs, we assumed that the USA placed the same average tariff as the European Union on Brazilian goods. We then ran exactly the same three experiments. The impacts on the Brazilian economy were roughly the same. In particular, the welfare gains were virtually unchanged.

The computational experiments we ran suggest that most welfare gains for the Brazilian people arise from the reduction of Brazilian tariffs and domestic tax rates. This finding has a striking implication regarding two particular policies. First, Brazil should open to trade and carry out tax reform regardless of whether its trade partners proceed in the same way or not.

Second, Brazil should improve its accounting systems to prepare for the benefits of tax reform. The results presented in this chapter have an enormous impact for tax accounting research in emerging markets. This article computes the effects of tax reforms and of free trade agreements on GDP and welfare. It shows how the tax system is important to wealth creation at a macroeconomic level, but in the model it is assumed that the value added tax (VAT) system proposed will work perfectly without significant transaction costs.

The accounting tax system plays a significant role in the functioning of the VAT system. A well-functioning accounting system is a necessary condition for the proposed solution to work. In other words, the model assumes that Brazil has an efficient accounting system guaranteeing the welfare gains stemming from the reforms. Unfortunately, this is not presently the case in several emerging markets and especially in Brazil.

This chapter is organized as follows. In section 15.2 we describe the model economy. In section 15.3 we define competitive equilibrium. In section 15.4 we carry out the experiments. In section 15.5 we discuss the implications of the results for accounting research for emerging nations and some adjustments we believe to be required to ensure that the accounting system works properly in an emerging economy.

15.2   The economy

There exist four countries: Brazil (b), Argentina (a), the USA (u), and the Rest of the World (r). The set of countries is represented by $I = \{a,b,r,u\}$. Each country produces a tradable good and a nontradable good. These goods are country specific.

Each nation i has a representative agent endowed with k_i units of capital and one unit of time that she can allocate to market and nonmarket activities (call it leisure). Capital is mobile across countries but labor is not.

Let c_{ij} denote the amount of the tradable good produced by country i and consumed in country j; c_i denotes the nontradable good of country i. The commodity space is $L = \Re^{13}$. A generic point in L is denoted by x,

$$x = (c_{aj}, c_{bj}, c_{rj}, c_{uj}, c_a, c_b, c_r, c_u, l_a, l_b, l_r, l_u, k),$$

where $j \in I$, c_{ij} is the good produced in country i and exported to country j, c_i is the nontradable good produced by country i, l_i is the amount of labor input in country i, and k is the capital stock.

The consumption set of a consumer in country $i \in I$ is:

$$X_i = \{x \in L_+ : l_i \leq 1; k_i \leq \bar{k}_i; c_j = l_j = 0 \qquad \text{for } j \neq i\}, \tag{15.1}$$

where l_i is the amount that a consumer from country $i \in I$ allocates to work and k_i is the amount of capital services that a consumer rents to firms, given that this consumer has $\bar{k}_i$ units of capital services to be rented.

15.2.1 Preferences

Preferences of a consumer of country $i \in I$ are represented by the utility function:

$$u_i(x) = [c_i^{\alpha_i} (c_{ai}^{\alpha_{ai}} c_{bi}^{\alpha_{bi}} c_{ri}^{\alpha_{ri}} c_{ui}^{\alpha_{ui}})^{1-\alpha_i}]^{\gamma} (1 - l_i)^{1-\gamma},$$

where $\alpha_{ai} + \alpha_{bi} + \alpha_{ri} + \alpha_{ui} = 1$, c_{ji} is the good consumed by the representative consumer in country i produced in country j, c_i is the nontradable good of country i, and l_i is the amount of consumer time allocated to work.

15.2.2 Technologies

In each country, firms operate two technologies, one that produces the nontradable good and one that produces the country-specific tradable good. The production set of the nontradable good of country $i \in I$ is:

$$Y_i(n) = \{y \in L_+ : y_i \leq k^{\theta} l_i^{1-\theta}; y_j = l_j = 0 \qquad \text{for } j \neq i; y_{ij} = 0\},$$

while the production set of the tradable good of country $i \in I$ is:

$$Y_i(t) = \{y \in L_+ : y_{ii} \leq k^\varphi l_i^{1-\varphi}; y_{ij} = y_j = l_j = 0 \quad \text{for } j \neq i\}.$$

The technological parameters satisfy $\theta, \varphi \in (0,1)$.

15.2.3 Government consumption and taxes

Government i levies proportional taxes at rate τ_{ji} on the imports from country $j \neq i$, at rate τ_{ii} on the consumption of domestic goods and at rate τ_{li} on labor income. The government uses its fiscal revenue to purchase some amount g_i of its country's nontradable good.

15.3 Competitive equilibrium

A tax system for country $j \in I$ is a vector $\tau_j = (\tau_{aj}, \tau_{bj}, \tau_{rj}, \tau_{uj}, \tau_{lj})$. An international tax system is an object $\tau = (\tau_a, \tau_b, \tau_r, \tau_u)$. Each component of τ is a tax system for a country. A price system for this economy is a vector:

$$P = (p_{at}, p_{bt}, p_{rt}, p_{ut}, p_a, p_b, p_r, p_u, -w_a, -w_b, -w_r, -w_u, -r).$$

We are abusing notation, since prices of nontradable goods from other countries are infinite. This abuse makes our notation easier and homogeneous across countries. The coordinates of P are before-tax prices. An after-tax price system for a country i is a vector:

$$P = (p_{ai}, p_{bi}, p_{ri}, p_{ui}, p_{an}, p_{bn}, p_{rn}, p_{un}, -p_{al}, -p_{bl}, -p_{rl}, -p_{ul}, -r).$$

The typical consumer from country $i \in I$ solves the following problem:

$$\max_{x \in X_i} u(x) \text{ s.t. } P_i \cdot x \leq 0.$$

The problem of a firm that produces the nontradable good in country $i \in I$ is:

$$\max_{y \in Y_i(n)} P \cdot y,$$

while the problem of a firm that produces the tradable good in country $i \in I$ is:

$$\max_{y \in Y_i(t)} P \cdot y.$$

345

Definition. A competitive equilibrium for an international tax system τ is an array $[P, (P_i, x_i, y_{in}, y_{it})_{i\in I}]$ such that:

1. Given P, y_{in} and y_{it} solve the problem of the respective firm.
2. Given P_i, x_i solves the maximization problem of consumer i.
3. P, P_i, and τ_i satisfy $(1 + \tau_{ai})p_{at} = p_{ai}$, $(1 + \tau_{bi})p_{bt} = p_{bi}$, $(1 + \tau_{ri})p_{rt} = p_{ri}$, $(1 + \tau_{ui})p_{ut} = p_{ui}$, $(1 + \tau_{ii})p_i = p_{in}$, and $(1 - \tau_{li})w_i = p_{il}$.
4. Each government balances its budget, i.e.

$$p_j g_j = \tau_{lj} w_j l_j + \tau_{jj} p_j c_j + \sum_{i\in I} \tau_{ij} p_{it} c_{ij}.$$

5. $(x_i, y_{in}, y_{it})_{i\in I}$ is feasible, i.e.

$$c_i + g_i = k_{in}^{\theta} l_{in}^{1-\theta},$$

$$\sum_{j\in I} c_{ij} = k_{it}^{\varphi} l_{it}^{1-\varphi},$$

$$l_{in} + l_{it} = l_i,$$

$$\sum_{i\in I} (k_{in} + k_{it}) = \sum_{i\in I} \bar{k}_i.$$

One may wonder why a balance-of-payment constraint was not considered in the above definition. It can be shown that the conditions we spelled out imply that each country satisfies its balance-of-payment constraint.

15.4 The experiments

The goal of this section is to evaluate welfare consequences and real effects of trade agreements and tax reform for the Brazilian economy. To carry out this task, we proceeded in the following way. First, we calibrated the model so that it matched some selected features of the actual Brazilian, US, Argentinian, and world economies (the calibration procedure is detailed in Cunha and Teixeira, 2004). Then, we computed the competitive equilibrium associated with the calibrated parameters. This equilibrium is our benchmark. Finally, we computed the competitive equilibria for three distinct international tax systems and compared the outcomes. The calibrated tariff and tax rates for Brazil, Argentina, and the USA are presented in Table 15.1. Note that each line indicates how a country taxes its domestic goods and the goods produced by other countries, as well as its tax on labor income.

Table 15.1 Calibrated tariffs and tax rates (% values)

Country	Argentina	Brazil	Rest of the World	USA	Labor income tax
Argentina	21	9.3	18.4	18.4	23.61
Brazil	0	16.2	23	23	18
USA	1.94	2.52	2.01	5.467	27.733

In the first experiment we simply lowered τ_{ba} from its original value (i.e. 9.3%) to 0. Observe that in this model economy a complete implementation of Mercosur amounts to setting both τ_{ab} and τ_{ba} equal to zero. Since the original (i.e. the calibrated) value of τ_{ab} is zero, we denoted this experiment as Mercosur.

In the second experiment we set $\tau_{ba} = \tau_{ua} = \tau_{ab} = \tau_{ub} = \tau_{au} = \tau_{bu} = 0$. This amounts to setting all intra-American trade tariffs in the model equal to zero. Therefore, we denoted this experiment as FTAA.

The third experiment combines the FTAA with a reduction of the consumption taxes in Brazil. We lowered τ_{bb} from its original value of 16.2% to 5.467% (the level observed in the USA). We called this experiment FTAA with tax reform. The main results are presented in Table 15.2.

We measured the welfare gain using equivalent variation as a percentage of benchmark GDP. All other figures in the table are percentage changes from the benchmark competitive equilibrium.

The equivalent variation is a standard measure of welfare gains and/or losses in general equilibrium analysis. Let P_b^0 be the price vector faced by the Brazilian consumer and u^0 the utility level she obtained before the reform. Let u^1 denote the post-reform utility level and $E(P_b, u)$ the expenditure function. The equivalent variation is given by the expression $E(P_b^0, u^1) - E(P_b^0, u^0)$. Observe that this difference tells how much extra income the consumer would need, at benchmark prices, to obtain the post-reform utility. For more on the equivalent variation and other welfare measures, see Varian (1992).

In the Mercosur experiment, the Brazilian trade deficit fell 2.39%. All other variables changed by less than 0.2%. The welfare gains for the Brazilian people were very modest. A factor behind the small impact of a drop in τ_{ba} in the Brazilian economy is the relative size of the countries. The Brazilian GDP is almost three times Argentina's GDP. Kehoe and Kehoe (1994b) stated that 'because Mexico's economy is the smallest, it will enjoy the biggest NAFTA-produced increase in economic welfare' and 'NAFTA's impact on the United States, although positive, is barely perceptible as a percentage of GDP'. Our finding is perfectly consistent with earlier studies.

Table 15.2   Experimental results

Variable	Mercosur	FTAA	FTAA with tax reform
c_{ab}	+0.18	+0.01	−0.97
c_{bb}	+0.01	−0.10	+9.76
c_{rb}	+0.05	−0.34	−1.32
c_{ub}	+0.05	+22.56	+21.35
c_b	+0.00	−0.02	+10.08
l_b	+0.02	−0.16	−0.63
l_{bn}	−0.02	−0.42	−5.48
l_{bt}	+0.11	+0.42	+10.13
k_{bn}	+0.06	−0.91	−7.34
k_{bt}	+0.19	−0.08	+7.97
$k_{bn} + k_{bt}$	+0.12	−0.54	−0.38
y_{bn}	+0.01	−0.60	−6.17
y_{bt}	+0.15	+0.16	+9.00
GDP at benchmark prices	+0.06	−0.32	−0.52
Trade deficit	−2.39	+10.88	+7.80
Consumer price index	+0.04	−0.69	−9.84
Real net wage	+0.04	+0.16	+8.71
Real net private income	+0.01	+0.32	+9.41
Welfare gain (% of GDP)	+0.00	+0.10	+2.42

Despite the small impact of the fall in τ_{ba} on the Brazilian economy, the Mercosur experiment provides some insights. Since both k_{bn} and k_{bt} went up, Mercosur generated a capital flow to Brazil. The physical output went up in both sectors. Hours worked went up as well. But the amount of labor in the nontradable sector went down. There was some reallocation of resources across the two sectors of the Brazilian economy. The consumption of all goods increased, the real GDP went up, the trade deficit fell, and CPI, real wages and real private income increased.

The FTAA experiment generated an increase of 10.88% in the Brazilian trade deficit. The welfare gain was 0.10% of the benchmark GDP. This is still a modest figure, but far larger than the Mercosur example. Brazilian consumption of the American tradable good (c_{ub}) increased by 22.56%. All other variables changed by less than 1%. Except for the trade balance and c_{ub}, the FTAA has small impacts on the variables.

Observe that both c_{ab} and c_{ub} went up, while l_b, c_b, c_{bb}, and c_{rb} fell. There was a reallocation of labor from the nontradable to the tradable sector of the Brazilian economy. Capital utilization was down in both sectors, and capital outflow took place.

The tradable output went up, while the nontradable one decreased. Both GDP and CPI decreased. Real wages and real private income experienced an increase.

We do not report these data here, but it is worth mentioning that the FTAA has negligible effects on the rest of the world. In particularly, k_{rn} and k_{rt} are roughly constant. Recall that in our artificial economy there is a fixed capital stock. Since there is almost no capital outflow or inflow to the rest of the world, the FTAA generated a reallocation of capital within Argentina, Brazil, and the USA.

The Mercosur experiment showed that when a trade tariff τ_{ij} is reduced, capital flows from country j to country i. In the FTAA experiment, several τ_{ij} values were simultaneously reduced. Thus, it is not possible to anticipate which country should receive or send capital abroad. It turned out that the USA received capital, while Brazil and Argentina lost capital.

These capital movements merit further discussion. Evidence from the formation of the European Union indicates that capital movement goes from richer countries to poorer ones. If the same were to happen with the FTAA, Brazil should benefit from a capital inflow.

Kehoe and Kehoe (1994b) discussed in detail the issue of capital flows in models of trade agreements. They showed that larger welfare gains take place when there is capital flow. However, any static model will hardly generate capital flow from a richer to a poorer country. What drives capital movement is the capital rate of return. Hence, a possible way that a model can generate capital flow to a poorer country is by means of a productivity increase.

Kim (2000) provided evidence that trade liberalization had a positive impact on the productivity of Korean manufactures. Tybout and Westbrook (1995) showed that a similar event took place in Mexico during the trade liberalization of the 1990s. Holmes and Schmitz (1995, 2001) and Herrendorf and Teixeira (2001) showed, from a theoretical point of view, that trade liberalization may have a positive impact on a country's productivity.

Even without capturing the productivity surge and capital flow associated with trade opening, the model still predicts welfare gains in both the Mercosur and FTAA experiments. We believe that these gains are lower bounds. We anticipate that a more sophisticated model will display even larger welfare improvements.

The observed GDP fall in the FTAA experiment also deserves attention (Table 15.3). That fall was driven by a drop in y_{bn}. Observe that when the Brazilian government reduces tariffs and tax rates, there is a fall in government fiscal revenue. This will lead to a decrease in g_b and a consequent fall in y_{bn}.

The aforementioned fall in g_b brings an important point to light. A reduction of the tax burden, as was done in the above experiments, has to be accompanied

Table 15.3 Experimental results for a higher initial US tariff on Brazilian goods

Variable	Mercosur	FTAA	FTAA with tax reform
c_{ab}	+0.18	+0.07	−0.91
c_{bb}	+0.01	−0.08	+9.77
c_{rb}	+0.05	−0.28	−1.27
c_{ub}	+0.05	+22.63	+21.42
c_b	+0.00	−0.02	+10.09
l_b	+0.02	−0.13	−0.61
l_{bn}	−0.02	−0.44	−5.50
l_{bt}	+0.11	+0.55	+10.26
k_{bn}	+0.06	−0.85	−7.27
k_{bt}	+0.19	+0.13	+8.20
$k_{bn} + k_{bt}$	+0.12	−0.40	−1.10
y_{bn}	+0.01	−0.59	−6.16
y_{bt}	+0.15	+0.33	+9.18
GDP at benchmark prices	+0.06	−0.25	−0.45
Trade deficit	−2.33	+8.00	+5.00
Consumer price index	+0.04	−0.64	−9.79
Real net wage	+0.04	+0.20	+8.75
Real net private income	+0.01	+0.34	+9.43
Welfare gain (% of GDP)	+0.00	+0.10	+2.42

by a reduction in government expenditure. An interesting exercise would consist of opening the Brazilian economy to international trade and raising some tax rates to compensate for the tariff reduction. This exercise is left for future research.

The FTAA with tax reform experiment generated a huge welfare gain (when compared to the previous two). There was a gain of the order of 2.42% of GDP. The Brazilian consumer substituted away from c_{ab} and c_{rb} toward c_{bb}, c_{ub}, c_b, and leisure.

Recall that our model is static. Thus, statements about capital flows have to be evaluated with care. It is interesting to see that in the FTAA experiment the sum $k_{bn} + k_{bt}$ decreased by 0.54%, while in the last experiment it decreased by a smaller amount (0.38%). Hence, this third experiment of the FTAA with tax reform suggests that tax reform may help Brazil to attract capital.

The third experiment generated a flow of production factors to the tradable sector. Both l_{bt} and k_{bt} increased. Resources left the nontradable sector. As a consequence of this reallocation of resources, y_{bt} grew and y_{bn} fell.

The aforementioned fall in GDP was larger than in the FTAA experiment. Again, this fall was driven by the reduction in g_b. The trade deficit increased, but less than in the FTAA simulation. On the other hand, the decrease in the CPI and the increase in net real wages and net private income were much larger.

Let us analyze the last experiment carried out in this paper. The calibrated value of τ_{bu} was 2.52%. As mentioned above in relation to the results presented in Table 15.1, this number is a weighted average of tax rates on Brazilian exports to the USA. This procedure does not take into consideration nontariff barriers as quotas. So, the effective tariff rate is clearly higher than 2.52%. To address this issue, we proceeded as follows: We assumed that τ_{bu} was equal to 8.1% (which is the average tariff that the European Union places on Brazilian products) and ran the three experiments again. Surprisingly, the results changed little (Table 15.3).

In the particular case of welfare gains, the differences are negligible. This finding has a striking policy implication. The model suggests that most of the gains Brazil can obtain from a trade agreement come from the reduction of Brazilian tariffs. More specifically, a unilateral reduction of Brazilian tariffs would increase welfare. Besides, if this unilateral reduction of tariffs were also followed by tax reform, the welfare gains would be substantial.

The conclusion that a reduction in domestic taxation induces larger welfare gains has an intuitive explanation. Consider the tariffs imposed by the USA on the goods imported from Brazil. Even when we increased this average tariff from 2.52% to 8.1% this tariff is still small when compared to the taxation that Brazil imposed on the consumption of the domestic good. That is, the distortions that the US government impose are too small compared to the distortion introduced domestically. Therefore, substantial welfare gains can be obtained by a unilateral reduction of Brazilian taxes and tariffs.

We should also keep in mind that we are likely underestimating these results, since we are working with a static model. Tax reduction should increase private investment, raising the gains computed above.

15.5 Conclusion: Implications of the results for tax accounting research in emerging markets

The results presented in this chapter have an enormous impact for tax accounting research in emerging markets. The chapter broadly states that tax reforms may have a greater impact on GDP and welfare than free trade agreements. It shows how the tax system is important to wealth creation on a macroeconomic basis. However, the model used assumes ex-ante that the value added tax (VAT) system proposed will work perfectly without significant transaction costs. The accounting tax system plays a significant role in the functioning of the VAT system. A well-functioning accounting system is a *sine qua non* condition for the proposed solution to work. Unfortunately, this is not the case in several emerging markets, especially Brazil. This section discusses some adjustments which are necessary to make the accounting system work in emerging markets, using Brazil as a special case.

This chapter states that a significant reduction in tax rates on consumption may have a greater impact on GDP and welfare than trade liberalization. This result only holds if the newly reduced tax rate is implemented de facto. This new tax must be calculated and consistently charged for the system to work. The general accounting system plays a significant role in both phases. The VAT is based on the value added to a certain product and involves a machinery calculation related to a margin over costs incurred to produce a certain product. To achieve this final number (the margin), firms must have an adequate cost accounting system that allocates costs to products on an appropriate basis. This allocation can be done using several methods. The allocation method is not the essential question. Full allocation, activity-based costing, etc., can be used. The central point is to guarantee that the chosen method is unbiased and used consistently through all the firms' activities.

It cannot, however, be assumed that all firms will have the same competence and compliance. To guarantee the execution of the calculation proposed, accountants must be well trained and an effective auditing process must be in place. Accounting education in emerging markets is a frequent cause for concern (Lopes, 2005). In Brazil, the accounting education system is based on a four-year bachelor degree, without an extensive certification program like the American (CPA) and British systems (ACA, ACCA). Most colleges only offer evening courses and the quality of education is generally perceived to be low. Profession education is virtually nonexistent. In addition, most of the tax work is conducted by accounting technicians who possess only a high-school level of education.

On a more general level, Brazil complies with four of the five criteria that Ali and Hwang (2000) showed to be related to the irrelevance of accounting data. First, Brazil has a bank-oriented (as opposed to market-oriented) financial system. In Brazil, few banks supply most of the capital that firms need and as a consequence there is a lower demand for published financial reports. Second, private sector bodies have no relation whatsoever with the standard-setting process. In Brazil, all accounting rules are issued directly by the central government or by one of the agencies that have responsibility for specific guidelines. The premise here is that government standard setters issue rules that are designed to serve government needs and not to inform equity investors. Third, Brazil is considered to be a continental model country because its accounting model is strongly influence by its Iberian colonizers. Fourth, tax rules have a strong influence on Brazilian financial reporting and sometimes it is indistinguishable. Tax laws are clearly influenced by a wider range of factors than the needs of equity investors. Recent research by Luyz and Wusteman (2004) suggested that the accounting loses relevance in countries that adopt a financial 'insider model'. An insider model is characterized when firms rely on special relationships and deals to obtain funding instead of using the public capital and credit markets. Publicly available financial accounting information is of no relevance in countries where this kind of arrangement is predominant. Brazil clearly adopts an 'insider model'.

To efficiently impose the new tax rate, an effective auditing process must be implemented. This is a problem in Brazil, since most firms need not submit to an extensive auditing system. Even very large firms are not audited in Brazil, because only public firms are subject to external auditing. This aspect may present an important obstacle to the implementation of the tax reforms proposed.

In summary, any attempt to improve the tax system in an emerging market demands a solid foundation on an effective accounting system. This system must encompass education and training of students and professionals, as well as profound reform in the auditing and assurance services. Otherwise, those important reforms will not leave the desks of academics.

References

Ali, A. and Hwang, L.S. (2000). Country-specific Factors Related to Financial Reporting and the Value Relevance of Accounting Data. *Journal of Accounting Research*, 18(1):1–25.

Bergoeing, R. and Kehoe, T. (2001). *Trade Theory and Trade Facts*. Federal Reserve Bank of Minneapolis Research Department, Staff Report 284. Available at http://minneapolisfed.org/research/sr/sr284.html.

Cunha, A. and Teixeira, A. (2004). The Impacts of Trade Blocks and Tax Reforms on the Brazilian Economy. *Revista Brasileira de Economia*, 58(3):325–342. Available at http://ideas.repec.org/a/fgv/epgrbe/5312.html.

Herrendorf, B. and Teixeira, A. (2001). How Trade Policy Affects Technology Adoption and Total Factor Productivity. Unpublished manuscript, Ibmec Business School, Sao Paulo, Brazil.

Holmes, T. and Schmitz, J. (1995). Resistance to New Technology and Trade Between Areas. *Federal Reserve Bank of Minneapolis Quarterly Review*, 19(1):2–17. Available at http://minneapolisfed.org/research/qr/qr1911.html.

Holmes, T. and Schmitz, J. (2001). A Gain from Trade: From Unproductive to Productive Entrepreneurship. *Journal of Monetary Economics*, 47(2):417–446.

Kehoe, P. and Kehoe, T. (1994a). A Primer on Static Applied General Equilibrium Models. *Federal Reserve Bank of Minneapolis Quarterly Review*, 18(2):2–16. Available at http://minneapolisfed.org/research/qr/qr1821.html.

Kehoe, P. and Kehoe, T. (1994b). Capturing Nafta's Impact with Applied General Equilibrium Models. *Federal Reserve Bank of Minneapolis Quarterly Review*, 18(2):17–34. Available at http://minneapolisfed.org/research/qr/qr1822.html.

Kim, E. (2000). Trade Liberalization and Productivity Growth in Korean Manufacturing Industries: Price Protection, Market Power and Scale Efficiency. *Journal of Development Economics*, 62(1):55–83.

Kydland, F. and Prescott, E. (1996). The Computational Experiment: An Econometric Tool. *Journal of Economic Perspectives*, 10(1):69–85.

Luyz, C. and Wusteman, J. (2004). The Role of Accounting in the German Financial System. In: *The German Financial System* (Krahnen, J.P. and Schmidt, R.H., eds). Oxford University Press, Oxford.

Lopes, A.B. (2005). *ROSC Project in Brazil*. Unpublished report. World Bank, Washington, DC.

Tybout, J. and Westbrook, M.D. (1995). Trade Liberalization and the Dimensions of Efficiency Change in Mexican Manufacturing Industries. *Journal of International Economics*, 39(1–2):53–78.

Varian, H. (1992). *Microeconomic Analysis*. W.W. Norton, New York.

Index